Experimenting with uncertainty
Essays in honour of Alan Davies

STUDIES IN LANGUAGE TESTING...11
Series editor: Michael Milanovic

Also in this series:

An investigation into the comparability of two tests of English as a Foreign Language: The Cambridge–TOEFL comparability study
Lyle F. Bachman, F. Davidson, K. Ryan, I.-C. Choi

Test taker characteristics and test performance: A structural modeling approach
Antony John Kunnan

Performance testing, cognition and assessment: Selected papers from the 15th Language Testing Research Colloquium, Cambridge and Arnhem
Michael Milanovic, Nick Saville

The development of IELTS: A study of the effect of background knowledge on reading comprehension
Caroline Margaret Clapham

Verbal protocol analysis in language testing research: A handbook
Alison Green

A multilingual glossary of language testing terms
prepared by ALTE members

Dictionary of language testing
Alan Davies, Annie Brown, Cathie Elder, Kathryn Hill, Tom Lumley, Tim McNamara

Learner strategy use and performance on language tests
James Enos Purpura

Fairness and validation in language assessment: Selected papers from the 19th Language Testing Research Colloquium, Orlando, Florida
Antony John Kunnan

Issues in computer-adaptive testing of reading proficiency
Micheline Chalhoub-Deville

Experimenting with uncertainty
Essays in honour of Alan Davies

**Edited by C. Elder, A. Brown,
E. Grove, K. Hill, N. Iwashita, T. Lumley,
T. McNamara, K. O'Loughlin**

Published by the Press Syndicate of the University of Cambridge
The Pitt Building, Trumpington Street, Cambridge CB2 1RP, UK

CAMBRIDGE UNIVERSITY PRESS
The Edinburgh Building, Cambridge CB2 2RU, UK
40 West 20th Street, New York, NY 10011–4211, USA
10 Stamford Road, Oakleigh, Melbourne 3166, Australia
Ruiz de Alarcón 13, 28014 Madrid, Spain

First published 2001

Printed in Great Britain at the University Press, Cambridge, UK

British Library cataloguing in publication data

University of Cambridge, Local Examinations Syndicate

Experimenting with uncertainty: Essays in honour of Alan Davies

Edited by C. Elder, A. Brown, E. Grove, K. Hill, N. Iwashita, T. Lumley, T. McNamara, K. O'Loughlin

1. Education. Assessment 2. Education. Tests. Setting

ISBN 0 521–772540 hardback
0 521–775760 paperback

WRITING OF TESTS

(with apologies to Henry Reed 'Lessons of the War:
1, Naming of Parts' (1946))

Today we have writing of tests. Yesterday
We had rater training, and tomorrow morning,
We shall have what to do after marking. But today,
Today we have writing of tests. Niphophila
Tremble like dancers on all of the Dandenong Ranges
And today we have writing of tests.

This is the ASLPR bandscales. And these
Are the IELTS bandscales, whose use you will see,
When you are given your specs. And these are the TOEFL bandscales
Which in your case you have not got. The sprinklers
Arc in the gardens their pulsing mysterious signals
Which in our case we have not got.

Alan Davies

(On the occasion of his retirement from the Language Testing
Research Centre, Melbourne 1998)

Contents

Series Editor's note **x**

Preface **xi**

Section One

The contribution of Alan Davies **1**

1. Alan Davies and British applied linguistics 2
Christopher Brumfit

2. Ten years of the Language Testing Research Centre 5
Tim McNamara

Section Two

Construct definition in language testing **11**

3. Communicative language testing: The art of the possible 12
Henry Widdowson

4. Fossilisation or evolution: The case of grammar testing 22
Pauline Rea-Dickins

5. The assessment of metalinguistic knowledge 33
Caroline Clapham

Section Three

Language testing for specific purposes and populations **44**

6. Three problems in testing language for specific purposes: Authenticity, specificity and inseparability 45
Dan Douglas

7. Assessing language skills for specific purposes: Describing and analysing the 'behaviour domain' 53
Elaine Tarone

8. The assessment of language impairment across language backgrounds 61
Rosemary Baker

9. A process for translating achievement tests 73
Charles Stansfield and Joan Auchter

Section Four
Judgement in language testing **81**

10. Revisiting raters and ratings in oral language assessment 82
Daniel Reed and Andrew Cohen

11. Establishing meaningful language test scores for selection and placement 97
Patrick Griffin

Section Five
The uses and usefulness of language tests **108**

12. Designing and developing useful language tests 109
Lyle Bachman

13. The formative and summative uses of language test data: Present concerns and future directions 117
Cyril Weir

14. Language assessment and professional development 126
Geoff Brindley

Section Six
Language test impact **137**

15. The need for impact studies of L2 performance testing and rating: Identifying areas of potential consequences at all levels of the testing cycle 138
Carolyn Turner

16. Impact and washback research in language testing 150
J. Charles Alderson and Jayanti Banerjee

Section Seven

Language testing in its policy context **162**

17. Prescribed language standards and foreign language classroom practice: Relationships and consequences 163
Rosamond Mitchell

18. Rendering ESL accountable: Educational and bureaucratic technologies in the Australian context 177
Helen Moore

19. The policy context of English testing for immigrants 191
John Read

20. Testimony from testees: The case against current language policies in sub-Saharan Africa 200
Eddie Williams

Section Eight

The ethics of language testing **211**

21. Cheating language tests can be dangerous 212
Bernard Spolsky

22. Ethics, fairness(es), and developments in language testing 222
Liz Hamp-Lyons

23. The ethical potential of alternative language assessment 228
Brian K. Lynch

Section Nine

Language testing and SLA **240**

24. Quantitative evaluation of vocabulary: How it can be done and what it is good for 241
Batia Laufer

25. Some thoughts on testing grammar: An SLA perspective 251
Rod Ellis

26. Measuring development and ultimate attainment in non native grammars 264
Antonella Sorace and Daniel Robertson

Section Ten

Beyond language testing **275**

27. Fossilisation: Moving the concept into empirical longitudinal study 276
Larry Selinker and ZhaoHong Han

28. The unbearable lightness of being a native speaker 292
John C. Maher

Section Eleven

The publications of Alan Davies **304**

Notes on the contributors 315
Author Index 326

Series Editor's note

Alan Davies has been centrally involved in Applied Linguistics and Language Testing for more than thirty years. Over that time he has also worked with UCLES on many occasions, most recently as a consultant, advisor and editor-in-chief of the SILT Volume 7, *A Dictionary of Language Testing*. Alan's contributions to our work in Cambridge have always been of the greatest help and it is with a sense of honour that we publish this volume as a token of our respect.

Michael Milanovic
Cambridge
September 2000

Preface

This volume pays tribute to Alan Davies' work in the field of language testing which spans a period of more than thirty years. His interest in this area began almost by accident when, on leave in the UK from an English teaching post in Kenya, he was offered the opportunity of working at Birmingham University on the development of the English Proficiency Test Battery (E. P. T. B.), later known as the 'Davies' test, commissioned by the British Council for the selection of overseas students for admission to higher education courses in the UK. His involvement in this project provided the data for his doctoral dissertation 'Proficiency in English as a Second Language' which was submitted in 1965. The project gave him the chance to acquire knowledge and skills in educational measurement, but its chief appeal was that it offered him a way to understand and build theory around the problems he had faced when applying English as a mother tongue assumptions to his practice as a teacher of English to L2 learners in East Africa.

It is this interest in language testing not as an end in itself but as a means of exploring or operationalising important issues in applied linguistics that characterises much of Davies' contribution to the field, together with his constant striving for the right balance between speculation and empiricism (Davies 1992a). He writes in the first issue of the journal *Language Testing* which appeared in June 1984:

> *The process of concurrent and predictive validities, the internal analyses and the external comparisons are time consuming but routine. ...in the end no empirical study can improve a test's validity. That is a matter for the construct and content validities. What is most important is the preliminary thinking and the preliminary analysis as to the nature of the language learning we aim to capture...*
>
> (p. 68)

Davies (1968b) has warned against allowing the necessary preoccupation with the psychometric properties of language tests to override the central issues of language, learning and evaluation which underlie the language testing enterprise. What sets his own books on testing, *Testing and Experimental Methods, Edinburgh Course in Applied Linguistics, Vol 4* (Allen and Davies 1977) and *Principles of Language Testing* (Davies 1990a), apart from others in the field is their attempt to bring language testing squarely under the umbrella of Applied Linguistics.

It is important to acknowledge (as do a number of authors in this volume) that Davies' interests and scholarly endeavours are by no means confined to language testing. He has written extensively about language teaching and learning, sociolinguistics, language planning, ideology and, more recently, about the nature and scope of the Applied Linguistic endeavour (see ***The publications of Alan Davies*** at the end of this volume). His originality lies in his capacity to draw these various strands together in his language testing work, to ask unexpected, but always pertinent, questions, to query whether a new trend is necessarily better than, or essentially different from, what has preceded it, and to draw attention to the wider implications of a particular test use or test outcome. We are acutely aware that the focus of this volume has meant that many who would have liked to mark their respect for Davies' contribution to the broader field of applied linguistics have felt unable to do so in this context. We are nevertheless happy that we have been able to attract contributors (e.g. Widdowson, Section Two; Tarone, Section Three; Sorace and Robertson, Section nine; Maher, Section ten) who do not see themselves as language testers but who nevertheless recognise the potential or actual links between this field and their own research interests and/or who are prepared to give us the benefit of the outsider's view.

The papers in this *Festschrift* have been collected by colleagues at the Language Testing Research Centre where Alan worked for several years before retiring in March 1998. (He remains attached to the Centre as Principal Fellow but has now returned to the University of Edinburgh where he is Honorary Fellow and Emeritus Professor of Applied Linguistics.) Its scope is deliberately broad. It presents a number of different 'angles' on language testing, most of which have been touched upon in Alan's writings over the years. There are 28 papers in all, divided into 10 sections covering issues which range from construct definition in language testing to the design and applications of language tests (including their importance as a means of exploring larger issues in Applied Linguistics) and the consequences (pedagogical, social and ethical) of their use. The papers have been grouped thematically but these groupings should be seen as *ad hoc* since it was clear from our editorial discussions that a number of alternative categorisations would have been possible.

Section One ***The contribution of Alan Davies*** contains two papers, *Alan Davies and British applied linguistics* and *Ten years of the Language Testing Research Centre,* which pay direct tribute to Alan's work over the last three decades in both Britain and Australia. The first, by Christopher Brumfit, outlines Alan's outstanding record in British applied linguistics and points to the profound 'humanising influence' of his work across the whole discipline.

The second, written by Tim McNamara in collaboration with the other editors of this volume, tells the story of a major research initiative in Australia with which Alan was associated and which would not have been possible without Alan's benign leadership, his prolific scholarly output and his capacity to encourage and inspire his younger colleagues.

The second section, ***Construct definition in language testing,*** deals with the controversial (and to Davies absolutely crucial) issue of constructs of language ability (e.g. Canale and Swain 1980, Bachman 1990) and how these are operationalised in language tests. It opens with a paper by Henry Widdowson, *Communicative language testing: The art of the possible,* which pays homage (through a personal anecdote) to Alan's admirable and sometimes unnerving capacity to 'disturb the settled certainties of conventional belief'. Widdowson, in similar vein, proceeds to mount his own challenge to current orthodoxy in language testing. He questions the adequacy of recent models of communicative competence (because of their failure to capture the interrelationships between the various components of competence that they identify) and casts doubt on the possibility that such competence, as currently defined, can be tested at all. Widdowson's doubt about the feasibility of communicative language testing echoes Davies' early scepticism in the face of what he saw as over-eager assumptions about the value of CLT.

> *Naturalism is a vulgar error: all education needs some measure of idealisation, and the search for authenticity in language teaching is chimerical ... Testing (like teaching) the communicative skills is a way of making sure that there are tests of context as well as of grammar; testing (and teaching) the communicative skills is not doing something parallel to or different from testing (and teaching) the linguistic skills – what it does is to make sure that they are complete.*
>
> (Davies 1978a)

His caution has proved to be well-founded. So too has his prediction that grammar, more powerful in terms of generalisability than any other language feature, would remain central to language testing (ibid). The practice of grammar testing, as Pauline Rea-Dickins reminds us in the second paper in this section, *Fossilisation or evolution: The case of grammar testing,* is still widespread. Her paper examines the prevalence of tests explicitly focused on grammar in a range of situations, concluding that grammar seems to hold a more prominent position when students are entering ESL/EAP courses than when they exit from them. She suggests that grammar has come to be defined much more broadly than as sentence level accuracy, and this is reflected in the range of integrative methods used to test it – here there are signs of evolution. On the other hand, the reasoning and practices associated with grammar testing in pedagogic contexts are much less clear, and suggest a more fossilised situation. She urges language testers to provide guidance to the language teaching profession by coming up with better definitions of grammar and by clearly operationalising their constructs.

The next paper, *The assessment of metalinguistic knowledge,* by Caroline Clapham, shows how exacting the task of construct definition can be. Her concern is with the metalinguistic knowledge of undergraduate foreign language learners and with how it can be tested – an important issue given a) the emphasis which university teachers place on explicit grammar teaching and on their students' understanding of grammatical terms, and b) current controversy in SLA about the role of knowledge about language in acquiring a second language. Clapham's study, which has since been partially replicated by Davies and colleagues in Melbourne (Elder *et al.* 1997), demonstrates how difficult it is to decide at what point a learner's understanding can be regarded as adequate. Her results indicate that language knowledge varies according to the task or context in which it is elicited and that what learners appear to understand in one language is not necessarily carried over into another.

In the third section, ***Language testing for specific purposes and populations***, we have grouped four papers which deal, in one way or another, with test design issues or, more precisely, with the matching of test tasks with test takers' particular backgrounds, abilities or needs. The first two are concerned with testing language for specific purposes and take up issues which have been foreshadowed by Davies in his work on the ELTS validation study (Criper and Davies 1988), on a medicine-specific listening test for the Professional and Linguistic Assessment Board (PLAB) (Davies 1986) and on LSP and performance testing generally (Davies and Brown 1990; Davies 1990a, 1995a).

The first paper, by Dan Douglas, *Three problems in testing language for specific purposes: Authenticity, specificity and inseparability,* offers an overview of the thorny problems surrounding LSP test development. Those which Douglas identifies as critical are the following: a) how to achieve the best fit between the test and the relevant domain of inference (= authenticity), b) how to achieve a balance between generalisability of test results and the tailoring of test tasks required to render them appropriate for a particular group of test takers (= specificity), and c) how (if at all) we can identify and measure the relative contributions of language ability and content knowledge to LSP test performance (= inseparability).

Elaine Tarone's article, *Assessing language skills for specific purposes: Describing and analysing the 'behaviour domain',* focuses more specifically on the methodology of specific-purpose testing and proposes a principled approach to the needs analysis stage of test development which draws on analytic frameworks and ethnographic techniques adopted for genre analysis.

These techniques, she suggests, can yield more accurate and meaningful descriptions of language behaviour in context and as such are a necessary first step in the design of both LSP tests and classroom activities. Whether the items or tasks thus derived would necessarily be performance based (in keeping with the central LSP testing position) or more indirect measures of the relevant skills and abilities (as Davies [1986] would have it) remains uncertain.

Another angle on test specificity is the question of how validly a test designed for a specific purpose can measure the performance of a particular subpopulation of test takers – an issue addressed by Davies (1991b) in relation to the performance of children from immigrant backgrounds on basic numeracy tests administered through the medium of English. A similar issue is taken up by Rosemary Baker in her paper, *The assessment of language impairment across language backgrounds*. Baker finds that language tasks of the types commonly used for the assessment of language impairment in age-related disease, when administered in English, can disadvantage patients from non-English-speaking backgrounds and result in diagnostic errors or virtual denial of access to speech pathology services. But Baker also warns against the assumption that non-native speakers of English necessarily perform better in their first languages and identifies a number of problems with direct translations of test content into other languages.

Stansfield and Auchter also deal with the issue of test equivalence across languages in their paper, *A process for translating achievement tests*. They describe the painstaking procedures adopted to translate tests from one language to another in such a way as to ensure that all items are valid and that the resultant instruments measure comparable constructs. Although the authors agree with Baker (above) that translation is not *ipso facto* a guarantee of item equivalence across different languages and cultures, they suggest that strict adherence to pre-established translation guidelines can reduce the risk of construct-irrelevant differences in test performance, and resultant biases in score interpretation.

The fourth section, ***Judgement in language testing***, deals with an issue which Davies regards as endemic to all attempts to study and measure language learning, namely, the inevitable subjectivity involved in making decisions about how a test is to be designed, how performances are to be rated and what inferences are to be drawn from test scores (see for example Davies *et al.* 1996b). The section contains two papers, a review article by Daniel Reed and Andrew Cohen on the issue of rater behaviour in language testing and a methodology paper by Patrick Griffin dealing with the notoriously problematic issue of setting cut-offs in language tests (see also Davies 1990b).

The Reed and Cohen paper contains a survey of the relevant literature on (a) the validity of different kinds of rating scales and procedures, (b) the characteristics of raters, and (c) rater behaviour and its amenability to training. The conclusion reached by the authors is that some of the most crucial questions about enhancing the validity of language test ratings have yet to be answered. They propose a research agenda into rater behaviour which encompasses both quantitative and qualitative methodologies, and advocate the construction of new types of rating scales which reflect test constructs more explicitly.

Griffin's paper, *Establishing meaningful language test scores for selection and placement,* proposes a practical means of accommodating rater variability and minimising the inevitable uncertainty involved in the setting of cut-scores on language tests through the combined application of the Angoff method and the Rasch partial credit model of measurement. The author however emphasises that the validity of this process rests ultimately on the validity of rater judgements. Griffin argues that meaningful cut-off scores can only be ensured if there is a close fit between the scoring method and the variable being measured, and if the raters concerned are both specialists in the relevant domain and trained in using the scoring procedure.

Section Five, ***The uses and usefulness of language tests***, contains three papers centred around the issue of how tests are used and how they can be rendered useful for their intended purposes.

Lyle Bachman, in his paper *Designing and developing useful language tests,* presents us with a theoretically-grounded framework in which considerations of test usefulness permeate the entire testing cycle, from inception to ultimate use. He sees a key element of test authenticity, and hence the construct validity of score interpretations, as being a demonstrable correspondence between the characteristics of target language use tasks and those of the test tasks, a view which appears on the surface to be quite contrary to that held by Widdowson. Further analysis of the two positions may however reveal considerable affinity between Widdowson's notion of 'valency' (see Section Two) and Bachman and Palmer's definition of 'interactiveness' as the extent and type of involvement of the test taker's individual characteristics in accomplishing a test task (Bachman and Palmer 1996: 25). Both, we suspect, would in the end agree with Davies' (1990a) conclusion:

> *The fundamental argument/debate in language testing over the last 24 years has been basically about the meaning/realization of language behaviour, how best to get at it. The issue is sometimes presented as if there were disagreement about language use. There is not. The disagreement is about the best way to capture control of that language use ...*
>
> (1990a: 137)

The topic of Cyril Weir's paper, *The formative and summative uses of language test data: Present concerns and future directions,* is highly appropriate to this *Festschrift,* given the number of evaluation projects which Davies has been involved in during the course of his career (e.g. Beretta and Davies 1985, 1986; Davies 1987, 1990a, 1991c). Weir, like Davies, is somewhat circumspect about the role of testing in the evaluation process although for different reasons. Davies makes modest claims about the value of tests in programme evaluation seeing them merely as 'a way of focusing attention, discussion and planning on the original and on the existing purposes' (1990a: 116). Weir is more concerned with the qualitative information about learning processes which may be lost or ignored as a result of undue faith in the testing product. Paradoxically, he points out, the reverse is the case in much formative evaluation where in many cases testing is not as central as it should or could be to the classroom monitoring of student language development.

The third paper in this section, *Language assessment and professional development,* by Geoff Brindley, is about test users, rather than test use. It takes on the important task of delineating what these users need to know about language testing (a task which has also been tackled by Davies and his colleagues through their video series: *Mark My Words: Assessing second and foreign language skills* (Davies *et al.* 1996a) and through the creation of a *Dictionary of Language Testing* (Davies *et al.* 1999).) Brindley outlines various ways in which social, economic and political forces have influenced policies and practices in educational assessment in recent years and considers the implications for teachers of this changing assessment environment. He concludes by drawing up an agenda for professional development programmes which will enable teachers to perform learner assessments in a competent manner and to be aware of the long-term impact of their testing practices (see Turner, and Alderson and Banerjee, below).

Test effects or test consequences are now widely believed to be a key aspect of test validity and of a tester's responsibility (Messick 1989) and it is perhaps for this reason that the papers in Section Six, ***Language test impact,*** demand that greater attention be paid to this phenomenon. Davies, however, while stressing the importance of professional accountability, has warned language testers against defining their responsibilities so broadly that they become unmanageable (1997b: 335–6). Carolyn Turner, in her paper, *The need for impact studies of L2 performance testing and rating: Identifying areas of potential consequences at all levels of the testing cycle,* argues that in order to better define where the profession's responsibilities start and finish, and also to maximise the beneficial impact of language tests, we should strengthen our understanding of the washback phenomenon through further empirical research.

J. Charles Alderson and Jayanti Banerjee, while acknowledging the importance of empirical work on test impact, stress the need for greater methodological rigour in its implementation. Their paper, *Impact and washback research in language testing,* concentrates on the validation of instruments used for data gathering purposes. The impact studies reviewed by the authors lacked any adequate treatment of validation issues – hence their recommendation that concepts from the field of language testing be used to develop a conceptual framework within which validity and reliability issues can be investigated. These proposals are illustrated with reference to an ongoing International English Language Testing Service (IELTS) impact study in which the authors are engaged.

In Section Seven, ***Language testing in its policy context,*** we have grouped papers which place testing or assessment issues in the context of national language policies in five different countries: the United Kingdom, Australia, New Zealand, Malawi and Zambia. The demand by governments for greater accountability in education is a near-global phenomenon (see Brindley, Section Five) and Rosamond Mitchell, in a paper entitled *Prescribed language standards and foreign language classroom practice: Relationships and consequences,* discusses the introduction of 'language standards' to foreign language (FL) teaching in England and Wales. The author examines the model of FL development underlying the National Curriculum and suggests that its failure to incorporate 'growth'-oriented beliefs about language use and interlanguage development is likely to stifle creativity and experimentation by both teachers and learners, thereby seriously hampering the achievement of communicative proficiency outcomes in FL classrooms.

Helen Moore's paper, *Rendering ESL accountable: Educational and bureaucratic technologies in the Australian context,* is also concerned with the issue of national frameworks for curriculum and assessment, this time in the context of adult migrant education. While conceding (similarly to Mitchell, above) that such state-mandated frameworks are reductionist and tend to induce conformity rather than foster creativity, she argues that they can at the same time offer important educational trade-offs. She demonstrates that the recently introduced Certificates in Spoken and Written English for adult learners of English as a second language, notwithstanding their limitations, provide a powerful authorising mechanism whereby teachers' professional aspirations can be realised and institutional claims for resources can be legitimised.

John Read's paper, *The policy context of English testing for immigrants,* documents the social impact of recent policy changes for immigrants to New Zealand including the introduction of a controversial pre-entry English language requirement and a financial penalty for those failing to meet this requirement within a given period of time. His paper is a welcome addition to recent writings on the politics of language testing in immigration contexts (e.g. Hawthorne 1997; Shohamy 1997; Brindley and Wigglesworth 1998) and nicely complements a paper by Davies (1997c) documenting the history (and questionable ethics) of using English language tests as a means of barring undesirable aliens from entry to Australia.

It is fitting that the final paper in this section, by Eddie Williams, is about the status of English in developing countries, a subject which Alan Davies has been interested in (Davies 1968a, 1987, 1991c) since his early days as an English teacher in Kenya. In contrast with the other papers in this section, Williams' article, *Testimony from testees: The case against current language policies in sub-Saharan Africa,* is concerned not with the social impact of language testing, but rather with what test outcomes tell us about the impact of language policy, in this case the policy of promoting English-medium instruction in primary schools in Southern Africa. While the rationale for the policy is one of modernisation and unification, Williams' analysis of test results (relating to literacy in both English and local languages) suggests that this policy is limited in its effectiveness. His findings are contrasted with public perceptions regarding the value of English as a vehicle for social advancement.

Section Eight, ***The ethics of language testing***, deals with some of the issues identified as critical by Davies (1997a and b) in a special issue of *Language Testing* (14,3) on test ethics and what he has called 'right conduct' of the professionals engaged in test development, use and validation. The section opens with a paper by Bernard Spolsky, *Cheating language tests can be dangerous*, which emphasises the fact that language test scores are at best 'a chance approximation of the ability we hope to measure'. Like Davies, he believes that some form of testing is generally better than no testing at all but goes on to argue (using the history of the industrialisation of TOEFL by way of illustration) that testers' energies have been misdirected: they have focused too much attention on the reduction of measurement error and too little on 'the more urgent task of learning how to use flawed instruments fairly'.

Defining what we mean by fair test use is however a complex matter, as Liz Hamp-Lyons, in her paper, *Ethics, fairness(es), and developments in language testing,* points out. She reflects here on her early struggles with the issue of ethics in language testing in response to Alan Davies' comments on her doctoral dissertation. She then goes on to describe the current difficulties she faces in ascribing a single meaning to the term fairness, given the large numbers of stakeholders involved in the testing enterprise and their sometimes conflicting views and needs. She issues a plea to language testers to pay greater attention to stakeholders' perspectives and to assume greater responsibility for the impact of the instruments they devise.

Some of the scenarios proposed by Hamp-Lyons are quite at odds with traditional thinking about language testing and suggest the need for an alternative assessment paradigm. Lynch, in *The ethical potential of alternative language assessment,* talks of an alternative assessment culture involving an integrated view of teaching and assessment, in which students have a key role in making choices about how they are assessed and what counts as evidence in this process. He argues that alternative systems require different approaches to validity and proposes a theoretical framework for such approaches.

Section Nine, ***Language testing and SLA***, takes the volume in a new direction, away from the consideration of tests and their social impact towards an investigation of their value as a tool for doing research into second language acquisition, including the measurement of vocabulary acquisition, grammatical development and ultimate attainment. The validity of empirical investigation in this area depends on satisfactory methods of measuring interlanguage development, as Davies (1990a), amongst others, has insisted.

The paper, *Quantitative evaluation of vocabulary : How it can be done and what it is good for,* by Batia Laufer, makes a case for using multiple quantitative measures of vocabulary acquisition both for practical purposes (e.g. to predict second language learners' future academic performance) and in acquisitional research. She describes a number of such measures and illustrates their potential as research tools with data from recent research.

The issue of grammar testing, which featured strongly in the second section of this volume (see papers by Rea-Dickins and Clapham) re-emerges in a paper by Ellis, *Some thoughts on testing grammar: An SLA perspective.* Ellis questions the validity of indirect system-referenced practices in grammar testing (as exemplified by the TOEFL), because they measure only one type of grammatical ability. He offers what appears to be a response to the problems identified by Rea-Dickins and Clapham in the form of a set of provisional 'specifications' for instruments which are sensitive to both explicit and implicit grammatical knowledge and to sources of variation in interlanguage development.

Sorace and Robertson in their joint paper, *Measuring development and ultimate attainment in non-native grammars,* describe a measurement technique principally employed in psychophysics, known as magnitude estimation, which allows them to quantify judgements of linguistic acceptability on interval (rather than the traditional dichotomous or Likert-type) scales and therefore to use the full range of parametric statistics in analysing their findings. They demonstrate that magnitude estimation is especially suitable to the investigation of non-native competence, since it is sensitive to one of the main distinguishing features of these grammars: namely, indeterminacy and optionality at all stages of development.

The final section of the volume, ***Beyond language testing,*** contains two papers which fall well within the realm of Alan Davies' interests and research activity but are not centrally about language testing. They nevertheless pose challenges to the language tester by identifying aspects of language behaviour which are not easily amenable to empirical investigation.

Selinker and Han's paper, *Fossilisation: Moving the concept into empirical longitudinal study,* presents a state-of-the-art discussion of the poorly understood phenomenon of fossilisation (which was touched on in Davies and his colleagues' early edited volume on Interlanguage (Davies, Howatt and Criper 1984)). The paper deals with both theoretical and definitional issues pertaining to the concept of fossilisation as well as the related concepts of stabilisation and multiple effects. The authors call for longitudinal studies as the only means of ascertaining that no change has occurred in an interlanguage form over time, and identify the need for context-sensitive language tests which can elucidate the complex nature of the fossilisation phenomena they identify. They argue as Davies has done (e.g. Davies 1998) for the importance of co-operation between language testers and SLA researchers.

John Maher's paper, *The unbearable lightness of being a native speaker,* is a fitting conclusion to this volume. It takes up and elaborates, in a fanciful but scholarly fashion, the tantalisingly elusive concept of the native speaker which Davies has written about extensively (Davies 1991a and d, 1992b, 1994, 1995c). The notion of the native speaker encapsulates the kind of paradox (ideal versus real, universal versus particular) which has captured Davies' imagination and which he has attempted to reconcile in much of his work in language testing and in applied linguistics more generally (see ***The publications of Alan Davies*** at the end of the volume). For testing, the challenge is to find a satisfactory compromise between principle and expediency (see Widdowson, Section Two) or, as Alan puts it, between uncertainty and explicitness.

> *Our view is that through its important contribution to the fundamental linguistic tension between uncertainty and explicitness the central role of language testing in applied linguistics can be generally agreed.*
>
> (Davies 1990a: 69)

References

Allen, J. P. B. and A. Davies. 1977. *Testing and Experimental Methods.* Volume 4 in *Edinburgh Course in Applied Linguistics.* Oxford: Oxford University Press.

Bachman, L. F. 1990. *Fundamental Considerations in Language Testing.* Oxford: Oxford University Press.

Bachman, L. F. and A. S. Palmer. 1996. Language Testing in Practice: Designing and Developing Useful Language Tests. Oxford: Oxford University Press.

Beretta, A. and A. Davies. 1985. Evaluation of the Bangalore Project. *English Language Teaching Journal* 39 (2): 121–127.

Beretta, A. and A. Davies. 1986. Evaluation of the Bangalore Project. *Journal of English Language Teaching (India)* 21 (4).

Brindley, G. and G. Wigglesworth (eds.). 1998. **access**: *Issues in Language Test Design and Delivery,* pp. 9–29. Sydney: NCELTR.

Canale, M. and M. Swain. 1980. Theoretical bases of communicative approaches to language testing. *Applied Lingustics* 1/1: 1– 47.

Criper, C. and A. Davies. 1988. *English Language Testing Service Research Report* 1 (1). ELTS Validation Project Report, British Council/UCLES.

Davies, A. 1968a. Oral English testing in West Africa. In A. Davies (ed.), *Language Testing Symposium,* pp. 151–179. Oxford: Oxford University Press.

Davies, A. 1968b. Introduction. In A. Davies (ed.), *Language Testing Symposium* (pp. 1–10). Oxford: Oxford University Press.

Davies, A. 1978a. Language testing: Part one. Survey article in *Language Teaching and Linguistics Abstracts* 11.

Davies, A. 1984. Validating three tests of English language proficiency. *Language Testing* 1 (1): 50–69.

Davies, A. 1986. Indirect ESP testing: Old innovations. In M. Portal (ed.), *Language Testing*, pp. 55–67. NFER/Nelson.

Davies, A. 1987. When professional advice and political constraints conflict: the case of Nepal. In *Focus on English.* Madras: British Council.

Davies, A. 1990a. *Principles of Language Testing.* Oxford: Basil Blackwell.

Davies, A. 1990b. Operationalising uncertainty in language testing. In J. de Jong and D. Stevenson (eds.), *Individualizing the Assessment of Language Abilities,* pp. 179–195. Clevedon: Multilingual Matters Ltd.

Davies, A. 1991a. *The Native Speaker in Applied Linguistics.* Edinburgh: Edinburgh University Press.

Davies A. 1991b. Performance of children from non-English speaking background on the New South Wales Basic Skills Tests of Numeracy. *Language, Culture and Curriculum* 4 (2): 149–161.

Davies, A. 1991c. An evaluation model for English language teaching projects in South India: The policy of change. *Australian Review of Applied Linguistics* 14 (2): 73–86.

Davies, A. 1991d. The notion of the Native Speaker. *Journal of Intercultural Studies* 12 (2): 35–45.

Davies, A. 1992a. Speculation and empiricism in applied linguistics. *Melbourne Papers in Language Testing* 1(2): 1–18.

Davies, A. 1992b. The notion of the native speaker. *Focus on English* 7 (2 and 3): 3–15.

Davies, A. 1994. Native Speaker. In *Encyclopedia of Language and Linguistics.* Oxford: Elsevier Science Ltd.

Davies, A. 1995a. Testing communicative language or testing language communicatively: what? how? *Melbourne Papers in Language Testing* 4 (1): 1–20.

Davies, A. 1995c. Proficiency or the Native Speaker: what are we trying to achieve in ELT? In G. Cook and B. Seidlhofer (eds.), *Principles and Practice in Applied Linguistics; Studies in Honour of H. G. Widdowson,* pp. 145–157. Oxford: Oxford University Press.

Davies, A. 1997a. Introduction: The limits of ethics in language testing. *Language Testing* [special issue] 14 (3): 235–241.

Davies, A. 1997b. Demands of being professional in language testing. *Language Testing* [special issue] 14 (3): 329–339.

Davies, A. 1997c. Australian immigrant gatekeeping through English language tests: how important is proficiency? In V. Kohonen, A. Huhta, L. Kurki-Suonio and S. Luoma (eds.), *Current Developments and Alternatives in Language Assessment: Proceedings of LTRC '96,* pp. 71–84. Jyväskylä: University of Jyväskylä and University of Tampere.

Davies, A. 1998. Preface. In A. Davies, A. Brown, C. Elder, K. Hill, T. Lumley and T. McNamara, *Dictionary of Language Testing.* Cambridge: Cambridge University Press.

Davies, A. 2000. *Introduction to Applied Linguistics: From Practice to Theory*. Edinburgh: Edinburgh University Press.

Davies, A. and A. Brown 1990. Designing instruments to measure language proficiency. In E. Wylie (ed.), *Assessment of Proficiency in Japanese as a Foreign Language*, pp. 94–103. Asian Studies Council, Canberra.

Davies, A., A. Brown, C. Elder, R. Evans, E. Grove, K. Hill, N. Iwashita, T. Lumley and C. O'Shannessy. 1996a. *Mark My Words: Assessing second and foreign language skills.* Melbourne: Multimedia Education Unit, University of Melbourne.

Davies, A., A. Brown, C. Elder, R. Evans, E. Grove, K. Hill, N. Iwashita, T. Lumley and C. O'Shannessy. 1996b. 'Video 4: Objective and subjective assessment' in *Mark My Words: Assessing second and foreign language skills*. Melbourne: Multimedia Education Unit, University of Melbourne.

Davies, A., A. Brown, C. Elder, K. Hill, T. Lumley and T. McNamara. 1999. *Dictionary of Language Testing*. Cambridge: Cambridge University Press.

Davies, A., A. Howatt and C. Criper (eds.) 1984. *Interlanguage*. Edinburgh University Press.

Davies, A. and T. Kansakar. 1986. English proficiency in the Kathmandu Valley Colleges: a preliminary investigation. *Indian Journal of Applied Linguistics* 12 (1–2): 127–136.

Elder, C., A. Davies, J. Hajek, D. Manwaring and J. Warren. 1997. Is grammar good for you? The relationship between metalinguistic knowledge and success in studying a language at university. *Melbourne Papers in Language Testing* 5 (1): 35–55.

Hawthorne, L. 1997. The political dimension of English language testing in Australia. *Language Testing* 14: 248–60.

Messick, S. 1989. Validity In R. L. Linn (ed.), *Educational Measurement (3rd ed)*, pp. 13–103. New York: American Council on Education.

Shohamy, E. 1997. Testing methods, testing consequences: Are they ethical? Are they fair? *Language Testing* 14 (3): 340–349.

Acknowledgements

A number of people, other than the editors and the contributors, worked very hard on the production of this volume. We would like to thank Samantha Green for tracking the contributors down, Natalie Stephens for collecting the abstracts and continuing the liaison work and Ruta Kanepe and Felicity Jensz for sending out reminders, circulating the incoming papers for comment and generally keeping the editors in line. Thanks also to Fiona Watson for her preliminary formatting of the volume.

The editors:
Catherine Elder, Annie Brown, Elisabeth Grove,
Noriko Iwashita, Tom Lumley, Kathryn Hill,
Tim McNamara, Kieran O'Loughlin
The University of Melbourne

Section One

The contribution of Alan Davies

1 Alan Davies and British applied linguistics

Christopher Brumfit
University of Southampton

For many applied linguists Alan Davies is identified with 'Testing', and undoubtedly he has been for many years the major British theorist in this field. But it would be quite wrong to see him as a researcher exclusively in this area; on the contrary, within British applied linguistics he has been a major humanising influence across the whole discipline. His publications and conference papers range across topics as diverse as language in Quaker meetings, the role of the native speaker, teaching methods, and the politics of English.

He has been of course, at different times, chair and committee member of the British Association for Applied Linguistics, head of the oldest and most distinguished Department of Applied Linguistics in UK at the University of Edinburgh, editor of *Applied Linguistics*, and sometime secretary-general of AILA. As a contribution to the internal and external politics of British applied linguistics that is an outstanding record. But his contribution was distinguished as much by his manner as his matter; his particular style gave British applied linguistics much of its character: grounded partly on empirical and technical work, closely allied to the world role of English, but humane and contextualised within a broadly classical tradition.

My own first encounter with Alan typifies his approach. My first ever paper to a BAAL conference, in Edinburgh in 1974, addressed the subject of the relationship between applied linguistics and teachers of English as a first language in UK. I argued that an applied linguistics without central interest in such work was failing to address its most important questions, and that English teachers without a similar central interest in applied linguistics were failing to address the central issues in their subject. As I crept away from this nerve-wracking initiation, Alan followed me. 'We'll never succeed, you know,' he said. 'However hard we try, we won't get them interested – English teachers are too suspicious and we are too tied to EFL.' A conversation developed, in which many of the themes of our subsequent meetings emerged. It was only many years later, after I had watched sympathetic questioning from the floor of many rough and ready papers from home and overseas students at BAAL conferences, that I realised how typical this was of Alan's style. First of all, he bothered to come and say something. Second, he immediately included the new and unknown speaker in the community of applied linguists – 'We'll never succeed.' Third, without being arrogant, it was clear he had been there before; he had thought about the same issues, and was anxious to continue the debate with anyone else concerned. Fourth, he was pursuing the interaction between academic matters and the socio-politics of applied linguistics activity. Fifth, he was mildly and deprecatingly pessimistic: applied linguistics could not offer grand and up-beat solutions to human problems. What we could do was try to be clearer about the nature of language, about where we stood as individuals, and about the role of language in society. If we did that, things just might be a little better than before.

Unlike most British applied linguists, Alan Davies came from a humanities and arts background rather than from modern languages. But (as he discusses in the preface to his 1991 book on *The Native Speaker in Applied Linguistics*) his Welsh background gave him an awareness of multilingualism – but of multilingualism attached to power. 'My South Wales had been part of what in Ireland is called the Pale. It included most of Southern Glamorgan and Southern Pembroke and had been settled by Normans, later by Flemings and Huguenots and always by English speakers' (p. vii). Note how resonant and how economical the 'always' is, and also how inclusive: it links his experience to those of his foreign students, of the receivers of English, those to whom it is done, rather than those who do it.

For in all his work, Alan retains the ambivalence which English-speaking applied linguists necessarily must have. Too individual and western to accept an inheritance of guilt from ancestors for whom he could not personally be held responsible, he none-the-less worries away at real issues of human ambition, personal choice, and language as an institution. His preface continues to point out how the Welsh learnt English, 'very rarely the other way round', how Welsh- and English-speaking groups intermarried and how Welsh declined 'as all languages have in the path of a juggernaut like English'. But he then develops the argument with a careful consideration of the pros and cons of access to English, from the point of view of individual speakers and their families, and links the discussion to worldwide issues, concluding an exploration of personal identity in his own return (in his forties) to learn Welsh with 'We all want to belong, we all want to be native speakers' (p. viii).

The book which emerges from this preliminary, personal account, explores a wide range of psycholinguistic and sociolinguistic literature to clarify the concept of 'native speaker', demonstrating that there are indeed psycholinguistic differences between native and non-native speakers, but that sociolinguistically these are not significant. He concludes with the assertion that 'if a non-native speaker wishes to pass as a native speaker and is so accepted then it is surely irrelevant if s/he shows differences in more and more refined tests of grammaticality' (p. 166). For him, applied linguistics exists firmly in the social world, and the impact of language on that world is central to his conception of the discipline.

Since this book was published, there has been much more discussion of the 'native speaker' issue, most of which is angrier than Alan Davies' book and none of which is more thoughtful. But unlike many of his contemporaries, he has never been a polemicist. Even when, as with his work on testing, the implications have been ideologically highly contentious, he has tended to accept that there is a job to be done, to define the issues and carefully explore the implications, but to leave it to individuals to decide on the best path for them to follow. Indeed, as he indicates in another autobiographical preface (to *Principles of Language Testing*, 1990) he almost came in to his work on testing by accident, having started to work on an MA on African writing in English, but being diverted by a paid research post developing the English language proficiency test. And if this appears to reflect passivity rather than activity in career creation, it also draws attention to one of Alan's strengths. He is indeed typical of his time, caught up inexorably in the astonishing spread of English since the second world war, and providing throughout his career a commentary on the academic preoccupations of those who are being driven along by a force which they cannot entirely control.

But it is a humane and civilised commentary. Like many of his generation, he left university to teach in Africa, returned to Britain for further study and found himself pulled into the EFL/ESOL machine, as publishers and the British Council provided the bases for student funding and the dissemination of research work. Particularly through the British Council, he travelled widely, and his movements (up to and including his recent connection with Australia) reflect the shifting centres of English language/applied linguistic activity in the late twentieth-century world. With his predecessor at Edinburgh, Pit Corder, he maintained a civilising influence on developments in language teaching by commenting from a standpoint where values came primarily from outside the work environment. If Pit Corder had one big idea and Alan Davies had many, their influence was similar, for each provided ways of conceptualising the enterprise, but more importantly provided a tone of careful clarification of specific problems, with an emphasis on getting the ideas right, and a suspicion of dogma. Both would have acknowledged that they were lucky in their times and institutions, but the tradition to which both were central figures, in different generations, is a powerful legacy for Edinburgh, and British applied linguistics, to have provided for the world.

References

Davies, A. 1990. *Principles of Language Testing*. Oxford: Blackwell.

Davies, A. 1991. *The Native Speaker in Applied Linguistics.* Edinburgh: Edinburgh University Press.

2 Ten years of the Language Testing Research Centre

Tim McNamara
University of Melbourne

The Language Testing Research Centre (LTRC) at the University of Melbourne was founded late in 1989, one of the fruits of the National Policy on Languages (Lo Bianco 1987). Ten years on it is a good time to review the history of the establishment of the Centre and its subsequent achievements, and to consider Alan Davies' contribution to both.

The founding of the LTRC was a stroke of extraordinary good fortune. It is a very Australian story, a happy combination of historical circumstance, idealism and improbability. It is necessary to appreciate something of the distinctive history of applied linguistics in Australia to understand the circumstances of the creation of the LTRC. Applied linguistics established itself as an area of teaching and research later in Australia than in Britain, the United States or Canada. Moreover its origins lay in the teaching of foreign languages (what came in Australia to be called Languages Other Than English or LOTE) rather than in the teaching of English; this alone distinguishes Australian applied linguistics from its counterparts in the UK and the USA.

Why an LTRC at Melbourne? The Melbourne applied linguistics programme, like others in Australia, had only been recently established. It was the creation of Terry Quinn, whose background was in French, and who was at the time Director of the Horwood Language Centre at Melbourne. Quinn had helped found the Applied Linguistics Association of Australia with other colleagues in French language teaching in the 1970s, and became the most influential thinker in Australia in the 1970s and 1980s on the teaching of foreign and second languages. He was active and influential in government language policy in the 15 years of rapid social and cultural change following the election of the Whitlam Labor Government in 1972. In this period he became a friend and mentor to Joe Lo Bianco, whose Master's thesis he supervised and with whom he interacted on key policy committees, and who subsequently became the leading Australian figure in language policy.

Although the origins of applied linguistics in Australia were in University foreign language teaching, the British tradition of applied linguistics was nevertheless a crucial intellectual influence. The first appointment to the Melbourne applied linguistics programme was Tim McNamara, a graduate of the University of London Birkbeck MA, who had an interest in language testing. McNamara encouraged Quinn to use the presence of international experts on language testing at the AILA conference in Sydney 1987 as the basis for an invitational colloquium on language testing in Melbourne following AILA (McNamara 1988). One of those invited was the eminent British scholar and expert in language testing, Alan Davies. Quinn secured further funding for Alan to return as a Faculty Visitor for eight weeks in 1988. As the senior figure in British language testing, and someone who epitomised the British research tradition in Applied Linguistics, he seemed a very fitting visitor for a newly established programme with a burgeoning research focus in language testing.

Meanwhile, Lo Bianco's remarkable document, the *National Policy on Languages*, which appeared in 1987, ushered in an unprecedented era of generous government support for research in many areas of applied linguistics, particularly those to do with LOTE. This area encompassed both community languages (the languages of indigenous and recent immigrant communities) and languages of strategic significance for the country, including traditional European languages and the languages of Australia's neighbours and main trading partners, Indonesia, Japan, China and Korea.

One of the outcomes of Lo Bianco's document was to be the establishment of what was initially known as the National Languages Institute of Australia (NLIA), a multi-site organisation with research centres in a number of states, each focusing on an aspect of applied linguistics research. After a year of tortuous negotiations, transformations, disappointments and deals, the NLIA came into being in 1989. The political realities had led to the creation of two centres for research on language testing.

The first was at Griffith University and was headed by Professor David Ingram, perhaps the best known language tester in Australia following his work in the late 1970s on the Australian Second Language Proficiency Ratings (ASLPR). This was an interview-based oral proficiency procedure designed to accommodate the needs of English teaching to adults within the context of Australian immigration.

The second was at Melbourne, to be known as the Language Testing Unit (LTU). Melbourne had been actively lobbying for involvement in the NLIA throughout the period prior to its establishment. But despite Lo Bianco's loyalty to Melbourne, it was politically difficult to justify funding a second testing research centre at Melbourne, given McNamara's junior status (Quinn had now retired owing to ill health), the seniority of Ingram, and the desirability of avoiding the creation of two research centres in language testing. The key to the success of the Melbourne bid to be included in the NLIA was an invitation to Alan Davies to act as Director of the Centre for an initial three-year period. He agreed, bringing the necessary seniority, vision, experience and maturity. His mixture of informality, sharp critical judgement, encouragement of junior staff and democratic administrative style was to set a stamp on the character of the Centre and strengthened its 'British' feel; this was melded with an Australian enthusiasm and idealism that was in stark contrast to the ailing mood in Britain after ten years of Thatcherism.

The University of Melbourne, without the advocacy of Quinn, was bemused by the project, happy to get the funding and the prestige but unsure what to make of an energetic junior lecturer and a very British professor, whose dry sense of humour was largely lost on the administrators with whom he had to deal. The University offered accommodation but no salaries; if the LTU could fund itself, then well and good; let it be seen but not heard. Regular external reviews heaped praise on its achievements, but did not succeed in substantially altering the nature or tenor of relations between it and the University at large.

The upshot was that the LTU was left to itself, largely ignored; this had the advantage that it had the freedom to determine its own fate. Core infrastructure funding was supplemented with project funds secured from State and Federal governments, largely for occupationally-based performance tests in a range of languages (following McNamara's PhD research on the development of the Occupational English Test for immigrant and refugee health professionals [McNamara 1990]). But who would do the work? The most likely source of recruits were the best graduates from the MA programme, which, once established, attracted the pick of language teachers and teacher educators in Melbourne, people who would have done MAs years earlier had a suitable programme been available. The first appointments were all graduates of the MA programme: Cathie Elder, a specialist in LOTE, with many years' lecturing experience in Italian and in LOTE teacher education at various universities in Melbourne; Annie Brown and Tom Lumley, British-educated Australians, friends and colleagues, both ESL specialists recruited from the English language programme at a Melbourne College of Advanced Education; Joy McQueen, a colleague from the same college; Kieran O'Loughlin, a senior ESL teacher at the leading adult migrant education centre in Melbourne. In time, most of these undertook PhDs in language testing, which they completed concomitantly with their work as research officers. The tradition of employing Melbourne graduates has continued with current staff members Lis Grove, Kathryn Hill and Noriko Iwashita. Former staff members who have also made a significant contribution to the life and work of the Centre include Jill Wigglesworth, Ruth Evans and Helen Lunt.

In time, the work of the LTU began to take many new directions. Major research projects were secured, in both LOTE and English, in each of the school, university and private sectors. A hallmark of the work was the extent of collaboration with other centres in Australia; this was in the spirit of the

National Languages Institute, but Melbourne did it more than any other Centre. It was a product of the youth, idealism and energy of the staff, who flourished under Alan Davies' benign leadership. The feeling in the Centre in its early years was of a family business; it was characterised by an extreme friendliness and level of good will; the feeling of neglect by the University only inspired people to greater efforts. As the operation grew larger – it had now become the Language Testing Research Centre (LTRC), after a favourable University review in 1993 – it necessarily grew more impersonal. At the height of its growth, in 1994, when the Centre was a partner in the development of the ***access:*** test (Brindley and Wigglesworth 1998), a major government initiative to test the English language proficiency of immigrants to Australia, the Centre employed some 20 research and administrative staff. It became fragmented, with staff being scattered both on- and off-campus because of space limitations.

The ending of this testing contract led to a resumption of the earlier scale of the operation, and a return to greater intimacy coinciding with a move to a small Victorian terrace house adjacent to the main University campus. This move also coincided with the return of Alan Davies for a second three-year period of Directorship. During his absence (when he returned to Edinburgh to take up a personal chair) the Directorship of the Centre had been taken over by Tim McNamara who now also found himself Head of the newly formed Department of Applied Linguistics and Language Studies. Ultimately, it became clear that a full-time Director was required and a decision was made to invite Alan to return. Alan served his second term as Director from 1995 to 1998.

The Centre now has a core staff of seven, with Cathie Elder as its third Director and its former Directors Alan Davies and Tim McNamara closely associated and supportive of its activities. The Centre remains affiliated to the National Languages Institute (now called Language Australia) but core funding has now ceased due to a general shrinking of Commonwealth funds to education. As of 1998 the Centre has been entirely reliant on funds secured through competitive tender and consultancy work. Current projects include a nationwide study of the comparative language proficiency attainments of school-age learners of Japanese, Italian, French and Indonesian over a five-year period, an evaluation of different programme models for delivering school-based minority language maintenance, and research into task-based language testing as part of the TOEFL 2000 project at ETS in Princeton. The early focus on performance testing continues with the recent development of a test of oral communication for ESL undergraduates admitted to Melbourne University's Faculty of Medicine. The Centre remains a marvellous place to work and to be associated with, never quite having lost its independence, humour, inventiveness and spontaneity, qualities which are attributable in large part to the style of its first Director, Alan Davies, and which stand out within the institutional setting of a traditional university.

The productivity of the Centre in terms of research has been extraordinary. In terms of Alan's contribution, this may be seen as a reflection of his commitment to scholarship above all else and to his own prolific output, but also to his encouragement of his younger colleagues, many of whom came to the Centre with little experience of academia. As measured by publications in *Language Testing* (the main refereed international journal in the field), the Language Testing Research Centre has emerged as highly prolific. At the annual Language Testing Research Colloquium, the main international language testing research conference, Melbourne has over a period of five years been responsible for more papers than any other centre in the world. Since its inception in 1996, the ILTA Robert Lado award for best graduate student presentation has been given each year to a member of the LTRC. The Centre has also made its presence felt on a regular basis at AAAL, AILA, SLRF, PacSLRF and, of course, closer to home, the Australian Applied Linguistics Association conference.

Melbourne Papers in Language Testing, a working papers series which has become essential reading for most serious language testing researchers, was established on the initiative of Annie Brown in 1992, and is still going strong. Important books on language testing by Davies (1990) and McNamara (1996) were published during the first years of the Centre. The Davies volume was at once a synthesis of Alan's previous work in the area of language testing and an attempt to position this relatively new discipline squarely within the realm of applied linguistics. McNamara's volume drew on the wealth of project work and research undertaken by himself and other members of the Centre to illustrate a theoretical approach to performance testing.

Particularly worthy of comment are two projects which reflect the spirit with which the Centre operates: highly collaborative, and employing the twin strengths of the Centre, a broad understanding of issues in testing theory, and years of practical experience in test development. In 1997, on an initiative of Alan Davies and following a survey of potential users, the Centre was awarded research funding which enabled it to create a series of 6 beautifully produced teaching videos entitled *Mark My Words* (Davies *et al.* 1996). Interest in the videos worldwide indicates a serious need for more such user-friendly materials to introduce graduate students and practising teachers to assessment theory.

But perhaps the most enduring achievement of the Centre coincides with its tenth anniversary: the publication by Cambridge in 1999 of the first *Dictionary of Language Testing* (Davies *et al.* 1999), prepared by Alan Davies and his Melbourne colleagues. The dictionary, like the video series, owes its existence entirely to Alan Davies' imagination, perseverance and commitment, and is likely to be the Centre's most enduring achievement. Work on the dictionary has served as a means of professional development for Centre staff and has involved years of intensive team work in a number of different locations, including a period in the basement of the Edinburgh Department of Applied Linguistics.

It has been a very good ten years, a wonderful opportunity to create a leading international research culture from scratch, and one unlikely ever to be replicated. Perhaps only in Australia would the goodwill, the resources, the energy and the sheer improbability of the enterprise have been possible. And without Alan Davies it would never have happened at all, or developed the character which has always distinguished it.

References

Brindley, G. and G. Wigglesworth (eds.) 1998. ***access*****:** *Issues in Language Test Design and Delivery*. Sydney: National Centre for English Language Teaching and Research.

Davies, A. 1990. *Principles of Language Testing*. Oxford: Blackwell.

Davies, A., A. Brown, C. Elder, R. Evans, E. Grove, K. Hill, N. Iwashita, T. Lumley and C. O'Shannessy. 1996. *Mark My Words: Assessing second and foreign language skills*. Multimedia Education Unit, University of Melbourne.

Davies, A., A. Brown, C. Elder, K. Hill, T. Lumley and T. McNamara. 1999. *Dictionary of Language Testing*. Cambridge: Cambridge University Press.

Lo Bianco, J. 1987. *National Policy on Languages*. Canberra: Australian Government Publishing Service.

McNamara, T. 1990. *Assessing the second language proficiency of health professionals*. Unpublished PhD thesis, University of Melbourne.

McNamara, T. 1996. *Measuring Second Language Performance*. London: Longman.

Section Two

Construct definition in language testing

3 Communicative language testing: The art of the possible

Henry G. Widdowson
University of Vienna

I first knew Alan Davies when we were at school together. He was (I should stress) the senior boy; so, naturally enough, he did not know me. I remember in particular an occasion when the sixth form organised a mock election, with boys assuming the role of candidates from different political parties. There was a speaker for the Labour Party, for the Communists, for the Conservatives. And there was Alan Davies: representative of the Welsh Nationalists. Plump and earnest, he spoke with eloquent conviction. But we were in Leicester, right in the middle of England and a long way from Wales. His arguments fell on deaf ears. He did not have a hope of winning, as he knew full well. The way to win was to champion established ideas. Instead, he chose to challenge them, and speak for an unpopular cause. But he did not set out to win: he was out to argue for alternative ways of thinking and so disturb the settled certainties of conventional belief. And he has been doing this ever since. In this respect he has not, I think, changed much over the years, though he may have done in others (age has withered him somewhat and he is not as plump as he was). He still retains a suspicion of orthodoxy, and is still ready to raise questions about it from an alternative point of view. He is naturally a dissenter and a doubter.

So in a way, it is odd that he should have gone in for language testing. For testing is surely all about establishing conventions of certainty, pinning things down, getting things measured. Tests are (surely) predicated on the assumption of conformity. How else can they be reliable? Testers are in the business of imposing patterns on behaviour and so reducing it to simple terms and manageable proportions. Doubts and misgivings are out of place if you want results: they just get in the way. But of course it may be that it is this very presumption that human affairs (linguistic and otherwise) can be so controlled and measured, that things can be made so definite, that makes testing an appealing subject for the sceptical and dissenting mind. It poses the continual dilemma of how the disparity between expediency and principle can be reconciled. So it is not so odd after all, perhaps, that Alan Davies should have been drawn to it: not for the solutions it provides, but for the problems it gives rise to. Or, more accurately, for the problems he can raise about it, for he has a way of assuming the role of Devil's Advocate and asking awkward questions, and not only about language testing.

In this contribution, I should like to assume the same role, and so pay tribute to Alan Davies (the senior boy), by following his lead. There is one problem about language testing that I myself find elusively troublesome, and this seems a good opportunity to explore it. I do so in a relatively informal and uninformed way. I am not a tester and have only a passing acquaintance with the literature, so the issue I wish to raise may, for all I know, have already been exhaustively debated elsewhere. It concerns the testability of communicative competence.

When, in the 1970s, those of us concerned with language pedagogy were busy promoting Dell Hymes' concept of communicative competence (Hymes 1971), we little knew what a Pandora's Box it would turn out to be. Hymes proposed four constituent features of such competence as kinds of judgement that one could be capable of making about a particular instance of use; whether, and to what degree, it was: possible, feasible, appropriate, done.

Since the possible was meant to be taken over from Chomsky's notion of linguistic competence, which was exclusively a matter of grammatical knowledge, it would follow that, in this formulation, part of communicative competence is the capability of distinguishing a grammatical from an ungrammatical sentence in isolation from context. So it would also follow that the much maligned structuralist approach to language teaching, and testing, focused as it was on the possible in this sense, was indeed dealing with communicative competence in part. But only in part. That was the problem. But by the same token, teaching and testing what is appropriate is only teaching it in part as well. The essential point is that if these are components of a competence, they are only components to the extent that they relate: the whole is a function and not a sum of its parts.

What Hymes does is to isolate four features. What he does not do is to indicate what their relationship is. But this is a crucial omission. For what is possible in isolation may be equated with Chomsky's concept of generative grammar, but what is possible in relation to what is appropriate (or feasible, or done) cannot be. For one thing, appropriateness to context applies as much to lexical as to grammatical choice, and, as corpus linguistics illustrates so abundantly, what is grammatically possible does not correspond at all with what is actually done in terms of lexical collocation. So you cannot talk about the formally possible in relation to the appropriate and the done without extending its scope into lexis. The other features that Hymes distinguishes are similarly interrelated. Expressions which would be judged unfeasible or impossible in isolation as manifestations of the language code (elliptical phrases, fragments of talk, and so on), are judged differently when they occur appropriately in context. So the point is that Hymes' notion was that communicative competence was a matter of making absolute judgements about the four features, but to do this is itself an analytic and non-communicative thing to do. Communication involves not identifying separate features, but exploiting relationships between them.

After Hymes, there have been other attempts to define communicative competence. Canale (1983), in his modification of Canale and Swain (1980), also proposes four features, namely: grammatical, sociolinguistic, discourse, strategic. The correspondence with Hymes' scheme is difficult to discern. The grammatical may be said to be a terminological variant of the possible, and the appropriate analysed into the two 'components', the sociolinguistic and the discourse. But the feasible and the attested seem to have disappeared. And again, the interdependencies are not apparent. Although grammatical competence is now said to incorporate lexical knowledge, we are not told how sociolinguistic knowledge acts upon it in the contextually appropriate choice of particular grammatical or lexical forms. Discourse is distinct from sociolinguistic competence and is said to account for how linguistic elements are combined to form larger communicative units (in speech or writing). But it would seem that this competence must involve reference to grammatical competence, if it is concerned with cohesion, and to sociolinguistic competence if it is to be concerned with coherence. The point, obviously, is that to be communicatively competent, the discourse side of things has to be a function of the relationship with both, for cohesion without coherence makes no sense. So one might argue (and I would argue) that discourse competence only exists as a function of the relationship between the grammatical and the sociolinguistic, and without this relationship, it has no communicative status whatever. But what of strategic competence? This is said to consist of verbal and non-verbal communication strategies that may be called into action to compensate for breakdowns in communication due to performance variables or to insufficient competence (Canale and Swain 1980: 30). And, more generally, to 'enhance the effectiveness of communication' (Canale 1983: 11).

So this is not really a competence at all, but the process of relating the others, of bringing them into pragmatic play as required for the occasion. As such, it is hard to see how it can be specified. It seems reasonable enough to talk about a knowledge of grammatical rules or sociocultural conventions, but knowing how to compensate for relative incompetence will surely often, if not usually, be a matter of expedient manoeuvre. We should note, too, that such compensatory behaviour is not confined to language learners; you can be competent in your language but not very capable (for one reason or another) of using it. Compensatory behaviour can indeed be said to be normal pragmatic practice. How people will draw on what they know, how they will exercise their ingenuity in exploiting what knowledge resources they have at their disposal would seem to be almost entirely unpredictable.

It seems to me that the 'competences' which Canale and Swain identify are a very mixed bag indeed. If we compare them with Hymes, the grammatical can be said to correspond with the possible, the appropriate with the sociolinguistic. Here one might reasonably talk about what people know (of the rules of their language and the conventions of its use). But discourse and strategic 'competences' have to do with how people act upon what they know in the immediate achievement of pragmatic meaning, and this involves a consideration of all kinds of contextual conditions. Indeed, all of the performance variables that Canale and Swain refer to as causing breakdowns in communication must be potentially implicated in successful communication as well.

The general difficulty about all this is that as soon as you begin to extend the concept of competence to include communication, it begins to unravel. As I have indicated elsewhere (Widdowson 1989), fault lines appear in Hymes' formulation when you submit it to scrutiny, and they become even more apparent in the Canale and Swain version. And this, we should note, is designed to be operational. Whereas Hymes' scheme is a general programmatic one, a piece of suggestive speculation about the scope of language description, that of Canale and Swain has a pedagogic purpose: it is expressly designed to provide a framework for language teaching and testing. It is meant to be applied to the specification of what should be taught and tested in language courses. But in the case of two of these 'competences', it is hard to see how, in principle, they can be so specified. On the other hand, if they are not brought pragmatically into operation to realise the other two in reaction to particular contextual requirements, no communication actually takes place. So if you teach and test grammatical and sociolinguistic competences on their own, there is no way of knowing whether you are getting at the learners' ability to communicate at all. Peter Skehan makes the following comment on the Canale and Swain scheme:

> *There is no direct way of relating underlying abilities to performance and processing conditions, nor is there any systematic basis for examining the language demands of a range of different contexts. As a result, it is not clear how different patterns of underlying abilities may be more effective in some circumstances than others, nor how these underlying abilities are mobilized into actual performance.*
>
> (Skehan 1998: 159)

The main motivation for proposing communicative competence in the first place was to bring linguistic description in touch with reality, and to extend its scope to account for what people actually do with their abstract linguistic knowledge. But if there is no way, direct or otherwise, of relating this underlying competence to actual performance, it cannot represent the reality of what people do with their knowledge when they communicate. To use a Firthian phrase, there is no 'renewal of connection'. But without such a connection, the model cannot be made operational: it remains an ideal analytical construct.

More recent formulations of the concept of competence (Bachman 1990; Bachman and Palmer 1996) do not resolve this difficulty. On the contrary, they exacerbate it. For now there is a proliferation of components of competence. Bachman separates strategic competence from language competence. Within the latter, sociolinguistic competence has been demoted to a subcomponent of pragmatic competence along with illocutionary competence, and grammatical competence is subsumed under organisational competence alongside textual competence, and these are further distinguished until we eventually arrive at no fewer than fourteen distinct components:

Figure 3.1

Components of language competence

(in Bachman (1990), *Fundamental Considerations in Language Testing*, p. 87, Oxford University Press)

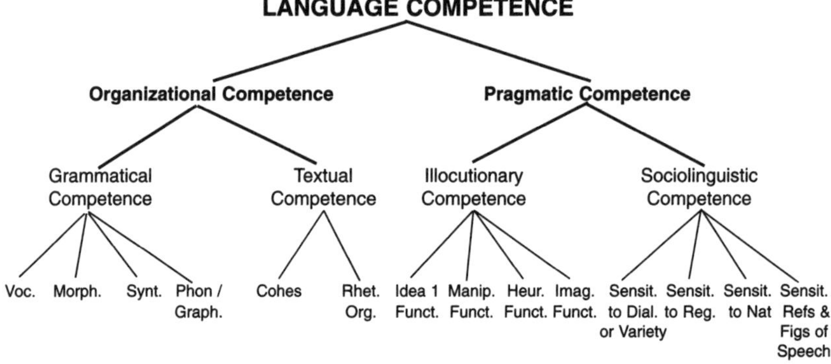

But of course the more distinctions you make, the greater the problem of accounting for the possible relationships between them. In fact, this kind of constituent analysis necessarily cuts the components off from any relational connection. So in the Bachman diagram, for example, the only way that any one terminal component can relate to any other is through some superordinate node. So knowledge of vocabulary on the extreme left, for example, is totally distinct and separate from, say, knowledge of rhetorical organisation, which belongs to another node, and even more remote from sensitivity to register. This would seem to suggest that this model of competence cannot account for how certain words might be used as markers of a particular rhetorical organisation, or as appropriate to a particular register. As before, it would appear that, as Skehan (1998: 159) puts it, 'there is no direct way of relating underlying abilities to performance'. Of course, it can be argued that it is strategic competence that does all that and makes the necessary contextual connection to achieve actual communication. But then we are back with the problem of defining what this competence actually is, and how it operates to bring about the expedient reaction to immediate contextual conditions that communication involves.

The problem with these different models of communicative competence is that they analyse a complex process into a static set of components, and as such cannot account for the dynamic interrelationships which are engaged in communication itself. As a consequence, when you make such models operational in language teaching and testing, you can only deal with the separate parts as discrete features, since the essential interrelationships that make the whole are missing. But to do this is not to depart radically from the structural approach, but rather to follow its example. The main criticism of this approach was that it taught, and tested, linguistic knowledge as something separate, and unrelated to the normal contextual circumstances of its use. Since linguistic knowledge is a component of communicative competence, this is tantamount to saying that this approach concentrated on only one component, and failed to show how it related to the others. But you do not remedy this deficiency by adding more components (textual, illocutionary, sociolinguistic, or whatever), for they are no more communicative, as separate components, than is linguistic competence.

As one deconstructs these models, one begins to have doubts as to whether any model of communicative competence can be made pedagogically operational as a framework for language testing. The assumption behind their development from Hymes to Bachman and Palmer seems to be that the more differentiations the analysis can yield, the greater its operational value. But this surely presupposes the very discrete item view of language testing that these models are designed to discredit. If you want to assess the ability to cope with the relational nature of communication, quite the opposite would seem to be true: the greater the differentiation of your analysis, the less operational it is likely to be. This is because it becomes more difficult to contrive reconstituted contexts which will systematically, and measurably, bring all the components into play. There seems to be a paradox: As frameworks for communicative testing develop to be more refined, the more remote they get from the phenomenon they are developed to test.

But then if these frameworks are rejected, what is the alternative? How else is communicative competence to be assessed? One might propose that the deliberate design of tests as contrived reconstituted contexts be abandoned altogether in favour of some simulation of an 'authentic' situation requiring a communicative outcome. There are obvious objections to such an *ad hoc* procedure. One is that there is no way of knowing how representative the particular situation is of more general communicative demands that might subsequently be made on the learner. There is no way either of knowing how representative the learner's performance is of a more general ability to communicate. The learner might be successful by the ingenious use of avoidance strategies, and these may not be distinguishable from an adherence to the least effort principle that characterises normal pragmatic uses of language. In this case, in effect, all you get is evidence of the so-called 'strategic competence' without knowing whether it is compensatory or not, or if it is, what it is compensating for.

So, it would seem that on the one hand we have a means of measurement which cannot of its nature measure communication, and on the other hand we have a means for eliciting communicative behaviour which cannot be measured. What, then, are we to do?

I want (in my role as Devil's Advocate) to advance the heretical proposal that one way out of this impasse is to recognise that communicative competence cannot, as such, be measured at all. I want to suggest that communicative tests are impossible in principle, which is why it is not surprising that they are so difficult to design. You just cannot test the ability to communicate, and so it is pointless to try. And you cannot teach it either, if it comes to that. All you can teach, and test, is some aspect of it. So the question to consider is not how many different components or features we have to specify to provide as comprehensive an account as possible of what constitutes communicative competence to be taught and tested, but which features have particular saliency or implicational value, in the sense that others are in some way dependent upon, or derivable from, them. If these could be established, they would provide a teachable and testable investment for learning. But which features would they be?

One obvious candidate is linguistic competence. The immediate objection to this might be that to focus attention on that is to go back to square one, and reinstate the discredited procedures of the discrete point testing of linguistic forms. But this is not so. As I pointed out earlier, if linguistic competence is to be a component of a more comprehensive competence, it cannot retain its Chomskyan character as a knowledge of the formal property of sentences in isolation, for it has to play its part, and it can only do that in relation with the other components. So the question we need to consider is how linguistic competence can be defined so that it does play its relational part: in other words, how can it be conceived as being a part of a more general ability to communicate? And this is a cue for Michael Halliday to make an appearance in the argument.

In Brumfit and Johnson (1979), Halliday is featured alongside Hymes as a seminal influence on the development of a communicative approach to language teaching. But whereas Hymes' influence is apparent in that, as we have seen, different models of communicative competence can be recognised as reformulations of his original programmatic scheme, evidence for the influence of Halliday is hard to find. The term 'communicative competence' is not even part of his vocabulary. The term 'meaning potential', however, very definitely is. And this indicates, I think, a crucial conceptual difference between him and Hymes. In Hymes' scheme of things, language seems to retain its Chomskyan independence as a code or formal system (the possible) and communication occurs when it comes into (appropriate) contact with context. So meaning is an external pragmatic function. This, as we have seen, leaves us with the problem of how this actually comes about, of what it is in the code that makes it relateable to context. There must be some potential in the code itself that is contextually realised. And this, of course, is where Halliday comes in. His conception is of a code that is functionally motivated: it is indeed the evolved encoding of features of its contextual use, a formal abstraction of contextual features (Halliday 1973, 1994 and *passim*). So what happens when code comes into contact with actual context is that certain internally encoded contextual features get activated and become externalised: the potential gets realised. To put it another way, communication is a matter of the conditional projection of code meanings, and it is the context which provides the conditions whereby some meanings are actualised and others not. Clearly, in this conception linguistic competence is indeed, and of its very nature, a part of the ability to communicate, and indeed the central part.

What, then, for Hymes is the possible, for Halliday is the potential. Linguistic knowledge is not something separately defined in formal terms with an unspecified relationship with other components, but is naturally integral in that it incorporates these components in condensed abstract form. Thus its combination with these other components is a realisation of its own potential. In this view, communication is immanent in the code as an intrinsic valency. According to the Oxford English Dictionary, the term *valency* denotes: the combining power of an atom measured by the number of hydrogen atoms it can displace or combine with. By analogy, we can conceive of the combining power of the possible, of the linguistic component of communicative competence, in terms of what aspects of the other components it can displace or combine with. We have a principled way of establishing, and measuring, the relationships which, as I have argued, have proved so elusive in the models I have passed under review.

If we can restore language to its essential centrality in this way, then this provides us with something specifiable to deal with, and language tests become, again, tests of language. Instead of analysing communicative competence into more and more disparate features, which not only misrepresent the very nature of communication, but become well-nigh impossible to incorporate into effective test design, the better course, I would suggest, is to adopt a unifying principle, and focus attention on the extent to which learners have internalised the communicative potential in language itself. The validity of the language test corresponds to the valency it measures. In this way, I think, language testing becomes (in two senses) the art of the possible.

And the same point applies to language teaching as well. If I may cite myself (Widdowson 1984), we are not in the business of teaching language as communication, but for communication. Our purpose is not to try to rehearse learners in patterns of performance appropriate to particular contextual conditions, which are for the most part impossible to pin down anyway, but to induce learners to invest in valency, or, as Halliday (1978) would put it, 'meaning potential': a general linguistic capacity for communication. How this potential gets realised in the particular circumstances of real-life communication is something learners will have to learn by engaging with it when the occasion arises. The only thing pedagogy can do is to prepare people to learn for themselves: it is concerned with what can be taught and not what will be learned. And you can only test what you can teach.

Such a view runs contrary, of course, to current orthodoxy, and in particular to the fashionable advocacy of authenticity. But my advocacy (devilish or not) would be quite the opposite. It seems to me that efforts to replicate communicative reality in language teaching and testing are, for the most part, a waste of time. And they deflect us from our main pedagogic task, which is to identify what constitutes the essential investment for our learners, and what activities we need to contrive (I use the word advisedly) in our teaching and testing to induce this process and evaluate its success. Such a minority view may not find much favour. It is likely to get as few votes as Alan Davies got for the cause of Welsh Nationalism all those years ago. But, as then, the arguments might provide food for thought nevertheless. And the fact is that Plaid Cymru is now thriving, and Wales already has its own regional autonomy. One should never be too sure about lost causes.

References

Bachman, L. 1990. *Fundamental Considerations in Language Testing*. Oxford: Oxford University Press.

Bachman, L. and Palmer, A. 1996. *Language Testing in Practice*. Oxford: Oxford University Press.

Brumfit, C. J. and Johnson, K. (eds.), 1979. *The Communicative Approach to Language Teaching*. Oxford: Oxford University Press.

Canale, M. 1983. On some dimensions of language proficiency. In J. W. Oller, (ed.), *Issues in Second Language Testing Research*. Rowley, MA: Newbury House.

Canale, M. and Swain, M. 1980. Theroretical bases of communicative approaches to second language testing. *Applied Linguistics* 1(1): 1–47.

Halliday, M. A. K. 1973. *Explorations in the Functions of Language*. London: Edward Arnold.

Halliday, M. A. K. 1978. *Language as Social Semiotic.* London: Edward Arnold.

Halliday, M. A. K. 1994. *An Introduction to Functional Grammar (2nd ed.).* London: Edward Arnold.

Hymes, D. 1971. *On Communicative Competence*. Philadelphia: University of Pennsylvania Press.

Skehan, P. 1998. *A Cognitive Approach to Language Learning*. Oxford: Oxford University Press.

Widdowson, H. G. 1984. *Explorations in Applied Linguistics Vol 2*. Oxford: Oxford University Press.

Widdowson, H. G. 1989. Knowledge of language and ability for use. *Applied Linguistics* 10(2): 128–37.

4 Fossilisation or evolution: The case of grammar testing

Pauline Rea-Dickins
University of Bristol

Introduction

For several decades 'grammar' has been a core component of many language test batteries, and there is much evidence to suggest that this is still the case across a range of testing contexts – in, for example, language proficiency and school examinations of English as a foreign language (EFL). However, the testing and teaching of grammar continues to generate controversy: what model of grammar should be taught and, hence, tested? How broadly, or narrowly, should grammar be defined? Can grammar tests that focus only on sentence level accuracy be justified? Should the role of grammar in language tests be different in some way in proficiency and in school-based progress and achievement measures? Should grammar be tested separately from other skills? What is the role of grammar testing in EAP/ESP skill-based programmes of instruction? Given the recent debates on the role of grammar in pedagogy, it is perhaps surprising to find little recent work on grammar testing from research, test development or pedagogical perspectives.

The discussion in this paper centres around two questions.

1 What is the role for a grammar test in language proficiency assessment?
2 In the area of pedagogy, what assumptions may lie behind different grammar testing practices?

Grammar in EAP language proficiency testing

University admissions and placement examinations

At one time, most English language proficiency examinations used for university admissions purposes included a grammar component. Examples of these are the EPTB (Davies 1964), ELBA (Ingram 1963), CELT (Harris and Palmer 1970), and the TOEFL.[1] In addition to more general contributions to test analysis from psychometrics, the shape of many of the proficiency measures of this period were influenced by Lado (1961), and by Carroll (1961) in the form of the 'discrete-point' approach to testing. Some of these examinations are more or less defunct, although the widely administered

TOEFL in its new computer-based format maintains its multiple choice subtest of structure and written expression. Overall, however, the situation in the late 1990s is rather different with a less prominent position given to the explicit and separate testing of grammar.

More recent English language proficiency examinations designed for placement/admission in English medium study contexts have not included a separate grammar component. The reasons for this are varied. One change is explained by the interest in communicative language teaching in the 1980s which marginalised grammar in certain ways. Another, more specific influence, is the way in which the construct of language proficiency for testing purposes has been characterised (e.g. Canale and Swain 1980; Bachman 1990). A further impetus for change has arisen from the perceived need to assess those language skills which are developed within an EAP/ESP language programme of instruction, in which students may be placed on the basis of proficiency test results. In the case of the ESLPE,[2] as an example, there was a deliberate replacement of the grammar-based construct of the earlier proficiency examination by one designed to measure a student's ability to use English in academic settings, e.g. 'to include academic skills such as: (1) the ability to write with fluency on an academic topic; (2) the ability to understand lectures ...'(Cushing Weigle and Lynch 1995: 60).

The development of the IELTS (International English Language Testing System, as a replacement for the ELTS) is interesting from the perspective of the role of grammar in reading comprehension and the possible overlap between tests of reading and tests of grammar. Following extensive consultation, including with language testing researchers, Alderson (1993) reports considerable support from the profession for including a test of lexis and structure. Thus a deliberate attempt was made to develop a separate grammar component and to differentiate this construct from that of reading. However, in spite of identifiably different test specifications, subtests and item formats, analysis of score patterns revealed a relationship between grammar and some of the other subtests, and a 'consistently close relationship to the reading tests' is reported (Alderson 1993: 210). Further, dropping the grammar test did not significantly affect the overall reliability of the test battery (with the exception of the General Training Module). There were also pragmatic considerations at play, with some pressure to shorten the overall length of the IELTS administration. Given the consistently demonstrated overlap with reading subtests and the fact that the reliability of the battery was not significantly reduced by eliminating the grammar test, the decision was taken not to include grammar as a separately identifiable subtest.

The construct validation studies of Alderson (1993) and Cushing Weigle and Lynch (1995) are not unique and a number of other studies have been conducted over the years in relation to specific examinations (e.g. Pike 1979) and to the construct of language proficiency more generally (e.g. Verhoeven and de Jong 1992). Findings have at times been ambiguous (see, for example, Angelis 1982; Stansfield 1986) making generalisability across contexts problematic. However, the test development studies reported above (see also Weir 1983) provide some indication of a move away from an explicit and separate grammar component in EAP proficiency testing.

Next, an analysis of testing practice in one specific EAP instructional setting is presented.

Grammar testing and EAP pedagogy

Some two to three months prior to the start of the academic year, many UK universities organise pre-sessional English language programmes which focus on improving academic study skills. Students usually come with proficiency test results, most commonly with band scores from IELTS or TOEFL. In 1996, I surveyed pre-sessional course directors on their testing practices: a questionnaire was sent to 64 institutions, with a 67% return. I wanted to find out (i) about assessment procedures administered within these programmes, in particular entry or exit tests, and (ii) whether grammar was tested and if so, how. Table 4.1 below summarises the frequency of entry and exit tests reported in the sample.

Table 4.1

Entry and exit tests administrations (N=43)

Entry test	Exit test
93%	58%

Ninety-three per cent of respondents indicated that they administered a test battery at the beginning of their programme. Just over half included some form of exit, or end of programme, procedure; a smaller number also reported use of coursework assessment.

To investigate the extent to which the bias of the instructional programme (i.e. the primary orientation on the development of academic study skills in English) was reflected in tests used, informants were asked about the components of their different entry and exit batteries. The findings are summarised in Table 4.2.

Table 4.2

Test components for entry and exit tests (N=42)

	Entry test	Exit test
N	40	40
Language elements	67%	41%
Language skills:		
Writing	67.4%	51.2%
Speaking	48.8%	27.9%
Listening	41.9%	34.9%
Reading	34.9%	30.2%

Tests of language elements (i.e. tests of vocabulary and grammar, of which the majority were identified as 'grammar' tests) and writing were cited as the most frequent component in the entry measures. The least assessed skill was reported as reading (34.9%). The pattern for the exit procedures is different. Writing is reported as the most frequently measured skill (51.2%), followed by language elements (41%) which has a higher frequency than listening, reading or speaking.

There was considerably more explicit testing of grammar reported in the entry tests (Table 4.3). Explicit testing refers to a separate component in which grammar is directly assessed. An indirect measurement of grammar is where it is integrated within a test of language skills, for example, grammatical accuracy as one of the marking criteria in a writing task.

Table 4.3

How is grammar tested in entry and exit tests? (N=42)

	Entry test	Exit test
Explicitly	67%	17%
Indirectly	36%	24%

At entry level, explicit grammar testing in separate subtests is favoured; in addition grammar testing is also integrated within skills-based tests. This trend is not replicated in exit measures. At the end of a programme, there is a trend towards less testing overall, as well as a less explicit focus on grammar, with a significant decline in the number of separately identifiable grammar subtests. Respondents also commented on or provided examples of the grammar tests used. Of those who tested grammar on entry to a course, 66% of these used commercially produced materials, many of which are of a discrete-point multiple choice format.

The data presented above have linked English language proficiency testing with English medium higher education study situations. The next analysis briefly examines proficiency tests which are more closely allied to school EFL language learning contexts. In view of their widespread use internationally (or variants of these tests), the UCLES suite of general English language proficiency examinations is chosen as an example. They also have a clearly defined construct of language proficiency detailed in their Handbooks.[3]

Grammar in general language proficiency testing

General EFL proficiency examinations

In the domain of general English language proficiency examinations, as demonstrated by the UCLES suite, grammar is clearly identifiable as a component, in several ways. For example, grammar forms the explicit focus of separate subtests (e.g. at FCE and CAE levels) in which candidates 'demonstrate knowledge of lexical and grammatical systems' (UCLES 1994: 5) and 'apply knowledge of the language system, including control of grammar, lexis, register, spelling, punctuation, coherence and formulaic language' (UCLES 1995: 51). At a lower level of proficiency, it is stated: 'PET corresponds closely to an active and communicative approach to learning English, without neglecting the need for clarity and accuracy' (UCLES 1995: 8), as well as an 'understanding of structural relationships at the phrase, clause, sentence or paragraph level …' (UCLES 1996: 20).

The status of grammar is further confirmed with comments on both the range and accuracy of structures used within speaking and writing tests. For example, 'Candidates will be expected to write grammatical prose with due regard to word order, subject/verb agreement and appropriate use of tense and voice' (UCLES 1996: 2), with 'accuracy of language, including spelling and punctuation' assessed on a general impression scale (UCLES 1995: 33).

Grammar and pedagogy: A classroom-based perspective

To discover more about practices in grammar testing, students at two universities in England, most of whom were following an MA in ELT, completed a questionnaire (N=70).[4] Most worked in the state sector: half as EFL teachers in primary or secondary schools; the other half as either EFL/ESL teachers at tertiary level or with adults. Sixty-seven (96%) reported that they tested grammar, of whom 61 (91%) did this explicitly. Grammar was also assessed indirectly through skill-based tests (N=27). The reasons given for testing grammar were wide ranging. Thirty respondents (43%) mentioned the importance of checking on basic mastery of the rules and accuracy.

Curricular reasons were also cited (N=28), e.g. feedback to teacher and learner, monitoring progress, and informing curriculum management. It is interesting to note that only four (6%) mentioned the role of grammar testing in establishing levels of language proficiency. Only one respondent felt that grammar should not be tested, with a further four observing that 'it depends on the circumstances', 'not on ESP courses' and that 'grammar is overtested'. The overwhelming majority were of the view that grammar should be tested.

Discussion

The revision of both the ESLPE and the IELTS (see also Weir 1983) has been cited as evidence of a trend in study-related English language proficiency examinations not to test grammar explicitly as a separate component (but see the UETESOL).[5] This pattern is to some extent paralleled in the pre-sessional exit assessment procedures summarised above. Where the focus is on establishing end-of-programme proficiency levels, grammar is less likely to appear as a separate subtest and more likely to be integrated within a variety of skills-focused assessment procedures. This suggests that where the purpose for testing relates to proficiency levels, and the adequacy of these for university study, the ability to integrate linguistic knowledge in study-related tasks is paramount.

The use of explicit and separate grammar subtests as part of pre-sessional programme entry procedures parallels the general EFL practice reported here where explicit grammar testing is favoured, often as an identifiably discrete subtest. The relative frequency of grammar testing on entry to the study skills/EAP programme, it will be recalled, is more marked when a comparison is made with the other test components (with the exception of writing, see Table 4.2). This further supports the view that assessment purpose (e.g. placement, informing teaching, checking progress) is influential in determining the approach to testing grammar. In the pre-sessional context, the need for a quick-to-administer placement measure may account for the marked use of multiple choice and gap filling items in the separate grammar subtests on entry. It may also reflect a view of grammar as a useful indicator of overall language proficiency, a point also made by some of the EFL teachers. Further, it may also be that course placement decisions are reversible if proved wrong, which is not the case with decisions about preparedness for university study, or other high-stakes assessment. In contrast with the placement context, high-stakes assessments require a more reliable and valid basis for decision making in the form of measures which characterise target language use (e.g. that assess the ability to develop an argument in writing) and which assume an adequate command of grammar.

The data also suggest that the representation of grammar in tests has changed in several respects. Firstly, grammar has been defined more broadly than sentence level accuracy to include textual competence such as cohesion, rhetorical organisation, as well as accuracy and appropriacy of language for tasks set. Secondly, there is considerable variety in texts used as well as actual test formats, (e.g. modified cloze, gap-filling passages, matching, unscrambling words and sentences, guided short answer and summary tasks). Thirdly, accuracy of language use frequently occurs as a criterion in the marking of written and spoken language linked to effectiveness of communication. In several instances, only inaccuracies of language which impede understanding are penalised. These, alongside the more traditional grammar item type, provide evidence of grammar being tested both as a body of 'knowledge' and 'a means to an end', with attention in the case of the latter to conveying appropriate meanings in messages rather than an exclusive emphasis on accuracy of form and structure.

In the two pedagogical contexts discussed, teacher perceptions of grammar testing reflect a wide variety of beliefs, e.g. discrete-point testing in one or several areas of grammar is justified for diagnostic purposes; checking the accuracy of grammatical knowledge is important, especially in the early stages of language learning or with future teachers of English; a variety of test formats should be used; and grammar should be tested in context. Another strong voice emerged for indirect grammar testing through skill-focused tasks: '... [the] testing of grammar [is] perceived as enabling students to do things, not just learn abstract rules and metalinguistic terms' (EFL secondary teacher, Sri Lanka).

There is also a pervasive sense of conservatism in the comments from both the ESP and general EFL contexts, and an argument that grammar testing is the result of an adherence to 'tradition' surfaces in various guises. For example: 'it's a relic of an old off the peg system designed for coursebooks in use ten years ago ... and has never been dropped' (English EFL teacher). Another reason put forward is that grammar has always been a part of tests and that students and administrators expect it, with face validity for stakeholder groups other than teachers considered to be important.

Some conclusions

It will have been noted that I have not attempted a definition of 'grammar testing' in this paper, although various views of the construct of grammar have emerged from the data. In response to an earlier publication of mine on the same topic (Rea-Dickins 1991), Davies observed (1991: 138) that whilst he agreed with my delineation of communicative grammar as 'central to the organisation of our language use' he would not want to call it 'communicative *grammar*', preferring 'discourse studies, cohesion/coherence or perhaps organisational skills'. He comments that 'One of the paradoxes of all language work is that naming is both trivial and at the same time profound.' This last point is noteworthy in several respects. In many ways little progress will be made by attempts to come up with a 'better' definition of grammar, to explain differences in the labels (such as English in Use, Use of English, Grammar, Editing, Structure, Proof Reading) for grammar tests, or to further refine a testing model that creates boundaries between grammar, discourse, cohesion/coherence, and organisational skills. On the other hand, in testing we have to operationalise our constructs and are expected to provide guidance to the language teaching profession. In this respect, naming may have profound implications. It thus becomes crucially important to be able to justify approaches to the testing of grammar in different teaching, learning and testing contexts.

Davies also maintains 'form in language ensures that order is maintained. Actual messages, actual meanings are conveyed through function; what form does is to package them' (1991: 142–143). This view is useful in identifying some of the parameters of grammar testing. In certain contexts – for example in the earlier stages of language learning, with test takers at lower levels of language proficiency, where course-related decisions are required, or with future teachers of English – it may be highly relevant to have explicit system-focused testing. In these situations, it may be crucial to uncover whether learners have the right packaging at their disposal in order to convey messages appropriately. Greater attention to form and structure, knowledge of rules, or accuracy of language use will thus be paramount.

At other times, where test takers demonstrate higher levels of language ability, the primary focus may be on target language proficiency levels of performance in reading, writing, listening and speaking. The EAP context provides one such example where grammar appears to assume a less prominent and explicit role at later stages in the instructional programme. The more indirect approach to assessing grammatical ability, observed above, may be premised on the assumption that the learners (should) have already acquired an adequate command of the language system to package messages appropriately. The evidence that is thus required is their ability to use grammar to convey ideas and intended meanings effectively in skill-based tasks.

Returning to the question raised in the title of this paper, a first reaction might be that grammar testing has fossilised since the late 1960s and early 1970s, with grammar in the form of multiple choice or objective formats still much in evidence as part of test batteries. Was it not as early as 1961 that Carroll advocated the use of integrated skills testing? However, there are discernible changes. There is evolution in the way in which the operationalisation of the construct of grammar has taken account of developments in applied linguistics, in particular extended models of language proficiency, with different representations of 'grammar' across language tests. There has also been change in terms of the range of text types used as the basis for a wider variety of item types for testing grammar. In addition, there are now a number of studies that contribute to our understanding of the construct relationships between grammar and other test battery components.

On the other hand, whilst there is evidence of evolution in terms of 'grammar' and language proficiency testing, there is a distinct lack of interest in grammar testing in relation to pedagogy, i.e. as part of school-based assessment. There is much that remains unclear. For example, to what extent is an observed grammar focus (variously labelled) driven by tradition, market forces or *ad hoc* decisions, rather than by explicitly articulated purposes for testing, by research findings, or informed through pedagogical analysis? Grammar will mean different things to different stakeholders at different times. These differences should be reflected through variations in approach to the assessment of grammatical abilities, the strategies for which should be specifically chosen, as opposed to some random selection. As one teacher observed, grammar tests should vary according to need (EFL secondary teacher, Slovakia). This raises the question as to whether the profession is sufficiently informed of the ways in which different contexts, testing and pedagogical, EAP/ESP or general EFL, different language levels of test takers, and so forth, affect the ways in which we test grammar.

This paper has set out to raise an awareness of some of the assumptions underlying the role of grammar tests in relation to pedagogical practice and recent developments in the design of language proficiency measures. Further investigation is required to determine the extent to which the representations of grammar testing identified here are widespread.

Acknowledgements

I would like to thank the editors for their constructive comments on the first version of this paper.

Notes

1 These acronyms refer to the English Proficiency Test Battery, the English Language Battery Assessment, the Comprehensive English Language Test and the Test of English as a Foreign Language.

2 The English as a Second Language Placement Examination, at the University of California, Los Angeles.

3 The University of Cambridge Local Examinations Syndicate (UCLES) administers a series of proficiency tests at five different levels: the Key English Test (KET), the Preliminary English Test (PET), First Certificate in English (FCE), Certificate in Advanced English (CAE) and the Certificate in Proficiency in English (CPE). A handbook for each of these examinations is available from UCLES.

4 I am exceedingly grateful to Tricia Hedge at Warwick and Caroline Clapham at Lancaster for their skill in gathering completed questionnaires from their students.

5 The University Entrance Test in English for Speakers of Other Languages (UETESOL) provides a counter example. In addition to tests in the four skills, it includes an Editing Skills section which carries 25% of the total available marks where 'particular attention will be paid to accuracy in grammar and vocabulary' (NEAB 1996: 2). This examination is largely used for school leavers in UK wishing to start undergraduate studies; this contrasts with the IELTS which has a largely overseas postgraduate target population.

References

Alderson, J. C. 1993. The relationship between grammar and reading in an English for Academic Purposes test battery. In D. Douglas and C. Chapelle (eds.), *A New Decade of Language Testing Research*, pp. 203–19. Virginia: TESOL, Inc.

Angelis, P. 1982. *Language Skills in Academic Study*. Final Report submitted to the TOEFL Research Committee. Princeton, NJ: Educational Testing Service. (Cited in Stansfield, C. 1986, p. 233.)

Bachman, L. F. 1990. *Fundamental Considerations in Language Testing*. Oxford: Oxford University Press.

Canale, M. and M. Swain. 1980. Theoretical bases of communicative approaches to second language teaching and testing. *Applied Linguistics* 1: 1–47.

Carroll, J. B. 1961. Fundamental considerations in testing for English proficiency of foreign students. In *Testing the English Proficiency of Foreign Students*, pp. 31–40. Washington DC: Center for Applied Linguistics.

Cushing Weigle, S. and B. Lynch. 1995. Hypothesis testing in construct validation. In A. Cumming and R. Berwick (eds.), *Validation in Language Testing,* pp. 58–71. Clevedon, Avon: Multilingual Matters Ltd.

Davies, A. 1964. *English Proficiency Test Battery*. London: The British Council.

Davies, A. 1991. Language testing in the 1990s. In J. C. Alderson and B. North (eds.), *Language Testing in the 1990s*, pp. 136–149. London and Basingstoke: Macmillan.

Harris, D. P. and L. Palmer. 1970. *Comprehensive English Language Test for Speakers of English as a Second Language*. New York: McGraw-Hill.

Ingram, E. 1963. English Language Battery (ELBA). Edinburgh: University of Edinburgh, Department of Linguistics.

Lado, R. 1961. *Language Testing: The Construction and Use of Foreign Language Tests*. London: Longman, Green and Co. Ltd.

Northern Examinations Board (NEAB). 1996. Syllabus for 1996: UETESOL. Manchester.

Pike, L. 1979. *An Evaluation of Alternative Item Formats for Testing English as a Foreign Language*, TOEFL Research Report 2. Princeton, NJ: Educational Testing Service.

Rea-Dickins, P. 1991. What makes a grammar test communicative? In J. C. Alderson and B. North (eds.), *Language Testing in the 1990s*, pp. 112–135. London and Basingstoke: Macmillan.

Stansfield, C. 1986. A history of the Test of Written English: The developmental year. *Language Testing* 3: 224–234.

University of Cambridge Local Examinations Certificate (UCLES). April 1994. *First Certificate in English: Handbook.*

University of Cambridge Local Examinations Certificate (UCLES). July 1995. *Certificate in Advanced English: Handbook.*

University of Cambridge Local Examinations Certificate (UCLES). January 1996. *Key English Test: Handbook.*

Verhoeven, L. and H. A. L. de Jong. (eds.) 1992. *The Construct of Language Proficiency: Applications of Psychological Models to Language Assessment*. Amsterdam: John Benjamins.

Weir, C. J. 1983. Identifying the Language Needs of Overseas Students in Tertiary Education in the United Kingdom. Unpublished PhD dissertation, University of London, Institute of Education.

5 The assessment of metalinguistic knowledge

Caroline Clapham
Lancaster University

Introduction

One of the important uses of language tests is to elicit responses which might throw light on the process of second language acquisition (SLA). One area of SLA which is generating much debate at present is that relating to students' knowledge about language: do language learners acquire a new language more readily if they know something of the grammatical rules that underpin the language? This controversy is bound up with research into the relative contributions of explicit and implicit language knowledge to second language acquisition (for example, Krashen 1981; Skehan 1986; Bialystok 1990), the Knowledge about Language movement (for example, Richmond 1990), and research into Language Awareness (see James and Garrett 1991).

In a recent study (funded by the Economic and Social Research Council of Great Britain), Alderson, Clapham and Steel (1997) investigated the metalinguistic knowledge of university modern languages students, and compared this knowledge with the students' level of foreign language proficiency. Correlations between the total scores on the different components of the Metalinguistic Assessment Test and tests of French proficiency led the researchers to report that the relationship between metalinguistic knowledge and linguistic proficiency was weak. This finding was supported by Elder *et al.* (1997), who widened the scope of the research by giving the Metalinguistic Assessment Test and tests of language proficiency to students learning three different languages, at elementary as well as advanced levels.

The purpose of the present paper is not to investigate the relationship between metalinguistic knowledge and language proficiency, but to explore in greater depth the nature of metalinguistic knowledge, and to show how performances on a variety of tasks will give a more accurate picture of a student's metalinguistic knowledge than will performance on a single task.

One of the aims of the Alderson, Clapham and Steel (1997) research was to assess the amount of metalanguage recognised by newly enrolled university students in order to show whether these students were sufficiently familiar with grammatical terms for university teachers to use these terms in their language classes. The researchers gave students the Metalinguistic Assessment Test, and reported on the number of students recognising the terms listed in Section 1 of the test (see below for a description of this test). However, a more detailed scrutiny of the test results suggests that reporting the ability of the students to recognise a single example of a grammatical term does not accurately represent their understanding of that term. Metalinguistic knowledge is so complex that students may appear to understand a grammatical term in one context, but fail to understand it in another.

The Metalinguistic Assessment Test

The Metalinguistic Assessment Test has three sections. In Section 1, students identify examples of different parts of speech such as noun, verb and adjective in an English sentence (henceforth referred to as the Complex English Sentence [CES]). They are then given four Simple English Sentences (SES) and have to identify an example of a different grammatical term in each sentence. Both these tasks were first used by Bloor (1986). The students then do two similar tasks, where the stimulus sentences are in French rather than English. These sentences will be referred to as the Complex French Sentence [CFS] and the Simple French Sentences [SFS]). The two Complex Sentences (English and French) have little in common because they are intended to assess the students' knowledge of terms of particular importance to the language concerned. The two sentences are:

1 CES: Materials are delivered to the factory by a supplier, who usually has no technical knowledge, but who happens to have the right contacts.
2 CFS: J'ai demandé deux jours de congé à mon patron et il ne pouvait pas me les refuser avec une excuse pareille.

The four Simple French Sentences, on the other hand, are designed to parallel the four English ones. For example:

1 SES: Poor little Joe stood out in the snow. (The students have to underline the 'subject' – Poor little Joe, Poor Joe, Little Joe, or Joe.)
2 SFS: La petite vieille dame avait perdu son chemin. (The students have to underline the subject – La petite vieille dame, La petite dame, La vieille dame, or La dame.)

Sections 2 and 3 of the test (inspired by work by Bialystok 1978 and Sorace 1985) consist respectively of 15 French and 15 English sentences. Each sentence contains a grammatical error, and students have to correct the error, and explain the rule that has been broken.

For example:

I often goes to the cinema.
Correct version: *go*
Rule: The verb must agree with the subject.

Although the students are not specifically asked to use metalanguage in their explanations of the errors, many do, and this has provided a wealth of data showing what the students understand by the metalinguistic terms, and how they think these terms should be used.

As part of their 1997 study, Alderson, Clapham and Steel gave this Metalinguistic Assessment Test to 509 undergraduates who were embarking on French degrees in seven British universities. Most of the students had had seven years of French tuition and had passed the General Certificate in Education Advanced Level French examination or its equivalent.

Results: Section 1

Table 5.1 gives the facility values (FVs: % correct) of those items which were tested twice in Section 1.

Table 5.1

Identification of grammatical terms

		% Correct (n=509)	
		English	**French**
From the Complex Sentences			
	noun	98	90
	adjective	86	84
	indefinite article	35	26
	preposition	64	68
	conjunction	62	61
	infinitive verb	72	81
	past participle	88	84
From the Simple Sentences			
	subject	97	85
	predicate	1	1
	direct object	62	64
	indirect object	72	72

On the strength of these results the researchers reported that although many students seemed unfamiliar with, for example, the 'indefinite article', where only 35% of the students identified it correctly in the English sentence and 26% in the French sentence, most students were familiar with 'noun', where the FVs were 98% and 90% respectively. Since most pairs of items have similar FVs (in seven out of eleven instances, the difference is no more than 4%), it appears at first glance as if the students were equally able or unable to identify the terms in the English and the French sentences. However this is often not the case. A closer inspection of the results reveals that the students frequently recognised the term in one sentence but not the other. (The correlation between the two components was .73; see Alderson, Clapham and Steel 1997.) Table 5.2 gives the number of students who correctly identified an example of a grammatical term in one of the two sentences but not the other.

Table 5.2

Inconsistent answers (n = 509)

Term	FV (Eng.)	FV (Fr.)	English √ French x	French √ English x	Total inconsis-tencies	Consistently right (√)	Consistently wrong (x)	Total consis-tencies
Noun	98%	90%	9%	1%	10%	89%	1%	90%
Adjective	86%	84%	7%	5%	12%	79%	9%	88%
Indef. article	35%	26%	13%	4%	17%	22%	61%	83%
Preposition	64%	68%	8%	12%	20%	56%	24%	80%
Conjunction	62%	61%	10%	9%	19%	52%	29%	81%
Infinit.verb	72%	81%	6%	15%	21%	66%	13%	79%
Past particip.	88%	84%	10%	7%	17%	78%	5%	83%
Subject	97%	85%	14%	0%	14%	83%	3%	86%
Predicate	1%	1%	0%	0%	0%	1%	99%	100%
Direct obj.	62%	64%	15%	16%	31%	47%	22%	69%
Ind. obj.	72%	72%	12%	12%	24%	60%	16%	76%

Key: √ = Right
x = Wrong

This table shows that, with the exception of 'predicate' (Total consistencies = 100%), which almost no one could identify, there were no terms which were consistently recognised or not recognised by students in the two sentences. Even in the case of 'noun' (FVs 98% and 90%), although 89% of the students consistently chose a correct example, 10% of the students differed in their response to the two sentences: 9% (47 students) identified a noun correctly in the English sentence but failed to identify one in the French sentence, and 1% (six students) identified it correctly in the French but not the English sentence. 'Direct object', the term which had the greatest number of inconsistent answers (31%), was identified correctly in the Simple English Sentence but not the French one by 15% of the students, and in the Simple French Sentence but not the English one by 16%. It seems that although some students may have a good understanding of the term as it used in one of the two languages, this knowledge does not automatically transfer across to the other. It is not safe to conclude, therefore, that if a student identifies the term successfully in one sentence, then that student understands the full meaning of the term, and it is clear that the FVs by themselves give an inflated idea of what the students know. This suggests that the figures reported by Alderson, Clapham and Steel, and those reported earlier by Bloor (1986), and Alderson and Steel (1994) give an over-generous picture of the students' metalinguistic knowledge (already described in those papers as variable and, on occasion, weak).

It could simply be, of course, that Section 1 is unreliable. In spite of the fact that the reliability index (Cronbach's alpha) for Section 1 is .86, which is reasonably high for a test of 37 items, some students could be guessing, and might, therefore, provide equally varied responses if the two parallel sentences were in the same language. It may not be possible to draw conclusions about students' metalinguistic knowledge by giving them only one opportunity to identify an example of a grammatical term. On the other hand, it might be that students consistently identify the terms in one language more successfully than in the other, either because of difficulties in understanding the French sentences, in which case the English FVs would be higher than the French, or because the terms had been taught during French rather than English classes, in which case the French FVs would be higher than the English. However, there is little evidence that either of these is the case here: three grammatical terms were more often correctly identified in the French sentences than in the English, and six were more frequently identified correctly in the English than in the French (see Table 5.1). However, when we look at the results of Sections 2 and 3 (see below), we will see that in some cases students seem to be able to use terms more successfully when these terms relate to French rather than English sentences.

Results such as those above are likely, of course, to depend on the context in which the terms appear, and by 'context', I mean the complexity of the sentence and the role of the grammatical item in that sentence. As far as complexity goes, the Complex English Sentence includes a passive, and two relative clauses, whereas the Complex French Sentence has no passive verbs, and comprises two simple sentences joined by a conjunction. The roles of the grammatical terms, too, differ, as can be seen if we look at the 'direct object' in the various sentences in which it appears. 'Direct object' is one of three grammatical terms which, in Section 1, have to be identified by the students not only in the two Simple Sentences but also in the Complex French Sentence. Although the 'direct object' stands out clearly in the two Simple Sentences (it is a single noun following an active verb, and could become the subject of a passive verb. see Quirk *et al.* 1985), the two examples of a direct object in the Complex French Sentence are more difficult to identify (see below for the text of the Complex Sentence). The first consists of a phrase of four words *(deux jours de congé)* and the second is a pronoun *(les)* which precedes the infinitive *'refuser'*. To be able to identify this second direct object correctly students need to have some understanding of the positioning of pronouns in French, and the different functions of *'me'* and *'les'* in this sentence. Not surprisingly, fewer students identified a direct object in this Complex Sentence than in the Simple Sentences (see below for more about this).

The three sentences in which a 'direct object' has to be identified are:

Identification of a direct object

1. *Simple English Sentence (SES)*
   The policeman chased Joe down the street. (Answer: 'Joe'.)
2. *Simple French Sentence (SFS)*
   Un jeune homme a offert ses conseils avec gentillesse. (Answer: 'ses conseils' or 'conseils'.)
3. *Complex French Sentence (CFS)*
   '*J'ai demandé deux jours de congé à mon patron et il ne pouvait pas me les refuser avec une excuse pareille.*' (Answer: 'deux jours de congé', or 'congé' or 'les'.)

Table 5.3 shows that although the two Simple Sentence FVs were almost identical, 62% and 64%, that of the Complex Sentence was much lower – 34%; the students did have difficulty identifying either of the two somewhat obscure examples in the Complex French sentence.

Table 5.3

FVs – Direct object

	English (SES)	**French (SFS)**	**French (CFS)**
Direct object	62%	64%	34%

However, once again, the individual responses were inconsistent. Table 5.4 shows how a subset of 122 students fared. These students comprised the Lancaster University sample from the seven universities which participated in the main study; their scores on the Metalinguistic Assessment Test were similar to those of the whole sample (n = 509), and their mean scores on the proficiency tests were similar to those of the whole sample (see Alderson, Clapham and Steel 1997).

Table 5.4

Inconsistencies across the three sentences

	'Direct Object' (n = 122)									
	Consistent			Inconsistent						
Sentences	EFC	EFC	Total	EFC	EFC	EFC	EFC	EFC	EFC	Total
R or W answers	√√√ All right	xxx All wrong		√√x	√x√	√xx	xx√	x√x	x√√	
Number of students	26 (21%)	14 (11%)	40 (32%)	29 (24%)	2 (2%)	15 (12%)	5 (4%)	18 (15%)	13 (11%)	82 (68%)

Key: Sentence E = Simple English Sentence; Sentence F = Simple French Sentence; Sentence C = Complex French Sentence. √ = Right; x = Wrong

The ticks and crosses in Table 5.4 relate to the three sentences, SES, SFS, CFS, and the numbers beneath the ticks and crosses show how many students fell into each category of right and wrong answers. For example, the √√ x group contains those students who identified the term correctly in the two Simple Sentences (E and F), and wrongly in the Complex French Sentence (C). The 26 students (21%) in the 3-ticks group were consistently right across the three sentences.

Not surprisingly, the largest group of students (24%) identified the direct object correctly in the two Simple Sentences, but failed to identify it in the Complex French Sentence, and only 4% of the students answered the Simple Sentence items wrongly while recognising the direct object in the Complex Sentence. The number of students in each of these categories supports the suggestion that ease of identification is affected by the context in which the item appears. It may also be affected by the task type – for example, it may be easier to identify a single example of a grammatical term in a sentence than to pick out examples of many different grammatical terms from a single sentence. However, once again, that may be only part of the answer: 11% failed to identify the direct object in the Simple English Sentence, but identified it correctly in both the Simple and the Complex *French* Sentences. This suggests that it may, after all, be the language of the sentence that affects the identification rates of at least some grammatical terms, and that the effects may vary according not only to such factors as guessing, test method effect, and complexity of sentence and task, but also according to the grammatical term. In any case, whatever the reason for these inconsistencies, it is clear that these students have only a partial understanding of what these terms mean, and that reporting simple FVs will not give an accurate picture of the students' knowledge. At the very least, future metalinguistic knowledge tests should ask students to identify examples of each grammatical term more than once and preferably in more than one context.

Results: Sections 2 and 3

In Sections 2 and 3 of the test students have to explain the rules that have been broken in faulty French or English sentences. (See p. 35 for an example of this task.) If we compare students' *recognition* of grammatical terms in Section 1 with their *use* of them in Sections 2 and 3, the inconsistencies in their answers become even more marked. For example, of the 26 Lancaster students who correctly *identified* the direct object in two or three sentences in Section 1, six *used* the term wrongly in Section 3. Since the students had not been specifically asked to use metalinguistic terms in their explanations of errors, these six students are likely to form the visible part of a more widespread uncertainty.

Section 3, Sentence 2 reads as follows:

English Sentence 2	*When her said that, Jack hit her.*
Correct version:	*When she said that, Jack hit her.*
Expected Rule:	Pronoun should be used in subject case / 3rd person singular feminine subject is *she*.

All the students in the Lancaster sample had accurately corrected this sentence, and four of the six students mentioned above had correctly identified the direct object in all three Section 1 tasks. However, in Section 3, these four students wrote the following explanations of the rule that had been broken:

a) 'Her is *possessive,* a direct object should be used.'
b) 'The direct object pronoun should replace the indirect object pronoun.'
c) 'The direct object pronoun has to be used.'
d) 'She needed as direct not indirect.'

The other two students, who had each correctly identified two of the three Section 1 examples, wrote:

a) 'Direct object.'
b) 'Direct object needed, not pronoun.'

What is interesting here is that all six students appear to be unaware of the difference between the subject and the object of a sentence. If it is the case that the students had learnt 'direct object' in French rather than English classes, and there is evidence to support this below, then this suggests that the students' French teachers had restricted their metalinguistic explanation of the 'direct object' to the difference between 'direct' and 'indirect', and that the students had failed to appreciate the difference between 'subject' and 'object'. Indeed, in their responses in Sections 2 and 3, the students used the term 'subject' wrongly almost as many times as the 'direct object' – 12 and 16 times respectively.

There is also evidence that the students' understanding of the term 'direct object' as it relates to the French sentences did not transfer to their understanding of the term in the English sentences. For example, when describing the rule that had been broken in another sentence (Sentence 14: *Give the spanner to I*), four of the explanations were:

a) 'I' is direct, but 'me' is used when the word 'to' is involved.
b) 'Me' is the direct object which must follow the imperative.
c) 'I' is subject, 'me' is the direct object.
d) 'Me' is a direct object, 'I' is not.

(It is interesting that Response (b) seems to be an attempt to transfer to English the rule governing the positioning of pronouns in French imperative sentences.)

Since Sentence 2 (English Sentences) does not warrant the use of the term 'direct object' in the explanation, there are no examples of its correct use in the responses to Sentence 2. Indeed in all 15 English sentences, the Lancaster sample never once refers correctly to the direct object. However, there are many examples of its accurate use in Section 2 (French Sentences). For example:

French Sentence 1:	*Maman a donné un petit pain à Paul et il a mangé le.*
Correct version:	*... il l'a mangé.*
Expected Rule:	Direct object goes before the verb.

Students' answers:

a) 'Direct object precedes verb.'
b) 'The direct object goes before *avoir* or *être* in the perfect tense.'

There were 14 examples of similar answers in the Lancaster data. (The only student in the sample who used the term wrongly did not seem to be able to discriminate between 'direct' and 'indirect' object. This student used the two terms four times altogether, twice correctly, and twice incorrectly.)

The fact that the students used the term so successfully when it was related to the French sentence suggests that the students had learnt the term in their French lessons. In French it is important to distinguish between direct and indirect objects because of their effect on word endings, and many teachers might therefore make a point of teaching students the difference between the two. However, it is likely that some attempts to transfer this knowledge to the English language have been unsuccessful because the students did not fully understand the term in question.

Conclusion

Although the purpose of this paper has not been to study the reasons for the inconsistencies in students' answers, one interesting finding relates to the transfer of metalinguistic knowledge across languages. There is some evidence from the data that, in the case of the 'direct object' at least, students attempt to transfer metalinguistic rules learnt in French to English. However, since, in many cases, these students have only a partial understanding of the term, they are unable to transfer this knowledge successfully. It is not yet clear how often such transfers are attempted, but it is likely to vary according to the term concerned, and whether it has been introduced to the students in a French or an English setting. More research is needed into students' transfer of metalinguistic knowledge from language to language.

The main purpose of this paper has been to show how complex the area of metalinguistic knowledge is, and how difficult it is to assess. It seems clear that the students' ability to recognise or produce appropriate grammatical terms varies from sentence to sentence not only according to the grammatical term concerned, but also to the language and context in which it occurs, and the way in which knowledge about this term is elicited. Any attempt to understand the extent of students' metalinguistic knowledge must not only take into account the above factors, but must require students to *recognise* more than a single example of any grammatical term, and must also require them to *use* this term themselves.

The original Alderson, Clapham and Steel (1997) study showed varying levels of metalinguistic knowledge among newly enrolled university students. It also showed a lack of relationship between metalinguistic knowledge and language proficiency. This paper goes further, and shows that students' metalinguistic knowledge seems to be even more uncertain than originally suspected. It is therefore crucial that further studies of the relationship between metalinguistic knowledge and language proficiency establish the quality, depth and consistency of such knowledge. The question of how students acquire a knowledge of metalinguistic terms, and to what degree they are able to transfer such knowledge from one language system to another is beyond the scope of this study, but is of concern to all those who feel, for one reason or another, that knowledge about language is a necessary component of foreign language learning.

References

Alderson, J. C., C. Clapham and D. Steel. 1997. Metalinguistic knowledge, language aptitude and language proficiency. *Language Teaching Research* 1: 93–121.

Alderson, J. C. and D. Steel. 1994. Metalinguistic knowledge, language aptitude and language proficiency. In P. Meara (ed.), *Proceedings of the 1993 BAAL Conference*. Swansea: UK.

Bialystok, E. 1978. A theoretical model of second language learning. *Language Learning*. 28: 69–83.

Bialystok, E. 1990. *Communicative Strategies*. Oxford: Blackwell.

Bloor, T. 1986. What do language students know about grammar? *British Journal of Language Teaching* 24: 121–160.

Elder, C., A. Davies, J. Hajek, D. Manwaring and J. Warren. 1997. Is grammar good for you? The relationship between metalinguistic knowledge and success in studying a language at university. *Melbourne Papers in Language Testing* 5: 35–55.

James, C. and P. Garrett (eds.) 1991. *Language Awareness in the Classroom.* London: Longman.

Krashen, S. 1981. *Second Language Acquisition and Second Language Learning*. Oxford: Pergamon.

Quirk, R., S. Greenbaum, G. Leech and J. Swartvik. 1985. *A Comprehensive Grammar of the English Language*. London: Longman.

Richmond, J. 1990. What do we mean by knowledge about language? In R. Carter (ed.), *Knowledge about Language and the Curriculum: The LINC Reader*. London: Hodder and Stoughton.

Sorace, A. 1985. Metalinguistic knowledge and use of the language in acquisition-poor environments. *Applied Linguistics* 6: 239–54.

Skehan, P. 1986. The role of foreign language aptitude in a model of school learning. *Language Testing* 3: 188–221.

Section Three

Language testing for specific purposes and populations

6 Three problems in testing language for specific purposes: Authenticity, specificity and inseparability

Dan Douglas
Iowa State University

Introduction

In discussing the issue of a lack of theory in LSP testing, Alan Davies argues that 'Tests of LSP/ESP are indeed possible, but they are distinguished from one another on non-theoretical terms. Their variation depends on practical and *ad hoc* distinctions that cannot be substantiated' (Davies 1990: 62). This complements Henry Widdowson's view that LSP/ESP as a field has been largely atheoretical: 'The problem about all the kinds of ESP that have been suggested is that they make up an observational list and have no status in theory' (Widdowson 1983: 8). It is one of the purposes of this paper to provide, in the context of discussing three vexing problems in LSP testing, some theoretical justification and frameworks for LSP testing that will take it out of the realm of narrowly focused behavioural assessment and bring it more in line with the theoretical underpinnings of communicative language testing that attempt to assess abilities that underlie communicative performance, generalisable from the test situation to non-test target situations.

Testing language for specific purposes (LSP) refers to that branch of language testing in which the test content and test methods are derived from an analysis of a specific language use situation, such as *Spanish for business, Japanese for tour guides, Italian for language teachers,* or *English for air traffic control.* LSP tests are usually contrasted with 'general purpose' language tests, in which 'purpose' is more broadly defined, as in the *Test of English as a Foreign Language*. It is important to note that tests are not *either* general purpose or specific purpose – all tests are developed for some purpose! – but there is a continuum of specificity from very general to very specific, and a given test may fall at any point on the continuum. I suggest that LSP testing is a special case of *communicative language testing*, since both are based on a theoretical construct of contextualised communicative language ability, and that LSP tests are no different in terms of the qualities of good testing practice from other types of language tests.

I offer the following definition of LSP testing:

> A specific purpose language test is one in which test content and methods are derived from an analysis of the characteristics of a specific target language use situation, so that test tasks and content are authentically representative of the target situation, allowing for an interaction between the test taker's language ability and specific purpose content knowledge, on the one hand, and the test tasks on the other. Such a test allows us to make inferences about a test taker's capacity to use language in the specific purpose domain.

This definition comprises a number of key concepts in LSP testing: the analysis of target language use situations in terms of characteristics that are likely to be shared across a number of similar situations; communicative language ability and content knowledge as the dual components of what I call *specific purpose language ability*; an interaction between this specific purpose language ability and the test tasks; and the goal of making inferences about the capacity to use language in a specific purpose domain.

Three aspects of LSP testing that may be said to distinguish it from more general purpose language testing are *authenticity of task, specificity of content,* and *the interaction between language knowledge and specific purpose content knowledge*. By authenticity of task, I mean that the tasks in an LSP test share critical features of tasks in the *target specific purpose language use situation* of interest to the test takers. The intent of linking the test tasks to non-test tasks in this way is to engage the test taker's language knowledge in carrying out the test task as far as possible in the same way it would be in responding to the target situation. Specificity of content refers to factors which affect the level of specificity of a written or spoken text in an LSP test. Clearly there are a number of such factors, including the amount of field specific vocabulary, the degree to which the specific purpose vocabulary was explained or not, the rhetorical functions of various sections of the text, and the extent to which comprehension or production of the text required knowledge of subject specific concepts. The interaction between language knowledge and background knowledge is perhaps the clearest defining feature of LSP testing, for in more general purpose language testing, the factor of background knowledge is usually seen as a confounding variable, contributing to measurement error and to be minimised as much as possible. In LSP testing, on the other hand, background knowledge is a necessary, integral part of the concept of 'specific purpose language ability'.

However, each of these three distinguishing characteristics of LSP testing is associated with theoretical and practical problems. The notion of authenticity has been a continuing thorn in the side of testing theorists (Bachman and Palmer 1996; Douglas and Selinker 1985; McNamara 1996,

1997; Skehan 1984), owing mainly to the difficulties of simulating the features of the target language use situation and of engaging the test takers' language knowledge and background knowledge in a testing situation. The problem of specificity centres around the questions of *how specific* specific purpose should be (Alderson 1981; Sajavaara 1992) and how to generalise from a specific purpose test situation to a target language use situation (McNamara 1996, 1997). Finally, the problem of the inseparability of language knowledge from field specific background knowledge calls into question whether communicative ability can be measured effectively in specific purpose contexts (Alderson and Urquhart 1985; Clapham 1993, 1996; McNamara 1997). I discuss each of these problems in more detail, and while I will not propose specific solutions to them, I believe the discussion itself will help us lay the groundwork for a principled approach to the testing of language in specific contexts of use.

The problem of authenticity

Since the publication of Widdowson's *Explorations in Applied Linguistics* (1979), language teachers and testers have come to view authenticity not as a property of spoken and written texts themselves, but rather as a quality conferred upon texts as a function of the uses people put them to. For example, a set of instructions for conducting a chemistry laboratory exercise is a perfectly authentic piece of material, but when used in a multiple choice language test as a vehicle for testing knowledge of vocabulary or the use of imperatives, it is not being used for the purpose intended by the author of the chemistry lab manual or in the way lab supervisors and their students would use it. A key concept in Widdowson's formulation is that authenticity is a function of an *interaction* between the language user and the text, and this notion is crucial to the characterisation of authenticity in specific purpose language testing.

Bachman (1991) proposes two aspects of authenticity: *situational* and *interactional*. The first aspect comprises authentic characteristics derived from an analysis of the target language use situation, the features of which are then realised as test method characteristics. Thus, situational authenticity can be demonstrated by making the relationship between the test method and the target specific purpose language use situation explicit. The second face of authenticity, the interactional aspect, involves the interaction of the test taker's specific purpose language ability with the test task. The extent to which the test taker is *engaged* in the task, by responding to the features of the target language use situation embodied in the test method characteristics, is a gauge of interactional authenticity. It is important in specific purpose language tests that *both* these aspects of authenticity are present. It is quite possible, for example, that a test task may be perceived by the test taker as having nothing whatever to do with her field of study, but which she nevertheless finds quite interesting and which engages her communicative language ability interactively. Performance on the task would be interpretable as evidence of her communicative language ability, but *not* in the context of the student's specific area of study. By the same token, a test task may contain all the contextual attributes of the target situation and yet fail to engage the test taker meaningfully in communicative language use. Mere emulation of a target situation in the test is not sufficient to guarantee communicative language use (Skehan 1984; Douglas and Selinker 1985, 1993).

The problem of specificity

While it is recognised that all tests have 'purposes', in LSP testing, it is the notion of *specificity* that distinguishes it from more general language testing. There are rhetorical, pragmatic, and sociolinguistic characteristics, as well as lexical, semantic, syntactic, and phonological ones, peculiar to any field, and these features allow for people in that field to speak and write more precisely about the field in a way that outsiders sometimes find impenetrable. It is this precision that is a major focus of specific purpose language use and is a major factor arguing in favour of specific purpose language tests. There is a problem inherent in this focus, however, leading to a dilemma: there appears to be on the one hand no way of determining how specific 'specific' needs to be, and on the other, no way of specifying the range of language forms that will be required in a specific purpose domain, thus making it difficult to generalise from the test performance to the target language use situation.

The first horn of the dilemma is presented when one begins to think about the degree of specificity that is possible: is a specific purpose language test for engineers good enough, or must we produce different tests for agricultural, automotive, chemical, civil, electrical, industrial, marine, mechanical, nuclear, and transportation engineers? We needn't stop there: within the field of mechanical engineering alone, for example, we might produce separate tests for those in combustion science, dynamics, fluid mechanics, metrology, microelectromechanical systems, nanostructures, tribology, and thermal engineering! Indeed, Charles Alderson has suggested that 'the ultimate specification of a test situation must be that of one individual at one point in time; above that level, a claim of specificity must be invalid for some individual at some point in time' (Alderson 1981: 5). More recently, Kari Sajavaara noted the theoretical specificity problem posed by LSP, but suggests that 'the problem of how specific LSP and LSP testing should be has no straightforward solution, because what is at issue here is the fundamental problem of how to categorize whatever there is in the world' (1992: 124).

The second horn of the dilemma is no less vexing: a criticism of specific purpose testing has been an assumption that if a test taker could perform the test task, she would be able to perform in the target language use situation. However, there are serious problems in demonstrating this to be the case. It has proven very difficult to make predictions about non-test performance in the 'real-life' target situation on the basis of a single test performance, no matter how true to 'real-life' the test tasks might be. This is so because language use, even in supposedly highly restricted domains, such as taxi-driving, accounting, welding, biochemistry, or waiting tables, is so complex and unpredictable that coverage, or sampling of tasks, will be inadequate. Bernard Spolsky reminds us that how speech acts are realised is the result of a complex interaction among many contextual variables, and although we might study pragmatic values and sociolinguistic probabilities of various forms appearing in different contextual environments, 'the complexity is such that we cannot expect ever to come up with anything like a complete list from which sampling is possible' (Spolsky 1986: 150). Lyle Bachman makes a similar point and offers an example of an attempt to produce a test of English proficiency for taxi-drivers in Bangkok by making lists of actual utterances the drivers might be expected to control. It soon became clear that the complexity involved in negotiating meaning even in this relatively narrowly defined context meant that 'there was probably an infinite variety of conversational exchanges that might take place' (Bachman 1990: 312). Peter Skehan notes a similar problem in another domain, that of a waiter in a restaurant: 'What range of customers needs to be dealt with? What range of food is to be served? . . . the well-defined and restricted language associated with any role is revealed to be variable, and requiring a range of language skills' (Skehan 1984: 216). This presents a real problem for specific purpose language testing: tests might contain tasks that mirror faithfully those of the target situation, and these tasks might meaningfully engage the test takers' language ability, and yet the test overall might not be truly *representative* of the target situation, since there are simply too many possible variations of situation to cover adequately in a test situation.

As a way out of the dilemma of never-ending specificity on the one hand and non-generalisability on the other, we can make use, I suggest, of the context and task characteristics referred to above, which are drawn from an analysis of a target specific purpose language use situation, and which will allow us to make inferences about language ability in specific purpose domains *that share similar characteristics*. In specific purpose language test development, what we must do is first describe a target language use situation in terms of characteristics of context and task, such as those outlined by Bachman and Palmer (1996), for example, then specify how these characteristics will be realised in the test method so as to engage the test taker in test tasks, performance on which can be interpreted as evidence of language ability with reference to the target specific purpose situation.

The problem of inseparability

I suggested at the outset that a defining characteristic of LSP testing is the inclusion of specific purpose background knowledge in the construct to be measured, as opposed to considering it to be a confounding variable as is the case in more general purpose testing. I thus define specific purpose language ability in LSP testing as *a construct that results from the interaction between specific purpose background knowledge and language knowledge*. But what does that concept mean in practice? A problem for LSP testers is establishing the relationship between language knowledge and background knowledge in test performance, for we are in the business of making inferences about the ability to use language in specific situations of use. We thus need to understand how language knowledge and specific purpose background knowledge interact and influence each other in language use (see Clapham 1996 for a detailed discussion). The question is whether it is possible to *distinguish* between the two types of knowledge – language knowledge and specific purpose background knowledge. It may sometimes be desirable to attempt to disambiguate language and background knowledge. In the case, for example, of trainee medical practitioners who perform poorly on a test of English for medical purposes, we might want to know whether their poor performance was due to a lack of English skills or a lack of medical knowledge. As Bachman and Palmer (1996) and Douglas (2000) have argued, it should be possible to give the trainees a test of medical knowledge, allowing us to control for background knowledge, as it were, in our interpretation of performance on the language test.

However, the problem for LSP testing is whether language knowledge and specific purpose background knowledge can be separated at all. I argue that they appear in principle to be inextricably intertwined. If indeed languages are learned in contexts of use, as Douglas and Selinker (1985), among others, have argued, then surely those contexts must influence the type of language that is learned. To then attempt to separate our understanding of what it means to know a language from the context in which it was acquired is at least questionable. I believe we must, in testing language for specific purposes, define specific purpose language ability as comprising both language knowledge and background knowledge, and, until we know more about how the mind deals with abilities and knowledge, leave it at that. Not a very satisfying theoretical stance, but given our present somewhat primitive level of understanding of the nature of human cognition, perhaps the best we can do.

Conclusion

In grappling with three problems in testing language for specific purposes, I first situated LSP tests within the larger theoretical framework of communicative language testing. I then argued that authenticity does not lie in the mere simulation of 'real-life' texts or tasks, but rather in the interaction between the characteristics of such texts and tasks and the language ability and background knowledge of the test takers. In other words, the solution to the problem of authenticity will be found only when the properties of the communicative situation established by the test instructions, prompts, and texts are sufficiently well-defined as to engage the test takers' specific purpose language ability in responding to the test tasks. With regard to the problem of the dilemma of overspecificity on the one hand and undergeneralisability on the other, I suggested that a solution might be to focus on characteristics that are shared by a number of relevant target language use situations. Finally, I suggested that our attempts to disentangle language knowledge from background knowledge may be misguided, given our current understanding of the nature of human cognition, and recommended that in LSP testing we continue to interpret test performance as evidence of the complex construct of specific purpose language ability, which includes both language knowledge and specific purpose background knowledge. I believe that our earnest attempts to come to grips with these three problems suggest ways to develop a conceptual basis for the field of specific purpose language testing and to distinguish LSP tests from one another on well-grounded theoretical terms.

References

Alderson, J. C. 1981. Report of the discussion on the testing of English for specific purposes. In J. C. Alderson and A. Hughes (eds.), *Issues in Language Testing* ELT Documents No. 111. London: British Council.

Alderson, J. C. and A. Urquhart. 1985. The effect of students' academic discipline on their performance on ESP reading tests. *Language Testing 2:* 192–204.

Bachman, L. 1990. *Fundamental Considerations in Language Testing*. Oxford: Oxford University Press.

Bachman, L. 1991. What does language testing have to offer? *TESOL Quarterly* 25: 671–704.

Bachman, L. and A. Palmer. 1996. *Language Testing in Practice*. Oxford: Oxford University Press.

Clapham, C. 1993. Is ESP testing justified? In D. Douglas and C. Chapelle (eds.), *A New Decade of Language Testing Research,* pp. 257–271. Alexandria, VA: TESOL Publications.

Clapham, C. 1996. *The Development of IELTS: A Study of the Effect of Background Knowledge on Reading Comprehension.* Cambridge: Cambridge University Press.

Davies, A. 1990. *Principles of Language Testing*. Oxford: Blackwell.

Douglas, D. 2000. *Assessing Languages for Specific Purposes.* Cambridge: Cambridge University Press.

Douglas, D. and L. Selinker. 1985. Principles for language tests within the 'discourse domains' theory of interlanguage. *Language Testing 2:* 205–226.

Douglas, D. and L. Selinker. 1993. Performance on a general versus a field-specific test of speaking proficiency by international teaching assistants. In D. Douglas and C. Chapelle (eds.), *A New Decade of Language Testing Research*, pp. 235–256. Alexandria, VA: TESOL Publications.

McNamara, T. 1996. *Measuring Second Language Performance*. London: Addison-Wesley Longman.

McNamara, T. 1997. Problematising content validity: The Occupational English Test (OET) as a measure of medical communication. *Melbourne Papers in Language Testing* 6 (1): 19– 43.

Sajavaara, K. 1992. Designing tests to match the needs of the workplace. In E. Shohamy and A. R. Walton (eds.), *Language Assessment for Feedback: Testing and Other Strategies*, pp. 123–144. Dubuque, IA: Kendall/Hunt.

Skehan, P. 1984. Issues in the testing of English for specific purposes. *Language Testing* 1: 202–220.

Spolsky, B. 1986. A multiple choice for language testers. *Language Testing 3:* 147–158.

Widdowson, H. 1979. *Explorations in Applied Linguistics*. Oxford: Oxford University Press.

Widdowson, H. 1983. *Learning Purpose and Language Use*. Oxford: Oxford University Press.

7 Assessing language skills for specific purposes: Describing and analysing the 'behaviour domain'

Elaine Tarone
University of Minnesota

Introduction: Language variation

The language produced in meaningful settings by second language learners appears to vary systematically across those settings. Dickerson (1975), Ellis (1985, 1987), Young (1991), Tarone and Liu (1995) and others suggest that this interlanguage (IL) variation across a range of social contexts is importantly related to change in the learners' IL knowledge over time.

Certainly, contextual variation is typical of all language use. Research in Languages for Specific Purposes (LSP) clearly shows that native speakers as well as fluent expert non-native speakers of any language form distinct discourse communities who pursue their common goals using distinct registers and 'genres' which are shaped to serve their communicative purposes (cf. Swales 1990 and Bhatia 1993). A genre is

> *a recognizable communicative event characterized by a set of communicative purposes identified and mutually understood by the members of the professional or academic community in which it regularly occurs. Most often it is highly structured and conventionalized with constraints on allowable contributions in terms of their intent, positioning, form and functional value.*
>
> Bhatia (1993: 13)

In such 'genres', grammatical choice is systematically conditioned by local, discourse-community-specific rhetorical purposes and conventions. As a native or fluent non-native speaker of a given language moves in and out of different discourse communities at any given point in time, that speaker will shift from genre to genre, from register to register. The nature of those shifts has been documented in research by such scholars as Trimble (1985), Swales (1990), Bhatia (1993), and Johns (1997). Clearly, even native speakers of a language have to acquire new registers and genres when they enter new discourse communities, and second language learners must learn to do so as well (cf. Selinker and Douglas 1985). It now seems clear that all second-language acquisition must start and end with specific second language (L2) learners who must function in the L2 in specific local social situations, and who therefore must acquire a set of L2 registers and genres.

Genre analysis and language assessment

To what extent can we assess the success of second language learners in mastering those context-specific registers and genres? To assess language skills for specific purposes, Davies (1990) states that what testers need is

> *a representative sample of the behavior domain to be measured' (Anastasi 1961: 27), upon which sample is performed 'a thorough analysis at an appropriate (macro)linguistic level [with] ... an awareness of the significance in language behaviour both of abstraction and of underlying ability ...*
>
> Davies (1990: 134–35).

This paper illustrates some techniques that have been proven useful in performing the sort of 'thorough analysis' of special purpose language use recommended by Davies. Those techniques have been extensively used by academic researchers in English for Specific Purposes (e.g. Bhatia 1993), performing *genre analysis*; these researchers have developed a useful analytical framework using ethnographic tools for the purpose of describing the identifiably different genres used by discourse communities in pursuing their communicative purposes. That framework encompasses the three areas Davies has identified: data collection, data analysis, and data interpretation. Bhatia (1993: 22–36) describes the procedure for genre analysis which is expanded to seven steps: (1) identifying a situational context; (2) surveying the existing literature; (3) refining the situational/contextual analysis; (4) selecting a corpus; (5) studying the institutional context; (6) analysing the text at the appropriate linguistic level; and (7) eliciting insights from specialist informants who are members of the discourse community being studied.

Ethnographic technique in genre analysis

According to Johnson (1992), a true ethnographic study has the goal of cultural explanation of the shared values and behaviours of the group as the group functions in its natural cultural context; this goal seems totally congruent with Davies' goal of establishing the 'significance in language behaviour both of abstraction and of underlying ability...'. But is an ethnographic model useful for the practical comparative measurement of individual students' learning and performance in distinct social contexts?

In spite of some reservations about the usefulness of 'true' ethnography for SLA research, Nunan (1992) argues that a number of ethnographic *techniques* can be extremely useful. Particularly in alternative assessment of L2 learning and performance for specific purposes, they can provide insights obtainable in no other way into the cultural values of the learner and those the learner interacts with. Nunan shows how practical steps can be taken to improve the validity and reliability of these techniques when they are used in the service of L2 assessment. The seven-step analytical procedure for genre analysis outlined by Bhatia (1993: 22–39) can make extensive use of such ethnographic techniques.

Use of ethnographic techniques for genre analysis in the assessment of learner performance in real situations includes careful observation of the learner's use of the L2 in actual cultural contexts (including audio and video recordings), a comparison of learner language use in those contexts with language use by genre 'experts'; interviews with the learner and those the learner interacts with, especially 'specialist informants' (cf. Selinker 1979; Tarone *et al.* 1985); and analysis of written products in the setting, both those the learner produces (such as journals, letters or written assignments) and those the learner has to read (such as textbooks). Analysis of these pieces of data can lead to an understanding of the degree to which the learner has or has not mastered the use of the L2 for the purposes required of her or him in the target situation, and can provide valuable insights into the learner's and native speaker's perspective on the process. See Parks and Maguire (1999) for such a study.[1] Such an analysis may offer a more valid assessment of language knowledge than more traditional structured forms of assessment.

Examples of teacher-executed genre analysis

For detailed descriptions of the process of genre analysis as carried out by academic researchers, the reader should refer to Swales (1990) and Bhatia (1993). But here, to provide some idea of the way genre analysis works, I will describe a few studies, not by expert researchers, but by ESL teachers and teachers-in-training. These studies show variation in the registers, genres and language skills needed in such different social contexts as the doctor–patient interview, the welfare office, telephone messagery and the basketball court. Such different social situations call for both native speakers and L2 learners to use and develop some areas of L2 proficiency more than others.

Medical English has been the focus of several published studies in ESP research. But teachers-in-training have also done useful genre analyses. Levine (1981), Ranney (1992) and Mori (1991) describe the doctor–patient office interview, both in terms of what non-native speakers (NNSs) need to know and what they in fact know. As Davies (1990: 131–137) suggests with regard to the description of 'medical English', such studies may be more or less directly focused on language performance in the target context. Levine (1981) did in fact tape, transcribe and analyse an actual doctor–patient interview between an elderly Russian immigrant with his daughter-translator and an American doctor. This study established that the patient often lacked health-related vocabulary to explain symptoms, and receptive understanding of English directives and recommendations. For example, the patient didn't know the word 'dizzy' and so in spite of several efforts to do so, never communicated to the doctor that his heart medication made him dizzy (Levine 1981). Ranney (1992) and Mori (1991) did not focus on actual learner performance in context in identifying other language-related issues in the doctor–patient interview; they elicited doctors' and patients' 'scripts' for the medical interview. 'Script' was defined as the participant's set of sociocultural expectations with regard to sequences of actions and utterances which she/he expected to take place in a typical medical interview. Learners were given tasks which elicited their scripts for medical interviews both in the US and in their home culture. Elicitation of such scripts enabled the researchers to go beyond surface performance to 'establish the significance of linguistic behaviour' in the medical interview (Davies 1990: 135). The differing sociocultural expectations of non-native and native speakers of English resulted in quite different interpretations of linguistic behaviours for this context.

For example, the Ranney and Mori studies found that the non-native speakers (NNSs) did not typically share the same script as native-speaker Americans as to what the goal of the interaction was; the Americans typically thought the goal was to reach a diagnosis or understanding of the nature of the problem, but the NNSs often thought the goal was not to obtain a diagnosis but rather a prescription, some medication to take out of the office. Another part of the script that was not shared involved the sort of evidence the doctor would be trying to collect during the course of the interview; the NS Americans expected the doctor to make direct measurements of temperature and blood pressure as well as elicit statements from the patient, but the NNSs often expected the doctor to obtain direct visual, tactile and even olfactory clues. In addition to the above, the NNSs did not expect that the doctor would be under substantial time pressure to get in and out of the office as quickly as possible, and that the patient would need to use negotiation skills and assertiveness in making clarification requests and confirmation checks. It seems clear that similar sorts of differences in the expectations of non-native speaker patients and American physicians are extremely likely to lead to difficulties in communication in the actual performance of a doctor–patient interview.

We can turn now to another genre which occurs in a different social setting: the social services (or 'Welfare Office') intake interview. This is a genre and situation which may be commonly encountered by recent immigrants, particularly refugees who enter the country with few resources, little English skill, and no family support, and it is an extraordinarily difficult and important communication situation to manage – yet to my knowledge, survival English curricula do not discuss it. Kuehn (1994) taped and described NS and NNS clients as they went through a social services intake interview in applying for social services to which they were entitled in rural Minnesota, and also elicited the social service intake interviewers' scripts for this 'genre'. Kuehn was a teacher researcher who had taught in rural Minnesota and had always had a number of recent immigrants who were legally qualified for social services but had a very difficult time with intake interviews. Fortunately this teacher had also worked herself as a social worker in the 'welfare office' and so was able to get permission to tape, transcribe and analyse two interviews. She was able, through observation, introspection and interview of other social services intake interviewers, to identify a highly ritualised prescribed script used in the social services financial intake interviews. In this script there were three major transactions, all areas in which the NNS had demonstrable language-related difficulties. The greatest difficulties the NNS client had were in understanding the structure of the script, in understanding the jargon used by the interviewer, and consequently in responding to confirmation requests and understanding directives. Kuehn was able to gather data on language use in a naturally-occurring social setting which had never been examined before, and to interpret the significance of this language behaviour in light of the differing sociocultural expectations of the participants. This information was helpful in designing several instructional tasks which might be used in the classroom to better prepare students to deal with this social context.

Rimarcik (1996) discovered that her students were having difficulties in listening and responding to automated voice response systems (AVRSs) on the telephone. AVRSs are computerised systems which answer the phone, list options for choice and ask you (for example) to press one to make an aeroplane reservation, two to find out about flight arrival and departure times, or three to find out about frequent flier miles. This genre is not to my knowledge covered in *any* commercial ESL textbook (or, presumably, assessment instrument), and yet it is ubiquitous these days for anyone who needs to use the phone. Rimarcik taped twelve messages, transcribed them, analysed their logical and linguistic structure, and then used them to design instructional tasks for her learners. She found that these messages imposed substantial memory burdens on her students. Rimarcik found that her students needed to understand the use of several variants of the conditional:

> If you wish/want/are/would like X, press Y.
> For X, press Y.
> To X, press Y.
> If you have N, press Y.

They also needed to know terms like 'pound key' and 'star key'. Interestingly, the AVRS which was longest, most complex linguistically, and most difficult to process cognitively was the one which was supposedly aimed at immigrants: the Immigration and Naturalization Service message system. It would be useful to use other ethnographic techniques in further study of the AVRS. One might elicit scripts for the AVRS genre from both native and non-native speakers of English. While the non-native speakers in Rimarcik's study typically appeared to have no experience with AVRSs, it seems very likely that experienced callers living in the US might have very specific scripts or expectations for the genre, and very specific strategies for dealing with it. For example, anecdotal evidence suggests that many experienced callers use the strategy of hitting the 0 or # key at the inception of an AVRS because they've learned that this terminates the procedure and provides immediate access to a human being.

In addition to these studies, teachers and teachers-in-training, in carrying out assessments of the needs of students in their classes, have used direct observation as well as other ethnographic techniques to study interactions ranging from academic discussions in university physics labs (Jacobson 1986) to 'trash talk' on the basketball court (Trites 1996) (the latter to meet the English-language needs of a Spanish-speaking draftee to a major-league American basketball team).

Conclusion: Genre analysis and language assessment

I have suggested that the process used in 'genre analysis' in LSP is a potentially useful tool for coping with language variation in language assessment. In particular, I have pointed out that genre analysis is consistent with recommendations made by Davies (1990) in that it uses a variety of ethnographic techniques in obtaining representative samples of target behaviour domains, analysing the samples thus obtained, and establishing the significance of that language behaviour for the discourse community. This approach is both a theoretically sound and useful way to deal with systematic language variation in eliciting and describing language use in context, and establishing the significance of that language behaviour. Its usefulness is supported by the fact that classroom teachers have been able to use the information gained through genre analysis to design classroom activities in teaching students to use new genres. The design of tests and procedures to measure learners' progress in mastering those genres may well benefit from the use of the same ethnographic techniques which have proven so productive in studies such as those described here.

Notes

1 Parks and Maguire (1999) document the process by which NNS nursing students acquire the genre of 'nursing notes'. This study makes good use of ethnographical techniques.

References

Bhatia, V. 1993. *Analysing Genre: Language Use in Professional Settings.* London: Longman.

Davies, A. 1990. *Principles of Language Testing.* Oxford: Basil Blackwell.

Dickerson, L. 1975. The learner's interlanguage as a system of variable rules. *TESOL Quarterly* 9: 401–07.

Ellis, R. 1985. Sources of variability in interlanguage. *Applied Linguistics* 6: 118–131.

Ellis, R. 1987. Interlanguage variability in narrative discourse: Style shifting in the use of the past tense. *Studies in Second Language Acquisition* 9: 1–20.

Jacobson, W. 1986. An assessment of the communication needs of non-native speakers of English in an undergraduate physics lab. *English for Specific Purposes* 5: 173–88.

Johns, A. 1997. *Text, Role and Context: Developing Academic Literacies.* Cambridge: Cambridge University Press.

Johnson, D. 1992. *Approaches to Research in Second Language Learning.* New York: Longman.

Kuehn, K. 1994. Form-structured discourse: A script of a welfare office intake interview for ESL learners. Unpublished MA Qualifying Paper, University of Minnesota.

Levine, L. 1981. Influence of social role on communication in a cross-cultural interview. Unpublished MA Qualifying Paper, University of Minnesota.

Mori, M. 1991. Script for the medical consultation: Comparison of the expectations between a Japanese and American. Unpublished Course paper, University of Minnesota.

Nunan, D. 1992. *Research Methods in Language Learning.* Cambridge: Cambridge University Press.

Parks, S. and H. H. Maguire. 1999. Coping with on-the-job writing in ESL: A constructivist semiotic perspective. *Language Learning* 49 (1): 143–175.

Ranney, S. 1992. Learning a new script: An exploration of sociolinguistic competence. *Applied Linguistics* 13: 25–49.

Rimarcik, JuLee. 1996. Automated Voice Response System (AVRS) telephone messages: Reality of the nightmare for international students. Masters Qualifying Paper, English as a Second Language, University of Minnesota. Unpublished MA Qualifying paper.

Selinker, L. 1979. On the use of informants in discourse analysis and language for specific purposes. *IRAL* 17: 189–215.

Selinker, L. and D. Douglas. 1985. Wrestling with 'context' in interlanguage theory. *Applied Linguistics* 6: 190–204.

Swales, J. 1990. *Genre Analysis: English in academic and research settings.* Cambridge: Cambridge University Press.

Tarone, E., S. Dwyer, S. Gillette, and V. Icke. 1985. On the use of the passive in two astrophysics journal papers. In J. Swales (ed.), *Episodes in ESP*, pp. 188–207. Oxford: Pergamon Press.

Tarone, E. and G. Liu. 1995. Should interlanguage variation be accounted for in a theory of second-language acquisition? In G. Cook and B. Seidlhofer (eds.), *Principles and Practice in Applied Linguistics: Studies in Honour of Henry Widdowson*, pp. 107–124. Oxford: Oxford University Press.

Trimble, L. 1985. *English for Science and Technology: A Discourse Approach.* Cambridge: Cambridge University Press.

Trites, J. 1996. English for basketball purposes. Unpublished MA Qualifying Paper, University of Minnesota.

Young, R. 1991. *Variation in Interlanguage Morphology.* New York: Peter Lang.

8 The assessment of language impairment across language backgrounds[1]

Rosemary Baker
Griffith University, Queensland

Introduction

One of the primary responsibilities of clinicians and researchers in speech-language pathology is to gather accurate, representative and interpretable information on the linguistic performance of people with known or suspected language impairment. Such information lies at the heart of correct diagnosis, appropriate treatment, and advances in our understanding of language disorders. It is usually obtained from a combination of case history, observation and formal testing. In this sphere (as in others), the results of language tests can have significant personal, social and vocational implications. The adequacy of test results for reflecting the nature and severity of language impairment is therefore an important ethical concern.

Professional bodies have alerted practitioners to the need to take account of cultural and linguistic diversity when assessing and providing therapy for language impairment (American Speech-Language-Hearing Association 1986; Australian Association of Speech and Hearing 1994). Tests are developed with reference to particular populations, and failure to recognise the potential impact of differences in cultural and linguistic background can lead to erroneous interpretations of results. Failure to provide appropriate language assessment for people from different backgrounds can result in diagnostic errors or virtual denial of access to speech-pathology services.

The present discussion is concerned with language assessment for Australian residents who are not monolingual speakers of English. In Australia, an estimated 75 – 100 'immigrant' languages are spoken (Clyne 1991), and approximately 15% of the population aged five years and over speak a language other than English at home (Australian Bureau of Statistics 1993).

About 20% of people aged 65 and over were actually born in non-English-speaking countries. Within this subpopulation there is considerable variation in educational level, length of residence in Australia, degree of acculturation, and language skills, ranging from those who speak only a language (or languages) other than English to those who can operate with ease in English plus one or more other languages. Health professionals concerned with age-related diseases thus find themselves dealing increasingly with people who are bilingual or multilingual to varying degrees, or who have limited English proficiency. Two clinical activities for which this has important implications are the assessment of aphasia (language disturbance) following a stroke, and the assessment of language and other cognitive abilities in determining the presence or severity of dementia.

Key questions

Assessment for aphasia and dementia in this setting is problematic. The options are limited by institutional constraints on expenditure, time, personnel, expertise and test materials. However, available resources could be used to best effect if clinicians had more evidence on which to base fundamental assessment decisions.

In which language(s) should people be tested?

Paradis (1995) considers it ethically unacceptable to test bilinguals and multilinguals with aphasia in only one of their languages, because it is not possible to predict which language will be most easily available to the patient, or which set of assessment data will best reveal the nature of the impairment. Assessment in all languages spoken by the patient is nevertheless the exception rather than the rule in the Australian setting, and those who are testable in English are often tested only in English.

In assessment for dementia it would be desirable to test in the language that optimises the patient's performance on the tasks, given that inferences about cognitive functioning are made on the basis of the responses. In practice, however, the management of assessment in languages other than English is very variable (Butcher 1996). At the very least, we need to know to what extent the language of assessment might affect the outcome.

What test materials should be used?

Translations of familiar materials from English may seem an obvious solution, but cross-linguistic research on aphasia has shown that language impairment manifests itself differently in different languages. Bates and Wulfeck (1989) describe differences in agrammatism (grammatical disturbance) in English, which has little inflectional morphology, and highly inflected, case-marked languages such as German. In English there is typically omission of grammatical morphemes, whereas in highly inflected languages there tend to be substitutions.

A similar point is made by Nilipour and Paradis (1995), in their study of English-Farsi bilingual aphasic patients. They note that different languages offer different opportunities for grammatical breakdown. For example, English articles are highly susceptible to omission, whereas Farsi has no articles to omit. The recognition that languages differ in their vulnerable features has obvious implications for aphasia test content. Further, Bates and Wulfeck (1989) argue that translating English language diagnostic instruments into other languages with little modification is not only inappropriate in terms of the information obtained, but that this practice also impedes progress in the understanding of aphasia across languages and in bilinguals.

Another possible solution would be to use published materials in different languages from other countries. However, clinicians first need to know whether these would be appropriate for migrant populations, particularly those who left their countries of origin many years ago, and those who received little formal education.

Who should administer tests?

The options for test administration in languages other than English are determined largely by available resources, but also in part by decisions regarding materials. For example, in the absence of prepared test materials, the clinician may ask interpreters or relatives to translate items from familiar tests in English. Even if one regards translation as an acceptable approach, this still places great reliance on the skills of the interpreter, as well as on the translatability of the item content.

If prepared or published materials are used, the need for translation is avoided, but assistance is still required with administration and scoring. Paradis (1987) claims that the Bilingual Aphasia Test (BAT), which has been published in many languages, can be administered by inexperienced people such as friends, relatives or hospital employees, using the explicit administration and scoring instructions provided before each task in the test booklet. However, given that formal test administration in most settings requires professional training and experience, the clinician may wonder whether the use of inexperienced assistants would affect the quality of the data obtained.

Studies conducted

Before test materials can be used to assess impairment, it must first be established that they would present no problem for 'normal' members of the target populations, i.e., people with no existing language disorder or known neurological impairment. In addition, unless patients are automatically to be assessed in all of their languages, we need to know the extent to which the language of administration might affect the scores. The first step in addressing the questions above, therefore, was to gather data on normal linguistic performance in the target populations, both in their first languages and in English.

Two related studies were conducted in the Brisbane area over a period of three years, involving Australian residents aged 60 years and over from some of the language backgrounds most common in this sector of the population. All participants were tested in their first language, and most were also tested in English. In some cases English testing was not possible, mainly for reasons of low proficiency or confidence, or lack of enthusiasm for further formal testing. Both studies included an assessment of hearing and spoken English proficiency, and all testing was carried out by the researcher and a team of trained research assistants who were native speakers of the participants' first languages. For full accounts of these studies, the reader is referred to Baker (1999) and Baker *et al.* (1998). Here, we summarise findings and observations that are of particular relevance to the questions highlighted above.

Study 1: Performance of normal seniors on the Bilingual Aphasia Test

The first study was designed to assess the potential suitability of the Bilingual Aphasia Test (Paradis 1989) for older people in the Australian multilingual setting. The BAT consists of 32 subtests. It includes task types found in widely used tests such as the Western Aphasia Battery (Kertesz 1982), as well as more recently developed tasks deriving from psycholinguistic models of language processing.

A total of 93 people aged 63–85, from Cantonese, Dutch, Greek, Polish and Vietnamese language backgrounds, were tested in these languages using published versions of the BAT. Of these, 69 were also tested using the English version.

Overview of results on Bilingual Aphasia Test tasks

To gain an overall picture of 'normal' BAT performance for these subjects, the percentage of the sample with perfect or near-perfect scores was calculated for each subtest in each language. The subtests on which more than 75% of the sample had achieved such scores were considered to have been generally performed well. On this basis, three categories of task emerged:

1 Tasks generally performed well both in the first languages and in English: pointing to named objects, naming objects, following short commands, making sensible sentences from given words, simple text listening

comprehension, reading words and sentences aloud, reading comprehension of single words, reciting series such as the days of the week, and giving words with specified initial sounds.

2 Tasks generally performed well in the first languages but less so in English: giving semantic opposites, following longer commands, visual auditory discrimination of single words, repeating real and nonsense words, repeating sentences, making grammatical sentences from given words, judging the semantic acceptability of sentences, comprehension of simple texts, single word dictation, and orally presented multiple choice items testing semantic odd-word-out.

3 Tasks causing varying degrees of difficulty both in the first languages and in English: syntactic comprehension (picture items requiring understanding of thematic roles in reversible sentences), judging sentence grammaticality, lexical decision, derivational morphology (requiring an understanding of the concept of 'adjective'), morphological opposites (e.g. adding suffixes), synonym and antonym recognition (orally presented multiple choice items), sentence dictation, and sentence reading comprehension (based on the reversible sentences used in the syntactic comprehension task).

The criterion scores set by Paradis (1987) were relaxed slightly here, in recognition of the generally low educational levels and relatively advanced age of these subjects. However, although about two-thirds of the BAT tasks were, in general, found to be suitable for use with these subjects, either in one language or both, the remaining third seemed to contain inherent difficulties, irrespective of the language of administration.

Potential influences on scores

The personal variables that one might expect to influence scores on a test such as this include age (particularly on tasks depending on memory), hearing (especially on tasks involving single, uncontextualised words), and levels of education, literacy and language proficiency. There were, however, some additional, unanticipated influences which became apparent during testing, and which represented potential sources of error.

Among these was the influence of the first language phonological system on responses to items in English involving comprehension, recognition or repetition of single words or non-words. In the lexical decision task, for example, two of the non-words in the English version are *rop* and *chetty*. During administration of these items, the answers 'Yes, rop, you tie', and 'Yes, I'm very chetty. I talk a lot' were noted, demonstrating that the non-words had been decoded through the first language phonological system as *rope* and *chatty*.

In the semantic opposites task, the stimulus word *wide* is intended to elicit the response *narrow*. However, some participants gave the answer *black*. Those who repeated the stimulus when giving this answer pronounced it as *wide* rather than *white*, which suggested that this error resulted from phonological transfer rather than mis-hearing.

In the visual auditory discrimination task, the person chooses, from a set of four pictures, the one which depicts the word spoken by the examiner. It was noted that some of the items in English hinged on phonemic contrasts that participants (depending on their language background) did not necessarily make in their English speech, for example *shin – chin*, *fan – van*, *sick – thick*. This resulted in some erroneous choices, even for these 'normal' subjects.

A second unanticipated factor concerned one of the scoring procedures itself. In general, the scoring was applied without difficulty by the (trained) research assistants who administered the various versions of the test. However, observation of testing sessions revealed some hesitation and confusion in the use of plus and minus signs in certain subtests. For most items, the examiner circles the plus sign for a correct answer and the minus sign for an incorrect one. However, in the judgement tasks, the plus sign signifies that the testee judged the stimulus word or sentence to be acceptable, and the minus sign that he or she judged it to be unacceptable. These judgements may or may not be correct; the responses are marked later, using an answer key. The most susceptible to error was the word repetition and lexical decision task, where the two meanings for each symbol are used alternately throughout. The person's repetition of the word (or non-word) is first marked as correct (+) or incorrect (-), and then the judgement as to whether it is a real word is recorded as yes (+) or no (-).

Task equivalence across languages

The tasks in the BAT are intended to be equivalent across languages. Some are essentially translation equivalents, while the content of others, e.g., those involving minimal pairs or non-words, necessarily varies according to the language (Paradis 1987).

This study raised some questions concerning the notion of cross-language equivalence. For example, in the English version of the morphological opposites task, words such as *legible*, *just* and *probable* have to be changed to *illegible*, *unjust* and *improbable*. The ten items in this subtest require the addition of different prefixes in English. In the Polish version, on the other hand, the opposites of all ten words are formed using a single prefix, *nie-*, for example, *cztelny – niecztelny*, *sprawiedliwy – niesprawiedliwy*, *mozliwy – niemozliwy*. Thus tasks which are ostensibly equivalent can differ markedly in their demands across languages.

In the verbal fluency task, testees are asked to say all the words they can think of beginning with each of three sounds in one minute. The research assistant who administered this task to the Cantonese speakers remarked on the great difficulty they had in understanding the task, despite the examples provided. Overall, very few words were given in Cantonese. Indeed, for this subgroup the task seemed better understood in relation to English, with one particularly educated participant remarking 'Ah, you mean alliteration'. As one might expect, the phonological awareness and segmentation skills required by this task did not seem to apply equally to alphabetic and non-alphabetic languages, thereby calling into question the 'equivalence' of particular metalinguistic skills across languages.

Study 2: Performance in first languages and English on modified tasks

The second study investigated a range of normal linguistic and communicative abilities, and related factors such as hearing, health and social networks, in a total of 193 people aged 60–90 from the following language backgrounds: Chinese (Cantonese and Mandarin), German, Italian and Latvian. Discussion here focuses on the comparison of performance on language tasks in participants' first languages and English, based on data from the 175 people who were tested in both. Some of the tasks were adapted from the Bilingual Aphasia Test and the Arizona Battery for Communication Disorders of Dementia (ABCD) (Bayles and Tomoeda 1993). Others were developed specifically for this study.

Tasks previously found to be problematic, or prone to unwanted effects, were either excluded from this study, replaced or revised. For example, the verbal fluency task based on initial phonemes was replaced by generative naming by semantic category (e.g. animals). Revisions were made to particular items to improve their suitability for this population: in the modified semantic opposites task in English, for example, the word *narrow* was used as the stimulus instead of *wide*, to avoid the confusion with *white* noted previously.

Also included in this study was immediate and delayed recall of a simple story read out by the examiner. The format was that of the story-retelling task in the ABCD (Bayles and Tomoeda 1993), but with content adapted from BAT listening comprehension texts. Such tasks have been found useful in differentiating even mild dementia from normal cognitive functioning. Among the new tasks developed were listening comprehension on medication instructions and reading comprehension on short newspaper articles.

Overview of results on modified tasks

Comparison of scores for first languages and English revealed that for those tested in both (n=175), mean scores were significantly higher ($p<.001$) for the first language than for English on the following tasks: naming objects, following commands, generative naming (animals), semantic opposites, listening comprehension and reading comprehension. (Bonferroni's correction yielded $p<.005$ for significance.) When this comparison was made only for participants whose spoken English had been rated as high in accuracy, fluency and appropriateness (n=106), the listening and reading comprehension tasks still yielded significantly higher mean scores for the first language ($p<.001$). On the immediate and delayed story-retelling tasks, however, scores for this subgroup were significantly higher in English ($p<.001$). Below we look in greater detail at examples of differential performance.

Differential performance on modified semantic opposites task

Both the direction and magnitude of the differences in people's scores in their first and second languages are important to decisions concerning the appropriate language(s) to test. Taking the 10-item modified semantic opposites task as an example, Table 8.1 shows the percentage of people in each language background group who 1) scored the same in their first language and English; 2) received a higher score in their first language than in English; and 3) received a higher score in English than in their first language. The numbers in parentheses show the range for the number of points difference between the pairs of scores.

Table 8.1

Performance in L1 vs English on modified semantic opposites task (10 items)

		% of group with same score for L1 and English	% of group with L1 score higher	% of group with English score higher
Italian	(n=47)	17%	72% (1–10)	11% (1–2)
Latvian	(n=50)	72%	20% (1–4)	8% (1–2)
Chinese	(n=30)	17%	63% (1–10)	20% (1–2)
German	(n=48)	54%	35.5% (1–4)	10.5% (1–4)

Note: Numbers in brackets show range for differences between L1 and L2 scores.

These results reflect group differences in degrees of bilingualism, and indicate that, in contrast with the Latvian and German speakers, relatively few of the Chinese and Italian subjects scored similarly in both languages. Furthermore, in cases where the score for English was higher, the difference was mainly one or two points. When the first language score was higher, this was sometimes by a considerable margin.

Differential performance on story-retelling task

Table 8.2 shows the corresponding results for the immediate story-retelling task. The testee scores one point for each of 12 pieces of information recalled. The different versions were designed to be equivalent in structure and information load, but content was varied to avoid any transfer of information from one language to the other. To ensure that the results reflected recall and not comprehension, it was necessary to exclude from the analysis those who could not understand the English story, or who did not fully grasp the requirements of the task. The total sample size here, therefore, is 158 instead of 175.

Table 8.2

Performance in L1 vs English on immediate story-retelling task (12 items)

	% of group with same score for L1 and English	% of group with L1 score higher	% of group with English score higher
Italian (n=40)	10%	55% (1-6)	35% (1-5)
Latvian (n=50)	22%	34% (1-3)	44% (1-6)
Chinese (n=20)	25%	45% (1-10)	30% (2-3)
German (n=48)	10%	19% (1-3)	71% (1-7)

Note: Numbers in brackets show range for differences between L1 and L2 scores.

Again, the groups vary in the extent to which equivalent information would be obtained by testing in different languages. In this case, however, the Latvian and German speakers tended to perform better on the English task than on those in their first languages. Again, the Italian and Chinese subjects showed something of an advantage when tested in their first languages. The differences between the scores for L1 and English varied quite widely, and in some cases were substantial. Given that poor performance on a task such as this can be indicative of dementia, it is important to be aware of the extent to which language of administration can influence scores.

Conclusions

We now consider the implications of these findings for assessment in the clinical contexts of aphasia and dementia.

Language(s) to be tested

The main implication is that testing in English alone can disadvantage members of these subpopulations, but that they will not necessarily perform better in their first languages. Even in the absence of neurological impairment, patterns of performance in the first language and English are not easily predicted, and are probably influenced by a multiplicity of factors relating to the person, the language and the task. In assessment for aphasia and dementia there is the added unpredictability of which language will be more easily accessible. In both cases, the difference between testing in one language rather than another might be enough to be misleading from a diagnostic point of view. On ethical grounds, then, the patient should perhaps be offered the opportunity to be assessed in all languages that are likely to contribute to an accurate picture of the nature and severity of impairment. At the very least, the choice of language(s) must take account of the individual's premorbid degree of bilingualism, in so far as this can be ascertained.

Test materials to be used

The findings suggest that a careful selection of subtests from the relevant versions of the Bilingual Aphasia Test (Paradis 1989) would be suitable for use in the Australian multilingual setting, provided that the choice of tasks and languages takes account of the individual's level of education and premorbid language proficiency. With appropriate revisions, particularly with regard to familiarity of vocabulary and register, one could probably broaden the applicability of the English version, without loss of information.

Several problems with direct translations of test content were exemplified in these studies. In the German semantic opposites task, the stimulus word *arm* (*poor*, translated from the English) gave rise not only to the expected response (*reich*), but also to *Bein* (*leg*), because of homophony with *Arm* (*arm*). Translation was also noted to change the nature and difficulty of tasks, as in the example concerning Polish and English prefixes. Furthermore, skills that may be important in the base language will not necessarily be equally relevant to the target language, and features not present in the base language (e.g., tone) will not be captured in a translation.

Thus the concept of task equivalence across languages is difficult to define, and even more difficult to implement. However, any translated or adapted tasks need to be trialled, so that unexpected answers can be discovered before they have the chance to contribute to misleading results in a clinical setting.

There is thus a need for materials in different languages prepared in advance, and shown to be appropriate for particular populations.

Personnel for testing in languages other than English

The pitfalls of direct translation of test materials have obvious implications for the use of interpreters, in that even accurate and appropriate translations made on the spot can result in flawed items. Asking relatives or hospital employees to act as interpreters introduces an unknown risk of inaccuracy, quite apart from the ethical issues raised by the involvement of a person other than a professional interpreter.

It was noted also that administration and scoring procedures which are straightforward for experienced examiners may not be so for untrained administrators. Even if present at testing sessions in all languages, the clinician would be unlikely to notice all errors entering into the data. Adequate training and experience are therefore desirable.

Finally, some of the problems observed during administration of certain tasks would not have been discernible from the completed test booklets alone. This highlights the value of having trained co-workers who can recognise and describe the significance of particular responses, and who can record incidental information that may be important to the valid interpretation of scores.

Notes

1 Based on a paper presented at the 19th Annual Language Testing Research Colloquium, Orlando, Florida, March 1997.

References

American Speech-Language-Hearing Association. 1986. Clinical management of communicatively handicapped minority language populations. In O. L. Taylor (ed.), *Nature of Communication Disorders in Culturally and Linguistically Diverse Populations*, pp. 285–93. San Diego, CA: College-Hill Press.

Australian Association of Speech and Hearing. 1994. *Speech Pathology in a Multicultural/Multilingual Society*. Melbourne: AASH.

Australian Bureau of Statistics. 1993. *1991 Census of population and housing*. Canberra: ABS.

Baker, R. 1999. Performance of normal elderly people of five language backgrounds on the Bilingual Aphasia Test. Manuscript submitted for publication.

Baker, R., A. J. Baglioni, L. M. H. Hickson and L. E. Worrall. 1998. Bilingualism in older migrant populations in Australia: implications for assessment of communication disorders. Manuscript submitted for publication.

Bates, E. and B. Wulfeck. 1989. *Comparative aphasiology:* A cross-linguistic approach to language breakdown. *Aphasiology* 3: 111–42.

Bayles, K. A. and C. K. Tomoeda. 1993. *The Arizona Battery for Communication Disorders of Dementia.* Tucson, AR: Canyonlands Publishing.

Butcher, L. S. 1996. *A Descriptive Study of the Process of Aged Care Assessment with Clients of Non-English-Speaking Background.* Brisbane: Ethnic Communities Council of Queensland.

Clyne, M. 1991. Overview of 'immigrant' or community languages. In S. Romaine (ed.), *Language in Australia,* pp. 215–27. Cambridge: Cambridge University Press.

Kertesz, A. 1982. *The Western Aphasia Battery.* New York: Grune and Stratton.

Nilipour, R. and M. Paradis. 1995. Breakdown of functional categories in three Farsi-English bilingual aphasic patients. In M. Paradis (ed.), *Aspects of Bilingual Aphasia*, pp. 123–38. Oxford: Elsevier Science.

Paradis, M. 1987. *The Assessment of Bilingual Aphasia.* Hillsdale, NJ: Lawrence Erlbaum Associates Publishers.

Paradis, M. 1989. *Bilingual Aphasia Test.* Hillsdale, NJ: Lawrence Erlbaum Associates Publishers.

Paradis, M. 1995. Epilogue: Bilingual aphasia 100 years later: consensus and controversies. In M. Paradis (ed.), *Aspects of Bilingual Aphasia,* pp. 211–23. Oxford.

9 A process for translating achievement tests

Charles W. Stansfield
Second Language Testing, Inc.
Joan E. Auchter
GED Testing Service of the American Council on Education

Introduction

The translation[1] of achievement tests into examinees' native languages is becoming more common as educators and testing organisations respond to the increasing diversity in student population in the United States and other countries. The vast majority of articles on test translation present the results of statistical comparisons and analyses of the dual language versions. Only a few publications on the test translation process are available. Generally, they focus on the translation of instruments other than achievement, such as measures of attitudes, intelligence, and personality traits. The constructs measured by such instruments can vary considerably across cultures. Achievement tests assess the mastery of a specified domain of knowledge. Therefore, such tests may be more amenable to direct translation, and the problems encountered in translating them may be of a somewhat different nature than is the case with tests of attitudes, intelligence, and personality.

The purpose of this project was to develop Spanish-language versions of the GED (General Educational Development) Tests that are parallel to the English-language versions so that the GED candidates' Spanish-language scaled scores are comparable to the scores of candidates who take the English-language GED Tests. This article describes the process followed by the GED Testing Service in translating five GED achievement tests.

Translatability study

Prior to translating the tests, the GED Testing Service contracted with a translation firm to conduct a preliminary study evaluating the feasibility of doing a direct translation of the English-language GED Tests into Spanish. The purpose of the study was to discern whether or not test items were amenable to translation to Spanish. In the study, all stimuli, items, and options in three forms of the GED were analysed for translatability. The study concluded that the entire battery could be directly translated with minor modifications. Complete analyses are included in the GED Direct Translation Feasibility Study (Colberg 1993).

Translation process

The translation of a test into another language is an important task. It is assumed by test score users that the translated items are equivalent in meaning and difficulty to the original version in English. This equivalence reinforces the claim for score comparability. If the translation is accurate, then the examinee will not be affected (assisted or disadvantaged) by the quality of the translation. Thus, the examinee's response to each item will reflect the ability to respond in his or her native language to the exact same item that was administered in English to English proficient students.

Similarly, a translation must be expressed in natural language, or in language that is as natural as the language used in the English original. If a translation is too literal, it will read like a translation as opposed to an authentic document in the target language. The lack of naturalness in the wording of the item often results in poor quality items which, generally, are more difficult. Haladyna (1994) points out that unedited, awkwardly written items tend to distract some test takers by causing them to lose concentration. Haladyna states: 'This inattention produces a bias in test scores that undermines the valid interpretation or use of test scores' (1994:64). Furthermore, research on item bias on the NTE (the National Teacher's Exam) has shown that it is often the least able examinee who is most disadvantaged by awkwardly-worded items (Wolfram, Figueroa and Christian 1991).

The same concerns are relevant to test translation. If a translation is too literal, then the meaning of the original item will be distorted because a critical distinction in the original may be simplified or not carried over to the translated tests. Normally, a distortion in meaning makes it less probable that the examinee will perform well on the item. The resulting loss of information usually makes the item harder to answer correctly. Sometimes, a translated document may be more clear than the original, because of efforts to improve its meaningfulness. This can actually result in easier items (Stansfield 1996). Sireci (1997) observes that a rigorous translation process may facilitate item equivalence across languages.

General guidelines in translation

While there are issues specific to each of the five subject-area tests, the following steps applied to all five tests.

Step One: Selecting three forms most appropriate for translation. Because multiple forms of the GED are created each year, there were many forms available for translation into Spanish. The initial task was to identify which forms would be translated. Two reviewers were selected to evaluate the existing forms to determine the most suitable ones for translation to Spanish. Both reviewers had a native command of Spanish, extensive test development experience, and experience as professional translators. Seven recent, equated, operational forms of the Science, Social Studies, Mathematics, and Interpreting Literature and the Arts Tests were selected for review. The criteria used to review the forms were 1) the degree to which the tests reflect recent changes in the test specifications; 2) the accessibility of test content to Hispanic examinees and 3) the ease with which the language of the test could be rendered into Spanish. Based on the review, the three forms of each subtest most suitable for translation were identified.

Step Two: Selecting translators. Once the test forms were identified, the primary translators were selected. The requirements for the selection of translators included 1) accreditation by the American Translation Association or an equivalent endorsement; 2) near-native reading and writing skills in English, the source language; 3) educated native writing skills in Spanish, the target language; 4) experience in the test development process – ideally, experience as an item writer; translators should be familiar with the mechanics and rules of item writing, including the role of grammatical clues in the wording of items, clang associations,[2] the length of the correct answer, and the homogeneity and parallelism of the options; 5) appropriate academic training and subject specialisation. Different translators were selected so that their area of specialisation matched the subject of each test.

Step Three: Translator orientation. Because tests represent a different kind of text than translators routinely handle, the proper and detailed orientation of translators is especially important. Prior to beginning the translation, translators were given basic information on the GED Testing Program and the test population. Translators also were given a copy of the test specifications for the tests they were translating, the *Technical Manual for the Tests of General Educational Development*, and the *Item Writer's Manual* furnished to English-language GEDTS item writers.

Translators were given a copy of the English-language versions of the tests, including graphics, and were requested to provide the translation of all text, including titles and footers. The importance of translating each message or proposition within each stimulus or task was emphasised. Translations from English into Spanish all too frequently retain the use of the passive voice when it would be more germane to a Spanish-language text to use the active voice. The result is an anglicised text that is structurally inappropriate, and, hence, more difficult to read and comprehend.

Translators also were coached to be aware of dialect and syntax issues. Since GED examinees are expected from all Spanish-speaking countries, the translators were advised to make a conscientious effort to use language that is not biased toward the peculiarities of any particular national speech. The language should be as clear to a person of Argentine roots as to one of Mexican or Spanish heritage. Terms that vary across dialects also pose a considerable problem that translators must address. In this case, it was decided to consider all possible variants of a word or phrase, and then to look for the variant that is most neutral or most widely understood across the Spanish-speaking world. An example is the word for *car* in Spanish. Depending on dialect, a speaker might commonly use *coche*, *carro*, or *máquina*. Each of these words could mean something different to speakers of the other dialect. Yet the word *automovil* would be understood by speakers of all these dialects.

Step Four: Initial forward translation. When translating a test, a testing company is faced with the issue of whether to contract for a back translation as a quality control mechanism. Back translation is sometimes used in the development of foreign language versions of tests and questionnaires. The literature on it comes not from the field of translation studies, but from cross-cultural psychology. Brislin (1970, 1976, 1986) has written extensively on back translation, claiming that it produces a high quality test translation. A number of other authors (Warner and Campbell 1970; Bernard 1988; Hambleton 1994; McKay *et al.* 1996) have written about it as well. Forward translation involves rendering a source document into the target language.[3] Back translation involves rendering the forward translation back into the source language. The back translation is then compared with the source document in order to identify discrepancies between the two. The forward translation is then examined to see if it is the cause of each discrepancy. When the forward translation is determined to be the cause of the discrepancy, the forward translation is revised.

Although back translation is portrayed quite favourably in the literature, it can present a number of problems. First, the lack of agreement between the original document and the back translation may be due to problems with the back translation, not to problems with the forward translation. That is, the back translation is as likely to contain translation errors or infelicities as is the forward translation. Errors in back translation are just as common as errors in forward translation. One is left with two translations and no verification of the quality of either.

Once the back translation is completed, the focus of work becomes a comparison of the two English documents (the original test and the back translation), as one searches for points of inconsistency. Next, one must analyse the two translations to determine the reason for the inconsistency. If the reason relates to the forward translation, only then does one begin to consider the solution to the problem. Thus, back translation introduces additional steps that can be a waste of time. A more direct evaluation of errors and infelicities is possible.

Because of these concerns about back translation, it was decided to use forward translation followed by successive iterations of review and revision. Each form of each subject-area test was translated from the source to the target language by the primary translator. The primary translators compiled a file of comments identifying any items in the tests that could not be translated, as well as any items or portions of the tests that posed special problems for translation, and how these were handled.

Step Five: Initial review. The initial translation and the translator's file of comments were reviewed by a primary reviewer, who was asked to judge the congruity of the translation with the English-language version of the test. Each reviewer was a specialist in the translation of the subject area of the test. The reviewer was asked to create a list of specific concerns and suggested revisions. This list was then returned to the project manager.

Step Six: Translation contractor review. Each test was returned to one of the two translation contractors who have extensive experience in test development and translation. After reading the translation, the translator's comments, and the reviewer's suggested revisions, each contractor's project manager discussed the issues with each reviewer and then with the primary translator. The primary translator revised the translation based on the suggested revisions. The primary translator kept a file on each suggested revision. The file indicated whether the revision was implemented or not. If the revision was not implemented, a justification for this decision was provided.

Step Seven: Secondary review. The revised translation was then reviewed by two secondary reviewers. The secondary reviewers were contracted directly by the GED Testing Service, rather than the translation contractor, in order to ensure their independence. These reviewers were selected because of their familiarity with the subject, and their sensitivity to Spanish dialects, and to regional and cultural differences in the Hispanic world. The secondary reviewers reviewed the translations for linguistic accessibility, equivalence of meaning, and naturalness of expression in Spanish. They described problems in a memorandum and suggested revisions where appropriate on the manuscript. These problems and suggested revisions were returned to each project manager, who, after reviewing them, returned them to the primary translator. Again, the primary translator either made the revisions or documented why the revisions were not made.

Step Eight: Key verification. With the translation in final form, the primary translator and one reviewer read each test and marked the correct response for each test item. The two keys were compared with each other and with the English original. This step provided additional verification of the accuracy of the translation and corroborated the viability of all correct answers and distractors, thus corroborating the preservation of the original instrument and the integrity of the translation.

Step Nine: Translation documentation. Because the quality of a translation is critical to the reliability, validity, and score comparability of a test, it is necessary to document the process that was followed to translate a test. Each translation contractor was required to document the process and the efforts that were made to ensure the quality of the translation of each form of each of the GED subject area tests, as well as the professional qualifications of the translators who performed the translations and the reviews. This documentation took the form of a formal report to the GEDTS by each contractor.

Conclusions

Test translation is ordinarily done long after the source language test is developed. Our experience suggests that the following guidelines for future development of test forms in English would smooth the way for translation of new GED test forms to other languages:

- Avoid stimuli that reference topics identified with American culture, such as baseball. For example, in baseball, which is not an international sport, there is no translation for 'shortstop'. A careful review of all stimulus texts should be done prior to developing items.
- When possible, select literary texts for which a translation already exists. By using texts that have published translations, the time spent translating stimulus texts can be saved.
- Add translation reviewers to the item and test review stages of test development. These reviewers can identify potential translation problems and suggest revisions during the test development stages. The resulting forms will be fully translatable, and no items in the English version will have to be replaced in order to create a version in another language.

While translation from one language to another does not automatically result in tests that are equivalent in both languages, careful attention to translation issues during the English language test development process and strict adherence to established translation guidelines can reduce the likelihood of introducing factors that can lead to differences in test performance, validity, and score comparability.

Notes

1 A distinction is made here between translation and adaptation. Adaptation involves modifications in test content so that the new version is not identical in content to the original. When all items are the same in both language versions, the new version should be called a translation, rather than an adaptation.

2 Clang associations is a term used by Hambleton (1994) and others. It refers to the construction of distractors based on the repetition of words that occur in the stimulus.

3 In translation studies, it is common to speak of the source language or document and the target language or document. The source language is the language of the original document; the target language is the language into which the translator renders the document. The verb 'render' is used to mean 'translate' in the translation literature. However, its usage implies that the task is not a process of word-for-word translation. Rather, 'rendering' involves creating a document with equivalent meaning and style appropriate to the target language. Rendering implies a document that does not read like a translation.

References

Bernard, H. R. 1988. *Research Methods in Cultural Anthropology*. Newbury Park, CA: Sage.

Brislin, R. W. 1970. Back-translation for cross-cultural research. *Journal of Cross-Cultural Psychology* 1: 185–216.

Brislin, R. W. 1976. Translation: Applications and research. NewYork: Halsted.

Brislin, R. W. 1986. The wording and translation of research instruments. In W. J. Loner and J. W. Berry (eds.), *Field Methods in Cross-cultural Research*, pp. 137–164. Newbury Park, CA: Sage.

Colberg, M. 1993. *Direct Translation Feasibility Study*. Washington, DC: GED Testing Service.

Haladyna, T. M. 1994. *Developing and Validating Multiple-Choice Test Items*. Hillsdale, NJ: Lawrence Erlbaum Associates Publishers.

Hambleton, R. 1994. Guidelines for adapting educational and psychological tests: A progress report. *European Journal of Psychological Assessment* 10 (3): 229–44.

McKay, R. B., M. J. Breslow, R. L. Sangster, S. M. Gabbard, R. W. Reynolds, J. M. Nakamoto and I. Tarnai. 1996. Translating survey questionnaires: lessons learned. New directions for evaluation. *Advances in Survey Research* 70: 93–104.

Sireci, S. G. 1997. Problems and issues in linking assessments across languages. *Educational Measurement: Issues and Practices* 16 (1): 12–19.

Stansfield, C.W. 1996. *Report to GEDTS on Translation Procedures Employed by Second Language Testing, Inc.* N. Bethesda, MD: Second Language Testing, Inc.

Warner, O., and D. T. Campbell. 1970. Translating, working through interpreters and the problem of decentering. In R. N. Cohen and R. Cohen (eds.), *A Handbook of Methods in Cultural Anthropology.* New York: American Museum of Natural History.

Wolfram, W., E. Figueroa, and D. Christian. 1991. *Investigative Research on Sociolinguistic Dimensions of the NTE.* Princeton, NJ: Educational Testing Service.

Section Four

Judgement in language testing

10 Revisiting raters and ratings in oral language assessment

Daniel J. Reed and Andrew D. Cohen
University of Minnesota

Introduction

'Agreement' is an ambiguous concept. It can refer to consent, or to mere consistency of any sort. Who agrees with whom? What with what? In second language performance assessment, which raters agree with which other raters? Which raters agree with the test's rating criteria and the reasoning behind them?

How does agreement relate to reliability and validity? It is commonly stated that reliability is essential to validity, but even this notion has been challenged, at least with respect to certain types of agreement. Raters may have reasons for disagreeing, and one might say that if their reasons are 'good', then their ratings are valid, despite the lack of inter-rater reliability. Of course, reliability still exists in the form of self-consistency. The disagreement is not random. But whose self-consistency matters most? How do we meaningfully interpret and report individual ratings by individual raters if the criteria used are not explicit?

How much does all this matter? Some well known rater effects are small, but they occur frequently. For instance, disagreement between Test of Written English (TWE) readers by more than one scale point is rare, occurring only 0.2 – 1.1 per cent of the time, yet disagreement by one scale point occurs about 30% of the time (ETS, 1996, see Table 4, p.14). Citing data from Linacre (1993) and from Stahl and Lunz (1993), McNamara (1996: 128–30) discusses cases of surprising differences between raw scores and scores adjusted for rater characteristics. These observations give rise to additional questions. Why do some tests appear to show greater consistency than others? Are they really more reliable? Or are the differences attributable to other factors, such as the different types of agreement just alluded to, different kinds of scales, different interpretations of scales and rating criteria, and different rating procedures? Given all these questions, and given the high-stakes uses of tests like the TWE, it is clear that issues related to raters and ratings merit the ongoing attention that they are receiving in the field of language testing. In what follows, the literature on raters and ratings is reviewed in order to identify emerging themes and research directions.

Themes emerging in the literature on raters and ratings

Three themes emerge in the existing literature: rating scales, rater characteristics and rater training.

Validity of current scales and possible alternatives

Analytic and holistic scales

The validity of holistic scales has been questioned in light of the need for the rater to force a disparate set of analytic ratings into one holistic score (Bachman 1988). It has been pointed out that using holistic single scales on the Oral Proficiency Interview (OPI) constitutes a simplistic solution to a complex testing problem (Shohamy 1990b).

While there have been repeated calls for empirical validation of ACTFL-type scale levels over the years (Lowe and Stansfield 1988; Young 1995), few rigorous efforts along these lines have been made. The wording of such scales has been seen to include fuzzy qualifiers like 'some', 'a few', 'many', and 'the majority' (North 1993). Research investigating the reliability of raters of written work using such scales have found broad discrepancies across raters who supplied verbal reports while rating essays (Vaughan 1991). Young (1995) criticises the assumption of linear development in such scales and their failure to properly account for interaction in performance.

Rater comparisons according to subscales

Another area of concern is that of whether raters need to agree on all subscales when an analytic approach is utilised. One study of speaking, for example, found raters to agree highly or relatively highly on oral reading pronunciation, idiomaticity of speaking, independence of language, and vocabulary, while intercorrelations across raters were lower for ratings of intonation in free speech, pronunciation, appropriateness of style, politeness and language correctness (Hasselgren 1997). Yet the point has been made that it may be beneficial not to have the raters agree – that is, if a variety of knowledge is involved, it may be important to have judges who are not expected to agree (Shohamy 1995).

Appropriateness of a single scale across tasks/tests/candidates

The appropriateness of using the same scales across different tasks, tests, and candidates has also been questioned (McIntyre 1995). One study, for example, found it problematic to use the same scale across speech situations that clearly elicited different kinds of language in terms of vocabulary and grammatical structures (Pavlou 1997). In response to this issue, research is beginning to indicate that it may be preferable to derive scales empirically according to the given test and audience (Chalhoub-Deville 1995). Chalhoub-Deville provided each rater with a holistic rating scale for every speech sample. She empirically derived three dimensions in rating: grammar–pronunciation, creativity in the presentation of information, and amount of detail. She found that her three rater groups – teachers of Arabic as a foreign language, non-teacher Arabs in the US, and non-teacher Arabs in Lebanon – emphasised three dimensions of speech performance differently. The teacher group favoured creativity in the presentation of information, the US non-teaching group emphasised all three with a slight favouring of amount of detail, and the Lebanese group emphasised the grammar–pronunciation dimension (Chalhoub-Deville 1995).

Transferability of ACTFL-type scales across languages

With regard to the transferability of ACTFL-type scales across languages, an assumption is generally made that descriptors on such scales are likely to be interpreted similarly across languages. This assumption has not had adequate empirical validation, however. The comparability of grammatical features like the negative in English and French, for instance, has been questioned (Hagiwara 1991).

Alternative types of scales

Given the dissatisfaction with the traditional scales and ratings, alternative avenues for assessment have been explored. One alternative scaling approach is to have an empirically-derived, ordered set of binary questions relating to boundaries between levels on the performance being evaluated. The rating depends on a series of decisions (Upshur and Turner 1995). Another approach is to use multitrait rating scales for making field-specific judgements, such as a non-native's ability to speak about chemistry or mathematics in English (Douglas and Selinker 1993). Yet another approach is to use scales for determining pragmatic ability (Hudson, Detmer and Brown 1994). Finally, semi-direct measures of speaking (referred to as the SOPI) have been generated in order to ascertain the functional ability to accomplish rhetorical tasks in various languages (Lazaraton and Riggenbach 1990). There is still the need to elaborate scales for assessing discourse phenomena – i.e. spelling out aspects to be assessed in measures such as the SOPI (Shohamy 1990a).

Characteristics of raters

The issues associated with rater characteristics include native/non-native speaker comparisons, raters' occupations, gender of raters, and personality fit between rater and candidate. Each of these issues will be considered in turn.

Native/non-native speaker comparisons

With regard to native/non-native rater comparisons, the literature is mixed. Some would suggest that native speakers are stricter raters (Barnwell 1989), for example, on politeness and pronunciation (Brown 1995). Another study, however, found native raters attached far less importance to grammar than non-natives (Van Maele 1994). Native raters were found to be more tolerant than non-native of grammatical inaccuracies and weak pronunciation when the English was communicative. While register and intonation were largely peripheral to the non-natives, they were central to native raters.

In addition, non-native raters have been seen to adhere more closely to the established rating criteria while natives are more likely to be influenced by an intuitive feeling not captured by the descriptors (Brown 1995). There may also be benefits from using non-native raters in contexts where the highest level of proficiency is defined in terms other than the native speaker ideal. For example, one study investigated whether native and non-native speakers rated the writing section of a test for proficiency among Indonesian teachers of EFL differently. The results confirmed the appropriacy of using non-native raters as assessors in English proficiency tests in contexts where the highest level of proficiency is defined in terms other than the native speaker ideal. Native-speaking Australian raters were harsher than non-native speakers, and inappropriately so, given the context (Hill 1997).

Raters' occupations

As concerns raters' occupations, raters who are foreign language teachers by profession have been found to rate both grammar and expression, and vocabulary and fluency harsher than tour guide raters, while the tour guides were harsher on pronunciation (Brown 1995). In comparing ESL teachers with subject specialists (math/science teachers), ESL raters were seen to focus more on the linguistically-oriented components, with least agreement between the two groups on accuracy and comprehension and the most on interaction and overall communicative effectiveness (Elder 1993). Another study found ESL teachers and medical practitioners to have broad similarities in judgements (Lumley 1995). Likewise, intercorrelations were high for electronics company supervisors in comparison to EFL teachers in a job interview. They were somewhat lower for nurses and EFL teachers in medical interviews, where the major concern for the medical personnel was with their ability to give accurate information (Meldman 1991).

Gender of raters

There is also some evidence that gender plays a role. Not only have male and female raters been found to rate differently, but also testees have been seen to respond differently to female/male interlocutors (Sunderland 1995; Porter 1991).

Personality fit between rater and candidate

Finally, there may be a lack of personality fit between one rater and another or between the rater and the candidate, just as Berry (1997) has found differences in candidates' output based on the pairing of extroverts and introverts. Pairing of extroverts with introverts may prejudice the performance of the extroverts on the task.

Behaviours of raters and behaviour modification through training

Rater behaviour issues that have been examined include rater leniency or bias, the effect of interviewer behaviour on the interview and the ratings, and the amount and nature of training.

Rater leniency (or bias)

There is considerable evidence of rater leniency or bias in favour of certain groups of candidates or with respect to certain items, tasks, subscales, language categories, or scale points (McNamara 1996; see especially Chapters 5 and 8 on raters and ratings). One study, for example, found subscale favouritism, where raters gave undue emphasis to a subscale, 'Grammar', which accounted for 60% of the shared variance, and yet it had been downplayed in rater training (McNamara 1990, 1996). Studies of bias have compared two statistical approaches to its measurement, Multifaceted Rasch measurement and Generalisability theory (Lynch and McNamara 1998). There was found to be a striking difference between the two: the first (FACETS) revealed extensive bias for rater-candidate and rater-item combinations, while the second (GENOVA) produced only negligible rater-candidate bias effect.

The effect of interviewer behaviour on the interview and the ratings

It is likely that the interviewer's behaviour during the interview will have some effect on the interview itself and consequently on the ratings themselves. It has been suggested that unequal interlocutor support may well lead to bias in ratings (Lazaraton 1996). Level and type of questions have, for instance, been found to influence ratings of the very same candidate when interviewed by different interviewers (Reed and Halleck 1997). Likewise, over-accommodation to lowest-proficiency candidates in an interview situation may diminish the power of the probe and may also subsequently bias the ratings (Ross and Berwick 1992).

A study based on data from the IELTS Oral Interview showed that interviewer styles and candidate styles can interact in ways that make it difficult for raters to distinguish the candidate's talk from the interviewer's talk (Brown 1998). For example, an interviewer claiming personal knowledge of a topic, as opposed to mere interest, might take away a candidate's reason for explaining. In this situation, a rater would not be able to assume that a scant response by a candidate indicated lack of ability to elaborate.

Amount and nature of training

Finally, there is the issue of the length of the training and its nature. Trained and untrained raters have been shown to disagree on scale points (Barnwell 1989). Certified OPI raters and trainees have been found to agree more on some levels (superior and intermediate mid) than on others (advanced high, advanced, and intermediate high) (Halleck 1996). Multifaceted Rasch techniques have been used with some success to train raters to avoid inappropriate severity (Wigglesworth 1994), though with limited success. While there was some initial evidence of improvement, follow-up studies have shown that such feedback, in fact, has little effectiveness (see McNamara 1996: 144, note 17).

While self-training has been introduced as an option for raters of the SOPI, the success of the self-training has depended on the background characteristics and motivation of the trainees. The SOPI investigators concluded: '... we learned that each trainee is unique, bringing to the task of self-training his or her own unique background, personality, and personal goals' (Kenyon and Stansfield 1993: 9). Previous familiarity with the ACTFL guidelines also appeared to have some effect on the success of the rater self-training.

Factors associated with variability in oral language assessment

Many factors have the potential to influence the nature of language performance and its evaluation in an assessment context. Ideally, though it makes the rating task even more daunting, raters should have some degree of awareness of these factors. Figure 10.1 illustrates some of the aspects of an assessment situation that raters need to keep in their heads while evaluating samples of language use. These factors would include a degree of 'self-awareness' of their own tendency to be lenient or severe, or to 'drift' towards use of personal criteria in between rater training sessions.

During an actual rating session, a rater must struggle under the weight of the many factors that are known to cast influence over the outcome of a particular assessment. Thus, in a sense, when evaluating a language performance, the rater, too, must perform. This performance by the rater is itself susceptible to empirical investigation, just as that of the candidate is.

It should be emphasised that, typically, it is not singular characteristics that affect variability, but rather particular combinations of characteristics. For instance, a candidate who possesses the ability to circumlocute, but who has a poor vocabulary, might fare better when paired with a rater who especially values functional ability than when paired with a rater who is inclined to be most impressed by the use of sophisticated vocabulary. Similarly, a candidate may appear to be advantaged when paired with an interviewer who shares specific common interests, such as a favourite music group or special affection for a particular city, town, or region.

Figure 10.1
Rater using both test and personal criteria to resolve uncertainties

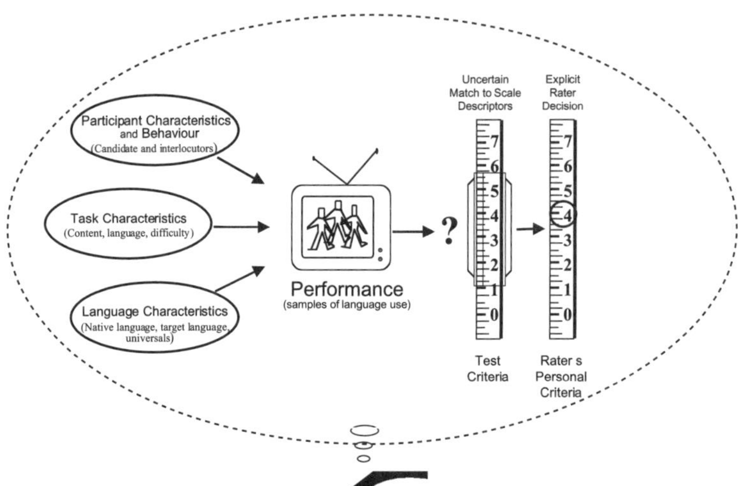

RATER

Figure 10.2 illustrates two hypothetical, sample scenarios that face a candidate about to have her or his oral language skills assessed. This candidate is a relatively shy high school student who likes music. In the top scenario, the candidate is interviewed by (or interacts with) Interlocutor X, who is a middle-aged professional who behaves in a relatively formal manner. The description of Rater X is nearly identical to that of Interlocutor X. It is possible that some candidates might be intimidated under these conditions, and that their performance might consequently be less impressive in the eyes of the distinguished Rater X.

In contrast, the lower scenario in Figure 10.2 shows what might happen to the candidate if the interlocutor and the rater were both closer in age, status, and had shared interests. We might imagine in this case that the candidate would be less intimidated, be more engaged by topics that came up, and have more to say. Furthermore, the content of this performance might well be valued more highly by Rater Y than by Rater X.

However, the question remains: which rating has greater validity?

One might be tempted to assume that the procedure in the upper scenario involving Interlocutor X and Rater X underestimates the candidate's level of ability. However, if the purpose of the test were to identify candidates who were able to perform negotiations for a government agency, or to conduct business in a corporate setting, then the opposite would be true. That is, for the purpose of selecting candidates for these professional positions, the procedure depicted in the lower scenario with Interlocutor Y and Rater Y would overestimate the candidate's ability. Thus, the validation of a performance-based test involves an understanding of how participant characteristics interact, and it also must take into account the purpose for doing the assessment.

The following discussion of factors related to variability is intended to be reflective and illustrative rather than exhaustive. The focus here is on the following four test features referred to in Figure 10.1: 1) participants, 2) language, 3) tasks, and 4) rating scales, criteria, and procedures.

Figure 10.2
The influence of participant characteristics on the assessment outcome

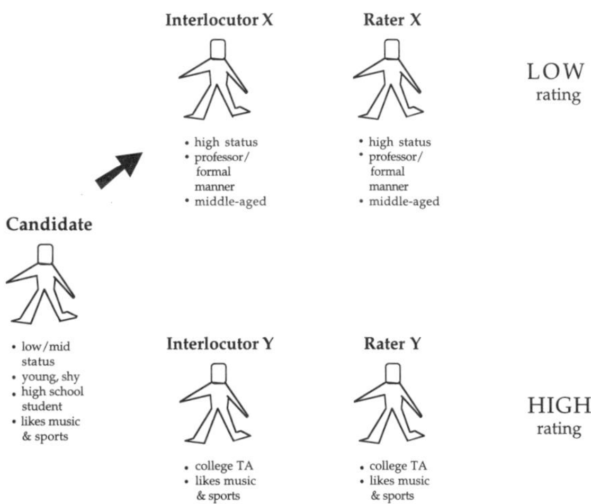

Participants

People have characteristics. This obvious point is especially important to bear in mind, because approaches to oral language assessment often call for the participation of more individuals than do traditional pencil-and-paper tests. Rather than just requiring a candidate and an instrument, a performance test might additionally call for an interviewer, or two interviewers, or actors serving as interlocutors in role plays, one or more raters, and sometimes an audience.

Whatever their role in the testing process, all of these individuals bring with them a certain amount of 'ability', and all of them (the candidate and the others) have the potential to vary how they play their role. The quality of their performance will likely be influenced by their motivation. It will also be influenced by other factors, such as their interest in, and knowledge of, the specific content areas covered during the assessment, their native language, gender, status, occupation, age, experience, education, and their familiarity with the test format. Whatever combination of these characteristics a candidate brings to the testing situation will be juxtaposed with the particular combinations of characteristics of the other participants.

Spolsky (1994) emphasises that testing complicates an already complex model of communication by adding multiple speakers, multiple texts, and hence the requirement of multiple interpretations. One implication is that funding agencies should take this consideration into account when providing money for research and development in language testing.

Language

Language has its own characteristics which may contribute to the variability of oral assessment measures. This fact is sometimes incidentally downplayed amidst the complexities associated with performance-based testing of contextualised language abilities. The fundamentals of phonology, syntax and semantics will always underlie the assessment of oral language performance in some manner. Without language, there would be no content or function. The definitions and weights assigned to categories such as accuracy and intelligibility may vary, but the influence will always be present to some degree. And, of course, what is known about these traditional linguistic levels must be integrated with features of language use that have been uncovered in areas such as pragmatics and sociolinguistics.

Chomsky (1973) was sceptical about whether linguistics proper would have specific implications for language teaching, but advised that teachers should be aware of fundamental, universal properties of language, such as its abstractness and complexity. As Davies (1988, 1990) has repeatedly reminded us, these are difficult notions to talk about with any precision. Thus, language also constitutes an area of 'uncertainty' in Davies' terms.

Tasks

Tests may vary in terms of how well tasks are explained. Instructions may be in either the native language or the target language. Instructions may be brief, or a rich context may be established. Both instructions and tasks involve language, and so are subject to the language characteristics just discussed. Tasks may be easy or hard. Sometimes raters are impressed by a candidate's attempt to respond to a difficult challenge. This tendency renders 'task difficulty' ambiguous. If we define task difficulty in terms of the mean ratings assigned, then certain tasks that are actually 'difficult' (as defined by an external framework) might be classified as moderate or easy, in the event that raters are so impressed that candidates even attempt to respond that they reward them with high ratings. Content, too, may range from general topics, superficially covered, to specific domains, covered in depth and requiring technical language.

Tasks may involve monologic or dialogic discourse. Some candidates will be better at 'co-constructing meaning' with an active interlocutor. Other candidates will be marked down by raters if they do not take long turns. In other words, there are different types of oral skills that need to be taken into account when constructing tasks to assess oral language ability.

Rating scales, criteria, and procedures

The presence or absence of particular scales will influence, to some degree, what raters pay attention to. However, the effect of this is not always straightforward. For instance, the presence of a scale for grammatical accuracy, along with a scale for task fulfilment, might result in undue emphasis on accuracy if too much weight is given to that scale in the computation of an overall score. On the other hand, if the accuracy scale is left out, raters might be tempted to mark candidates down in the 'task fulfilment' category, since that would be the only way to register their impression of a shortcoming with respect to accuracy. Such an action would blur the assessment of task fulfilment.

Other rating concerns relate to fatigue and motivation. Raters can lose sight of criteria, or shift the balance of their use of rating categories (the test's or their own). Thus, characteristics of rater training and retraining are important. Training must be motivating, and motivation must be present throughout actual rating sessions. In addition, rater behaviour during rating sessions must be monitored. If second ratings are not possible for all tests, then at least a subset of random and crucial cases (e.g. cases close to a cut-off point) could be double-rated.

Areas for further research

One area for research concerns the construction of new types of rating scales that reflect more explicitly the abilities that we wish to assess. Certain types of scales and criteria are well known. Essays, for example, may be evaluated with the use of holistic, primary trait, multitrait, or analytic scoring techniques (Cohen 1994). The exploration of new scales might help to provide an appropriate emphasis on abilities that are considered to be important by test developers, teachers, candidates and other stakeholders.

One interesting, principled approach to the development of a language proficiency scale involved the use of an item-banking methodology and the Rasch rating scale model to produce stand-alone criterion statements with known difficulty levels (North and Schneider 1998).

A second area for further investigation would be into the ways in which raters actually conduct ratings. Raters should be included in basic research and involved during all phases of test development and use.

At the level of basic research, rater input could be crucial to gaining an understanding of the various ways raters might react to, or evaluate, samples of performance, regardless of the test's explicit criteria. Since the rating process is already cumbersome for raters, audio-taping rater comments might result in richer input than having raters write down comments. Think-aloud protocols would seem to hold promise in this type of research (cf. Van Maele 1994; Meiron 1998). Think-aloud protocols could be used in a number of contexts: during initial collaborative sessions to establish potential criteria, during rater training, and during practice interviews.

A third area for research would be into ways for improving the fit among the purpose and context of the assessment, the choice of rating scales, and the selection and training of the raters. The general suggestion being made here is not that research could reveal all possible criteria by which raters make decisions. Rather, the assumption is that the set of commonly used criteria is restricted enough that choices of criteria could be managed in useful ways. Shohamy (1998) advocates a 'multiplism' view with choices made at several levels, including choices regarding purpose, knowledge definition, assessment procedure selection, items and tasks, administration, analysis of sample, examination of quality of procedures, reporting and audience.

Characteristics of a score report are not to be overlooked. Administrators are typically after a bottom-line conclusion: is the person good enough or not? Thus, no matter how much effort went into producing a meaningful assessment result, it could end up all but washed out if the score reporting is too simple.

Finally, effective communication is an important part of the improvements being suggested. In order to avoid some of the major disadvantages of external, standardised testing, certain information regarding test content and rating criteria should be made available to teachers, students, and other stakeholders. One problem is that technical reports and user manuals are often hard to understand and would not necessarily be looked at even if they were made more reader-friendly.

In summary, we have proposed that the rater has a critical role to play in the creation of '... the compromise between the underlying uncertainty of language testing and its need for explicitness' (Davies 1990: 7). Specifically, we have suggested that the rater play a part in basic research and in all phases of test development. We also observed that raters have the difficult task of interpreting and applying rating criteria in a manner that is true both to the theoretical framework of the test and to their own intuitions. We conclude that raters can do this if the criteria are explicit and not too distant from their own understanding of what it means to demonstrate language ability.

References

Bachman, L. F. 1988. Problems in examining the validity of the ACTFL Oral Proficiency Interview. *Studies in Second Language Acquisition* 10: 149–64.

Barnwell, D. 1989. 'Naive' native speakers and judgements of oral proficiency in Spanish. *Language Testing* 6: 152–163.

Berry, V. 1997. Ethical considerations when assessing oral proficiency in pairs. In A. Huhta, V. Kohonen, L. Kurki-Suonio and S. Luoma (eds.), Current Developments and Alternatives in Language Assessment: *Proceedings of LTRC 96*, pp. 107–123. Jyväskylä, Finland: University of Jyväskylä and University of Tampere.

Brown, A. 1995. The effect of rater variables in the development of an occupation-specific language performance test. *Language Testing* 12: 1–15.

Brown, A. 1998. Interview style and candidate performance in the IELTS Oral Interview. Paper presented at LTRC, Monterey: March.

Chalhoub-Deville, M. 1995. Deriving oral assessment scales across different tests and rater groups. *Language Testing* 12: 16–33.

Chomsky, N. 1973. Linguistic theory. In J. W. Oller, Jr. and J. C. Richards (eds.), *Focus on the Learner: Pragmatic Perspectives for the Language Teacher*, pp. 29–35. Rowley, MA: Newbury House Publishers, Inc.

Cohen, A. D. 1994. *Assessing Language Ability in the Classroom*. Boston: Heinle and Heinle.

Davies, A. 1988. Operationalizing uncertainty in language testing: An argument in favour of content validity. *Language Testing* 5: 32–48.

Davies, A. 1990. *Principles of Language Testing*. Oxford: Basil Blackwell.

Douglas, D. and L. Selinker. 1993. Performance on a general versus a field-specific test of speaking proficiency by international teaching assistants. In D. Douglas and C. Chapelle (eds.), *A New Decade of Language Testing Research*, pp. 235–256. Alexandria, VA: TESOL.

Educational Testing Service. 1996. *TOEFL Test of Written English Guide*. 4th Edition. Princeton, NJ: ETS.

Elder, C. 1993. How do subject specialists construe classroom language proficiency? *Language Testing* 10: 235–54.

Hagiwara, M. P. 1991. Assessing the problems of assessment. In R.V. Teschner (ed.), *Assessing Foreign Language Proficiency of Undergraduates*, pp. 21–41. Boston: Heinle and Heinle.

Halleck, G. B. 1996. Interrater reliability of the OPI: Using academic trainee raters. *Foreign Language Annals* 29: 223–238.

Hasselgren, A. 1997. Oral test subskill scores: What they tell us about raters and pupils in A. Huhta, V. Kohonen, L. Kurki-Suonio and S. Luoma (eds.), *Current Developments and Alternatives in Language Assessment: Proceedings of LTRC 96*, pp. 241–256. Jyväskylä, Finland: University of Jyväskylä and University of Tampere.

Hill, K. 1997. Who should be the judge? The use of non-native speakers as raters on a test of English as an international language. In A. Huhta, V. Kohonen, L. Kurki-Suonio and S. Luoma (eds.), *Current Developments and Alternatives in Language Assessment: Proceedings of LTRC 96*, pp. 275–290. Jyväskylä, Finland: University of Jyväskylä and University of Tampere.

Hudson, T., E. Detmer and J. D. Brown. 1994. *Developing Prototypic Measures of Cross-Cultural Pragmatics (Technical Report #7).* Honolulu: University of Hawaii, Second Language Teaching and Curriculum Center.

Kenyon, D. and C. W. Stansfield. 1993. Evaluating the efficacy of rater self-training. Unpublished manuscript. Washington, DC: Center for Applied Linguistics.

Lazaraton, A. 1996. Interlocutor support in oral proficiency interviews: The case of CASE. *Language Testing* 13: 151–72.

Lazaraton, A. and H. Riggenbach. 1990. Oral skills testing: A rhetorical task approach. *Issues in Applied Linguistics* 12: 196–217.

Linacre, J. M. 1993. Many-facet Rasch measurement and the challenges to measurement. Unpublished manuscript. Chicago: Department of Education, University of Chicago.

Lowe, P. Jr. and C. W. Stansfield. 1988. *Second Language Proficiency Assessment: Current Issues*. Englewood Cliffs, NJ: Prentice Hall Regents.

Lumley, T. 1995. The judgements of language-trained raters and doctors in a test of English for health professionals. *Melbourne Papers in Language Testing* 4: 74–98.

Lynch, B. and T. McNamara. 1998. Using G-theory and Many-facet Rasch measurement in the development of performance assessments of the ESL speaking skills of immigrants. *Language Testing* 15: 158–180.

McIntyre, P. 1995. Language assessment and real-life: The ASLPR revisited. In G. Brindley (ed.), *Language Assessment in Action,* pp. 113–144. Sydney: NCELTR, Macquarie University.

McNamara, T. 1990. Item response theory and the validation of an ESP test for health professionals. *Language Testing* 7: 52–75.

McNamara, T. 1996. *Measuring Second Language Performance*. London: Longman.

Meiron, B. 1998. Understanding raters' thought processes in holistic oral proficiency test scoring: A triangulated study. Paper presented at AAAL, Seattle: March.

Meldman, M. A. 1991. The validation of oral performance tests for second language learners. In M. E. McGroarty and C. J. Faltis (eds.), *Languages in School and Society: Policy and Pedagogy*, pp. 423–38. Berlin: Mouton de Gruyter.

North, B. 1993. Towards a common framework scale of language proficiency: Preliminary discussion and potential problems. *Thames Valley University Working Papers in English Language Teaching* 2: 72–110.

North, B. and G. Schneider. 1998. Scaling descriptors for language proficiency scales. *Language Testing* 15: 217–62.

Pavlou, P. 1997. Do different speech interactions in an oral proficiency test yield different kinds of language? In A. Huhta, V. Kohonen, L. Kurki-Suonio and S. Luoma (eds.), *Current Developments and Alternatives in Language Assessment: Proceedings of LTRC 96,* pp. 185–201. Jyväskylä, Finland: University of Jyväskylä and University of Tampere.

Porter, D. 1991. Affective factors in the assessment of oral interaction: Gender and status. In S. Anivan (ed.), *Current Developments in Language Testing*, pp. 92–102. Singapore: SEAMEO Regional Language Centre.

Reed, D. J. and G. B. Halleck. 1997. Probing above the ceiling in oral interviews: what's up there? In A. Huhta, V. Kohonen, L. Kurki-Suonio and S. Luoma (eds.), *Current Developments and Alternatives in Language Assessment: Proceedings of LTRC 96*, pp. 225–38. Jyväskylä, Finland: University of Jyväskylä and University of Tampere.

Ross, S. and R. Berwick. 1992. The discourse of accommodation in oral proficiency interviews. *Studies in Second Language Acquisition* 14: 159–76.

Shohamy, E. 1990a. Discourse analysis in language testing. *Annual Review of Applied Linguistics* 11: 115–31.

Shohamy, E. 1990b. Language testing priorities. *Foreign Language Annals* 23: 385–94.

Shohamy, E. 1995. Performance assessment in language testing. *Annual Review of Applied Linguistics* 15: 188–211.

Shohamy, E. 1998. Evaluation of learning outcomes in second language acquisition: A multiplism perspective. In H. Byrnes (ed.), *Learning Foreign and Second Languages: Perspectives in Research and Scholarship*, pp. 357–97 New York: The Modern Language Association.

Spolsky, B. 1994. Comprehension testing, or can understanding be measured? In G. Brown, K. Malmkjer, A. Pollitt and J. Williams (eds.), *Language and Understanding*, pp. 139–52. Oxford: Oxford University Press.

Stahl, J. A. and M. E. Lunz. 1993. A comparison of Generalizability Theory and multi-faceted Rasch measurement. Unpublished manuscript. Evanston, IL: Computer Adaptive Technologies, Inc.

Sunderland, J. 1995. Gender and language testing. *Language Testing Update* 17: 24–35.

Upshur, J. A. and C. Turner. 1995. Constructing rating scales for second language tests. *English Language Teaching Journal* 49: 3–12.

Van Maele, J. 1994. Native speaker assessment of oral proficiency in Advanced Speakers. Unpublished manuscript. Brussels: Katholieke Universiteit Brussel.

Vaughan, C. 1991. Holistic assessment: What goes on in the rater's mind? In L. Hamp-Lyons (ed.), *Assessing Second Language Writing in Academic Contexts*, pp. 111–125. Norwood, NJ: Ablex.

Wigglesworth, G. 1994. Exploring bias analysis as a tool for improving rater consistency in assessing oral interaction. *Language Testing* 10: 305–335.

Young, R. 1995. Discontinuous interlanguage development and its implications for oral proficiency rating scales. *Applied Language Learning* 6: 13–26.

11 Establishing meaningful language test scores for selection and placement

Patrick Griffin
The University of Melbourne

In testing, it is common to interpret the scores for a range of purposes. These purposes include student placement, selection, diagnosis and monitoring of development. Placement and selection based on test scores have been common for decades and a range of approaches have been used to identify the test score most appropriate for each of these decisions. The International English Language Testing System (IELTS) is one such system that establishes important cut-scores that can determine the life chances of students seeking admission to university programmes. Since its early evaluation, the potential tendency for fallible judgements of levels and their applications has continued to be an issue (Criper and Davies 1988). The central idea of the IELTS is the specification and measurement against standards of English language proficiency that is required and demanded of students in an English-speaking university. The process of establishing the standards and the related test-based cut-scores, however, has remained the province of professional judgement and mysterious, but apparently successful, procedures steeped in intuition and the history of the testing systems.

In an educational context, standards are important. When standards are linked to assessments or measurement, a cut-score or decision point is required. The process of arriving at this decision point has been problematic. Before approaching this problem, it is important to make a distinction between cut-scores and performance standards because, in education practice, setting standards usually involves establishing cut-scores for a test. A cut-off score is defined as a point on the score scale, and standard is defined as the minimally adequate level of performance for some purpose. This is described here as the 'limen (or absolute threshold) ability level' (Guilford 1954: 22). According to Kane (1994), a standard is the conceptual version of the desired level of competence, and the cut-score is the operational version of that desired level.

Judgement-based methods of cut-score definition, such as Angoff's summed probabilities, determine the cut-score independent of performance data. It may be decided on the basis of a review and scrutiny of the items themselves, leading to the judgement that the lowest acceptable limit or cut-score should be set at some agreed-upon value. The probability of a person being at the limen ability (a person at the precise threshold ability limit) arises from Guilford's (1954) discussion of limens and judgements.

The Angoff method has not proven to be acceptable in the past because of its lack of a variable definition. However, when coupled with the Rasch partial credit model and applied to a mixture of rating scale and dichotomous items, it has the capacity to provide meaningful interpretations of cut-scores used for placement or selection. This paper discusses the extension of the Angoff procedure for criterion-referenced interpretation of language performance test scores and presents an example to illustrate the method.

Regardless of the methods used, it is clear that cut-scores need to be informed by the purpose of the measurement and the decision to be made. The variable that is operationalised in the measurement process should have meaning at points along a continuum and enable interpretation by reference to stages of increasing competence. Usually the variable is operationalised by a test, a questionnaire, a performance appraisal or a product or portfolio. Once the observations are calibrated, they can define the variable and enable us to decide how much is 'enough'. The variable and the continuum enable us to identify what represents 'more' and 'less'. Two identifiable points of the continuum need to be defined – the location of the student or person and the point at which the decision of 'competence' can be made. It is this point that has bedevilled assessment in almost every domain. Despite a literature of cut-scores, standards, minimal competency and even litigation on the issue, it remains largely unresolved. The trivialising of a curriculum based on mastery test scores led to the demise of the competency based teaching and learning movement (Griffin 1995).

Wright and Gross (1993) used a simple procedure for the National Board of Examiners in the United States. Items were shown to the specialist examiners. Their task was to select the item that in their judgement represented the limen ability of a representative applicant. Each judge selected a set of items that met the criterion representing a specified point on the variable where the person has a 50% chance of success. The person's ability equals the task difficulty at this point. Gross showed that there was a spread of judges' standards as well and this was used to establish upper and lower limits (standard error) around the cut-point. It points to the fact that decisions need to take into account the uncertainty and imprecision of the judge as well as the errors of the assessment procedure. Those below the minimal level should be obviously incompetent and those above should be clearly competent. The mid-range of competency is arguably an area that calls for further observation and verification. What it suggests is that reliance on a single cut-point and a dichotomy of competency is unworkable and ignores errors of measurement and variability of judgement.

Extending the Angoff method

Angoff (1971) presented a technique which involved asking each judge to state the probability that the 'minimally acceptable person' would answer each item correctly. In effect, the judges would consider a number of minimally acceptable persons and estimate the proportion that would answer each item correctly. The sum of these probabilities, or proportions, would then represent the minimally acceptable score (Angoff 1971: 515).

In doing so, the cut-score is determined independent of performance data. It may be decided on the basis of a review and scrutiny of the items themselves, leading to the judgement that the lowest acceptable score (cut-score) should be set at some agreed-upon value. With a number of judges independently making these judgements it would be possible to decide by consensus on the nature of the scaled score conversion without actually administering the test. The estimates are averaged over judges to get each item probability. These are then summed over the items in the test to get a required cut-score.

Judges' estimates can be used to establish the cut-score for a test to represent the level required for a successful selection. The group members need to be specialists in order to examine every item on a test and estimate the probability of success on each item for a student of limen ability. In this worked example for a dichotomous item set, there are seven items on a test. The vertical line represents the limen of ability for the test's purpose as shown in Figure 11.1. The curves are Item Characteristic Curves (ICCs) relating the student ability to the probability of success on the item.

The vertical line intersects the seven ICCs. Each ICC represents the relationship between the probability of a correct response to an item and student ability. Horizontal lines are drawn from each point of intersection between the limen ability level and an ICC. The probability (Pr(m)) of a correct response (M+1) by a limen ability student is obtained by reading the values on the vertical axis for each of the seven items. These are reported in Table 11.1.

Figure 11.1
Limen ability level for student selection

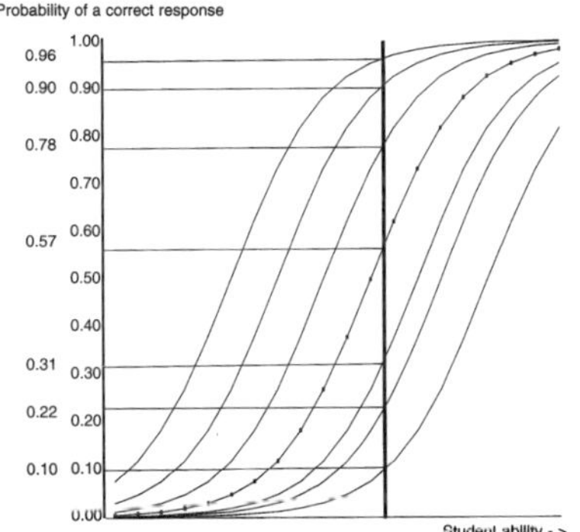

Table 11.1
Probabilities of correct response

Item	Probability =(Pr(m))
1	0.96
2	0.90
3	0.78
4	0.57
5	0.31
6	0.22
7	0.10
Total	$\sum_{m=1}^{7} \mathbf{Pr}(m)\mathbf{=3.84}$

By summing the probabilities of success we can develop an expected test score for that student of 3.84. Hence, the expectation is that any student who scores more than 3.84 (4, for example) would be considered competent. In this way, probabilities can be used to establish standards.

In this example, we added the probabilities to derive an expected score. For the dichotomous case, the formula to sum the probabilities for correct responses is shown in equation 1.

$$(1)\ \sum_{i=1}^{k} (\Pr(\ x = 1 \setminus ß_{v}) = r_{v}$$

Summing probabilities and linking these to the Rasch (1980) model opens up many possibilities. However, it is not restricted to scores derived from multiple choice items scored as either correct or incorrect (1 or 0). It can also be applied to partial credit or rating scale items by summing the product of the probability and the rating as we see in equation 2.

$$(2)\ \sum_{i=1}^{k} \sum_{x=0}^{m} (\Pr(\ x_{i} > m\ ) = r_{v}$$

Equation 2 enables the computation of the expected score for the sum of probable scores over k items with m ordered categories. This is a generalisation of the special case in the dichotomously scored example of equation 1. It is possible to use any number of items with a range of scoring categories in a true partial credit model.

In a second example the procedure is applied to a set of rating scale items. Possible scores are 0, 1 and 2. The levels are identified as decision points and, as a consequence, two cut-scores can be identified for item 1. There are also three score categories (0, 1 and 2). The first cut-score is an ability level marked 'C' or competent; and the second is marked 'HC' or highly competent. Persons representing these levels could be expected to obtain the following scores using the same procedure as shown in Figure 11.1.

The expected cut-score *on this item* for the C-person would be 0.45. For the HC-person the cut-score is 1.86. These figures are reported in Table 11.2.

Figure 11.2
Cut-scores on a single rating scale performance assessment task

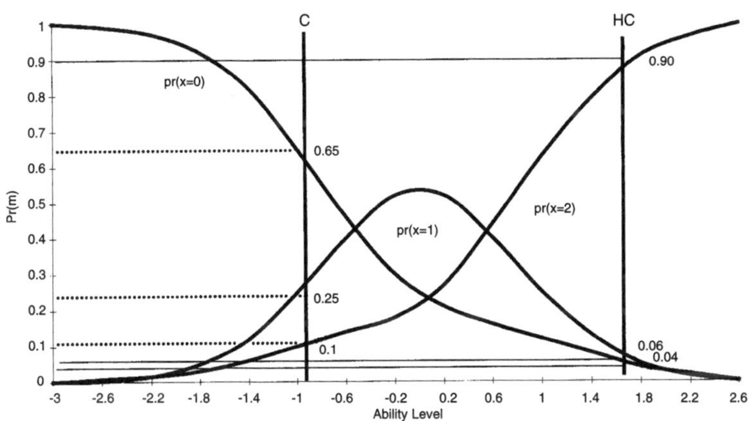

Table 11.2
Calculating cut-scores from a 3-point rating scale item

	C-person		HC-person	
m	Pr(m)	m*Pr(m)	Pr(m)	m*Pr(m)
0	0.65	0	0.04	0
1	0.25	0.25	0.06	0.06
2	0.1	0.2	0.9	1.8
$m\sum_{m=0}^{2} * \mathbf{Pr}(m)$		**0.45**		**1.86**

A second rating scale item is added to the assessment. This item provides a different set of characteristic curves for the 0, 1 and 2 point rating scale, but the cut-points for the C-person and the HC-person are at the same limen ability levels. These are shown in the next figure.

Figure 11.3
Cut-scores on a single rating scale performance assessment task

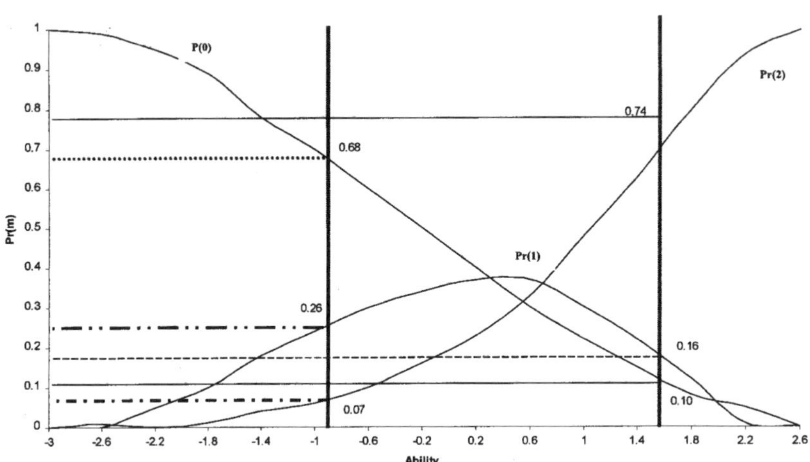

The expected scores for this item and the same limen ability levels are also derived using the same procedures as for Figures 11.1 and 11.2.

Table 11.3
Second example of cut-scores on a 3-point rating scale item

	C-Person		HC-Person	
m	pr(m)	m*pr(m)	pr(m)	m*pr(m)
0	0.68	0	0.1	0
1	0.26	0.26	0.16	0.16
2	0.07	0.14	0.74	1.48
$m\sum_{m=0}^{2} \Pr(m)$		**0.40**		**1.64**

On this item the C-person would be expected to score 0.4 and the HC-person, 1.64.

The overall total expected score for the two limen ability levels would be obtained by summing the expected scores for each item over all items.

Table 11.4
Summed item scores to obtain a subtest cut-score

Item	C	HC
1	0.45	1.86
2	0.4	1.64
$\sum_{i=0}^{2}\sum_{m=0}^{2} m\Pr(m)$	**0.85**	**3.5**

Hence on the two tasks or items, the C-person would be expected to score at least 1 of a total possible of 4 and the HC-person would be expected to score 4, since fractional scores are not possible. By adding more items, the summation over items continues and the refinement of the cut-scores becomes more feasible.

An example

The example below illustrates the procedure based on a student-writing task used in a literacy-assessment project. The students completed four tasks based on two prompts. The first prompt presented a newspaper article on the topic of bullying eliciting opinions. The second prompt presented stereotypical greeting cards and elicited impressions. The responses were each scored on two four-point scales, yielding eight scores altogether. The scores were then calibrated using a partial credit Rasch model (Wright and Masters 1982) using software developed by Adams and Khoo (1995).

In addition, a separate series of judges, experienced in assessing student work and experienced in teaching at these year levels, were used to estimate cut-scores. They made judgements about the likelihood that a student who was at a limen ability level for Year 7 could provide responses as described in the scoring prompts. There were nine judges. They worked independently and pooled their results. This was part of the training programme for the judges to familiarise them with the scoring rubrics and to moderate differences among them as raters as an initial verification process. The raw data for the exercise were as shown in Table 11.5 below together with the calculations based on equation 2.

The variable map in Figure 11.4 on page 105 shows the threshold values for each of the four tasks, independent of any other tasks on the test. The expected cut-score for a limen ability Year 7 student was established to be 16 in raw score terms. This is obtained by summing the threshold scores in the variable map starting from the bottom and working progressively upwards until a score of 16 is achieved. The overall standard error of the cut-score is based on the judges' variance of estimates and is calculated as +/-2.5 score points. This indicates variability among the judges, but a 95% confidence interval around the mean cut-score shows a smaller error than other procedures are reported as producing. A cut-score range between 18.5 and 13.5 is obtained. In this figure, the limen ability corresponding to a raw score of 16 is set at a logit value of approximately -1.1 Rasch units (logits) and the standard error extends the range to values between -0.7 and -1.7 logits. This level of uncertainty is common and illustrates the dangers of a single and discrete dichotomising decision point. It does however increase the certainty of judgement differences for students outside this range. A difference of 1 logit between the upper and lower groups has odds of approximately 3:1 that the decision is correct.

Table 11.5
Summed item scores over a partial credit, 4-task performance assessment

Item		score category (m) 0	1	2	3	4	Σm*Pr(m)
1.	pr(m)	0.07	0.17	0.26	0.36	0.16	
	m*pr(m)	0.00	0.17	0.51	1.07	0.62	2.37
2.	pr(m)	0.13	0.36	0.29	0.19	0.03	
	m*pr(m)	0.00	0.36	0.58	0.57	0.13	1.63
3.	pr(m)	0.07	0.24	0.29	0.36	0.04	
	m*pr(m)	0.00	0.24	0.58	1.07	0.18	2.07
4.	pr(m)	0.07	0.30	0.32	0.28	0.03	
	m*pr(m)	0.00	0.30	0.64	0.83	0.13	1.91
5.	pr(m)	0.06	0.18	0.26	0.37	0.15	
	m*pr(m)	0.00	0.18	0.51	1.10	0.58	2.37
6.	pr(m)	0.13	0.37	0.28	0.20	0.02	
	m*pr(m)	0.00	0.37	0.56	0.60	0.09	1.61
7.	pr(m)	0.06	0.25	0.28	0.37	0.04	
	m*pr(m)	0.00	0.25	0.56	1.10	0.18	2.09
8.	pr(m)	0.07	0.29	0.32	0.28	0.04	
	m*pr(m)	0.00	0.29	0.64	0.83	0.17	1.94
					$\sum_{i=0}^{k}\sum_{m=0}^{m} m\mathrm{Pr}(m)$		**15.99**

The decision region (-1.7 to -0.7) and those levels above and below the point can also be operationalised into performance descriptions for the students. It is clear, for example, that the criterion or threshold region is predominately associated with scores of 2. Those below are characterised by scores of zero or 1. Based on an interpretation of the scoring rubrics, it is apparent that the competent student needs to be able to do more than literal reproduction of the prompt and a clearly competent student is able to infer and draw from a prompt defensible opinions and inferences. The advantage of linking the Angoff procedure to item response theory is that once the calibration set of tasks is used to establish the cut-score, and converted to logits, any combination of tasks can be used to establish whether the student has reached the limen ability level. This then adds the sample free properties of the Rasch model to the Angoff procedure for establishing standards and cut-scores.

In this example, it is clear that approximately half the year level cohort would be considered to be below even an upper limen ability level for writing established by an experienced judging panel. In their judgement, approximately half the students are incapable of extending beyond the literal translation of prompt materials.

Figure 11.4

Ability variable map and threshold error band scores for year 7 writing

Logits	Students	Item score thresholds	Ability
5.0			Draws inferences that go beyond the surface features of textual or visual prompts and supports these inferences with well-sustained arguments.
		7.4 8.4	
		2.4 9.4	
		3.4 4.4 5.4	
4.0			
	X	1.4	
		7.3	
3.0	X		
	XX	5.3	
	XX		
	XXX		
2.0	XXX	8.3	
		9.3	
	XXXXXX		
	XXXXX		
1.0	XXXXXX	3.3 4.3	
	XXXXXXX	1.3 2.3	Goes beyond surface features and writes about personal opinions. Supports opinions with evidence and facts drawn from the prompt.
	XXXXXXXXX		
	XXXXXXXXXXXX		
0			
	XXXXXXXXXXXXXXXXX		
	XXXXXXXXXXXXX		**Reads at a literal level and emphasises this in writing. Writing tends to be descriptive relating only surface features of visual or written prompt.**
		5.2 7.2	
	XXXXXXXXXXXXXXXXXXX		
-1.0	XXXXXXXXXXXXXX	8.2	
	XXXXXXXXXXXXXXXXX	3.2 9.2	
	XXXXXXXXXXXXXXX		
	XXXXXXXXXXXXXXXXXX		
-2.0	XXXXXXXXXXXXXXX	4.2	
	XXXXXXXXXXXXXXX	1.2	
	XXXXXXXXXXXXXX		
	XXXXXXXXXXXXXXX	2.2	
-3.0	XXXXXXXXXXXXX		
	XXXXXXXXXXXX		
	XXXXXXXXX		
-4.0	XXXXX	3.1	
	XXXXXXX		Provides little information indicating an understanding of the visual or written prompt. Reactions are based on irrelevant materials and can be unrelated to the task.
	XX		
	XXXX		
-5.0	XX	1.1 5.1	
	XXXX	4.1 7.1	
	X		
-6.0		2.1 9.1	
	XX	8.1	
-7.0	X		Insufficient materials provided to form an assessment of writing ability.

Conclusion

Standards are difficult to set. They always require a set of specialists familiar with the subject area and with expected standards. In this regard, a standard setting exercise cannot be separated from the norm-referenced framework of the specialist judges. Indeed in this project the judges were using their knowledge of Year 7 students derived from many years of experience marking papers and teaching students at or around the target level. Their expectations could well have been established by these experiences.

Notwithstanding this emphasis on norms to establish standards, these procedures show how expectations can be used to derive an empirical elaboration of the Angoff procedure for establishing cut-scores. Identifying a range between upper and lower limits can accommodate the variability between the judges. The steps outlined in this procedure combined the Angoff procedure with the Rasch calibration to establish the limen ability level. After this has been done the number and nature of the tasks undertaken by the students does not matter. A complete data set is required, however, for the initial calibration using the Rasch procedure. The uncertainty arising from the use of judgements is represented by the error band and should warn about the dangers of setting a single cut-score or situating the cut-score only at the mean.

The process also makes other demands on the scoring procedure and the expertise of the judges. First, it requires that the scoring procedures reflect the variable being measured. Second, it requires that the judges are trained in using the scoring procedure and that they are specialists in the domain. Unless both conditions are fulfilled the extended Angoff, procedure cannot be successfully applied to partial credit and performance tasks and interpretation of performance levels and cut-scores are difficult to interpret and use. Once these conditions are met, however, the procedure can provide a useful approach to standard setting that is independent of the performance data and possible to set before the performance data are collected.

The simple example presented in this paper could be quite readily extended to a mixture of multiple choice, short answer and extended response tasks as well as performance tasks as used in the IELTS. At present the cut-scores for IELTS are decided through a mixture of experience, tradition and expert judgement. By and large the IELTS cut-score level has proven to be reasonably accurate for predicting a lack of extreme or debilitating difficulties in studying in an English medium environment. That fundamentally is the purpose of the test battery. However, the link between the test score and the IELTS level, especially in the reading and listening tests, is not fully established (Griffin 1990; Griffin and Gillis 1997).

References

Adams, R. and Khoo, S. T. 1995. *Quest: An Interactive Item Analysis Program.* Melbourne: Australian Council for Educational Research.

Angoff, W. H. 1971. Scales, norms, and equivalent scores. In R. L. Thorndike (ed.), *Educational Measurement*, pp. 508–600. Washington, DC: American Council on Education.

Criper, C. and A. Davies. 1988. *ELTS Validation Project Report. ELTS Research Report* 1. Cambridge: The British Council and University of Cambridge Local Examinations Syndicate.

Griffin, P. 1990. A latent trait approach to reliability in the evaluation of IELTS. *Australian Review of Applied Linguistics* 4 (2): 21–32.

Griffin, P. 1995. Competency Assessment: Avoiding pitfalls of the past. *Australian and New Zealand Journal of Vocational Education Research 3* (2): 34–59.

Griffin, P. and Gillis, S. 1997. Results of trials: A cross-national investigation. In Clapham, C. and Alderson, J. C. (eds.), *Constructing and Trialling the IELTS Test*, pp. 26–38. Cambridge: University of Cambridge Local Examinations Syndicate.

Guilford, J. P. 1954. *Psychometric Methods.* New York, NY: McGraw Hill.

Kane, M. 1994. Validating the performance standards associated with passing scores. *Review of Educational Research* 64 (3): 425–61.

Rasch, G. 1980. *Probabilistic Models for Some Intelligence Attainment Tests.* Chicago, IL: University of Chicago Press.

Wright, B. D. and M. Gross. 1993. How to Set Standards. *Rasch Measurement Transactions* 7 (3): 1–3.

Wright, B. D. and G. Masters. 1982. *Rating Scale Analysis*. Chicago: MESA Press.

Section Five

The uses and usefulness of language tests

12 Designing and developing useful language tests[1]

Lyle F. Bachman
Department of Applied Linguistics and TESL
University of California, Los Angeles

Introduction

When we consider using a language test, it is generally because we have some particular use or purpose in mind. For example, we may need to select the most qualified individuals from among a pool of job applicants, or we may need to place students into an appropriate level in a language programme. Whatever the specific purpose for which we need to use a language test, this purpose is likely to fall into one or more of the following general categories of test use: 1) to make inferences about language ability; 2) to make predictions about test takers' ability to use language in contexts outside the test itself; and 3) to make decisions about individuals, based on these inferences or predictions. The primary consideration in developing a language test, then, is the use for which it is intended. It would thus make sense to ask the question, 'What makes a given test useful for its intended purpose?' or 'What are the qualities that we need to consider when evaluating the usefulness of a given test?'

Another question that we need to ask is, 'What is the setting in which we will make our inferences, predictions and decisions?' We usually want our inferences about language ability to generalise beyond the test itself, so that we need to carefully consider the extent to which the performance we elicit in a language test corresponds to the language that is used in non-test language use settings. The way we specify these non-test language use settings or domains will have important implications for the validity of our uses of the test results. And unless we can demonstrate that the inferences or predictions we make on the basis of language tests are valid, we have no justification for using test scores for making decisions about individuals.

In this paper, I provide an overview of an approach to developing test tasks that Adrian Palmer and I describe in our book, *Language Testing in Practice* (Bachman and Palmer 1996). This approach is aimed at ensuring that language test tasks are useful for their intended purposes and correspond in demonstrable ways to language use tasks.

Test usefulness

Since the most important consideration in designing and developing a language test is the use for which it is intended, it would make sense to have some way of considering, in the way we design and develop a language test, the extent to which it is likely to be useful for its intended purpose. Traditionally, language tests have been evaluated in terms of several qualities, such as reliability, validity and practicality, with these qualities considered to be more or less independent of, or even conflicting with, each other. What has been lacking, I believe, has been a theoretically grounded, unified approach to evaluating the usefulness of a given language test. To this end, Adrian Palmer and I have developed a framework of test usefulness that we believe provides a guiding principle that must underlie any development and use of language tests (Bachman and Palmer 1996). Because of space limitations, I can only sketch the broad outlines of our notion of test usefulness, which we define as an overall quality that results from the appropriate balance among several individual qualities: reliability, construct validity, authenticity, interactiveness, impact, and practicality. We believe that the issues involved in maximising overall test usefulness, and finding an appropriate balance among the different qualities of usefulness, can most appropriately be addressed in specific language testing situations. Furthermore, we believe that the evaluation of test usefulness can and must be considered throughout the test development process, and not simply after the fact, when the test has already been given and used. We thus believe that test usefulness provides not only a metric by which we can evaluate the tests we use, but also an essential basis for quality control throughout the entire test development process.

Correspondences between language test performance and language use

In order to justify using the scores from a language test to make inferences, predictions and decisions about individuals, we must be able to *demonstrate* how performance on that language test is related to language use in specific situations other than the language test itself. This correspondence is illustrated in Figure 12.1.

Figure 12.1

Correspondences between language use and language test performance

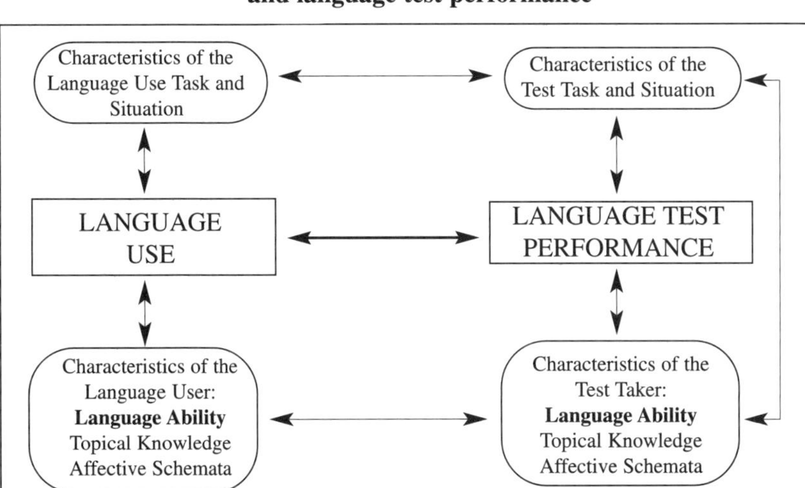

(Bachman and Palmer 1996: 12)

In order to demonstrate this relationship, we need a conceptual framework that will enable us to treat performance on a language test as a particular instance of language use. Using such a framework, we can describe the distinctive features of both language use tasks and language test tasks with the same characteristics. Bachman and Palmer (1996) propose a framework that includes two sets of characteristics that we believe affect both language use and language test performance and that thus need to be considered when we design a language test: 1) characteristics for describing language use tasks, on the one hand, and test tasks, on the other; and 2) characteristics for describing the individuals who are language users, on the one hand, and test takers, on the other.[2]

We need to consider task characteristics in order to demonstrate the ways in which our test tasks correspond to language use tasks. This correspondence is relevant to the test usefulness quality of *authenticity*, which Bachman and Palmer (1996) define as 'the degree of correspondence of the characteristics of a given language test task to the features of a TLU [target language use] task' (p. 23). Considering the characteristics of individuals enables us to investigate the extent to which these characteristics, particularly their language ability, are involved in language use tasks and test tasks. The characteristics of individuals are relevant to the *construct validity* of any inferences we make about language ability. Construct validity can be defined as the meaningfulness and appropriateness of the interpretations of language test scores as indicators of language ability (APA 1985; Messick 1989). Another correspondence that is of particular interest in designing language tests is that between the characteristics of the test task and the characteristics of the test taker. This correspondence pertains to the quality of *interactiveness*, which Bachman and Palmer (1996) define as 'the extent and type of involvement of the test taker's individual characteristics in accomplishing a test task' (p. 25).

A framework of task characteristics

The various types of items, or tasks, that are commonly found in language tests are not single wholes, but consist of collections of characteristics. Multiple-choice test items, for example, may vary in their length, grammatical complexity and topical content. Similarly, composition prompts can differ in characteristics such as the intended audience, the purpose, and the specific rhetorical style requested. Therefore, in order to specify test tasks precisely, we need a descriptive framework of task characteristics. These task characteristics provide the link between tasks in the domain of the language test and those in the domain of language use, and permit us to select or design test tasks that correspond in specific ways to language use tasks.

Two notions that are central to our approach to language test development are *language use task* and *target language use domain*. Drawing on the literature in both measurement (e.g. Carroll 1993) and applied linguistics (e.g. Crookes and Gass 1993a; Pica, Kanagy, and Falodun 1993, Duff 1993); Bachman and Palmer (1996) define a *language use task* as 'an activity that involves individuals in using language for the purpose of achieving a particular goal or objective in a particular situation' (p. 44). Language use tasks can be thought of informally as constituting the elemental activities of language use. Language use, by its very nature, is embedded in particular situations, or domains, and in most language testing situations we want to make inferences about test takers' ability to use language in a particular language use domain. Bachman and Palmer (1996) define a *target language use (TLU) domain* as 'a set of specific language use tasks that the test taker is likely to encounter outside of the test itself, and to which we want our inferences about language ability to generalize' (p. 44).

The framework of task characteristics that Bachman and Palmer (1996) describe builds on the framework proposed by Bachman (1990), and consists of a set of features for describing five aspects of language use tasks and language test tasks: setting, rubric, input, expected response, and relationship between input and expected response. These can be described briefly as follows:

- **setting:** the physical circumstances under which either language use or language testing takes place. It can be characterised in terms of its physical characteristics, the participants involved, and the time of the task.
- **rubric:** the context for the task. It includes those characteristics of the test or language use situation that provide the structure for the task, and constrain how language users or test takers are expected to respond to these tasks.
- **input:** the material contained in the task, which test takers or language users need to process in some way, and to which they are expected to respond. Input may be either aural or visual or both; it may include verbal or non-verbal visual material, or both. If the input includes verbal material, this can be characterised in terms of its linguistic characteristics, as well as its topical content.
- **expected response:** the language use that is expected, given the way in which the rubric, or context, for the task is configured, and the particular input that is provided.
- **relationship between input and response:** reactivity, which is the degree of reciprocity, or interaction involved; scope, which is the amount and range of input that needs to be processed in order to respond; and directness, which is the extent to which the response can be made by using information in the input by itself, or whether the language user or test taker must also rely on information in the context or in his or her own real world knowledge.

This task characteristics framework can be used in a variety of ways, and I will focus on one of the most important of these in this paper: describing the characteristics of target language use tasks as a basis for designing and developing test tasks.

Describing target language use tasks

In order to demonstrate the correspondence between the language used in the test and that used in a specific (TLU) domain, we begin by describing test tasks in the relevant TLU domain. This involves three kinds of activities: 1) *identifying* the tasks in the relevant TLU domains, 2) *selecting* TLU tasks as a basis for designing test tasks; and 3) *describing* these TLU tasks in terms of their task characteristics, using a framework such as that presented earlier.

Identifying tasks in the relevant TLU domain can be accomplished by conducting a needs analysis, which involves the systematic gathering of specific information about the language needs of learners, and the analysis of this information, for purposes of language syllabus design. The amount of time and effort spent in identifying tasks will depend on the demands of the particular testing situation; high-stakes testing situations will generally require a more detailed needs analysis than low-stakes situations.

The next step in test development is to select some of these TLU tasks for use in designing test tasks. There are several reasons why we generally need to select some tasks in the TLU domain and avoid others as a basis for designing test tasks. In some cases, certain TLU tasks may be essential to performing the job, and in such cases, we will want to make sure we include these critical tasks in our task analysis. A reason for not selecting some TLU tasks is that some tasks can be carried out with little or no use of the areas of language ability that we want to measure. Another reason for not selecting some TLU tasks is that these may not be appropriate for all of the test takers. This may happen when the TLU domain may require specialised topical knowledge, and if we include test tasks that correspond, in level and areas of topical content, to specific tasks in the TLU domain, these could be considered unfair to test takers who do not already have the levels of specialised knowledge such tasks require.

Once the TLU tasks to be used for developing test tasks have been selected, the next step is to describe these in terms of the characteristics that are common to these particular TLU tasks and that distinguish them from other sets of TLU tasks. Bachman and Palmer (1996) refer to this set of characteristics as *distinctive task characteristics*, which define task 'types' and provide the templates for developing actual test tasks. In some cases the test developer may find the task characteristics framework described above to be satisfactory for describing TLU tasks. In other cases, this may need to be modified to meet the needs of the particular situation. Regardless of what specific task characteristics are used, the main point is that some sort of task characteristics framework and systematic analysis is useful for bringing precision to describing the characteristics of TLU tasks.

Developing test tasks

Once the TLU tasks that will be used for test development have been described in terms of their distinctive task characteristics, we are ready to begin developing test task specifications based on these. There are two general strategies that we can use in developing these specifications: we can modify the characteristics of TLU task types, or we can create original test task specifications based on the characteristics of TLU task types.

In most cases, because of considerations of test usefulness qualities such as reliability, construct validity and practicality, we need to modify the TLU task types to accommodate the demands of testing. When TLU task types are modified in developing language test tasks, the specific characteristics of the test tasks will differ somewhat from those of TLU tasks. Because of the importance we attach to authenticity and interactiveness in our approach to test development, we give the highest priority, in developing test tasks, to maintaining those characteristics of TLU task types that are considered to be distinctive.

In other situations, specific TLU tasks may not be an appropriate place to *begin* to develop test tasks. This may be the case when the TLU domain is very large and contains a variety of different task types, none of which by itself is sufficiently representative of the tasks in the entire domain. In such circumstances, we may want to create original test tasks whose characteristics nevertheless correspond to the *distinctive characteristics* of TLU tasks.

Irrespective of which strategy we use – modifying TLU tasks or creating original test tasks on the basis of distinguishing characteristics of TLU tasks – we believe that our approach will yield relatively authentic and interactive language test tasks, whose distinctive characteristics correspond very closely to those of TLU tasks. We also believe that such tasks will provide a basis for obtaining reliable measures upon which we can base valid inferences and make decisions that are fair and defensible, given the values of the society and business setting in which the test is used.

Conclusion

I have described an approach to language test development that is based on the fundamental principle that if we are going to use the results of language tests to make inferences, predictions, or decisions about individuals, we must be able to *demonstrate* how performance on that language test corresponds to language use in specific situations other than the language test itself. One essential component of this approach is a framework for implementing considerations of overall test usefulness throughout the entire test development effort, from test design to test use. Another key element is the correspondence between the characteristics of target language use tasks and those of test tasks, and this correspondence pertains to the quality of authenticity. The mechanism for demonstrating this correspondence is a framework of task characteristics.

I believe that our approach to language testing will provide test developers with a theoretically grounded and principled basis for developing and using language tests. I believe it also provides test developers with an understanding that will enable them to make their own judgements and decisions about either selecting or developing a language test that will be useful for their particular language testing situations. I further believe our approach makes a contribution to language testing practice because it requires language test developers to take into consideration, in the design and development of language tests, the fundamental correspondence between language test performance and non-test language use. It is this correspondence which provides the basis for demonstrating both the construct validity of score interpretations and the authenticity of test tasks.

Notes

1 This paper is a revised version of a presentation made at the international symposium 'Language Testing and Human Resources Management' held in Antwerp, 20–21 November 1997, sponsored by The Scientific Research Community on Language Testing.

2 There are a number of individual characteristics that need to be considered, such as personal characteristics, background or topical knowledge and affective schemata. In language tests, of course, the characteristic in which we are most interested is the language ability of the individuals.

References

American Psychological Association, American Educational Research Association, and National Council on Measurement in Education. 1985. *Standards for Educational and Psychological Testing.* Washington, DC: American Psychological Association.

Bachman, L. F. 1990. *Fundamental Considerations in Language Testing.* Oxford: Oxford University Press.

Bachman, L. F. and A. S. Palmer, 1996. *Language Testing in Practice: Designing and Developing Useful Language Tests.* Oxford: Oxford University Press.

Carroll, J. B. 1993. *Human Cognitive Abilities: A Survey of Factor Analytic Studies.* Cambridge: Cambridge University Press.

Crookes, G. and S. Gass. 1993a. Introduction. In G. Crookes and S. Gass (eds.), *Tasks in Language Learning: Integrated Theory and Practice*, pp.1–7. Clevedon, Avon: Multilingual Matters.

Crookes, G. and S. Gass (eds.) 1993b. *Tasks in Language Learning: Integrated Theory and Practice.* Clevedon, Avon: Multilingual Matters.

Duff, P. 1993. Tasks and interlanguage performance: an SLA research perspective. In G. Crookes and S. Gass, (eds.), *Tasks in Language Learning: Integrated Theory and Practice,* pp. 57–95. Clevedon, Avon: Multilingual Matters.

Messick, S. 1989. Validity. In Linn, R. L. (ed.), *Educational Measurement* 3rd ed., pp. 13–103. New York: American Council on Education and Macmillan.

Pica, T. R., R. Kanagy and J. Falodun, 1993. Choosing and using communicative tasks for second language instruction. In G. Crookes and S. Gass (eds.), *Tasks in Language Learning: Integrated Theory and Practice,* pp. 9–34. Clevedon, Avon: Multilingual Matters.

13 The formative and summative uses of language test data: Present concerns and future directions

Cyril J. Weir
University of Reading

The formative and summative uses of language test data in educational programmes and projects: Some cause for concern

Summative evaluation of language programmes or projects, the judgement of their impact or value added at a terminal or intermediate stage of their life, is often seen principally as a matter of the collection of student test results and their statistical analysis, interpretation and comparison. The demands of accountability and value for money have led in some cases to the narrow use of tests as measures of the performance levels of students exiting a programme or project, and on the basis of these data alone, for evaluating the worth of what has been achieved. Test data are often used to enable authorities to assess the 'cost of input' against the 'value of output'.

Initiators of outsider evaluation for contractual accountability tend to favour the use of test data because they are hard data; measurable with the veneer of quantifiable objectivity. For example, the baseline evaluation of the effectiveness of the secondary language teacher training project in Nepal (see Weir and Roberts 1994) started from the premise that, with a control group of comparable classes taught by teachers who had not received training and an experimental group of the classes of trained teachers, it should be possible to administer and readminister relevant tests to these two groups of students over a period of time and examine whether significant differences emerged. In designs of this type, if greater improvements in the scores of the students taught by trained teachers are recorded, then it might be inferred that it was worth continuing the training of teachers. More crucially, if no differences were observed between the test scores of the two groups then one might want to review the continuation of the funding.

Though such a quantifiable approach might appeal through its simple elegance and its reliance on 'hard' data, it would not necessarily give us a valid picture of the impact of teacher training in a project or the quality of teaching in a particular programme. If no differences emerged in the summative gains in test scores between students in control and experimental groups, this approach does not tell us why it is the case. We would, for example, need to monitor the classroom practice of both trained and untrained groups of teachers in order to interpret the test data. One needs a comprehensive picture of what has happened in a project before one can offer possible explanations.

In the past project evaluation has tended to favour quantifiable information rather than qualitative judgement. This is largely due to the desire of funding agencies for hard data so that 'single truths' may be identified as a basis for decision making. For contractual accountability purposes, using test data is an attractive proposition. Unfortunately, using test data is not as simple, clean or conclusive as its advocates might wish to believe. There are a number of key issues that must be addressed by those wishing to use test data to make summative judgements on language programmes and projects and it is to these issues we now turn. They are not sufficient reason to abandon testing (especially, given the lack of any better alternative tool), but they serve as a caution against an unquestioning acceptance of the absolute value of using this methodological procedure for summative purposes.

Parallel tests

Funding agencies and recipients might reasonably ask for test data to be elicited at the beginning and end of a project or programme to show the extent of language improvement, as a first step in calculating 'value added'. Without constructing parallel (equivalent) tests, however, making definite statements as to how much students have improved as a result of following a course of language instruction is difficult.

To establish test equivalence is a time-consuming and expensive process as is evidenced by the fact that few examination Boards in Britain or abroad (TOEFL and the College English Test in China are notable exceptions) have ever taken this on board. In the absence of complex IRT equating, it is necessary to trial both versions of the test on a representative sample of the target population. The tests then need to be balanced so that one can confidently administer either test at the beginning or end of treatment and measure improvement in performance as the difference between the performances on the two parallel forms. Unfortunately, the construction of parallel tests is out of the question for most language projects because of the time and resources required to do it effectively. Statistical equating is not problem free either, and considerable effort is still required to develop sound anchor items.

The alternative of administering the same test at the beginning and end of the study raises the objection that improvement may be in part due to practice effect. In single group studies the use of the same test at the beginning and end of a language programme may not satisfy funding agents. However, given that the purpose in an experimental design is to compare the performance of two groups, we might reasonably assume that the practice effect benefits both groups equally, especially if there is a sufficient gap between the two administrations and students do not know they will be taking the same test again. If we take scores on the first test into account in the analysis of the second administration this enables us to contrast gains made by the two groups. If there is a difference between the two groups in performance on the second test administration, it can be reasonably inferred that the training has had some effect.

What is a meaningful difference?

Statistically significant differences are on occasion mistakenly seen as constituting evidence of the success of a programme or project. There is, of course, an important distinction to be made between statistically significant difference and meaningful difference. We have the schema for the former but not the latter.

Questions relating to the magnitude of any differences that might emerge are problematic, in particular the contentious issue of whether what has been achieved is in fact worthwhile. In the first instance one has to say what any improvement represents. This may not be too difficult in the cases of direct 'real life' tests of speaking or writing, because one has a product to make qualitative judgements about. However, the interpretation of gain does seem to be problematic in tests of general proficiency (such as tests of lexical or grammatical knowledge) or less direct tests of listening and reading where one has to move from a quantitative score on the test to a qualitative description of performance, for example, in tests involving dictation, response elicitation or listening recall, selective deletion gap filling or cloze.

Even the judgement to be made on size of gain is problematic when dealing with quantitative scores. If the gain is large the interpretation is better grounded, but what does a ten-point difference on a thirty-item dictation test really tell us beyond that there was a ten-point difference? The case for direct tests and criterion referencing in summative evaluation studies is strong (Brindley 1989).

Tests and acquisition

It may well be that tests such as gap filling and dictation, because they focus on specific linguistic items, may be testing constructs which take a long time to develop in learners. There is a possibility that gains in linguistic competence may take a longer time to appear in comparison with skills/strategies development and performance. It may be that in those cases where it is feasible to use tests of spoken language ability, gains in proficiency might be more evident over a shorter period of time. This is an area which is in urgent need of research. The practicality and reliability problems in testing skills such as spoken interaction cannot be ignored, however, and the limitations this imposes on evaluation studies are evident.

Value of tests in summative evaluation studies

Despite these problems, using language test data to monitor gain in student language achievement is likely to be more reliable and valid than any other methodological procedure. The spin-offs are important too. The design process underlying the construction of valid, reliable and practical tests requires project staff to be very clear about what it is that the project should achieve. Language tests have to be developed with great attention to their appropriacy and relevance to the objectives of a programme. The washback from this often promotes much needed rigour in course design and delivery.

So far we have looked at testing largely in connection with summative evaluation for accountability purposes. We now consider how it is perceived in relation to developmental evaluation in the classroom. We will argue that testing does not seem to have much formative effect on what happens in the classroom and suggest that this is a cause for concern.

The formative value of testing: The swing to accountability

In recent years there has been a tendency to link language testing to summative evaluation and, as a result, the important formative capacity of testing in the classroom has often been overshadowed. The increased expectation that providers of educational services should be made accountable to external bodies for the impact of their work has been a powerful driving force behind this. It has encouraged a swing from viewing tests as instruments for assisting in the development and improvement of student language ability to treating them as indicators of performance for outside agencies.

In evaluating student progress, achievement of objectives, curriculum success or school performance, the focus now appears to be summative, on the product(s), rather than formative, on the process(es) of educational interventions; the league tables of summative school examination results in the UK are a case in point. In more enlightened circumstances evaluators may take account of what the situation was like at the start of the process to allow meaningful comparisons to be made at the end, and a more accurate picture of 'value added' in terms of test gain scores may be available as a result. They may even have collected data on a range of variables which influence the dependent variable (the test scores), such as contextual features of the school environment, teacher language levels, and hours of tuition.

Irrespective of the soundness of such evaluation procedures, the focus is still on using tests to provide data on the extent to which the students have successfully mastered a language syllabus, whether this is expressed in terms of tasks, structures, lexis, functions or skills. It is essentially a product driven approach to testing and education. The central area of interest for funding agents and authorities often appears to be in the summative results and not the learning process or the learners *per se*.

A formative role for testing?

Teachers often have a different, more immediate agenda than accountability. They need information on student progress during the life of a course as well as summative assessments of ability at the end. Teachers need to evaluate formatively to make appropriate decisions concerning modifications to teaching procedures and learning activities and to steer their way through the syllabus in action, i.e. to shape and influence the process. Teachers need to decide when to move on in a unit or to the next unit. If the next units are dependent on what has gone before, then the teacher needs to be sure the students have mastered the objectives of a particular unit before proceeding. They need to know whether new material is being introduced too quickly or too slowly. If it is, the effectiveness of learning may well be diminished.

There is a need to monitor the developing performance ability of students, a need to establish as clearly as possible what it is they can do. This can lead to a descriptive profile of a learner's communicative performance or a record of achievement. Formal tests devised for monitoring achievement can be extremely helpful to individual students, can help identify areas of strength or weakness and provide a focus for future learning objectives. In addition, if learner autonomy is to be pursued, then there is a need to provide students with more effective self-assessment techniques to monitor their own progress and facilitate decisions on how best to improve. Tests can be motivational by providing students with a sense of progress.

Formative testing: The freedom to choose

Where tests are used for reasons of summative accountability, there is often no choice of what instruments are to be employed, let alone the option to participate or not. Such decisions are normally taken by stakeholders who are higher up the authority ladder than teachers and sometimes far removed from the classroom. In contrast, teachers potentially have the freedom to choose in their classrooms whether to use tests for formative purposes or not. The focus of the investigations reported in this section is therefore on the formative rather than the summative use of testing.

Our interest is whether, in those situations where teachers have the opportunity to use tests for formative purposes, they exercise that option. There is a strong theoretical case for using tests for formative purposes in the classroom, but the issue is whether this actually takes place.

Activities such as administering tests for formative purposes in the classroom are mediated through the personal constructs of those involved. The data reported below represent an initial attempt to establish some of the parameters of the constructs associated with testing for developmental purposes in the classroom. The data reported below are derived from both secondary and primary sources. They are an attempt to summarise the opinions provided by those involved in the teaching and learning process.

Testing for formative purposes has accepted value. But does it happen?

The profession was first alerted to the possibility that all was not well with testing in the classroom by the work of Geoff Brindley in Australia. Brindley (1989), in a study of 131 teachers in the Australian Adult Migrant Education Programme, found a tendency to rely very much on informal methods of ongoing assessment, such as observation followed by recycling of work, and verbal feedback in informal discussions with learners about their progress. Brindley found that:

> *this does not seem to be sufficiently explicit to meet the expectations and requirements of either administrators or learners for more formal information on learners' achievement of the objectives of a course or a unit ... The informal methods of ongoing assessment favoured by teachers do not provide the kind of explicit information on achievement required by learners and administrators.*
>
> (Brindley 1989: 43)

Many of the teachers Brindley surveyed regarded formal assessment as someone else's job and as a potentially threatening process. He found that teachers preferred informal feedback rather than formal use of tests within the classroom.

Our own surveys in Malaysia, Turkey and the UK of stakeholder perspectives on language testing have also cast some doubt on the degree to which formal testing is universally perceived as having formative value in the classroom. A number of stakeholders in the language learning field (heads, teachers and students) were asked their views on the value of language testing in the classroom. Our data sources were group reports by 106 Principals/School Heads attending a series of workshops conducted in Malaysia on testing and evaluation by the author and Mary Gill of the Centre for British Teachers (CfBT) and group reports by MATEFL students at the CALS University of Reading. Reference is also made to a questionnaire survey of attitudes to testing carried out by the Testing and Evaluation Unit, Bilkent University School of English Language (BUSEL), Ankara, Turkey with 80 teachers/300 students/16 administrators replying.

The statements on student perceptions below reflect self-reported views, actual statements of teachers, as well as the students themselves. The comments listed under teacher perceptions were taken from the poster presentations at the staff seminars and from the returns to the BUSEL staff questionnaires. The comments have been selected subjectively simply to illustrate the range of views we encountered in the staff seminars and in the written returns to the BUSEL staff and student questionnaires. No claims are made for the representativeness of our sampling, and we make no attempt to generalise beyond our limited opportunistic sample. We merely use some comments from these self-reports to raise awareness of the possibility that all is not well with testing in the classroom.

The data suggest lack of a 'feelgood' factor concerning testing in a number of the responses to the question: What is the value of language testing in the classroom for students and teachers? The picture is not all negative however and it is clear from the data that testing is already for some stakeholders fulfilling a valuable formative role. We therefore list both positive and negative responses in our selection from the data in Figure 13.1.

Figure 13.1

Some typical views on the value of testing

Perceived value for students

Positive:
- can lead to praise, self confidence, builds self esteem
- can motivate (good) students; leads to better grades; helps pass exams
- helps in self assessment, in learner independence, measures progress; encourages revision, shows skill(s) have to work on

Negative:
- tests are difficult; boring; a burden; a punishment; have no purpose
- for slow learners can cause fear of comparison and ridicule
- takes time away from teaching; does not contribute to learning
- students interested in the mark, not in learning from their mistakes

Perceived value for teachers

Positive:
- measures achievement of course objectives
- assesses students' strengths and weaknesses; helps plan remedial/follow up lessons
- useful for streaming and grouping, motivates teachers
- plays an important role in moving up levels

Negative:
- something which is imposed from above
- BUSEL study indicated that ideally 91% of the teachers thought testing could in theory be valuable but in practice only 65% thought it actually did have any value
- burden of marking/preparation/analysis; wastes teaching time
- students not interested in going back over something they have done already
- students not aware of value of assessment
- BUSEL survey 51% said ideally test results should motivate students but only 16% of teachers thought they did
- stressful
- can cause fear of exposing failures in one's own teaching; fear of comparison with other teachers
- insufficient testing skills to do it properly; problems in diagnosing student weaknesses through tests and in how to provide feedback

---

Clearly the formative value of testing is recognised by many stakeholders but this view is far from universal. Furthermore, there appears to be a strong suggestion that formative testing is all very well in an ideal world, but in practice it is different.

Conclusion

There is a pressing need for more work on formative as against summative testing given the scant attention paid to it in many language classrooms. The emphasis needs to be on how we can make such tests more useful and useable in the provision of feedback for developmental purposes. Without testing there are only limited, impoverished data to feed into the process of learning and to enable learners and teachers to modify their behaviour. Without testing there is a danger of 'going through the motions' of learning. There is a need to focus on the development of progress-sensitive performance tests for use during courses. Testing must be related to the developmental stages in language learning.

As regards summative evaluation, testing also has a vital role to play in providing high quality information on impact. But perhaps in the summative dimension, the product has again overshadowed the process. To understand fully the outcomes of language programmes and projects we need data on what has actually taken place, a wider sociolinguistic frame of reference. Testing alone is insufficient.

So in the 1990s we somehow seem to have got our testing wires crossed. The potential formative value of testing as a tool for giving us true estimates of our students' abilities seems to have become chimerical for many classroom teachers. In contrast, summative evaluation testing has been elevated to a position whereby it is seen as the arbitrator of success or failure in many language programmes and projects. In summative evaluation too much is expected of testing, in formative evaluation too little. In the next millennium the focus needs to switch from the arrival to the journey as far as language testing is concerned.

Acknowledgements

I am grateful to Shigeko Amano, Mary Gill, Rita Green, Don Porter and Eddie Williams, for comments on an earlier version of this paper, and in particular to Jon Roberts, who co-authored *Evaluation in ELT* (Weir and Roberts 1994) on which the first part of the paper draws.

References

Brindley, G. 1989. *Assessing Achievement in the Learner Centred Curriculum.* Sydney: National Centre for English Language Teaching and Research, Macquarie University.

Weir, C. J. and J. Roberts. 1994. *Evaluation in ELT.* Oxford: Blackwell.

14 Language assessment and professional development

Geoff Brindley
National Centre for English Language Teaching and Research, Macquarie University, Australia

Introduction

In recent years, testing and assessment issues have begun to figure with increasing prominence on the agenda of educational authorities around the world. In the wake of greater demands for public accountability, an increasing concern with standards and the imposition of more stringent reporting requirements, educational institutions have introduced a variety of testing and assessment procedures in order to make decisions on selection, certification and achievement. These range from standardised proficiency tests to outcomes-based systems which require teachers to report learners' progress and achievement against predetermined attainment targets (Brindley 1998).

One consequence of these developments is a growing need for language teachers to be familiar with the principles and practice of testing and assessment in order to conduct their own assessments and to participate in debates about external tests and examinations. However, although there has been a considerable amount of research in general education into teachers' assessment practices, levels of training and professional development needs (see, for example, Brookhart 1994; Cizek *et al.* 1995; Harlen and James 1997), there have been relatively few investigations of these questions in the context of language teaching programmes.

The aim of this chapter is therefore to identify some of the issues and problems involved in developing professional development programmes in assessment aimed at practising language teachers. Although the examples and observations offered here are largely based on my own experience in conducting courses for teachers of adult immigrants and secondary school foreign language learners in Australia, the findings and general conclusions will hopefully be transferable to other populations and contexts.

In order to examine the relationship between assessment and professional development, I will focus on four central themes. These are 1) teachers' assessment practices; 2) teachers' knowledge and skills in assessment; 3) teachers' professional development needs; 4) the content of professional development programmes on assessment.

Language teachers' assessment practices

Evidence from studies conducted in a range of educational contexts suggests that teachers prefer to use informal and flexible methods of assessment such as observation, *ad hoc* tests, oral corrective feedback and recycling of work, rather than formal tests (Brindley 1989; Mavrommatis 1997; Stiggins and Conklin 1992). Usage patterns, however, appear to vary according, *inter alia*, to teachers' experience, their views of the role of assessment in the curriculum, collegial expectations and external reporting demands (McCallum *et al.* 1995; Breen *et al.* 1997). Notwithstanding these individual differences, one common theme which emerges from studies of assessment practices is that teachers see assessment as an activity which is integrated into the curriculum with the aim of improving learning, rather than as a 'one-off' summative event. This seems to be the case even when they are working in contexts which prescribe summative testing (Cizek *et al.* 1995).

What do language teachers know about assessment?

According to Stevenson (1985: 112), 'we are still far distant from our ideal of the classroom language teacher with a firm knowledge of at least the fundamental principles of language testing and assessment'.

One possible reason for this state of affairs may be the relative lack of emphasis which is given to assessment issues in teacher education courses in general (Cizek *et al.* 1995). Another is the inaccessibility of much of the language testing literature and its perceived irrelevance to the daily assessment practices of teachers. Professional books and journal articles, by and large, have tended to concentrate heavily on theoretical and statistical aspects of test validity and reliability and are most often written by academics or educational measurement specialists who are primarily concerned with large-scale test construction and validation. This can only serve to create a situation where testing is considered by many teachers as the somewhat arcane province of 'experts' and of marginal relevance to everyday classroom concerns.

It would be wrong, however, to see teachers as ignorant of assessment issues merely because they lack familiarity with measurement techniques used for test analysis. They are usually familiar with the tests that are used within their institution, and are in a good position to evaluate their predictive validity and/or reliability since they have to use the results (e.g. placement tests). In addition, as the studies cited previously demonstrate, they assess constantly through such means as observation, recycling of work, diagnostic testing, learner self-assessment, various forms of corrective feedback and *ad hoc* tests. With experience, many teachers become skilled judges and observers capable of evaluating the quality of language performances and making fine-grained diagnoses of learners' difficulties. (In this regard, it is significant that experienced teacher judgement is still used as the benchmark in many studies of criterion-related validity. It is also worth noting that many examination boards and testing authorities employ teachers to write items for high profile language proficiency tests.)

These observations have clear consequences for professional development. Since teachers are very experienced in evaluating language performances, professional developers can capitalise on this fact by using teachers' experience as a starting point from which to extrapolate general principles of assessment.

What should teachers know about assessment?

The American Federation of Teachers, National Council on Measurement in Education and the National Education Association (1990) propose the following set of standards for teacher competence in educational assessment of students:

- Teachers should be skilled in choosing assessment methods appropriate for instructional decisions.
- Teachers should be skilled in developing assessment methods appropriate for instructional decisions.
- Teachers should be skilled in administering, scoring and interpreting the results of both externally-produced and teacher-produced assessment methods.
- Teachers should be skilled in using assessment results when making decisions about individual students, planning teaching, developing curriculum and institutional improvement.
- Teachers should be skilled in developing, using and evaluating valid student grading procedures which use student assessments.
- Teachers should be skilled in communicating assessment results to students, educational decision makers and other concerned stakeholders.
- Teachers should be skilled in recognising unethical, illegal, and otherwise inappropriate assessment methods and uses of assessment information.

These standards constitute a comprehensive and ambitious agenda for teacher professional development in assessment. However, it should also be recognised that different individuals will require different levels of knowledge according to the nature and extent of their involvement in assessment issues. For example, whereas some teachers in an educational organisation might need to know in detail how to develop and analyse formal tests, others may be concerned only with knowing how to construct their own informal instruments for classroom use. It is therefore important that professional development programmes are flexible enough to allow teachers to acquire familiarity with those aspects of assessment that are most relevant to their needs.

Developing professional development programmes in assessment

Given what is known about teachers' assessment practices and levels of knowledge, then, it would seem that any programme aimed at practitioners should 1) begin with a focus on curriculum-related assessment; 2) capitalise on teachers' existing knowledge; and 3) be adaptable to meet a wide variety of needs.

The essential components of what such a programme might look like are outlined briefly below. The programme could be delivered in a modular fashion, in the form of a short course, series of seminars/workshops or individual seminars/workshops, depending on the needs of the participants and the resources available.

i) The social context of assessment (core unit)

This unit deals with the social, educational, and political aspects of assessment in the wider community, including questions of accountability, standards, ethics and the role in society of standardised competitive examinations and tests. Activities include an examinination of the role and purpose of assessment in the participants' own teaching situation.

ii) Defining and describing proficiency (core unit)

This unit aims to address the crucial question of 'what it means to know how to use a language' (Spolsky 1985). It involves a consideration of the ways in which judgements of human performance are made, followed by a range of activities which require participants to examine the theoretical basis of language tests and assessment procedures. In this way, the concepts of validity and reliability can be introduced in an accessible way, thus providing teachers with a basis both for the construction of assessment instruments and the critical evaluation of tests. This unit also provides an opportunity for discussion and critical evaluation of theoretical models of language ability such as those proposed by Canale and Swain (1980) and Bachman and Palmer (1996).

iii) Constructing and evaluating language tests

This unit aims to provide participants with skills in test development and analysis. For those who need to be able to construct their own tests and analyse the results, an introduction to classical item analysis and item response theory is included, using actual examples of test analysis. Although some testers have expressed concern about the accessibility of statistical concepts to language teachers (Stevenson 1985), a range of materials is now available which contains user-friendly descriptions of the use of statistical procedures in test construction and validation. These make the task of presenting techniques for test analysis considerably easier than it would have been a decade ago (see, for example, Alderson *et al.* 1995; Brown 1996; McNamara 1996).

iv) Assessment in the language curriculum

This component explores the notion of criterion-referencing in language learning programmes and looks at a range of methods for constructing criterion-referenced procedures for assessing progress and achievement. Participants begin by considering various ways in which objectives and outcomes can be stated, thus emphasising the close link between objectives and assessment. They are then given the opportunity to examine and evaluate a range of methods for monitoring and assessing progress and achievement, and to construct examples appropriate to their own circumstances. The different methods examined include observation schedules, portfolios, conferences, project work, journals, self-assessment techniques, and progress and achievement profiles. Samples of student performance are examined and ways of monitoring the quality of assessments are discussed.

v) Putting assessment into practice

This component requires teachers to map out a follow-up strategy to the workshop by specifying an action plan through which the issues raised in the course or workshop can be further explored and documented. These plans might include proposals for test construction projects, assessment-related classroom research or recommendations for policy development.

Professional development on assessment: Some guiding principles

On the basis of conducting courses and workshops along the lines outlined above over a number of years, I have found that a number of principles can usefully inform professional development on assessment, particularly in institutional contexts. These are as follows:

Involve the whole system

Professional development which takes place in institutional contexts should recognise the fact that assessment is a shared responsibility. For this reason, I have found it useful to involve decision makers from the beginning in whatever form of professional development that takes place. Although this is often difficult for logistical reasons, it is particularly important to have decision makers present if a change in the assessment system is imminent. If they are asked to make a statement concerning the role of assessment within the organisation, they can then deal with any concerns on the part of teachers – it is not the job of the professional developer or visiting 'expert' to explain the role of assessment and accountability in the system or to allay teachers' fears about the potential adverse consequences of assessment reform.

Related to these system concerns, as I have indicated already, it is important to include a component in which assessment is dealt with in its broader social context. Assessment does not happen within a vacuum. It is driven by a range of economic, social and political considerations which are now beginning to receive a good deal more prominence in the literature (see McNamara 1998 for a review). For this reason, professional development in assessment is not a question merely of demonstrating the technical 'tricks of the trade'. Teachers also need the opportunity to see how assessment within their own organisation fits into the broader social context. This will usually involve a consideration of different perspectives on accountability, which, in turn, may engender political and philosophical debate. These issues cannot be avoided, however unpalatable they may be to some administrators or funding bodies. In fact, they have to be confronted if teachers are to come to grips with the key question of the purpose of assessment.

Capitalise on existing practices

Since most teachers are not engaged in the construction of formal tests, there are strong arguments for placing the emphasis in professional development programmes – at least initially – on the role of assessment in the learning process rather than on theoretical and statistical issues in testing. With the move towards task-based syllabus design which has taken place in language teaching assessment, it is relatively easy to make the connection between teaching tasks and assessment tasks. Forms of assessment and monitoring such as observation, learner self-assessment, profiling and portfolios which directly reflect learning are therefore more likely to be of interest and relevance to teachers than 'curriculum-free' proficiency tests. However, it is important to note that teachers need to be aware that their assessment procedures still need to possess basic measurement properties if they are to be used as 'can-do' statements of people's ability which are communicated to an outside audience. As Carroll (1991: 25) points out, it is not sufficient for test constructors to say that assessment has a beneficial effect on teaching. Authentic-looking assessment tasks which reflect what has been taught still need to have their validity and reliability established through the accepted empirical procedures. Issues such as the relationship between authenticity and validity and the consistency of subjective judgements are therefore topics which merit thorough coverage, even in contexts not involving formal tests.

Recognise and deal with the reality and constraints influencing teachers' assessment practices

Teachers' assessment practices are heavily influenced by a range of practical constraints, including time, funding, expertise and demands for external accountability (Black and Broadfoot 1982: 15). Where curriculum-related assessment is concerned, the time factor assumes particular importance. Here, it has frequently been pointed out that continuous assessment erodes teaching time, since it can be extremely time-consuming to construct appropriate instruments, devise marking and grading systems, administer them and give students feedback on the results (Barrs 1992; Breen *et al.* 1997; Cumming 1997).

If teachers are to assume greater responsibility for assessment, then, they require sufficient time and resources to do the job properly. Unfortunately, policy makers and programme administrators may not be aware of how time-consuming assessment can be, particularly when it involves the construction of formal tests. This constitutes another reason for involving them in professional development activities where they can see the amount of time, expertise and effort required to develop high quality tests and assessment tasks. Another way to demonstrate the impact of increased assessment duties on teachers' day-to-day work is to encourage teachers to pilot the new tests or assessments over a reasonable length of time, documenting the kinds of assessment-related tasks performed by teachers and how long they take (Gunn 1995; Barrs 1992). Once it becomes clear what demands a new form of assessment makes on teachers' time, an argument can then be made if necessary for a corresponding reduction in teaching loads or the injection of extra resources.

Encourage a research orientation to professional development

One way of ensuring the skills and knowledge acquired through attending professional development activities is to encourage teachers to map out a follow-up project which involves collecting data and systematically monitoring and/or changing their assessment practices in their own workplace. If possible, others in their own institution should also be involved and support provided (time for discussion with peers, reflection on practice and consultation with external advisers).

Professional development workshops and courses can lead to the formation of teacher support networks through which the skills and knowledge gained from the workshops can be pursued collectively. For example, through some of the professional development workshops described above, groups of teachers were formed to undertake small-scale research projects into assessment issues in their own workplaces. The sorts of issues teachers nominated for investigation included the use of self-assessment in job-seeking skills programmes; ways of demonstrating gains over a short course of instruction; reasons for misplacement of learners; and introducing criterion-referenced assessment into beginner ESL classrooms. The outcomes of some of these projects were reported to peers in local staff development sessions, while others were documented and published in professional journals or books (see, for example, Lewis 1990; Gunn 1995). This process of networking and support thus led to the wider involvement of colleagues and generated an interest in assessment which would probably not have come about had the issues been dictated by system needs alone.

Plan for change

One of the aims of most professional development workshops (although not always explicitly stated) is to encourage teachers to change some aspect of their classroom practice. In this respect, changing assessment practices or adopting new tools is no different from introducing a new curriculum or a new textbook. It is an exercise in change management which by definition means trying to plan for the implementation of whatever change is proposed as a result of the professional development experience. If professional developers are concerned with the long-term effects of what they do, then they need to be aware of this. This is not to suggest that they should be personally responsible for following through the implementation of the ideas they sow. However, workshops which have as a projected outcome some kind of change in individual or institutional practices (for example, the introduction of a new type of assessment procedure) should at the very least try to build in a component which allows participants the opportunity to consider the practical implications of the change. These include institutional factors which will affect the extent to which the planned change can occur and the type and amount of support they will need. Even if the professional developer cannot provide this support, he or she might be able to make suggestions as to where it might be obtained.

Conclusion

In this chapter, I have examined some of the issues involved in designing and conducting professional development activities on second language assessment for language teachers. Based on available information on teachers' assessment practices and professional development needs, I have sketched out the structure of a programme which would be flexible enough to meet a variety of different needs.

I have also suggested that in planning professional development on assessment, it is important to be aware that learning how to construct tests and assessment tasks is only part of the picture – assessment also has a wider social, political and institutional dimension which also needs to be built into the programme by involving decision makers and by carefully considering the resources needed to implement new assessment practices. Proceeding in this way can significantly increase the long-term benefits of professional development in assessment for both teachers and the educational institutions in which they work.

References

Alderson, J. C., C. Clapham and D. Wall. 1995. *Language Test Construction and Evaluation.* Cambridge: Cambridge University Press.

American Federation of Teachers. 1990. *Standards for Teacher Competence in Educational Assessment of Students.* Washington: American Federation of Teachers.

Bachman, L. F. and A. S. Palmer. 1996. *Language Testing in Practice.* Oxford: Oxford University Press.

Barrs, M. 1992. The Primary Language Record: what we are learning in the U.K. In C. Bouffler (ed.), *Literacy Evaluation: Issues and Practicalities.* Sydney: Primary English Teaching Association.

Black, H. and P. Broadfoot. 1982. *Keeping Track of Teaching.* London: Routledge and Kegan Paul.

Bouffler, C. (ed.) 1992. *Literacy Evaluation: Issues and Practicalities.* Sydney: Primary English Teaching Association.

Breen, M., C. Barratt-Pugh, B. Derewianka, H. House, C. Hudson, T. Lumley and M. Rohl. 1997. *Profiling ESL Children. Volume 1: Key Issues and Findings.* Canberra: Department of Employment, Education, Training and Youth Affairs.

Brindley, G. 1989. *Assessing Achievement in the Learner-Centred Curriculum.* Sydney: National Centre for English Language Teaching and Research.

Brindley, G. 1998. Outcomes-based assessment and reporting in language programmes: a review of the issues. *Language Testing* 15 (1): 45–85.

Brookhart, S. 1994. Teachers' grading: practice and theory. *Applied Measurement in Education* 7 (4): 279–301.

Brown, J. D. 1996. *Testing in language programs.* Upper Saddle River: Prentice Hall Regents.

Canale, M. and M. Swain. 1980. Theoretical bases of communicative approaches to second language teaching and testing. *Applied Linguistics* 1 (1): 1–47.

Carroll, J. B. 1991. Resistance to change. In J. C. Alderson and B. North (eds.), *Language Testing in the 1990s*. London: Macmillan.

Cizek, G., S. Fitzgerald and R. Rachor. 1995. Teachers' assessment practices: preparation, isolation and the kitchen sink. *Educational Assessment* 3 (2): 159–179.

Cumming, A. 1997. *Grade 9 teachers' uses of language standards.* Paper presented at AAAL, Orlando, Florida: March.

Gunn, M. 1995. Criterion-based assessment: a classroom teacher's perspective. In G. Brindley (ed.), *Language Assessment in Action.* Sydney: National Centre for English Language Teaching and Research, Macquarie University.

Harlen, W. and M. James. 1997. Assessment and learning: differences and relationships between formative and summative assessment. *Assessment in Education* 4 (3): 365–79.

Lewis, J. 1990. Self-assessment in the classroom: a case study. In G. Brindley (ed.), *The Second Language Curriculum in Action.* Sydney: National Centre for English Language Teaching and Research, Macquarie University.

McCallum, B., C. Gipps, S. McAlister and M. Brown. 1995. National Curriculum assessment: emerging models of teacher assessment in the classroom. In H. Torrance (ed.), *Evaluating Authentic Assessment.* Buckingham: Open University Press.

McNamara, T. F. 1996. *Measuring Second Language Performance*. London: Longman.

McNamara, T. F. 1998. Policy and social considerations in language assessment. In W. Grabe (ed.), *Annual Review of Applied Linguistics*, 18. New York: Cambridge University Press.

Mavrommatis, Y. 1997. Understanding assessment in the classroom: phases of the assessment process – the assessment episode. *Assessment in Education* 4 (3): 381–399.

Spolsky, B. 1985. What does it mean to know how to use a language: an essay on the theoretical basis of language testing. *Language Testing* 2 (2): 180–191.

Stevenson, D. 1985. Pop validity and performance testing. In Y. P. Lee, C. Y. Y. Fok, R. Lord and G. Low (eds.), *New Directions in Language Testing*. Oxford: Pergamon.

Stiggins, R. and N. Conklin. 1992. *In Teachers' Hands: Investigating the Practices of Classroom Assessment.* Albany: State University of New York Press.

Section Six

Language test impact

15 The need for impact studies of L2 performance testing and rating: Identifying areas of potential consequences at all levels of the testing cycle

Carolyn E. Turner
McGill University

Introduction

In the last decade, there has been an increased awareness in the field of language testing concerning the impact of tests. This concept, often referred to as 'washback' in second language (L2) education, generally refers to the influence of a test or other evaluation procedures on teaching and learning. The effects can be positive or negative. In the literature, there is much discussion pertaining to definition, scope and nature of this concept, and not always with consensus. Recently, Hamp-Lyons (1997) has criticised the term 'washback' as being too narrow, and points out that general education and educational measurement employ the broader term of 'impact', which includes effects beyond the classroom as well, such as effects on the educational system and society as a whole. Within the scope of this paper, the term 'washback' will be used in a general sense to represent the effects of tests and will be used interchangeably with the term 'impact'.

Even though there is much discussion in the literature, empirical evidence as to the nature of washback remains scant. It is true that an increasing number of studies are being carried out, but there remains a void particularly pertaining to studies using qualitative inquiry with the intent of investigating participants within a certain classroom community, educational system and social structure (Wall and Alderson 1996). Due to the culturally situated phenomenon of washback (e.g. Watson-Gegeo 1988; Watanabe 1996), it would appear that the triangulation of quantitative and qualitative methods could be relevant and insightful (e.g. Alderson and Banerjee 1996). Until such voids are filled, it is difficult to address the increasing discussion and ongoing debate in the language testing literature on test consequences. Hamp-Lyons

(1997: 302) states that 'the responsibility of language testers is clear: we must accept responsibility for all those consequences which we are aware of'. Davies (1997b: 335–36) discusses limiting the ethical demands on language testing. He provides the following view:

> *... the apparent open-ended offer of consequential validity goes too far. I maintain that it is not possible for a tester as a member of a profession to take account of all possible social consequences ... In other words, limited and predictable social consequences we can take account of and regard ourselves as responsible for.*

Such dialogue hopefully generates awareness and/or at least consideration of the consequences of our actions as language testing participants. Until enough evidence is forthcoming, however, to support and help define the assumed impact of tests, it is difficult to address these issues directly.

Within the context of second language testing, we are finding that the concept of washback cannot be articulated in a simple theory. The studies available are beginning to demonstrate the many areas in which washback may occur, resulting in an evolving definition of a multifaceted concept (e.g. Alderson and Hamp-Lyons 1996; Cheng 1997; Shohamy *et al.* 1996). Turner (1998), Turner and Upshur (1996a, b) and Upshur and Turner (1999), in their work with empirically derived rating scales, have observed that in performance testing, washback effects on certain participants appear to take place not only as a result of the final test product, but during the test development stages as well. This has not been documented systematically, only observed as a by-product of other studies. Such a study is presently being initiated and the rationale and context are described as part of this paper. If such evidence is borne out, we may need to consider the potential of washback effects at different times throughout the testing cycle (i.e. anywhere decisions need to be made concerning evaluation – needs analysis, purpose of test, objectives of instruction, item/task writing, developing scale/evaluation criteria, teacher training, administration of test, interpretation of scores, use of scores, etc.).

This paper will focus on the concept of washback in L2 performance testing and evaluation in educational settings. It will: 1) review pertinent literature on test impact and awareness/responsibility of test consequences, and call for a research agenda that includes potential consequences at any point throughout the testing cycle; 2) discuss observations within the context of other studies which led to a research proposal on washback; and 3) briefly mention a proposed study whose purpose is to identify potential areas of impact on participants during the construction, validation, standard setting and implementation of empirically derived rating scales.

Background

Discussion on the concept of washback can be found in the literature in both general education and second language education. It refers to the role that external tests play (i.e. tests external to the classroom such as provincial exams or standardised tests) in influencing classroom activity. More recently, there has been a call to include alternative assessment procedures in this definition as well (Hamp-Lyons 1997). It is to be noted that other terms besides 'washback' are employed when referring to the relationship between testing, teaching and learning. Shohamy (1993) summarises them as: 'measurement-driven instruction', the notion that tests should drive learning; 'curriculum alignment', the connection between testing and the teaching syllabus; and 'systemic validity' (Frederiksen and Collins 1989), the integration of tests into the educational system to improve learning. The notion of washback also overlaps with test validation. Currently, validity is viewed as a unitary concept (Messick 1989; Bachman 1990) with test validation seen as an ongoing process involving the accumulation of various types of validity evidence. Messick (1989) examines the concept of washback as an instance of the consequential aspect of construct validity (i.e. consequential validity).

It is interesting to note how the reporting on test impact has evolved. It has expanded from just reporting on perceived classroom activity, outcomes and teacher reactions to external tests, to include a raised consciousness of language testers/researchers and other participants/stakeholders in a testing effort asking questions such as, 'Who is responsible for test consequences?' and 'How can beneficial/positive washback be promoted?' Several studies focus on the negative impact of tests, and call for a focus to work towards positive washback. An expansion in research methodology to include more qualitative and ethnographic-type approaches than had been common is evident. As awareness is raised to potential washback effects, such approaches are employed to capture the social dynamics between tests and the participants. This evolving context can be demonstrated by tracing a few pertinent studies. (For an extensive overview of recent research on impact and washback in language testing, see Wall 1997.)

In general education, the most quoted study is entitled *The Effects of Standardized Testing* by Kellaghan, Madaus and Airasian (1982). This was a collaborative study between the USA and Ireland in which the impact of introducing standardised tests in Irish schools was investigated. Results demonstrate that the use of these tests was beneficial to the schools. Several criticisms were voiced but the main one concerned methodology and a lack of classroom observation.

Most other general education studies can be criticised for data collection methodology as well (e.g. Frederiksen 1984; Haladyna, Nolen and

Haas 1991; Paris *et al.* 1991). The main criticism is with the absence of classroom observation data. Claims made in such studies, however, are worth noting and mainly concern negative washback: for example, narrowing of the curriculum, lost instructional time, reduced emphasis on skills that require complex thinking or problem solving, and increases in test scores without a corresponding rise in the ability of the construct being tested (Alderson and Hamp-Lyons 1996: 281). Smith (1991), as an exception to other general education studies, did use classroom observation as well as interviews. She found that elementary teachers were concerned about test score accountability, and that data from classroom observations revealed that test programmes reduced instruction time, limited curriculum and modes of instructions, and reduced teacher ability to focus on content or methodology that is incompatible with the standardised test formats.

In second language education, empirical studies concerning washback are slowly increasing, but they are still scarce and even less prevalent than in general education. The most cited study is Alderson and Wall (1993), *Does washback exist?* It describes an empirical longitudinal investigation in Sri Lanka concerning the impact of a secondary-school English exam on classrooms, and explicitly breaks down the simplistic notion of a washback hypothesis into 15 possible hypotheses recognising its complexity. Alderson and Wall report that impact was demonstrated on the content of teaching, but no evidence was found for effects on how teachers taught. The inclusion of classroom observation as methodology was considered paramount to this study and to any study concerning influences of a test on classroom activity.

Studies which have followed are beginning to incorporate such research techniques. Using classroom observation and teacher/student interviews, Alderson and Hamp-Lyons (1996) studied washback in preparation courses for the English proficiency test TOEFL (Test of English as a Foreign Language). Their results showed that 'the TOEFL affects what and how teachers teach, but the effect is not the same in degree or in kind from teacher to teacher ...' (p. 295). Within the context of an ongoing washback study in Japanese English foreign language (EFL) classrooms, Watanabe (1996) argues 'that an approach informed by the principles of ethnographic research is an appropriate way to deepen our understanding of the nature of washback' (p. 233). He stresses a process that is systematic, detailed and rigorous. More recently, Cheng (1997, 1998) reported on the washback effect of public examination change on classroom teaching of English in Hong Kong secondary schools. Her research framework included a variety of participants (e.g. policy-makers, textbook publishers, teachers, students) and multiple data sources (e.g. questionnaires, interviews, classroom observation, student exam performance, textbook content). Analysis involved both qualitative and quantitative approaches. Superficial and conceptual changes in the participants and the process were identified, which brought to light the complexity of investigating any potential washback situation.

The above studies demonstrate that, in order to capture the complex nature of test consequences, there is a need for both qualitative and quantitative approaches to empirical studies. A concern about appropriate methodology is becoming more and more prevalent in the language testing community. An informative series of papers concerning methodological techniques can be found in the research design plans for an impact study of the EFL exams provided by the University of Cambridge Local Examinations Syndicate (UCLES) (Milanovic and Saville 1996). One of the papers focuses on instrument validation (Alderson and Banerjee 1996).

More attention has been paid to test impact since the arrival of the communicative era (performance-based tasks) and the expanded notion of validity which includes consequential validity. There is concern that the alleged negative washback of external-to-classroom tests (as discussed above) is also due to a mismatch between the instructional practice and the actual test. In other words, in some instances performance-based teaching is taking place, but traditional tests (e.g. multiple choice formats) are being used to assess those contexts.

As L2 performance testing is progressively being implemented, however, new features are introduced into an assessment situation such as: 1) raters (usually teachers in an educational context), and 2) a procedure which involves the development and use of a rating scale (i.e. scoring criteria). Within the context of consequential validity, these add new dimensions to the potential impact of tests (McNamara 1996).

Therefore, due to the influence of several factors, it appears that the consciousness of the language testing community has been raised concerning the potential consequences of tests. To summarise, the factors are:

1 the slow, but steady, increasing number of impact studies in general education and more specifically in L2 education;
2 the ongoing discussion of this assumed phenomenon;
3 the growing prevalence of performance testing; and
4 current views on an expanded definition of validity (which include consequential validity).

A demonstration of this concern is that the journal *Language Testing* devoted a complete special issue in 1996 to the notion of 'the washback effect'.

It appears that an extended research agenda is needed in order to help promote positive washback in L2 educational settings. Even though it has been stated that a 'vigorous research program is underway' to investigate washback assumptions (McNamara 1998: 308), a collaborated effort or consensus on direction is not yet evident in the literature. Possibly this is due to the increasing awareness of the complexity of the concept. We are still in the initial stages of identifying potential areas for washback. An example: as mentioned above, Turner and Upshur (1996a, b) have observed potential washback effects in yet another area of the testing cycle, that is, at the level of test development. Such effects have been on participant (i.e. teachers, educational administrators, government educational testing people) attitudes, perceptions and behaviour due to their involvement in empirical derivation of speaking and writing scales and the setting of standards for performance testing. Possibly in an attempt to bring language testers into focus on the complexity of washback assumptions, Hamp-Lyons (1997: 300–301) suggests starting with the development of 'a logical model for exploring the consequential validity of performance assessments', then using it to develop a framework of expected classroom behaviours, and finally investigating the existence of those behaviours. These examples help illustrate the readiness, timing and need to provide more empirical evidence concerning washback assumptions, their scope and complexity.

Observed washback effects at the level of test development

Elder and Wiggleworth (1996: 2) define the testing cycle as a series of stages, 'from the test's inception, when the need for the test is identified and its purpose is conceptualized, through to the final stage of the testing process: namely a test's washback effect (or presumed effect) on the teaching situation in classrooms which prepare students for the test'. I would alter this definition by stating that it seems washback effects can potentially occur, not only during the final stage, but during any stage depending on the nature of the particular context and participants.

During my involvement in procedures concerning empirically derived rating scales in high-stakes performance testing, I have observed participant comments and behaviour that I would categorise as consequences of the testing process. These observations have not been the focus of any study, but have been by-products. These recorded patterns have been frequent enough to lead to a research proposal to investigate the impact of second language performance testing and rating scale development on educational settings.

Project and research settings

In the province of Quebec, English as a second language (ESL) is a required subject beginning in Grade 4 in the French-speaking school system. The Ministry of Education (MEQ) requires that communicative skills are tested at various points in the ESL programme through the means of high-stakes exams. In recent years, university researchers have been asked to participate in the construction of empirically derived rating scales for these exams. It is during these scale-making procedures that apparent consequential effects were recorded.

The empirically derived scale procedures involve extensive preparation and planning and include staff from the MEQ, educational administrators, teachers and researchers. A representative data sample of student exam performances is first collected and organised. Teachers are selected for the scale-making procedure which initially lasts for two full days (a detailed account of this procedure can be found in Turner and Upshur 1996a). Scales are validated with other groups of teachers and then performance standards are set through an exercise which involves a large group of the provincial teachers. This whole process can be categorised as part of the test development stage, but it must be noted that it includes the end users, the teachers. It is within this process that apparent consequential effects from teacher feedback were observed and documented.

Example 1

Turner and Upshur (1996a) describe a project that involved developing two speaking tests which included performance tasks and empirically based rating scales. We worked with a group of elementary school English as a Second Language (ESL) teachers. The tests were to be used for high-stakes performance assessment at the end of the year within a provincial school board. We report that in follow-up sessions with the teachers, we learned that this experience had caused a positive washback effect on teaching methodology. The teachers began using more performance tasks, particularly ones which involved speaking into a tape recorder. The students enjoyed the independent speaking practice (which they had not had previously) and the teachers profited from having extended discourse samples of their students for formative evaluation purposes. This contributed to meeting the objectives of the programme and to preparing the students for the speaking exam. Teachers believed that the rating scale criteria they had developed as a team were important to instruction. They felt the scales incorporated requirements for scoring on the basis of what they valued and were able to recognise in their students' performances.

Example 2

Turner (1998) describes a project that included developing empirically based rating scales for the provincial ESL writing tasks in the secondary leaving exam. This project also involved standard setting and planning for teacher training concerning the new scale. I reported on the discourse of the teachers developing the scales as well as follow-up sessions with teachers and staff from the MEQ. This data revealed potential effects of washback on teacher perceptions concerning teaching and evaluation criteria. In addition, MEQ people voiced their changing views on exam tasks and instructions after working with the data (i.e. student writing performances) and observing the development of the rating scale.

To set the context for this example it is to be noted that much discussion is involved in the scale-making process because it includes working with actual student performances (writing samples in this case) and coming to a consensus within a team of developers as to ability levels and the salient characteristics that distinguish those levels (see Turner and Upshur 1996a). In other words teachers need to work out differences. The criteria for the rating scale emerge from the following considerations: the general abilities that are agreed upon to measure from the outset, the actual salient characteristics that are identified in the data, and the lengthy discussions that surround the procedure and coming to consensus.

As an example in this specific context, it soon became evident from the data and discussion that 1) student writing placed at the top of the scale was not necessarily perfectly accurate, but did need to be coherent and 2) writing off topic would not be tolerated. These characteristics were reflected in the scale. Teachers voiced how these would now be implemented into their teaching strategies so as to help students in learning and in preparation of any writing performance evaluation.

As the scale has been introduced to teachers across the province, written accounts by teachers concerning use have been invited. Feedback patterns reveal that 1) teachers share and use the scale directly with students to help them understand the nature of the evaluation criteria, 2) teachers discover that the criteria are pertinent to what they find in their student writing, and 3) teachers find that the criteria reflect the programme objectives and the curriculum they are working with.

In addition to the above, the MEQ staff involved in the scale-making process realised that certain problematic characteristics for evaluation that had been identified in the data patterns might be controlled better through more precise exam instructions. Such changes were implemented (e.g. overtly stating minimum requirements for length of a written text and the necessity to write on topic).

Such feedback led to the possible assumption that the testing cycle stage of developing empirically based rating scales could potentially have washback effects on both the instruction and the assessment procedures. These observations contribute to the potential complexity of the washback concept, but need to be investigated systematically, taking into account the current views on methodological approaches (e.g. to include classroom observation).

A proposed study

A further project with the MEQ involves the development of empirically based speaking scales for the ESL secondary leaving exams. This project provides a context conducive to research concerning the impact of performance testing and rating on L2 educational settings. A brief description follows.

The purpose of the study is to investigate and identify potential areas of impact on participants during the construction, validation and implementation of empirically derived rating scales for speaking. Does the fact that MEQ staff, teachers and even students are involved in various stages of the testing cycle make a difference in promoting beneficial washback in terms of teaching strategies/content, testing strategies/content, participant perceptions, and learning strategies and learning outcomes? More specific questions to be asked are: Is there an effect and what is the nature of the effect if:

1 ESL experts from the milieu (with knowledge of the L2 programme and objectives) are participants in scale-making or are not?
2 teachers are participants in standard setting or are not?
3 the rating scale and testing procedures are introduced to teachers early on in the process or are not?
4 teachers in turn share and work with this material with their students or do not?

Participants will include teachers, students and educational administrators from different regions of Quebec, as well as MEQ personnel and researchers. Data sources will include interviews, questionnaires, classroom observation, classroom materials and rating scale and exam analysis. Baseline data will be collected before the rating scale development process and before the new testing procedures are introduced. Further data will then be collected during and after these periods.

The above describes only a few brief points concerning a washback study proposal. The anticipated results can enhance our understanding of the concept of washback in performance testing and rating settings, and inform decisions as to how to promote the beneficial impact of tests in large educational systems.

Conclusion

The intent of this paper was to demonstrate how we need to learn much more about the impact of testing procedures on teaching and learning, and more globally on educational systems and society as a whole. Already in the literature there is a consensus that the widely-asserted phenomenon of washback is lacking empirical evidence. As we focus increasingly on performance testing, we must now also include the new variables that are introduced into testing procedures and become aware of the potential for consequences at different points in the testing cycle. For those of us who are committed to second language testing, there needs to be a concerted effort to investigate this concept in all its complexity. Shohamy (1997) stresses that the true power of tests is that of offering pedagogical benefits (i.e., promoting beneficial washback). This is exemplified in involving teachers in the test development process, and improving teaching through testing by considering concepts coming from innovation theory (Wall 1996). It appears, however, that before such statements are credible, more evidence is needed. With more inquiry, we will be better positioned as language testers to deal with ongoing issues so as firstly, to work in the same direction for beneficial impact, and secondly, to realise the extent 'within reason' (Davies 1997a: 238) of our responsibility in terms of test consequences.

References

Alderson, J. C. and Banerjee, J. 1996. How might impact study instruments be validated? A paper commissioned by The University of Cambridge Local Examinations Syndicate (UCLES) as part of the IELTS Impact Study. Cambridge: University of Cambridge Local Examinations Syndicate.

Alderson, J. C. and Hamp-Lyons, L. 1996. TOEFL preparation courses: a study of washback. *Language Testing* 13 (3): 280–97.

Alderson, J. C. and Wall, D. 1993. Does washback exist? *Applied Linguistics* 14: 115–29.

Bachman, L. F. 1990. *Fundamental Considerations in Language Testing*. Oxford: Oxford University Press.

Cheng, L. 1997. How does washback influence teaching? Implications for Hong Kong. *Language and Education* 11 (1): 38–54.

Cheng, L. 1998. The washback effect of public examination change on classroom teaching. Paper presented at the 20th Language Testing Research Colloquium, Monterey, CA: USA: March.

Davies, A. 1997a. Introduction: The limits of ethics in language testing. *Language Testing* 14 (3): 235–41.

Davies, A. 1997b. Demands of being professional in language testing. *Language Testing* 14 (3): 328–39.

Elder, C. and G. Wigglesworth. 1996. Perspectives on the testing cycle: Setting the scene. In Wigglesworth and Elder, pp. 1–12.

Frederiksen, J. R. and A. Collins. 1989. A systems approach to educational testing. *Educational Researcher* 18 (9): 27–32.

Frederiksen, N. 1984. The real test bias: Influences of testing on teaching and learning. *American Psychologist* 39 (3): 193–202.

Haladyna, T. H., S. B. Nolen, and N. S. Haas. 1991. Raising standardized achievement test scores and the origins of test score pollution. *Educational Researcher* 20 (5): 2–7.

Hamp-Lyons, L. 1997. Washback, impact and validity: Ethical concerns. *Language Testing* 14 (3): 295–303.

Kellaghan, T., G. F. Madaus, and P. W. Airasian. 1982. *The Effects of Standardized Testing*. London: Kluwen, Nijholf.

McNamara, T. 1996. *Measuring Second Language Performance.* London: Longman.

McNamara, T. 1998. Policy and social considerations in language assessment. *Annual Review of Applied Linguistics* 18: 304–19.

Messick, S. 1989. Validity. In R. L. Linn (ed.), *Educational Measurement* (3rd edi.). pp. 13–103. New York, NY: American Council on Education.

Milanovic, M. and N. Saville. 1996. *Considering the Impact of Cambridge EFL Examinations.* Cambridge: University of Cambridge Local Examinations Syndicate.

Paris, S. G., T. A. Lawton, J. C. Turner, and J. L. Roth. 1991. A developmental perspective on standardized achievement testing. *Educational Researcher* 20 (5): 12–19.

Shohamy, E. 1993. The power of tests: The impact of language tests on teaching and learning. *National Foreign Language Centre Occasional Papers.* Washington, DC: The National Foreign Language Centre.

Shohamy, E. 1997. Critical language testing and beyond. Plenary talk presented at AAAL, Orlando, FL: USA.

Shohamy, E., S. Donitsa-Schmidt, and I. Ferman. 1996. Test impact revisited: Washback effect over time. *Language Testing* 13 (3): 298–317.

Smith, M. L. 1991. Put to the test: The effects of external testing on teachers. *Educational Researcher* 20 (5): 8–11.

Turner, C. E. 1998. Describing the discourse of scale developers: A closer look at the process of empirically derived scales. Paper presented at 20th Language Testing Research Colloquium, Monterey, CA: USA: March.

Turner, C. E. and Upshur, J. A. 1995. Some effects of task type on the relation between communicative effectiveness and grammatical accuracy in intensive ESL classes. *TESL Canada Journal* 12 (2): 18–31.

Turner, C. E. and Upshur, J. A. 1996a. Developing rating scales for the assessment of second language performance. In Wigglesworth and Elder, pp. 55–79.

Turner, C. E. and Upshur, J. A. 1996b. *Scale development factors and facets of method.* Paper presented at the 18th Language Testing Research Colloquium, Tampere, Finland: August.

Upshur, J. A. and Turner, C. E. (1999). Systematic effects in the rating of second language speaking ability: Test method and learner discourse. *Language Testing* 16 (1): 82–111.

Wall, D. 1996. Introducing new tests into traditional systems: Insights from general education and from innovation theory. *Language Testing* 13 (3): 334–54.

Wall, D. 1997. Impact and washback in language testing. In C. Clapham and D. Corson (eds.), *The Encyclopedia of Language and Education. Vol. 7. Testing and Assessment*, pp. 291–302. Dordrecht: Kluwer Academic Publishers.

Wall, D. and J. C. Alderson. 1996. Examining washback: The Sri Lanka impact study. In A. Cumming and R. Berwick (eds.) *Validation in Language Testing*, pp. 194–221. Clevedon, Avon: Multilingual Matters Ltd.

Watanabe, Y. 1996. Investigating washback in Japanese EFL classrooms: Problems of methodology. In Wigglesworth and Elder, pp. 208–39.

Watson-Gegeo, K. A. 1988. Ethnography in ESL: Defining the essentials. *TESOL Quarterly* 22 (4): 575–92.

Wigglesworth, G. and C. Elder (eds.) 1996. *Australian Review of Applied Linguistics:* Series S, No. 13. *The Testing Cycle: From Inception to Washback.* Melbourne: ARAL.

16 Impact and washback research in language testing

J. Charles Alderson and Jayanti Banerjee
Lancaster University

Introduction

In this chapter we problematise the validation of data collection instruments used in impact and washback studies. In doing so we assert the need for research to establish the validity and reliability of the instruments.

It is our contention that applied linguistic researchers can learn a great deal about the validation of their instruments and procedures from the work and thinking of language testers. Having discovered a remarkable lack of concern in social science research generally, and within applied linguistics particularly, for methods of establishing the validity and reliability of instruments like questionnaires, interview and observation schedules, we have turned to concepts of validity and reliability within language testing to explore what the implications might be for instrument validation in applied linguistics in general.

The issues we address arose during the development of instruments to assess the impact of a language proficiency test, the International English Language Testing System (IELTS) test, developed by the University of Cambridge Local Examinations Syndicate (UCLES), the British Council and IDP Australia. The Impact Study is part of a programme of test validation being developed at UCLES, which is concerned to investigate not only test validity as it is narrowly conceived, but also the impact and use of IELTS.

Lancaster University was asked to develop an Impact Study with four sub-projects, which would require the development of instruments, as follows:

Project One: Impact on the classroom

1 Classroom observation schedule
2 Teacher's post-observation questionnaire/interview schedule
3 Students' post-observation questionnaire

Project Two: Impact on materials design

1 Textbook analysis instrument

Project Three: Impact on attitudes towards IELTS

1 Administrators' questionnaire
2 IELTS teachers' questionnaire
3 EAP post-IELTS teachers' questionnaire
4 Questionnaire for subject teachers (in accepting institutions)
5 Questionnaire for students currently studying for IELTS
6 Questionnaire for students who have taken IELTS

Project Four: Test takers' language learning behaviour

Test takers' background questionnaire, including sections on: attitudes to learning English and taking tests; how you learn English; what you do when you learn English; and what you do in language tests.

The design of the instruments

The procedure for developing the instruments is extensively documented in Banerjee (1996), Herrington (1996), Horak (1996) and Winetroube (1997), and included the following stages:

1 close examination of the (confidential) test specifications, sample test material, and textbooks intended to prepare students for IELTS;
2 extensive consultation with testing researchers and masters and doctoral degree students;
3 a detailed review of the literature on instrument design;
4 discussion, extensive revision and editing of draft instruments through a minimum of six iterations; and
5 trialling of the instruments followed by further revision and editing.

Once this process was complete, the instruments were formally handed over to UCLES. However, before the instruments were to be used in live studies of IELTS impact, it was considered important to investigate and if possible establish their validity.

Validation rather than piloting

We contend that a distinction must be made between validation and piloting. Regular piloting methods such as editing rules and pilot surveys (Foddy 1993: 183–85) are aimed at indicating where respondents might have difficulty responding for any number of reasons, including that they have misunderstood the questions, or because the questions made them uncomfortable.

It might also be possible to run statistical analyses on pilot data, but what the statistical indicators would look like needs some consideration. For instance, a low level of response to any particular item is more likely to indicate that it is not a commonly held opinion than that it is an invalid question. Furthermore, unbelievable responses are not necessarily identified or explained through a statistical index.

It is also unclear whether these procedures uncover respondents' true interpretations of questions and response scales. They do not provide sufficiently detailed information to establish the validity of the instruments. Nor do they provide information about the reliability of an instrument.

The literature search

Based on a review of the literature on instrument design and validation, Alderson (1992) calls for much more thought to be given to methods of establishing instrument reliability and validity. Building on Alderson (1992), we have looked for guidance beyond the field of language teaching and research. Questionnaires, interviews and classroom observation schedules are widely used in social science research; there is much documentation as to how instruments might be constructed and worded, but much less on how validity and reliability have been or might be established.

For instance, Hughes (1976), Hoinville *et al.* (1977) and Oppenheim (1992) all emphasise the need for good questions, but they do not directly address the topics of questionnaire reliability and validity at any great length, largely confining themselves to statements about their importance.

Similarly, textbooks on research design and data analysis such as Hatch and Lazaraton (1991) deal only briefly with methods of establishing the reliability and validity of questionnaires, and do not exemplify their suggestions with reference to actual research. Nash (1973) and Allwright (1988) demonstrate how data sources might be triangulated to cross-check information, but there is still no established set of procedures for confirming an instrument designer's belief that the instruments can indeed capture the information required to answer his/her research question and will capture that information reliably.

We argue therefore that, despite commentary to this effect by Chaudron (1988) and Brumfit and Mitchell (1990), and in spite of recent research by Low (1988, 1995, 1996a, 1996b), the documentation of studies of the reliability and validity of data collection instruments is limited, and researchers are overwhelmingly concerned with issues of construction. In fact, it seems generally to be believed that a carefully constructed questionnaire is a good (i.e. valid and reliable) questionnaire. Therefore, what we consider next is what validation procedures might aim to achieve and the procedures available.

Considerations in the development of a validation procedure

Validation procedures for data collection instruments like questionnaires, interviews and classroom observation schedules are likely to focus on whether respondents have understood the questions the way they were intended to be understood and whether they are comprehensive, i.e. they capture all the information being sought. Consequently, such validation procedures are likely to have the following aims:

1. that the questions in a questionnaire/interview schedule mean the same thing to their respondents as to the researcher(s) who wrote them and the categories in an observation schedule mean the same thing to all the observers as they do to the instrument designer;
2. that the order of the questions is not adversely affecting the type/quantity of responses;
3. that the responses do actually help the researcher(s) to answer their research question/s;
4. that the construct the researcher(s) are trying to measure/describe actually exists;
5. that the respondents will give the same answers each time they complete the questionnaire/are interviewed and the observers will capture the same data each time the same event is observed.

It is, of course, unlikely that any single method could meet all these aims and this argues for the development of validation procedures which incorporate more than one method.

In the absence of categories specific to the validation of questionnaires or observation schedules, we adopt the categories used in the testing literature as a framework for identifying promising methods for validating the IELTS Impact Study instruments. In doing so, we confine ourselves to a discussion of those categories which seem most promising for these instruments.

Preliminary procedures

The first step in the validation process is to establish the profile of responses to be expected if the IELTS test is having washback on the various domains being explored by this suite of instruments. It will then be possible to compare these expectations with the actual responses (and check for 'fit'). 'Fit' or its lack can then be followed up by discussions with respondents to the instruments.

It is also useful to explore the development of discrimination indices for items, based upon characteristics of respondents or patterns of response. Thus, for example, it might be predicted that candidates who have already taken the IELTS test would make different responses to certain items than candidates who have not taken the test. A contrast of responses of the two groups could be expected to reveal such differences. Similarly, respondents to an instrument can be characterised in terms of the pattern of their responses (for instance, exhibiting a generally favourable attitude to IELTS or some component of the test). An index of this characteristic can be developed based upon responses to relevant items; respondents can be classified according to such an index; and then their responses to individual items on the instrument can be calculated in terms of their match to the index. This might give a measure of the extent to which an item discriminated appropriately.

Reliability

The most promising of the methods we have considered for establishing the reliability of the Impact Study are the measurement of internal consistency, test-retest, and intra-rater and inter-rater agreement.

Internal consistency (K-R20)

Litwin (1995) and Fitz-Gibbon and Morris (1987) recommend that internal consistency (split-half) reliability be established in order to see how well different items measure the same issue. The argument is that if the internal consistency is low (as measured by K-R20), then steps could be taken to determine whether this is because some of the items are inadequate. The main feature of internal consistency, however, is that it assumes item homogeneity, and as Alderson (1992) points out, questions might actually be designed to 'behave differently to each other' (1992: 3).

However, this method is helpful in the case of attitude questionnaires (where a group of concepts might be checked across a number of items) and could be calculated for the IELTS attitude questionnaires. The consistency of responses could also be checked qualitatively by considering the plausibility of a respondent's answer to one question in the light of other related responses, keeping in mind that consistency of response may not indicate a more valid questionnaire.

Test-retest

The procedure of test-retest (Alderson 1992; Fitz-Gibbon and Morris 1987; Litwin 1995) can check whether respondents will give the same answers each time they complete the instrument, and is applicable in the case of the attitude questionnaires of Projects 3 and 4 and the teachers' and students' questionnaires of Project 1. In all cases respondents could complete the questionnaire on one day and then again on the following day.

This procedure does, however, rely on the assumption that constructs are stable (a problematic scenario in the case of attitude measures). This could pose particular problems with the teachers' and students' questionnaires of Project 1 where some questions are lesson-specific. It is important, therefore, not to let too much time intervene lest respondents forget the specific lesson experience or their perceptions of that experience change.

Nevertheless, Alderson (1992) used the test-retest method successfully in his study of responses to an ERASMUS Exchange Questionnaire. He argues in its favour as long as responses are not aggregated across items, but responses to each individual item are compared (1992: 20). As Alderson points out, this is because it is more usual for the responses to individual items to be of interest in a questionnaire. Aggregation of responses could result in the loss of information.

Rater consistency (intra-rater)

Apart from an extremely brief reference in Litwin (1995), there is no discussion of this in the literature. Nevertheless, it would seem a promising area for further investigation, particularly in the case of classroom observation instruments (Project 1) where raters could observe a video-recorded class on two separate occasions and their observations could then be compared for consistency.

However, since observation is dependent on inference, 'inconsistencies' could be due to either the instrument or its application. Certainly, if the instrument cannot 'cope', this could have some bearing on its validity.

Rater agreement (inter-rater)

Litwin (1995) suggests that inter-observer reliability be checked in the case of instruments which capture observations of what might be a common experience. This is particularly applicable to the textbook analysis instrument of Project 2 and the classroom observation instrument of Project 1. Inter-rater reliability measures have actually been built into the design of the latter and observation is conducted in pairs with each pair of observers being required to document areas of agreement and disagreement. In the case of the former, a group of raters could train with one textbook and then analyse a second. Their individual analyses could then be compared.

This procedure may also provide insight into whether differences in observations/ratings are caused by differences in interpretations of the lesson/textbook being analysed or differences in interpretation of the instrument (its wording). It may also be necessary to consider whether agreement during training had been forced by one rater.

Validity

In what follows, we treat the traditional validities as distinct. We are aware that current thinking considers construct validity to be a superordinate concept, to which the various traditional validities contribute. Nevertheless, we consider that in discussing the literature and its application to the instruments, it is helpful to discuss the various validities separately.

As with our discussion of the methods of establishing reliability, we would like to concentrate on the validities we deemed most promising in the context of the IELTS Impact Study. These were content, concurrent, response and construct validity.

Content validity

This involves the seeking of expert judgements and implies an interest in 'getting the wording right'. To achieve this Litwin (1995) recommends that the instrument be given to a selection of the people for whom it has been designed. They should then be asked to rate each question and scale according to its appropriateness and relevance to the research question being addressed. It is unclear, however, how Litwin intends such ratings to be organised.

We suggest two possible ways. The first develops on the inter-rater consistency exercise suggested for the textbook analysis and classroom observation instruments, where raters are asked to discuss their analyses, their agreements and their disagreements (see above). Here we would need to consider the extent to which the instrument is able to cope with differences of interpretation of the textbook or lesson.

The second involves contacting textbook writers to discuss what they might include in an IELTS preparation textbook and what they think constitutes IELTS washback. They could then be given the textbook instrument and asked whether they thought it would capture the impact of the test on their textbook design. Their initial statements about what they consider constitutes IELTS washback could also be compared to the actual instrument.

A similar procedure could be conducted with teachers who complete the attitude questionnaires of Project 3 or the teachers' questionnaire from Project 1. In either case they could first be asked to discuss what they do when they teach an IELTS preparation class and what they think constitutes IELTS washback. They could then read the instrument and say whether it would capture the impact of the test on their classes. However, since it is possible that teachers' statements about what and how they teach to a test do not necessarily match what actually happens in the classroom, the same teachers should be observed and then debriefed to investigate possible apparent discrepancies.

Finally, in the case of the teachers' and students' questionnaires of Project 1, discussions could be held with groups of students with and without the teacher and observer in order for similarities and differences in responses to be explored. This discussion could reveal gaps in the questionnaire, indicate the questions which are badly worded and illustrate the inadequacies of the method of collecting data.

Concurrent validity

In the absence of a 'gold standard' against which to measure the validity of the IELTS Impact Study instruments, we recommend that concurrent validity be investigated only in the case of the classroom observation instrument (Project 1) where there could be two pairs of observers. A discussion of the purpose of the observation could be held beforehand, but one pair of observers could take notes on the class without having the instrument to refer to. Their observations could then be compared to the observations made by the two observers who conducted the observation with the instrument. If the discussion resulted in additions being made to the instrument, this would indicate 'construct under-representation' and would amount to construct validation as well.

Response validity

Investigating response validity involves capturing the introspection or retrospection (or both) of respondents on their answers to questions in the instrument. However, the methodology available for investigating response validity (think-aloud protocols; having respondents rephrase each question in their own words) is problematic. For instance, having attempted think-aloud protocols with respondents to a survey of ERASMUS students Alderson (1992) commented that respondents rarely 'think-aloud' since few are naturally able to do this. He recommended 'training' respondents to use the method.

Another approach is suggested by Foddy (1993) where respondents are asked to rephrase questions in their own words, after which the responses are coded according to four parameters:

1 fully correct – leaving out no vital parts
2 generally correct – no more than one part altered or omitted
3 partially wrong – but indicating that the respondent knew the general subject of the question
4 completely wrong and no response.

(Foddy 1993: 186)

These methods are promising and should be applied to all the instruments, for they may be able to supply information about what the questions mean to the respondents and whether the order of the questions is appropriate. They may also go some way to indicating whether the responses are going to answer the research question(s).

Nevertheless, they can only indirectly address the issue of whether the construct they are trying to measure actually exists.

Construct validity

This has two aspects, first as another measure relating particularly to the theory the instrument is trying to tap, and second as an overarching validity. Both aspects relate to the theory which has informed the construction of the instrument and establishing this can be problematic if the design of the instrument has not foregrounded the theory being drawn on.

Indeed, Litwin (1995) terms this 'the most valuable yet most difficult way of assessing a survey instrument. It is difficult to understand, to measure, and to report' (1995: 43). This is certainly true of the instruments in this study. For instance, the construct validity of the textbook analysis instrument might be investigated by using it to analyse first an IELTS textbook and then a TOEFL textbook. The assumption here would be that the two analyses will not correlate closely (an indication of divergent validity). In the case of the attitude questionnaires, students in different types of classes can be compared (IELTS/non-IELTS) as can teachers who are teaching different types of classes (IELTS/non-IELTS) in order to investigate divergent validity. However, while similarities might indicate invalidity, they might also validly indicate that the two textbooks or classes are indeed similar!

Alternatively, convergent validity can be investigated by seeking another source of opinions in order to determine whether the questionnaire is tapping the respondents' attitudes comprehensively. For instance, in the case of the attitude questionnaires, teachers' reports of discussions with students and interviews with students can be used to explore responses to the students' questionnaire. In the case of the teachers' questionnaire, other sources of opinions could be the teachers' colleagues or their supervisor. However, even here doubts remain, for if the measures do not coincide, it is still not possible to tell which of the measures is the valid one.

Even statistical procedures such as item-level factor analysis are problematic. Alderson (1992) expresses doubt about the 'validity of the technique [and] the interpretability of the results' (1992: 4). Technical problems include the use of a set level for the cut-off of eigenvalues for item level analysis, the method of factor extraction and rotation, and the use of confirmatory rather than exploratory techniques in cases where we might be said to be investigating specific hypotheses about the relations among items in the instruments. However, these are dwarfed by problems of the complexity of most results, and the lack of secure procedures for establishing the nature of the factors. For such reasons, the use of factor analysis in instrument validation has to be seen as tentative and suggestive, at best.

Indeed, the most promising approach to construct validation might be if content groupings of questions or categories within each instrument were established, including items or groups of items that contradict or are the opposite of other items/groups. Responses can then be cross-checked within groups for consistency of response and across groups for expected differences. This can also be seen either as a content validation procedure, or as a check on the consistency/reliability of responses.

Triangulation

It should be stressed that the validation procedures we have suggested would be largely exploratory since there is little discussion, much less consensus, over which established procedures are most fruitful.

Certainly, one issue that has underlain our discussions in this paper needs to be made explicit at this point, and that is the extent to which validation is or is not separate from the compilation of research results. To what extent can the examination of the results of the validation procedures discussed above be considered to lead to substantive findings about impact *per se*? To take an example: the proposal that two different textbooks, one aimed at IELTS preparation, one at TOEFL preparation, be examined as part of the validation of the textbook instrument. If the results of such a comparison show that there is little difference between the two supposedly different textbooks, then at least two conclusions are possible. One is that the instrument is invalid since it fails to capture 'known' differences. But, of course, such differences are not really 'known': they are simply hypothesised. They have not been established: that is precisely why the Impact Study has been developed. An alternative interpretation of such a result would be that IELTS has relatively little impact on textbook design. Such a conclusion would be strengthened if other procedures intended to validate the same instrument came up with similar conclusions.

Furthermore, given current thinking about construct validity as being attested from a multitude of perspectives, all of which contribute to, but do not individually determine, the validity of an instrument, it is clear that triangulation of data sources and instruments is essential. This is a point frequently made in the social science research literature, but rarely stressed in the reporting of validation results. Such triangulation would entail cross-checking of information, and it can, arguably, be seen as a measure of reliability also. Consequently, the instruments have been designed with a view to triangulation with items which cross-refer across respondent groups.

It is, however, important to stress that if views across instruments diverge, the sources of this divergence could be various. For example, while the divergence of views could indicate that one or more of the instruments was not working, it could also be because respondents had given inaccurate responses or because the phenomenon being investigated only affects some of the participants.

Conclusion

In this paper, we have argued that social science research instruments need to be validated, just as tests are. Our review of the literature revealed very little discussion of suitable methodologies for validation, and indeed rather weak and scarce evidence is reported for the reliability and validity of instruments. We have proposed a framework for validation, taken from language testing, but applied to the different aims of the instruments developed for an impact study. Finally, we have illustrated in detail possible procedures for establishing the validity and reliability of particular instruments. Experience with the procedures proposed should throw light on their value. We insist on the need for adequate validation procedures, and we hope that the future will see more exploration of how language testing concepts can help applied linguists more generally to develop and experiment with suitable validation procedures.

References

Alderson, J. C. 1992. *Validating Questionnaires.* CRILE Working Paper Series. No. 15. Lancaster: Lancaster University.

Allwright, D. 1988. *Observation in the Language Classroom.* New York, NY: Longman.

Banerjee, J. V. 1996. *UCLES Report: The Design of the Classroom Observation Instruments.* Unpublished report. Cambridge: UCLES.

Brumfit, C. and R. Mitchell (eds.) 1990. *ELT Documents 133: Research in the Language Classroom.* Devon: Modern English Publications and the British Council.

Chaudron, C. 1988. *Second Language Classrooms: Research on Teaching and Learning.* Cambridge: Cambridge University Press.

Fitz-Gibbon, C. T. and L. L. Morris. 1987. *How to Analyse Data.* Newbury Park: Sage Publications.

Foddy, W. 1993. *Constructing Questions for Interviews and Questionnaires: Theory and Practice in Social Research.* Cambridge: Cambridge University Press.

Hatch, E. and A. Lazaraton. 1991. *The Research Manual: Design and Statistics for Applied Linguistics*. Boston: Heinle and Heinle.

Herrington, R. 1996. Test-taking strategies and second language proficiency: Is there a relationship? Unpublished MA dissertation. Lancaster University.

Hoinville, G., R. Jowell and Associates. 1977. *Survey Research Practice.* London: Heinemann.

Horak, T. 1996. IELTS Impact Study Project. Unpublished MA assignment. Lancaster University.

Hughes, J. A. 1976. *Sociological Analysis: Methods of Discovery.* London: Thomas Nelson and Sons.

Litwin, M. S. 1995. *How to Measure Survey Reliability and Validity.* Thousand Oaks, CA: Sage Publications.

Low, G. D. 1988. The semantics of questionnaire rating scales. *Evaluation and Research in Education* 2 (2): 69–79.

Low, G. D. 1995. Answerability in attitude measurement questionnaires: an applied linguistic study of reactions to 'Statement plus Rating' pairs. Unpublished PhD thesis. University of York.

Low, G. D. 1996a. Intensifiers and hedges in questionnaire items and the lexical invisibility hypothesis. *Applied Linguistics* 17 (1): 1–37.

Low, G. D. 1996b. Validating research questionnaires: the value of common sense. *Research News* (the Newsletter of the IATEFL Research SIG) 9: 1–8.

Nash, R. 1973. *Classrooms Observed: The Teacher's Perception and the Pupil's Performance.* London: Routledge and Kegan Paul.

Oppenheim, A. N. 1992. *Questionnaire Design, Interviewing and Attitude Measurement.* New Edition. London: Pinter Press.

Winetroube, S. 1997. The design of the teachers' attitude questionnaires. Unpublished report. Cambridge: UCLES.

Section Seven

Language testing in its policy context

17 Prescribed language standards and foreign language classroom practice: Relationships and consequences

Rosamond Mitchell
University of Southampton

Introduction

This paper examines the introduction of 'language standards' to modern foreign language (MFL) teaching within schools in England. In this British case, 'language standards' take the form of so-called Attainment Targets and Level Descriptors within the framework of the National Curriculum (NC), progressively introduced since the late 1980s. First, we will be critically examining one of the Attainment Targets in order to clarify the underlying model of FL development which underpins the language standards. Then we examine data from an observational study of classroom teaching conducted during 1994–6, for its degree of 'fit' with the new standards. Finally we will evaluate some of the possible longer term consequences for the declared aim of raising general levels of achievement.

The National Curriculum for modern foreign languages

The turbulent development of the National Curriculum for England and Wales since the late 1980s has been described elsewhere (DES/WO 1988; Kelly 1990; Chitty and Simon 1993; Daugherty 1995; Lawton 1996). Here we concentrate on the subject-specific curriculum for MFLs. (One foreign language must be studied from age 11–14.) In response to changing political imperatives, there have been three successive attempts at defining the MFLs curriculum (DES/WO 1990, 1991; DFE 1995). On each occasion, the work was done by an expert panel working on a very short time scale, and was not underpinned by any programme of empirical research.

The current NC document for MFLs is brief (DFE 1995). It comprises the so-called 'Programme of Study', and four discrete 'Attainment Targets' (Listening, Speaking, Reading and Writing), each presented as a ladder of eight 'Level Descriptors'.

The Programme of Study specifies the range of situations and language functions which are to be addressed, though this is done in very broad terms. It also specifies learning strategies and cultural awareness strands, and sets out a short list of topic domains. A set of specimen activities intended to illustrate implementation of the Programme was published subsequently (SCAA 1997).

The Programme of Study itself raises many implementation problems. However, here our main concern is with the Attainment Targets and associated Level Descriptors. These are intended to be the defining statements about learner progress, and comprise the main assessment yardstick. Schools have responsibility for devising their own assessment tools against this yardstick, though sample assessment materials have also been published (SCAA 1996a, b). As we have seen, separate Attainment Targets exist only for the traditional 'four skills'; intercultural awareness, metalinguistic knowledge, and learning strategies are not assessed.

Progression in FL 'speaking'

The Attainment Target for 'Speaking' is shown as Figure 17.1; the remaining Attainment Targets are designed on similar principles. A number of assumptions are discernible, regarding the nature of progression:

1 Firstly, it seems that learner progression relates to the length of individual utterances, and also of conversational exchanges. Up to Level 4, at least, formal limits are set to expectations of learner performance on both fronts.
2 The model assumes a sequential relationship between the use of fixed phrases/unanalysed expressions, and creative construction of target language utterances. Thus oral production from Levels 1–4 is seen as depending primarily on the former, whereas from Level 5 onwards, creative construction is seen as the primary mechanism underpinning spoken TL use.
3 Finally, a linear relationship is assumed between the development of formal accuracy in spoken TL use, and overall progression (see especially Level 5 onwards).

Figure 17.1
National Curriculum for Modern Foreign Languages
(England and Wales)
Attainment Target 2: Speaking (DFE 1995)

Level 1	Pupils respond briefly, with single words or short phrases, to what they see and hear. Their pronunciation may be approximate, and they may need considerable support from a spoken model and from visual cues.
Level 2	Pupils give short, simple responses to what they see and hear. They name and describe people, places and objects. They use set phrases for purposes such as asking for help and permission. Their pronunciation may still be approximate, and the delivery hesitant, but their meaning is clear.
Level 3	Pupils take part in brief prepared tasks of at least two or three exchanges, using visual or other cues to help them initiate and respond. They use short phrases to express personal responses, such as likes, dislikes and feelings. Although they use mainly memorised language, they occasionally substitute items of vocabulary to vary questions or statements.
Level 4	Pupils take part in simple structured conversations of at least three or four exchanges, supported by visual or other cues. They are beginning to use their knowledge of language to adapt and substitute single words and phrases. Their pronunciation is generally accurate and they show some consistency in their intonation.
Level 5	Pupils take part in short conversations, seeking and conveying information and opinions in simple terms. They refer to recent experience and future plans, as well as everyday activities and interests. Although there may be some mistakes, pupils make themselves understood with little or no difficulty.
Level 6	Pupils initiate and develop conversations that include past, present and future actions and events. They are beginning to improvise and paraphrase. They use the target language to meet most of their routine needs for information and explanation. Although they may be hesitant at times, pupils make themselves understood with little or no difficulty
Level 7	Pupils give and justify opinions when discussing matters of personal or topical interest. They adapt language to deal with some unprepared situations. They speak with good pronunciation and intonation. Their accuracy is such that they are readily understood.
Level 8	Pupils show increasing confidence in dealing with unpredictable elements in conversations, or with people who are unfamiliar. They discuss facts, ideas and experiences, using a range of vocabulary, structures and time references. They speak confidently with good pronunciation and intonation, and their language is largely accurate with few mistakes of any significance.
Exceptional performance	Pupils discuss a wide range of factual and imaginative topics, giving and seeking personal views and opinions in informal and formal situations. They speak fluently, with consistently accurate pronunciation, and show an ability to vary intonation. They give clear messages and make few errors.

These assumptions run counter to much research evidence on the early course of FL learning. There is evidence that even early learners can engage in extended TL interactions, and successfully negotiate mutual understanding, provided appropriate levels of interlocutor support are forthcoming. (On adult learners, see e.g. Bremer *et al.* 1996; on child learners, see Mitchell and Dickson 1997.) From this point of view, 'progression' has to do with an increase in communicative autonomy and decreasing dependency on interlocutor support.

Secondly, it is clear that the spoken productions of both L2 and FL classroom learners are a mix of prefabricated routines and 'chunks' (the result of both direct teaching and of indirect socialisation into classroom routines), and creatively constructed utterances. (For L2 learners, see e.g. Ellis 1984, Willett 1995; for FL learners, see Myles, Hooper and Mitchell 1998.) Indeed, Myles *et al.* argue that interactions between these two types of productions are a significant factor in classroom FL development. Over time, the relative significance of creative construction and prefabrication will change; but there is evidence from corpus-based studies that even fluent language users' productions continue to incorporate prefabricated elements (Stubbs 1996: 35–44). Thus the NC assumption that a phase of largely prefabricated productions precedes, and is effectively superseded by, a phase of creative construction, very much oversimplifies the relationship between these two phenomena in learner language.

Thirdly, it is clear from much interlanguage research that the development of formal accuracy in the target language is non-linear, and that complex trade-offs exist between the development of accuracy, fluency and complexity/ambition in TL production; standard accounts are readily available, e.g. Larsen-Freeman and Long (1991: 88–96), or Ellis (1994: 73–117).

In several key respects, therefore, the model of progression which underlies the British NC language standards reflects a one-sided preoccupation with accuracy, which is clearly at odds with research-based views of interlanguage development.

Accounting for preoccupations with accuracy

Why is it that the British standards have been drafted in such controlled terms? Why is it that only fully accurate TL productions can be 'rewarded' with progression up the scale, even if this involves restrictions a) on the quantity of language, and b) on the degree of creativity? The extremely limited expectations of the earlier levels can partly be explained by the 'squeezed up' nature of the scale, with a ladder of eight levels to be climbed in the course of only three school years. A fuller explanation lies in wider professional debates about the FL curriculum in the UK context, as well as in political discussions around the whole NC project.

These debates cannot be fully reviewed here. Briefly however, the 20th century history of FL teaching in the UK context has been deeply affected by the rise of English as a global language. In these special circumstances, the last 30 years have witnessed a struggle by FL professionals to establish their subject as a compulsory curriculum element, under the slogan 'Languages for All' (Hawkins 1996); this principle was finally established with the introduction of the NC.

However, establishing clear curriculum goals and expectations for British FL teaching has not been straightforward, in the absence of clear instrumental motivation. The late 1970s and early 1980s were a period of considerable local experimentation with FL schemes of work and curricula, especially for the 11–14 age group. At that time, some local projects experimented with ambitious functional syllabuses, while others effectively restricted themselves to situational syllabuses and phrasebook-style learning (Utley, Mitchell and Phillips 1983; Clark 1987; Page 1996).

While recent years have seen strong centralisation of curriculum planning, the 1970s situational syllabuses have left clear influences on current norms and expectations, and provide a partial explanation for the restricted communicative expectations of the lower NC Levels. Further explanations can be found in the charged ideological debates surrounding the National Curriculum overall. By the mid 1990s the politicisation of educational policy had an impact even on FL teaching (see e.g. Phillips 1996), so that it is tempting to interpret the emphasis on accuracy in recent NC documentation partly as a defensive reaction to external political pressures.

Links between language standards and FL classroom practice

Between 1994 and 1996, the author jointly directed a two-year longitudinal study of a cohort of 60 children learning French, in two English secondary schools.[1] As well as tracking the children's interlanguage development, through a termly series of oral assessments, the project involved a regular programme of classroom observations. This gave the opportunity to observe a relatively large group of FL teachers working to implement the NC language standards with the 11–14 age group. Here we comment briefly on the work of a subset of five teachers, called Teachers C, D, E, N and O, each observed on around 20 individual occasions, over two years.[2] We explore the degree of congruence of these teachers' classroom practice with the new language standards, concentrating on their work with beginners, and on three selected issues already raised in our comments on the 'Speaking' Attainment Target:

1Control vs creativity in target language use;
2Learner dependence/autonomy;
3The pursuit of accuracy in TL production.

Control vs creativity

As we have seen, given the overall emphasis on the brevity of spoken exchanges, and on the rehearsed/memorised strand in learners' talk, the NC standards can be expected to weigh in on the side of control as far as learners' target language productions are concerned. Table 17.1 shows the overall pattern of activities observed in the five classrooms under consideration, during Year 7 (the first year of secondary schooling, when children would presumably be assessed using the lower end of the NC scale). We see a strong focus on oral activities, but we also see that the form-focused category of 'practice FL' predominated (comprising essentially the rehearsal and memorisation of situationally useful prefabricated expressions, or slot-and-filler exercises).

Table 17.1
Teachers' use of 'practice' and 'communicative' activities (number and % of observed minutes, Year 7 lessons)

Teacher		PFL activities (to nearest minute)	CFL activities	Other	Total
C	n	461	127	45	633
	%	72.8	20.1	7.1	100.0
D	n	375	219	13	607
	%	61.8	36.1	2.1	100.0
E	n	423	147	23	593
	%	71.3	24.8	3.9	100.0
N	n	309	129	0	438
	%	70.6	29.5	0.0	100.1
O	n	171	150	19	340
	%	50.3	44.1	5.6	100.0

The first lesson extract given below gives a flavour of this kind of form-oriented oral rehearsal, which we have categorised as 'practice FL'. Here, Teacher O and her class are looking at diagrams of apartments:

[1]

TO: Ouvrez vos livres alors à la page 82 où il y a quatre plans, 'un plan de mon appartement'... ce sont des appartements, ce sont des appartements ... lève la main si tu habites dans un appartement, moi j'habite dans un appartement, lève la main si tu habites dans un appartement ... regardez bien plan A. Combien de chambres y-a-t-il? Plan A, combien de chambres y-a-t-il? Elizabeth? (Open your books then on page 82, where there are four plans, 'a plan of my apartment'... these are apartments, these are apartments ... put up your hand if you live in an apartment, I live in an apartment, put up your hand if you live in an apartment ... have a good look at plan A. How many bedrooms are there? Plan A, how many bedrooms are there? [E]?)
E: Trois chambres (three bedrooms)
TO: Trois chambres, très bien (three bedrooms, very good)
E: Un salon (a living room)
TO: Il y a aussi un salon (there is a living room too)
E: Salle à manger? (a dining room?)
TO: Une salle de jeux, là où il y a un nounours, là où il y a un nounours, ça c'est une salle de jeux, voilà, trois chambres, une salle de jeux, un salon, c'est tout? (A playroom, there where there is a teddy bear, there where there is a teddy bear, that is a playroom, so, three bedrooms, a playroom, a living room, is that all?)
E: Une cuisine (a kitchen)
TO: Oui, il y a une cuisine (yes, there's a kitchen)
E: Une salle de bains (a bathroom)
TO: Il y a une salle de bains aussi, très bien (there is a bathroom too, very good)

Despite the incidental question about pupils' own homes, this extract has a clear focus on vocabulary rehearsal. It is unusual only in that pupil E is expected to complete the full cycle of room-labelling with scaffolded support from the teacher; more typically, in such whole-class interactions, individual pupils contributed to single question–answer (QA) exchanges, and the 'turn' then passed to another child.

Activities with some focus on meaning were also found with reasonable frequency (represented by the 'communicative FL' column in Table 1), but the degree of unpredictability and creativity required within these activities was low, typically involving choice between a small number of possible answers to a familiar question. The following extract from another lesson with Teacher C gives a flavour of activities recognised as 'communicative' in this sense:

[2]

TC: (...) Et dis-moi [A], qu'est-ce que tu fais mercredi? Qu'est-ce que tu fais mercredi? (And tell me [A], what do you do on Wednesdays? What do you do on Wednesdays?)
A: Umm on Wednesday I play ...
TC: Non non non non ... qu'est-ce que tu fais mercredi? Je pose la question en français (No no no no ... what do you do on Wednesdays? I am asking the question in French)
A: What are you doing on ...
TC: Oh, je pose une question. Donne-moi une réponse ... qu'est-ce que tu fais mercredi? (Oh, I am asking a question. Give me an answer ... what do you do on Wednesdays?)
Pupils: (Confused noise, helping out [A])
A: Mercredi je joue sur mon ordinateur (On Wednesdays I play on my computer)
TC: Bravo, excellent, un peu de problème de comprehension là, good, well done. Mercredi je joue sur mon ordinateur. Et dis-moi, qu'est-ce que tu fais samedi? [V], qu'est-ce que tu fais samedi? (Bravo, excellent, a small comprehension problem there, good, well done. Wednesdays I play on my computer. And tell me, what do you do on Saturdays? [V], what do you do on Saturdays?)
V: Samedi je vais à la piscine (On Saturdays I go to the swimming pool)
TC: Excellent, samedi je vais à la piscine. [K], qu'est-ce que tu fais mardi? (Excellent, on Saturdays I go to the swimming pool. [K], what do you do on Tuesdays?) (Etc.)

This exchange continued in this way around the class, in classic Initiation–Response–Feedback mode, with 13 pupils in all answering similar individual questions, and teacher feedback consisting in an almost unvarying 'Excellent'. Only at the very end, when the questioning finally returned to Pupil [A], was there any attempt to link one response with another:

[3]

TC: Qu'est-ce que tu fais samedi matin? [A]? (What do you do on Saturday mornings? [A]?)
A: Samedi matin je joue sur mon ordinateur (On Saturday mornings I play on my computer)

TC: Comme toujours! et samedi après-midi? Qu'est-ce que tu fais samedi après-midi? (Like always! and Saturday afternoons? What do you do on Saturday afternoons?)

A: Samedi après-midi je joue au foot (On Saturday afternoons I play football)

TC: Ah phew! Je joue au foot, ce n'est pas sur ton ordinateur? (Phew! I [sic] play football, it is not on your computer?)

A: Non (no)

TC: Non, ah c'est bien, c'est bien, très très bien (no, that's good, that's good, very very good)

Tasks which challenged pupils to engage in any more sustained cumulative interaction of a non-predictable kind, even with scaffolded support from the class teacher, were effectively absent from the corpus of observed lessons. The data-gathering procedures of the research project involved regular one-to-one sessions with the target pupils, in which they engaged in FL-medium interviews, story-telling or problem-solving tasks with a member of the research team. With liberal amounts of adult scaffolding these procedures worked successfully, but they attracted considerable comment from the teachers, who viewed the children as 'unprepared' by their ordinary lessons for these; this suggests to us that the controlled nature of the observed lessons, and in particular the brevity of the interactions in which individual pupils became engaged, were not untypical.

Table 17.2
Organisational patterns and skill focus
(numbers and percentages of observed minutes, Year 7 lessons)

Teacher		Whole class/ speaking	Pairs/ speaking	Tapes/ listening	Reading	Writing	Other	Total
C	n	427	27	0	11	123	45	633
	%	67.5	4.3	0.0	1.7	19.4	7.1	100.0
D	n	418	38	10	24	104	13	607
	%	68.9	6.3	1.6	4.0	17.1	2.1	100.0
E	n	385	41	20	23	101	23	593
	%	64.9	6.9	3.4	3.9	17.0	3.9	100.0
N	n	252	27	65	37	57	0	438
	%	57.5	6.2	14.8	8.5	13.0	0.0	100.0
O	n	181	49	64	9	18	19	340
	%	53.2	14.4	18.8	2.6	5.3	5.6	99.9

Learner dependence/autonomy

Table 17.2 presents a further analysis of interactional patterns within the same set of lessons. Here we see a very high degree of teacher control, with most oral work orchestrated as a whole-class activity centred on the teacher, for example. (Typical examples of the resulting interactions have been cited above as Extracts 1–3, from lessons taught by Teachers C and O.) The listening comprehension activities which featured in the lessons of Teachers N and O were also always conducted as whole-class activities. As Table 17.2 shows, the incidence of individual reading was strikingly rare; writing was the main individual activity, but was again very controlled, consisting almost always of copywriting, or slot-and-filler exercises.

The very limited use of pair- or group-work is an obvious feature of this lesson corpus, and the proportion of time spent in this way had declined substantially, compared with evidence from a somewhat similar study conducted ten years earlier (Mitchell 1988). When they did occur, pairwork episodes were typically brief, involving a few moments' practice of a single Q–A exchange. For example, the following extract shows Teacher O setting up a pairwork activity, using family photographs brought in by the pupils:

[4]

TO: Alors vous allez travailler avec un partenaire. La question, 'qui est-ce?' La réponse, 'c'est mon père', 'c'est mon frère', 'c'est mon grand-père', ou peut-être 'c'est ma mère', 'c'est ma soeur', 'c'est ma grand-mère'. OK, qui n'a pas de partenaire? (So you are going to work with a partner. The question, 'who is it?' The answer, 'it's my father', 'it's my brother', 'it's my grandfather', or maybe 'it's my mother', 'it's my sister', 'it's my grandmother'. OK, who hasn't got a partner?)

In spite of the personalised nature of the stimulus pictures, the teacher's instructions made it clear that only certain specific expressions were required (and gender concord is signalled in advance as a formal concern). In practice, the pupils actually went a little beyond these instructions, e.g. adding people's names to their brief descriptions; they were generally commended ('vous travaillez bien'/ 'you are working well'), but given no incentive to be more adventurous. Indeed, in a following pairwork activity about pets, a pupil preparing a question for her partner asked Teacher O for the word 'chicken'.

Her reply was negative:

> *Tu uses [sic] les mots que tu connais, des animaux comme par exemple 'lapin' (just use the words you know, animals like 'rabbit', for example).*

The pursuit of accuracy

As we have seen, the NC standards provide some very clear signals for teachers regarding accuracy. Teachers are expected to model large amounts of correct input; they should also aim consistently for accuracy in learners' TL output. The ability to approximate one's meaning, and to develop shared understandings through processes of negotiation and repair, earns learners no credit on the assessment ladder for 'Speaking'.

In response to these pressures, our teachers all invested very significant effort in promoting the accurate memorisation and production of a wide range of prefabricated expressions – clearly a highly rational strategy, if their aim is to 'push' pupils quickly to NC Levels 3 or 4 (see Figure 17.1).

Their error feedback was somewhat more varied, in response to learners' more creative TL utterances. The experienced teachers in the group all produced error feedback systematically, though with some variations. For example, Teacher O typically produced recasts only, and did not insist on learners' immediate self-correction, while others were much more persistent in eliciting corrected TL productions. (See Lyster and Ranta 1997 for detailed discussion of these tactics.) Extract 5 gives a flavour of the highly active correction style used by Teacher E during an episode describing imaginary characters:

[5]

TE:	Elle a des frères ou des soeurs? (She has brothers or sisters?)
P:	Oui, j'ai une (Yes, I have one)
TE:	Non, non, c'est pas 'j'ai' (No, no, it isn't 'I have')
P:	Il a deux frères (He has two brothers)
TE:	C'est pas 'il'... ce n'est pas 'il' (It isn't 'he'... it isn't 'he')
P:	Elle a deux frères (She has two brothers)(...)
H:	J'ai a un chat (I have has a cat)
TE:	Ce n'est pas 'j'ai', c'est Lucille (It isn't 'I have', it is Lucille)[Other pupil] Elle a (She has)
H:	Elle a ... elle a un chat (She has she has a cat)(...)
TE:	Elle aime quel animal? (She likes what animal?)
R:	Elle j'aime les oiseaux (She I like birds)

TE: Ce n'est pas 'j'aime' ... on parle de Lucille (It's not 'I like', we are talking about Lucille) [Other pupil] Elle (She)
TE: Elle (She)
R: Elle aime les oiseaux (She likes birds)

Here we see a sustained push by Teacher E to ensure correct pronoun–verb concord, in pupils' own productions. She produces no recasts herself; though other pupils are allowed to help, the original speaker is consistently required to rework the faulty expression, until a correct version is produced.

Only one of the observed teachers, a new entrant to the profession (Teacher D), clearly did not feel obliged to give systematic error feedback at all times, and positively defended this stance in interview, giving an explicitly 'developmental' interpretation of the role of error in interlanguage development.

Conclusion

Overall then, the teaching described here was broadly congruent with the language standards coming into force, at least as far as 'Speaking' was concerned. Of course, as we have seen, the standards themselves show considerable continuity with assumptions already current in many British schools prior to the NC developments. Thus both the new standards, and the observed teaching practices, share common roots.

In this situation, the immediate 'backwash' effects of the standards on classroom practice will not initially be very dramatic. However, their longer-term impact will certainly be to reduce diversity and experimentation (as is indeed intended!). In the case of FLs, given the way the standards are presently drafted, what we seem likely to lose are the more ambitious and more experiential interpretations of communicative language teaching, which have also historically been found at local level, associated with more ambitious targets for eventual communicative proficiency. Thus for example, a young teacher like Teacher D will not get any very systematic support for her tentative 'growth'-oriented beliefs about language use and interlanguage development from these standards, nor is she so likely to receive guidance and training in the management of more creative and extended TL interactions, in a profession dominated by the need to demonstrate success in terms of these particular NC targets. Thus the eventual consequences of these language standards may actually be to lock FL teaching in English schools into a cycle of too-low expectations, restricted classroom experiences, and 'survival competence' as the typical learning outcome. This would seem an ironic outcome, from an initiative with the declared aim of raising classroom achievement all round.

Notes

1 The 1993–1996 'Progression in Foreign Language Learning' project was co-directed by Rosamond Mitchell of the University of Southampton and Peter Dickson of the National Foundation for Educational Research. It was funded by the Economic and Social Research Council, award no. R000234754.
2 A fuller account of these observations is available in Mitchell and Martin (1997).

References

Bremer, K., C. Roberts, M.-T. Vasseur, M. Simonot and P. Broeder. 1996. *Achieving Understanding: Discourse in Intercultural Encounters*. Harlow: Longman.

Chitty, C. and B. Simon (eds.) 1993. *Education Answers Back*. London: Lawrence and Wishart.

Clark, J. L. 1987. *Curriculum Renewal in School Foreign Language Learning*. Oxford: Oxford University Press.

Daugherty, R. 1995. *National Curriculum Assessment: A Review of Policy 1987–1994*. London: Falmer Press.

Department of Education and Science/Welsh Office. 1988. *Task Group on Assessment and Testing: A Report*. London: DES/WO.

Department of Education and Science/Welsh Office. 1990. *Modern Foreign Languages for Ages 11 to 16*. London: DES/WO.

Department of Education and Science/Welsh Office. 1991. *Modern Foreign Languages in the National Curriculum.* London: HMSO.

Department for Education. 1995. *Modern Foreign Languages in the National Curriculum (Revised)*. London: HMSO.

Ellis, R. 1984. Formulaic speech in early classroom second language development. In J. Handscombe, R. Orem and B. Taylor (eds.), On *TESOL '83: The Question of Control*. Washington, DC: TESOL publications.

Ellis, R. 1994. *The Study of Second Language Acquisition*. Oxford: Oxford University Press.

Hawkins, E. (Ed.) 1996. *Thirty Years of Language Teaching*. London: CILT.

Kelly, A. V. 1990. *The National Curriculum: A Critical Review*. London: Paul Chapman.

Larsen-Freeman, D. and M. H. Long. 1991. *An Introduction to Second Language Acquisition Research*. Harlow: Longman.

Lawton, D. 1996. *Beyond the National Curriculum*. London: Hodder and Stoughton.

Lyster, R. and E. Ranta. 1997. Corrective feedback and learning uptake: Negotiation of form in communicative classrooms. *Studies in Second Language Acquisition* 19: 37–66.

Mitchell, R. 1988. *Communicative Language Teaching in Practice*. London: CILT.

Mitchell, R. and P. Dickson. 1997. *Progression in Foreign Language Learning*. CLE Occasional Papers 45. Southampton: University of Southampton.

Mitchell, R. and C. Martin. 1997. Rote learning, creativity and 'understanding' in the foreign language classroom. *Language Teaching Research* 1: 1–27.

Myles, F., J. Hooper and R. Mitchell. 1998. Rote or rule? Exploring the role of formulaic language in classroom foreign language learning. *Language Learning* 48: 323–63.

Page, B. 1996. Graded Objectives in ML (GOML). In Hawkins, pp. 99–105.

Phillips, M. 1996. *All Must Have Prizes*. London: Little, Brown and Company.

School Curriculum and Assessment Authority. 1996a. *Exemplification of Standards: Modern Foreign Languages, Key Stage 3*. London: SCAA.

School Curriculum and Assessment Authority. 1996b. *Optional Tests and Tasks: Modern Foreign Languages*. London: SCAA.

School Curriculum and Assessment Authority. 1997. *Managing the Programme of Study Part 1: Learning and Using the Target Language*. London: SCAA.

Stubbs, M. 1996. *Text and Corpus Analysis*. Oxford: Blackwell Publishers.

Utley, D., R. Mitchell and J. A. N. Phillips. 1983. *Hear/Say: A Review of Oral/Aural Graded Tests*. London: Methuen Educational.

Willett, J. 1995. Becoming first graders in an L2: An ethnographic study of L2 socialisation. *TESOL Quarterly* 29: 473–503.

18 Rendering ESL accountable: Educational and bureaucratic technologies in the Australian context

Helen Moore
University of Toronto

> *... power is not exercised by some agents who possess it for their own ends against other agents who lack it. Rather, the goals and exercise of power are effects of the deployment of those intellectual and political technologies that render reality calculable as an object of administration.*
>
> (Hunter, 1993: 182)

Introduction

Accountability has become a watchword in public sector enterprises. It is one of several themes – others being, for example, programme outcomes, cost efficiency, tax reform and small government – that are symptomatic of the late twentieth century loss of confidence in the state as a provider of services. Nowhere have demands for accountability become more strident than in education.

Macpherson (1998) notes that, in the British educational context, accountability was first defined in 1977 in terms of evaluating school performance by reference to student achievement (pp. 67–68). Using measures of student achievement in specific programmes and high-stakes examinations promises a straightforward way to monitor large and complex education systems. Where not entirely replacing other more interpersonal procedures such as inspection, it offers them a seemingly unproblematic investigative focus (Puscy 1981; Lingard 1990; Broadfoot 1996). In accounting for educational 'outcomes', student achievement measures are now central.

In this chapter, I will discuss the formation of a comprehensive curriculum, assessment and reporting framework used in the Adult Migrant English Program (henceforth the AMEP)[1] in Australia, namely *The Certificates in Spoken and Written English* (Hagan *et al.* n.d.; henceforth the CSWE). The AMEP provides English as a Second Language (henceforth ESL) courses for newly arrived adult immigrants in Australia.[2] The CSWE specifies the 'competencies' to be achieved within AMEP courses.[3] These competencies are elaborated in terms of their component elements, relevant criteria for evaluating performances, 'range' statements relating to contextual factors that affect performance (e.g. teacher support, resources that can be used), and sample tasks. Assessment is carried out by classroom teachers. It is criterion-referenced and performance-based (there are no standardised tests or examinations), on the assumption that this form of assessment provides indicators of outcomes that are 'relevant' to the 'real world' (Employment and Skills Formation Council 1992). These assessments are the basis for reporting to learners, employers and funding authorities on student achievement. Reports on the basis of the CSWE have become one of the main vehicles by which the AMEP is deemed by state authorities, teachers and possibly learners to be held accountable.

My interest here is not in the CSWE's assessment techniques or implementation (see, for example, Brindley 1994; Bottomley, Dalton and Corbel 1994; Burns and Hood 1994; Hagan 1994). Rather, I am concerned with developing an understanding of how this framework came to be adopted as a method of 'accounting' for ESL programmes, that is, in the words of the quotation heading this chapter, as a technology for rendering the AMEP 'calculable as an object of administration'. Following a sketch of some useful theoretical perspectives on accountability, my discussion will draw from interviews I conducted with people involved in the CSWE's development.[4]

Theoretical perspectives on educational accountability

Macpherson (1998: 68–69) reviews three influential contributions to the literature on accountability. Firstly, Becher (1979) has distinguished between five related forms of educational accountability: *moral* (answerability to clients), *professional* (responsibility to self and colleagues), *contractual* (accounting in terms of an employment contract), *political* (accounting to political masters) and *public* (accounting publicly in terms of the public interest). Secondly, Kogan's (1986) 'seminal analysis' identifies three main models of accountability – *public, professional* and *consumerist* – each proposing different 'partners', 'processes', and 'sources of criteria'. Lastly, Halstead (1994) differentiates between various approaches along two key dimensions of *contractual* and *responsive* accountability. Macpherson's review indicates that accountability is not at all straightforward, despite contrary assumptions by politicians. It allows us to recognise that there are multiple accountabilities. These give rise to both complementary and conflicting claims about who is accountable to whom and for what.

Using Halstead, Macpherson contrasts *contractual 'neo-centralist'* procedures enforcing school-based management with *responsive* approaches based on 'the encouragement, development and celebration of diverse problem-solving structures' ('pluriformity') coupled with 'collegiality and co-operative action between diverse member units for the common good' ('complementarity') (p. 70). This contrast underpins his investigation of parental attitudes in Tasmania, which demonstrates that although contractual procedures have been instituted in the name of accountability to parents, the actual preferences of most of the surveyed parents lie with responsive approaches. The study provides important evidence that claims about how the education system should be held accountable reflect – and disguise – relations of power between the claimants (for example, politicians or teachers) and those on whose behalf they purport to speak (for example, taxpayers, parents and students).

Broadfoot (1996) focuses on these power relations and particularly the ideologies that drive them. For her, accountability is 'the means by which the controlling interests in society monitor the operation of the education system as a whole and make it responsive to the needs of society, as they define them'(p. 56). She offers a compelling analysis of the social role of educational assessment in industrial societies, and its instantiation of scientific rationalism and technocratic instrumentalism. She argues that it is not legal or bureaucratic enforcement but rather 'the normative assumptions on which ... [professional] interaction is based that are the real source of power, albeit unremarked and unopposed, since they carry the power to determine selectively the way in which issues are discussed and solutions proposed' (p. 225). Broadfoot's focus on the way assumptions become normative provides a basis for understanding how the CSWE became a solution to the problem created by an assumption that accountability, educational outcomes and student achievement transparently represent each other. As a solution to the problem of how to 'account' for educational expenditures in terms of learning 'outcomes', the CSWE did not, and could not, question the assumption that learning can and should be accounted for in this way. It is part of what Smith (1990) calls an 'ideological circle' (pp. 93–100).

However, the case of the CSWE also demonstrates that ideological colonisation is not a one-way street from 'the controlling interests in society' (however nominated or defined) to educators. Moreover, although legal and bureaucratic enforcement was an important factor, it worked as much in complementary as oppositional fashion with educators' self-imposed standards. The quotation heading this paper, which draws from the work of Foucault, provides a means of probing how this was possible. It proposes that the power of 'the state' lies in specific 'intellectual and political technologies' employed to render domains of human activity 'calculable' as objects of administration. These technologies constitute what Foucault (1991) calls 'governmentality'. Governmentality – a play on the word 'government' and 'mentality' – is defined as an

> *ensemble formed by the institutions, procedures, analyses and reflections, the calculations and tactics that allow the exercise of this very specific albeit complex form of power, which has as its target population, as its principal form of knowledge political economy, and its essential technical means apparatuses of security.* (1991: 102)

The technologies of governmentality are not the exclusive property of state authorities. Rather, they are 'widely dispersed in social space – across medical, educational, insurantial, managerial, therapeutic, bureaucratic, ethical, fiscal sites – forming many local centres of calculation and intervention' (Hunter 1993: 182). Foucault rejects the search for particular agencies or sites as 'the real source of power', for example ruling classes or 'the state', and does not allow us to assume an essential opposition between bureaucratic and educational 'technologies' of governing. He opens up questions about the specific technologies used by different agencies in rendering particular realities accountable, arguing that their study should 'begin from a particular point in time', and that the focus should be how they '*reveal* their political usefulness and ... lend themselves to economic profit', and thus 'as a natural consequence, all of a sudden, they came to be colonised and maintained by global mechanisms and the entire State system' (1980, p. 101, my italics). In this chapter, my focus is the 'ensemble' of intellectual and political 'technologies' described by one of the authors of the CSWE and how their political usefulness became apparent to state authorities.

The context

The AMEP began with post-war mass immigration to Australia in 1949. In 1979, it was placed on a stable, triennially funded basis. Until approximately 1991, the AMEP's mandate was for almost all ESL provision for adults, including intensive ESL courses for newly arrived and long-term residents, specialist English for academic and professional purposes, English in workplace settings, a volunteer Home Tutor programme and correspondence courses. [5]

The programme is administered by a small designated section within the federal department responsible for immigration (henceforth Immigration).[6] Until 1997, the bulk of the programme was delivered through State/Territory level organisations, known as Adult Migrant English Services (henceforth AMES), the largest of which was in New South Wales. The stability of the AMEP funding and its specific focus generated a personally-based hierarchy of control that permitted responsiveness up and down the line (although this did not always occur) through day-to-day interactions, formal reporting, and professional meetings and conferences. As the 1980s progressed, a key component in Immigration's accountability mechanisms became a national information management system which, by the late 1980s, was computerised. Teaching centres entered data into a designated, centrally linked computer terminal. These reports allowed all students in the AMEP to be tracked according to entry and exit assessments (using the Australian Second Language Proficiency Rating Scale, Wylie and Ingram 1995; henceforth ASLPR), courses undertaken, and subsequent entry to employment or further education. The data base also included information on demographic and linguistic backgrounds, financial support, child-care arrangements, staff–student ratios, and costs per tuition hour (Sturgess 1996). It was probably the most comprehensive means of monitoring any educational endeavour, at any level, in the country, and the largest database of ESL learners in the world.

Now in its third edition (1st edn. 1992), the CSWE is one of many investments in professional development that also resulted from the programme's stability and focus. From the beginning of the 1980s, the AMEP has consistently set the pace for Australian adult and child ESL in teacher professionalism, classroom practices, and materials development.

Paradoxically however, the CSWE was developed in a climate that threatened the AMEP's stability and professional leadership. In 1983, a Labor government was elected that took as its pre-eminent goal – and definition of its own accountability as a government – restructuring the Australian economy to meet what it saw as the imperatives of global markets.[7] The economic restructuring agenda became the rationale, in 1987, for instituting a radical new ensemble of institutions, principles and procedures which made 'outcomes' (directed to economic restructuring) the central tenet by which accountability would be determined. The government's new vision of accountability required resetting directions for all sectors of education, as determined by specially appointed government committees (consisting of political, bureaucratic, union and industry representatives) and enforced through closer bureaucratic control. For post-school, non-university education, these committees designated the intellectual technology of 'competency-based training' as the key to educational reform, defined as focused on vocational 'outcomes', rather than 'inputs'; for example, what a person can do, rather than how long they spend in training (Employment and Skills Formation Council 1992: 8). A specific competency rubric was set in place by national accreditation procedures. Adherence to these procedures by 1995 became a precondition for course funding. Employment and career paths in a wide range of industries were formally tied to individuals' certification in accredited courses.

Initially the AMEP seemed insulated from these requirements by its guaranteed triennial funding, but from approximately 1991 onwards, they began to take effect. Space does not permit exploration of the arcane and complex interdepartmental and political processes that effectively destabilised the programme. Their key ingredients were 1) restriction of client eligibility for the AMEP to 510 hours in the first year after immigration for learners tested as being at beginner levels – these entitlements were enshrined in legislation; 2) reductions in immigration intakes and the imposition of English language requirements for some categories; 3) re-allocation of responsibility for the English in the Workplace programme to the federal Department of Employment Education and Training (henceforth DEET); 4) massive increases in DEET's funding for 'labour market training' for jobseekers, approximately $400 million of which was allocated to ESL programmes, thus placing the bulk of ESL provision within DEET-administered programmes; 5) distribution of DEET funds through short-term competitive contracting, open to anyone including AMEP providers, and awarded on the basis of 'cost efficiency', with a prerequisite being course accreditation.

In 1996, the incoming Liberal – National Party coalition abolished DEET's labour market training programmes. At the same time, separately contracted, on-the-job instruction modules begin to radically displace accredited curricula (of all kinds) – and hence professionalised teachers – in the post-school, non-university sector. Direct government-funded adult ESL provision in Australia remained only in the 510 hour programmes of the AMEP, which were protected by law.[8] In 1997, the AMEP was put out to competitive contract. The organisational unity and stability underpinning the programme's direction, synergy and professional leadership were replaced by a new governmental ensemble whose key technologies were centrally mandated curriculum and procedures to regulate competition between providers.

The conjunction of educational and bureaucratic technologies

The CSWE was developed by the professional development team of New South Wales AMES (henceforth NSW AMES) initially for use in that State but later, as we shall see, mandated by Immigration to be used nationally. The following narrative by one of its authors provides a description of both professional and political motivations for its development:

C: The timeline you have to consider with the development of the CSWE is really from 1988 with the National Curriculum Project ... because that was the beginnings of a fairly major shift in the dominant pedagogical approach. That was the beginning of the end of the strong progressive model of curriculum in adult ed., which was really no model at all, in fact [laughs]. ... It [= the National Curriculum Project] ... aimed to provide guidelines for teachers, to encourage them to actually set objectives, and program with particular profiles of learners in mind, and assess and so on. ... there was a kind of unwillingness to [pause] impose anything on the field, so it was a tentative move in a way, because teachers had been accustomed to having almost total autonomy in terms of what they did in their particular classroom, program and so on. So 1987 was the research year, when teachers nationally were encouraged to contribute descriptions of their course design process and so on. And then in 1988, teams of experienced teachers were pulled together to actually write up frameworks around particular profiles of students. As I said, the frameworks were presented as guidelines, very much standing back and saying 'We're not saying you're to do this, but here is an example of how you might go about programming for your students.' So there was a real push towards encouraging teachers to set objectives and it was really a professional development exercise in course design as well.

... the next big move was in 1989, when particularly people like ... Judy Colman[9] *were important in taking it another step, and saying 'Look, we've really got to get more systematic about what we're doing.' ... Initially, it was really just finding common ways of talking about who our students were, a sort of common language for description of students. ... And then 1990, in New South Wales AMES we had a project to begin to try and systematise it a bit further ...*

Then, with the opportunities to accredit curriculum and the National Training Board development of frameworks for competency-based curriculum –... [her boss] was actually really important there. There's often people who just seem to realise 'Hang on, there's an opportunity here' or this presents a way for us to position ourselves in a slightly more powerful or secure or whatever way. So there was a pedagogical kind of drive, which was towards more consistency, and actually addressing the need for some programming, the need for some sense of outcomes ... and then there was this policy change ...

So she and I sat down one day, and we had a model of a competency-based curriculum, which was something like pastry cooks ... It was probably the only one they had in print, making petits fours or something. So [laughs] she said 'Look, is there any way that – what we're thinking about in describing outcomes of stages – can we talk about it in these ways? can we fit into these kinds of frameworks?' ... And then that generated another project where a couple of experienced teachers were involved in spending a year putting it together.

H: So, at the time, what do you remember feeling?

C: Cautious [laughs].
H: Cautious.
C: Mm. I mean you could say well, OK, what we're [pause, sighs] – yes, very cautious. So you're always thinking, well hang on, how's this going to be interpreted, and how's it going to be read, and are we just, you know, are we, are we, um, yeah – I mean, how can I describe it? You're thinking are you doing a disservice to your profession, and are you reducing what you know language is to something artificial in some way. But ... we were always sure that what we were doing was fundamentally motivated by pedagogic concerns.[10]

This narrative provides a description of the technologies commonly used by educators to render the reality of their teaching governable. Their development within the AMEP was one aspect of the professionalisation of its teachers during the 1980s. Teachers were encouraged to develop syllabuses, some of which became national exemplars. Both the diversity and commonalities of these exemplars brought to light the need for 'common ways of talking about who our students are', which, in turn, generated a 'pathways' project to facilitate the sequential progression of learners through various AMEP courses, and thence into other post-school education and employment.

Organising teaching content appropriately for students, i.e. syllabus development, is seen by most teachers as central to the management of their teaching. For content to be appropriate, some form of student progression is necessary. Syllabuses and paths for student progression are arguably teaching's foundational technologies. Like many forms of governmentality, they provide a double-edged sword. On the one hand, they are constraining. On the other, they assist in producing an orderly and stable environment conducive to learning and creativity. Syllabuses and paths for student progression also require the co-operation – and/or regulation – of groups of teachers and their students. In the diffuse post-school, non-university sector, where this regulation is not performed by a localised institutional structure, and in which the AMEP was situated, it is arguable that the move to pathways inevitably entailed the bureaucratic technologies of course outcomes specifications and accreditation. Thus the state-mandated accreditation of competency-based training provided, as the speaker says, an important 'opportunity' – that is, a quite specific technology, including a powerful authorising mechanism – for the realisation of professional aspirations for improving the AMEP.

The CSWE is not, however, simply the product of an inevitable conjunction of educational and political-bureaucratic requirements. Its authors had very strategic and particular intellectual, administrative and material technologies that enabled them to respond to Labor's new regime of governmentality. Going back to the early 1980s – and with a history that ostensibly had nothing to do with competency-based training – the NSW professional development team had a strong commitment to, and were, to some extent, architects of so-called Australian 'genre theory'.[11] The speaker's dismissal of 'progressive' education reflects her highly critical stance towards 'natural' language development theories and the associated 'progressive' and 'process' approaches to teaching that had been widely adopted in Australia during the late 1970s and 1980s. In contrast, genre theory is predicated on an assumption of social constructionism and offers a highly developed intellectual technology for text description. As the speaker indicates, genre theory not only accommodated the content of the competency-based approach (a specification of language behaviours) and the directive teaching style it implies, but could also elaborate this approach in professionally sophisticated (although not universally accepted) ways.

Organisationally, the NSW structure reflected and complemented this intellectual orientation. Unlike the professional development team in its sister organisation in Victoria (the second largest AMES), whose energies were directed to stimulating diverse grass-roots teacher initiatives, the NSW group played a strong leadership role and were virtually able to mandate AMEP curriculum in the State. They also had a vigorous publications arm. Thus NSW AMES had both the organisational-political and material technologies to develop and deliver curriculum to meet the requirements of the new accreditation regime. Moreover, because AMES NSW were more autonomous within State-level educational structures than other State/Territory AMESes, they could act quickly. By the same token, the absence of wider protective institutional structures made them more vulnerable and acutely sensitive to threats to the AMEP.

Beyond NSW, the CSWE was not unanimously and immediately accepted by other AMEP teachers, many of whom did not favour genre theory or centralised curriculum development. However, the reductions to the AMEP in 1991 were seen as a substantive threat to employment. It was clear that DEET's short-term contracts (which, in any case, favoured accredited courses) were only a temporary respite. Resistance to the CSWE was negligible when teachers realised that it offered both a professionally credible and state-accredited avenue for the AMEP to accommodate the new governmentality quickly. Somewhat paradoxically, the strong grass-roots networks in Victoria were utilised to institute the CSWE as the standard curriculum throughout that State in the space of a year (Bottomley, Dalton and Corbel 1994), a move that was duplicated almost everywhere.

At the bureaucratic level, as we have seen, those managing the AMEP within Immigration faced problems arising from the new accountability regime. These problems, and the solution offered by the CSWE, were described by the responsible public servant as follows:

I: ... there was an expectation, as a result of the introduction of 510 hours, that our clients should all be able to get to functional English within 510 hours, and, of course, the disappointment started to emerge, that the AMEP, as a program, is set up to fail. How could you set a benchmark of functional English and only 17 per cent of your clients get there within the entitlement that they've got? ... And what we needed to do was try and recognise the gains that people were making in the AMEP, and the only way we could do that was to end up with a much more refined way of measuring outcomes. ... when you look at the structure of CSWE, and indeed other competency frameworks, it gives you the opportunity to look very closely at what clients achieve whilst they're in the program, in terms of competencies and certificates.

It was the CSWE's authors who took the initiative in demonstrating that the CSWE was not only compatible with Immigration's computer-based accountability system but allowed for its considerable refinement:

C: We set up the data-base and did some sample reports from a six month period. And ... [the responsible public servant] – like a light bulb went off. One of the things they'd always been concerned about is very low level students with minimal education not making any gains on the ASLPR. And so what they got from this data was how you could show progress, and you actually were talking about it in ways that made sense to people, ... and they could look at aggregating data which would actually show that the students had achieved certain competencies, modules, certificates, levels and so on. And that data could be broken down into learner profiles, years of education, etc. etc., language background, age and so on, all these reports show different ways in which students were progressing. So he basically took the decision that this was something they could work towards, so they developed the data base, and now teachers can report outcomes and it's all aggregated. So, they'll be reporting to Finance next year [1997] on the CSWE.

Recognition of the CSWE's potential led to the Immigration department specifying its use as a requirement in their 1997 contracts, and hence its national adoption as the basis of all AMEP curriculum and assessment – reflecting Foucault's (1991) picture of particular technologies revealing their usefulness, and their colonisation and maintenance by 'global mechanisms and the entire State system'. Research is now proceeding to specify 'benchmarks' for student achievements related to student types (e.g. age, ethnicity, education) within specific time frames, while other work is directed to improving quality control in teacher assessments (– both bearing out Foucault's description of 'the global functioning of ... *a society of normalisation*' 1980, 107, his italics). This dynamic indicates the CSWE's potency in bringing together an 'ensemble' of institutional, procedural and analytical technologies for the government of ESL teaching, teachers and learners.

Postscript and conclusion

Educators' responsiveness to political-bureaucratic accountability requirements does not necessarily ensure their personal survival. Ironically, NSW AMES failed to gain three of the five 1997 contracts for that State, the remainder of which were awarded to a private language organisation owned and operated by former AMEP and Immigration personnel.[12] Competitive contracting is liable to prove parasitic on individuals, groups and professional culture, rather than sustaining of them. As the dynamic of competitive contracting in conjunction with competency-based training plays itself out, its long-term effect is a new governmentality in which professional educators' culture of accountability is not simply colonised but is completely displaced by bureaucratic and hierarchical forms. The CSWE co-author's 'caution' above indicates her uneasy sense of this possibility.

These developments remind us that examples of an easy fit between educational and bureaucratic governmental technologies should not be taken as evidence for their homogeneity. Teaching is the reality which teachers seek to render 'calculable'. The economy and what Foucault (1991) calls 'population' are the realities on which state authorities are focused.

The CSWE is an example of how educational and political-administrative technologies can complement each other, despite the different realities they are designed to govern. As an educational technology of government, the CSWE is a syllabus, a method for regulating student progression, a research and development project, a theory and ideology, a professional development focus and a publication. Politically and administratively, it allows an increasingly detailed quantification of educational outcomes and the establishment of norms for state expenditures. As with most forms of governmentality, both advantages and disadvantages flow for those involved. Rendering ESL 'calculable as an object of administration' necessarily removes incentives for creativity and induces conformity. However, these calculations not only legitimate claims for resources by interested parties but can also authorise state authorities to grant them. Thus the accounts provided using the CSWE can be used to demonstrate the inadequacy of current adult

ESL provision, just as the legislated 510 hour tuition entitlement both limits and protects this provision.

In the development of the CSWE, we see an interplay of bureaucratic and professional governmentalities that created the conditions for the normalisation of outcomes-based accountability measures. The CSWE assumed these norms, and became a 'solution' to a situation that was born of them. Educational technologies anticipated and initiated ways forward for the bureaucratic hierarchy. The coercive ingredients in this situation did not generate resistance from teachers but rapid compliance. The power of the CSWE lies precisely in the way the different and differential powers of educators and bureaucrats complemented each other, and were harnessed to render the reality of the AMEP accountable.

Notes

1 A list of acronyms is provided as Appendix A.
2 Over the two-year period 1993–1994, 24,199 people undertook AMEP courses (Sturgess 1996: 24).
3 The CSWE began as a single certificate with four levels that are now separate certificates (the higher levels of which contain specialist strands for Vocational English, Further Study and Community Access). It is customary to speak of the whole scheme (pronounced 'the /sezwi/') in the singular. This convention will be maintained here.
4 My complete database consists of 50 interviews concerning five ESL curriculum and assessment projects, including the CSWE. Due to space limitations, the interview material cited here is confined to limited extracts from three informants. However, much of my analysis draws from other parts of these and other interviews. I am profoundly grateful for the generous gifts of time and insight my informants have given me. I also wish to thank Kari Delhi for suggesting that I look to the notion of 'governmentality' for an analytical approach and Don Plimer for valuable feedback.
5 Some universities and technical colleges also provided ESL support and courses from within their recurrent grants.
6 The actual names of the department have varied and reflect interesting shifts in 'governmentalities'. An early title was 'Labour and Immigration'. The 'employment' aspect of 'labour' was allocated to the Department of Employment, Education and Training in 1987. The department is currently called the Department of Immigration and Multicultural Affairs (DIMA) but for some of the time of the events narrated here was also called the Department of Immigration, Local Government and Ethnic Affairs (DILGEA).
7 Labour remained in office until 1996, when it was succeeded by the conservative Liberal – National Party coalition.

8 Other ESL classes could be funded from within institutions' (shrinking) recurrent grants. See note 5.
9 Colman (1991).
10 In presenting extracts from interviews, I have edited transcripts to include punctuation, and eliminate repetitions, grammatical infelicities and pauses unless these seemed to be significant. The conventions used are as follows:

...	material deleted.
italics	*emphasis by the speaker.*
[ ]	editorial comment from me.
=	speech interrupted.

11 Australian genre theory is derived from Halliday's model of systemic linguistics (Halliday 1985). Those developing and promoting it were Halliday's former students in Sydney University Linguistics Department.
12 This organisation had blossomed under DEET's labour market's programmes (as had also, to a lesser extent, the AMES's). The new contract saved approximately 300 teachers' jobs. AMES NSW lost approximately 350 teachers.

Appendix A

AMEP	Adult Migrant English Program (= the national program)
AMES	Adult Migrant Education Services (= State/Territory organisations that delivered the AMEP)
ASLPR	Australian Second Language Proficiency Rating (scale)
CSWE	Certificates in Spoken and Written English
ESL	English as a second language
DEET	Department of Employment, Education and Training
NSW	New South Wales

References

Becher, T. 1979. Self-accounting, evaluation and accountability. *Educational Analysis,* 1 (1): 63–5.

Bottomley, Y., J. Dalton and C. Corbel. 1994. *From Proficiency to Competencies*. Sydney, NCELTR: Macquarie University.

Brindley, G. 1994. Competency-based assessment in second language programs: Some issues and questions. *Prospect* 9 (2): 41–55.

Broadfoot, P. 1996. *Education, Assessment and Society: A Sociological Analysis*. Buckingham/Philadelphia: Open University Press.

Burns, A. and S. Hood. 1994. The competency-based curriculum in action: Investigating course design practices. *Prospect* 9 (2): 76–89.

Colman, J. 1991. Towards a coherent curriculum frame: Learner pathways in the NSW Adult Migrant English Service. *Prospect* 7 (1): 28–42.

Employment and Skills Formation Council, NBEET (L. Carmichael: Chair). 1992. *Australian Vocational Certificate Training System.* Canberra: Australian Government Publishing Service.

Foucault, M. 1980. Two lectures. In C. Gordon (ed.) *Power/Knowledge: Selected Interviews and Other Writings 1972–1977 Michel Foucault,* pp. 78–108. NY: Pantheon.

Foucault, M. 1991. Governmentality. In G. Burchell, C. Gordon and P. Miller (eds.) *The Foucault Effect: Studies in governmentality with two lectures by Michel Foucault,* pp. 87–104. Chicago, University of Chicago Press.

Hagan, P. 1994. Competency-based curriculum: The NSW AMES experience. *Prospect* 9 (2): 30–40.

Hagan, P., S. Hood, E. Jackson, M. Jones, H. Joyce and M. Manidis. n.d. *Certificates in Spoken and Written English I–II, III, IV.* (3rd edn.) 3 vols. Sydney: NSW Adult Migrant English Service.

Halliday, M. A. K. 1985. *An Introduction to Functional Grammar.* London: Edward Arnold.

Halstead, M. 1994. Accountability and values. In D. Scott (ed.) *Accountability and Control in Educational Settings*, pp. 146–65. London: Cassell.

Hunter, I. 1993. Personality as a vocation: The political rationality of the humanities. In M. Gane and T. Johnson (eds.) *Foucault's New Domains,* pp. 153–92. London and NY: Routledge.

Kogan, M. 1986. *Education Accountability: An Analytic Overview.* London: Hutchinson.

Lingard, B. 1990. Accountability and control: A sociological account of secondary school assessment in Queensland. *British Journal of the Sociology of Education* 13 (2): 171–88.

Macpherson, R. J. S. 1998. Contractual or responsive accountability? Neo-centralist 'self-management' or systemic subsidiarity? Tasmanian parents' and other stakeholders' policy preferences. *Australian Journal of Education* 42 (1): 66–89.

Pusey, M. 1981. The control of education in the 1980s. *Politics* 16: 223–4.

Smith, D. 1990. *The Conceptual Practices of Power: A Feminist Sociology of Knowledge.* Toronto: University of Toronto Press.

Sturgess, A. 1996. Commonwealth ESL arrangements and the Adult Migrant English Program. *Prospect* 11 (2): 15–27.

Wylie, E. and D. Ingram. 1995. *Australian Second Language Proficiency Ratings (ASLPR): General Proficiency Version For English.* (3rd edn.) Nathan, Queensland, Australia: Centre for Applied Linguistics (CALL), Griffith University.

19 The policy context of English testing for immigrants

John Read
Victoria University of Wellington

English-speaking countries have a long and often disreputable history of language policy making in their dealings with immigrants from non-English-speaking backgrounds. In the past a large proportion of these migrants worked hard in low-status jobs requiring limited if any proficiency in English in order to provide better educational and economic opportunities for their children and grandchildren. However, in recent years national immigration policies have shifted in favour of attracting successful, well-educated people who can apply their professional and entrepreneurial skills for the benefit of the host society. This raises the question of how to assess whether these new migrants have adequate proficiency in English to practise their profession or conduct their business.

Applied linguists – and language testers in particular – have become involved in initiatives to address the question, both as critics of inappropriate assessment procedures and as participants in testing projects. Cumming (1993) surveys various issues that have arisen in this area in Canada, but some of the most significant developments have occurred in Australia, including tests for foreign-trained health professionals (McNamara 1996: Chapter 4) and teachers (McDowell 1995). Another major Australian initiative in 1993 was the incorporation of mandatory English language assessment into the selection procedures for skilled migrants, by means of the specially commissioned Australian Assessment of Communicative English Skills, or **access:** test (Brindley and Wigglesworth 1997). Hawthorne (1997a, 1997b) outlines the political context in which the test was introduced and points out that, whatever technical merits it may have as a language test, any evaluation of its validity had to take account of its role as an instrument of the government's immigration policy.

The same applies in the case of a similar decision by the New Zealand Government in 1995 to require certain categories of migrants to take an English test before being admitted to the country. Rather than commissioning a test of their own or using the Australian one, the New Zealand Immigration

Service adopted the General Module of the International English Language Testing System (IELTS), the British-Australian test designed primarily to assess the proficiency of international students. The suitability of IELTS for use with immigration applicants is certainly an issue, but it needs to be considered in the broader context of the rationale for the English language requirement and the consequences for applicants who failed to achieve the minimum level in the test.

Background

The New Zealand immigration policy framework introduced in 1991 established two categories of targeted migrants: the General Skills category, for applicants with professional or technical skills and experience; and the Business Investor category, for those with a proven record in business and funds to invest in the country. The new policy led to a substantial influx of new migrants, especially from 1993 to 1995, when the country was experiencing strong economic growth. During that period the target number of immigrants was greatly exceeded, and the government initiated a policy review to better manage the flow of applications, to refine the mix of skills among migrants who were accepted, and to address concerns about the social and economic impact of the large numbers of new immigrants who had already arrived (New Zealand Immigration Service 1995: 4).

Thus in July 1995 the Minister of Immigration announced a package of policy changes, which were based on the assumption that New Zealand would continue to be an attractive destination for migrants and was in a position to select from a pool of well-educated, skilled and experienced applicants. Among the changes was the introduction of IELTS as the test which would determine whether applicants in the targeted categories had a minimum level of English proficiency, defined as Level 5 in the General Module. Principal applicants were required to pass the test in all four skills before arriving in New Zealand. Other members of the family (or 'non-principal applicants') aged 16 and over were also expected to achieve the same level. However, they could be admitted to the country without doing so, upon payment of a fee of NZ$20,000 each. The fee was refundable as follows:

1 A full refund would be given if IELTS Level 5 was achieved within three months of arrival.
2 The sum of $14,000 would be refunded if the required level was reached from three to twelve months after arrival.

After that, the full $20,000 was to be retained by the government. The official announcement stated that the fee was intended to act 'as an incentive for a person to rapidly acquire basic English language skills' (New Zealand Immigration Service 1995: 10).

After the policy changes were announced, the English proficiency requirement was the main focus of public debate. There were really two interconnected issues: the suitability of the IELTS test, and the justification for imposing such a large fee. Let us consider each of these in turn.

The suitability of IELTS

The first question is why IELTS was selected as the official proficiency measure. One point worth noting initially is that the adoption of a professionally developed language test represented a significant advance over previous practice. Until 1995, only principal applicants were assessed for English proficiency and this was done by means of an interview with an immigration officer to determine whether the applicant had a level of English comprehension equivalent to that of an eleven-year-old New Zealand child. It was obvious that some more appropriate assessment of language proficiency was required.

The Minister of Immigration's (1995) paper to the Cabinet on the policy changes reveals that three options were considered. One was to develop a New Zealand equivalent to the Australian **access:** test, the second was to adopt **access:** itself and the third option was to choose IELTS. The first two were ruled out largely on the basis of cost. The Australian Department of Immigration and Ethnic Affairs (as it then was) indicated that, if its New Zealand counterpart were to opt for **access:**, it would charge 'a contribution to development costs of A$4M and/or a royalty payment' (Minister of Immigration 1995: 2, fn 2) for the use of the test. This also reflected how much a separate New Zealand test would have cost, assuming it were to be adequately funded. The Cabinet paper makes it clear that a major thrust of the 1995 policy review was to contain the costs of providing ESOL tuition and unemployment benefits to migrants with limited English. Thus, the choice of IELTS was attractive, because the Management Board of IELTS indicated that it would not seek any payment from the New Zealand Government. The testing costs would in effect be borne by individual applicants through the fee they paid to the local centre for taking the test.[1]

Since IELTS was little known in New Zealand when the policy changes were announced, much of the early public comment on the English requirement centred on the nature of the test. There was understandable confusion between the Academic and General Modules of IELTS and a general uncertainty about what Level 5 represented in terms of functional language skills. Initially, the minister and his agency tended to quote the official descriptor for Level 5:

5 MODEST USER

Has partial command of the language, coping with overall meaning in most situations, though is likely to make many mistakes. Should be able to handle basic communication in own field.

(The IELTS Handbook 1998: 18)

Later, copies of the IELTS specimen materials pack were distributed to the news media and one journalist conducted an informal trial of the specimen reading test with native-speaking students in three Wellington secondary schools (Swain 1995). From a language testing perspective, these were obviously unsatisfactory ways to demonstrate test validity. Since the adoption of IELTS for testing migrants represented a distinctly different use of the test, it should have been properly re-validated to establish its appropriateness for the new purpose (cf. Bachman 1990: 70–71; Read 1991).

The cabinet paper quoted above shows that more steps were taken than were revealed at the time of the public announcement. The New Zealand immigration office in Bonn, Germany, had conducted a trial of IELTS involving 400 applicants from the former Yugoslavia and the Middle East, 90 per cent of whom achieved at least Level 5 in the General Module. The trial apparently satisfied the Immigration Service that IELTS Level 5 was an appropriately 'modest' level, similar to the standard expected by immigration officials in their existing interview procedure. The paper also noted that a comparison of the General Module of IELTS and **access:** showed there were many similarities between the two tests. In addition, the Ministry of Education had provided an 'assessment' of IELTS and other English language tests.

Thus, the publicly available evidence for the validity of IELTS for immigration purposes fell short of what language testers would consider an adequate standard, but further discussion of its validity from a technical point of view is beyond the scope of this chapter.

The justification for the fee

The reality is that judgements of the quality of the test as a proficiency measure were overshadowed by its broader social impact, in the context of the policy which imposed a $20,000 fee for failure to pass the test and a twelve-month deadline to qualify for at least a partial refund. As noted earlier, the official rationale for the imposition of the fee was to give incoming migrants a strong incentive to acquire English quickly.

The Minister's Cabinet paper reveals an interesting difference between the Immigration Service and other government agencies on the issue of when adult family members other than the principal applicant should meet the English requirement (Minister of Immigration 1995: 3). The Immigration

Service considered that the required standard should be reached before migrants were allowed to enter the country in order to reduce the risk that they would be unemployable and dependent on the social welfare system for support in their early years of residence. However, both the Treasury and the Ethnic Affairs Service took the view that this requirement would be unduly restrictive. They considered that lack of English proficiency should not in itself be a basis for excluding people who would otherwise be desirable migrants. Thus, Treasury recommended that such applicants be allowed to enter the country upon payment of a bond, which would be refundable if the required level of English proficiency was achieved within a specified period.

This view prevailed and thus the $20,000 fee was instituted as part of the 1995 policy changes. It is instructive to compare the New Zealand provision with a similar charge paid by immigrants to Australia who do not achieve what is defined as 'functional English' before their arrival. First, the maximum Australian fee in 1998 was A$4,485 (Department of Immigration and Multicultural Affairs (DIMA) 1998), which was about a quarter of the New Zealand one. Secondly, it was explicitly linked to the provision of English classes in the Australian Migrant Education Program (AMEP). Migrants were entitled to as many as 510 hours of tuition to assist them to achieve the functional level of English proficiency (Hawthorne 1997a: 15). By contrast, the payment of the New Zealand fee did not give any comparable entitlement to English teaching and, at the time the policy changes were first announced, the Minister of Immigration was reported as saying that there were no plans to invest the fee revenue in English language programmes (Boyd 1995). His department continued to view the fee simply as a financial incentive for applicants to learn the language before they came to New Zealand.

In fact, though, the new English language requirement had quite different effects from the ones intended. First, it deterred potential applicants from even applying to migrate to New Zealand, judging by the fact that the number of approved applications in the targeted categories declined from 40,272 in the year ending June 1996 to 17,420 in the following year (New Zealand Immigration Service 1997: 2). On the other hand, a significant number of adult migrants entered the country without having achieved Level 5 on IELTS. ESOL teachers and IELTS examiners observed firsthand the stress that many of these new immigrants experienced as they struggled to improve their English and pass the test before the twelve-month deadline, in order to qualify for a refund of the fee. Sympathetic accounts of their plight also appeared in the news media. Adding to the stress was the fact that the migrants were required to achieve Level 5 in all four skills rather than simply in the averaged overall score and had to repeat the whole IELTS test each time they attempted it.

From the perspective of these new immigrants, the issue was how feasible it was for them to go from limited or no English ability to Level 5 on IELTS within one year of arrival. The Treasury officials who recommended the fee mechanism envisaged that such migrants would be strongly motivated learners with a high level of language learning aptitude (Minister of Immigration 1995: 3). While motivation and aptitude are undoubtedly factors in successful language acquisition, applied linguists are well aware that motivation involves more than just having a monetary incentive and that other affective variables play a very significant role. Migration is a stressful experience even for those who are proficient in the language of the host country and new migrants can face all kinds of problems in adjusting to a new society and culture. In this respect, the carrot-and-stick strategy adopted in New Zealand contrasted with the Australian approach, as revealed in this excerpt from a pamphlet on English learning opportunities for new migrants to Australia:

> *If you don't want to start going to classes or doing distance learning straight away, that's OK. Maybe you or a family member are ill, you have small children to care for or you have to go to work. It's still important to register [for the AMEP]. Just explain why you want to delay your learning.* (DIMA 1997)

The feasibility of achieving IELTS Level 5 in a short time depended on migrants' prior opportunities to acquire English. Applicants could be exempted from taking IELTS if they had received all or part of their education through the medium of English. Thus, native speakers had an obvious advantage, as did those educated in places like Singapore, India and Hong Kong. On the other hand, passing IELTS represented quite a hurdle for citizens of South Korea, Taiwan and China, which have been significant sources of New Zealand immigrants in this decade. The issue was a sensitive one in the Chinese community in particular because New Zealand – like Australia – has a history of xenophobic legislation to discourage the entry of Chinese immigrants (New Zealand Official Yearbook 1990: 188). Chinese community leaders described the English requirement as discriminatory and insulting.

Some potential migrants from East Asia were in a better position to meet the English requirement than others. Principal applicants in the General Skills category were likely to have studied English up to university level, used English language reference materials in their work and perhaps obtained a postgraduate qualification in an English-speaking country. However, their spouses and other adult members of their families might have had none of these opportunities to acquire the language. And applicants in the Business

Investor category often had quite a different educational background from General Skills migrants. Professor Kuan Goh, a Chinese community leader in Christchurch, pointed out that many successful business people in Asia left school at the age of 14 or 15 without achieving any significant competence in English and owed their success to hard work and a wealth of practical experience. It was unrealistic to expect them and their spouses to be able to achieve even the 'modest' level of proficiency required for immigration within a limited period of learning time (Goh 1996). This view was supported by a big decline in the number of business migrants accepted, from more than 500 in 1995 to just 63 in the first nine months of 1997 (Young 1997).

By the end of 1997, the government recognised that the English language requirement was having a negative effect, particularly on potential Business Investor applicants and, as an interim measure, the standard required for migrants in this category was reduced to Level 4 in IELTS. Then in October 1998 the Minister of Immigration announced an overhaul of the immigration policy, including the abolition of the $20,000 fee. In his press release, he acknowledged that the fee had not worked as intended: of 184 migrants who had paid it in 1996/97, 101 had forfeited the entire amount by not passing the test within twelve months. The fee was to be replaced by a system of 'pre-purchased English language training'. Principal Business applicants and non-principal applicants in both categories who had not reached the required level in IELTS could be admitted by paying an amount ranging from NZ$1,700 to NZ$6,650, which would entitle them to ESOL tuition over a period of about three years after they entered the country.

Conclusion

Much of the controversy surrounding recent New Zealand immigration policy has focused on 'the English test'. There are questions which can be raised about the validity of Level 4 or 5 in the General Module of IELTS as a measure of whether new and intending migrants have achieved a threshold level of proficiency in English. However, criticisms of the test have been strongly coloured by its role in the overall policy and the consequences for individual applicants of failing to achieve the required standard. Therefore, it was unrealistic to try to evaluate the test without considering the validity of the assumptions on which its introduction was based and the discriminatory effects on non-English-speaking applicants of being required to pass it.

The English requirement, and the $20,000 fee in particular, gave a clear message to non-English-speaking migrants that becoming at least 'modestly' proficient in English was their private affair and they were not really welcome in New Zealand until they had achieved it. Far from acting as an incentive, the fee contributed to a continuing drop in the number of applicants. Thus, in order to reverse the decline, the government was obliged to take a more realistic view of the language background of potential migrants and the time it would take them to acquire a working knowledge of English. It remains to be seen whether the most recent policy changes will improve the country's attractiveness as a place to settle and allow the government to reach its immigration targets once again.

Acknowledgement

I wish to express my appreciation to Alison Hoffmann for her encouragement and assistance, particularly in providing me with a copy of the Minister of Immigration's 1995 Cabinet Committee paper.

Note

1 In 1998 the Australian Department of Immigration and Multicultural Affairs terminated the **access:** programme and switched to IELTS as the test to assess the proficiency of immigration applicants. Thus, in retrospect, the New Zealand decision to adopt IELTS three years earlier can be seen as a realistic one, given this evidence of the difficulty of sustaining a worldwide specific-purpose testing programme on a long-term basis.

References

Bachman, L. F. 1990. *Fundamental Considerations in Language Testing.* Oxford: Oxford University Press.

Boyd, S. 1995. Migrants to face tougher entry laws. *The Evening Post.* Wellington: 20 July.

Brindley, G. and G. Wigglesworth (eds.) 1997. ***access:*** *Issues in Language Test Design and Delivery.* Sydney: NCELTR.

Cumming, A. 1993. Criteria, issues, and developments in language assessment for recent immigrants to Canada. Paper presented at AILA, Amsterdam.

DIMA. (Department of Immigration and Multicultural Affairs). 1997. *Learning English in Australia – Adult Migrant Education Program (AMEP).* Form 1064i. URL: <www.immi.gov.au/allforms/pdf/1064i.pdf>

DIMA. 1998. *Charges–July 1998.* Form 990i. URL: <www.immi.gov.au/allforms/pdf/990i.pdf>

Goh, K. M. 1996. English-language test for Asian migrants — Have we got it right? *The Press.* Christchurch: 11 September.

Hawthorne, L. 1997a. English language testing and immigration policy. In Brindley and Wigglesworth (eds.).

Hawthorne, L. 1997b. The political dimension of English language testing in Australia. *Language Testing* 14: 248–60.

McDowell, C. 1995. Assessing the language proficiency of overseas-qualified teachers: The English language skills assessment (ELSA). In G. Brindley (ed.), *Language Assessment in Action*. Sydney: NCELTR.

McNamara, T. F. 1996. *Measuring Second Language Performance*. London: Addison Wesley/Longman.

Minister of Immigration. 1995. Adjustment to 'targeted' immigration policy: The General Category. Paper CIE (95) 49 for the New Zealand Cabinet Committee on Enterprise, Industry and Environment: March. [Released under the Official Information Act.]

New Zealand Immigration Service. 1995. *New Zealand's Targeted Immigration Policies: Summary of October 1995 Policy Changes*. Wellington: NZ Immigration Service.

New Zealand Immigration Service. 1997. *Background Questions and Answers*. URL: <www.immigration.govt.nz/about/announcements>, 19 December.

New Zealand Official Yearbook. 1990. Wellington: Department of Statistics.

Read, J. 1991. Response to A. Olde-Kalter and P. Vossen: *EUROCERT: An International Standard for Certification of Language Proficiency*. In J. H. A. L. de Jong (ed.), *Standardization in Language Testing*, pp. 106–7. (AILA Review, No. 7). Amsterdam: Free University Press.

Swain, P. 1995. Immigrants' English test no problem for third formers. *The Evening Post*. Wellington: 5 August.

The IELTS Handbook. 1998. Cambridge: University of Cambridge Local Examinations Syndicate.

Young, A. 1997. Bradford opens up to investors. *New Zealand Herald*. Auckland: 20 December.

20 Testimony from testees: The case against current language policies in sub-Saharan Africa[1]

Eddie Williams
University of Reading

Introduction

In most sub-Saharan African countries two important political objectives have, since the 1960s, been national unification and modernisation. One arena where governments have attempted to implement these objectives has been that of the public education system. Considerable evidence now suggests, however, that the policies of using English (or other ex-colonial languages) as a medium of instruction have been counterproductive as regards unification and modernisation. The evidence in this paper is provided by test results from Malawi and Zambia, but the state of affairs revealed is representative of many other sub-Saharan countries. However, governments generally ignore test results because of the political imperatives, and blame falls upon the teachers and pupils, rather than the policy. The paper briefly reviews previous research, then describes the country background and the present research, and finally discusses the findings against the framework of the political objectives.

Research on the effect of the medium of instruction on educational achievement does not, at first sight, present a consistent picture. In the USA, for example, Cummins (1979) claims that instruction in L2 of minority language children has resulted in poor academic achievement, while Skutnabb-Kangas (1981) makes the same claim for Europe. Counter-evidence from French immersion programmes in Canada is not entirely convincing. They are successful primarily in that immersion pupils perform as well as their English peers (in English medium education) in content subjects, while outperforming them in French. However, a number of studies (cited in Cummins and Swain 1986: 45) indicate clearly that their productive capacity in French is below that of their French peers. Furthermore, the content tests were 'typically administered in English' (ibid: 38). Further counter-evidence (Wagner, Spratt and Ezzaki 1989) from Morocco, consists of the finding that, although at year 1, Arabic L1 children scored higher on an Arabic reading test than Berber L1 children, 'such differences virtually disappeared by year 5' (ibid: 31). Apart from the fact that five years is a long time, another crucial factor is that the Berber speakers were improving their Arabic 'daily' through interaction with their peers. It need hardly be pointed out that the situation for the majority of schoolchildren in sub-Saharan Africa is very different from those obtaining in these Canadian and Moroccan cases.

Research data from Africa on the problems occasioned by the dominance of English as a medium of instruction has long indicated cause for concern. Criper and Dodd (1984, cited in Yahya-Othman 1989: 49) report that of 2,419 pupils tested in Tanzania 'at all levels of the educational system, only 29% had attained a level for easily following studies at their respective levels'. In Zambia, Sharma (1973) administered an English reading recognition test to 3,298 year 3 pupils, using a list of 40 words from the year 1 to 3 coursebooks. He found that only 7.2 per cent could read all the year 1 and 2 words correctly and 5.36 per cent could not read a single word. While the validity of the investigative instrument is debatable, the findings are suggestive. Chikalanga (1990: 69) reports the conclusion of another 1973 Zambian study of 583 pupils at year 5, namely that 'there is a large group of very poor readers in most classes and they are unlikely to be able to cope with the English course ... nor be able to do much of the work in other subjects'. A Zambian review found in 1992 that 'Too early an emphasis on learning through English means that the majority of children form hazy and indistinct concepts in language, mathematics, science, and social studies. A number of studies show that children's subsequent learning has been impaired by this policy' (Ministry of Education 1992: 28). For Malawi, there seems to be no published research in this field prior to the present work, although informal reports suggested there were similar difficulties. The research reported in this paper was therefore prompted by the need for a recent assessment of pupils in both countries in order to see whether such concerns were justified.

Country background

Malawi and Zambia are southern African countries, with a common border, and shared historical backgrounds, both gaining independence from Britain in the 1960s. Both countries are predominantly rural, and economically weak. Zambia has 'slightly over 20 more or less mutually unintelligible clusters of "languages", (Kashoki 1990: 109). Seven languages are officially designated as subjects to be studied in schools. The proportion of speakers of these (L1 and L2) is estimated (Kashoki 1990: 117) to be:[2]

Table 20.1
Distribution of seven Zambian languages

	Bemba	Kaonde	Lozi	Lunda	Luvale	Nyanja	Tonga
L1:	30.8%	3.4%	9.3%	2.9%	5.9%	16.0%	16.1%
L1+L2:	56.2%	7.1%	17.2%	5.3%	8.1%	42.1%	23.2%

Estimates of the number of indigenous language varieties in Malawi vary. Sichinga (1994) estimates the distribution of the three principal languages as follows:

Table 20.2
Distribution of three Malawian languages

	ChiChewa	**Chiyao**	**Chitumbuka**	**Others**
L1:	27%	19%	11%	43%
L1+2:	80%	20%	15%	not available

ChiChewa and Nyanja are different labels – which came about for historical and political reasons – for what is essentially the 'same' language (Kishindo 1990: 59), with minor variations in spelling and lexis.

Primary education in Zambia is free and consists of a seven year programme available to all children between the ages of seven and fourteen. English is, officially the language of instruction in primary education from year 1 for all subjects apart from spiritual instruction and one of the seven local languages. There are eight years of primary schooling in Malawi, with children officially starting at age six.[3] The language of instruction for the first four years is ChiChewa, with English as a subject;[4] for the last four years English becomes the language of instruction, and ChiChewa a subject.

Data sources

The quantitative data for this paper are the results of reading tests in English and local languages; qualitative data are from discussion and reading investigation sessions with selected testees, carried out in the local languages.

For all three languages (English, ChiChewa, Nyanja) modified cloze tests were used, with four or six deletions per paragraph, and the appropriate words (plus two additional 'dummies') supplied in a box above each paragraph.[5] All three versions had a total of thirty deletions. Both local language tests were taken from the same Zambian school text with the Malawian version very slightly modified in terms of spelling and lexis. For the reading investigation sessions an English passage (119 words) was concocted using language from year 4.[6] The local language reading investigation passage (71 words) for both Malawi and Zambia was taken from the year 5 Zambian coursebook.

In each country test data were collected from year 5 pupils in four rural schools and two urban schools. Year 5 is when Malawi switches to English medium, and where any inter-country differences might be maximised. A total of 290 pupils were tested in Malawi, and 227 in Zambia. All the children claimed to be able to speak ChiChewa and Nyanja respectively,[7] and the investigations were carried out in areas where these were the predominant local languages.

Data for the discussion and reading investigation sessions[8] come from 24 pupils in each country, 12 high-scoring, and 12 low-scoring, with girls and boys selected from each of the six schools. High- and low-scoring groups (based on English test results) were established relatively, not absolutely, for each school. The high scorers' range was 13–30 in Malawi, and 19–30 in Zambia, with the low scorers' range 3–9, and 0–8 respectively.

Findings for English

The cloze tests each had a maximum score of 30 points; descriptive statistics[9] are:

Table 20.3
Results of English reading test for Malawi and Zambia

	N	Mean	SD	Max	Median	Min
Malawi	290	12.84	6.22	30	12	1
Zambia	227	11.72	9.48	30	8	0

The means are very slightly in favour of Malawi, but not at a statistically significant level, and suggest that there is no difference in reading ability in English between children in Zambia and children in Malawi. It seems that Zambian children who have officially had the first four years of education through the medium of English are not superior to Malawian children who have officially had ChiChewa as a medium of instruction for those years.

English reading investigation sessions

During the structured discussions with the Zambian testees that preceded the reading, eight out of 12 high scorers in Zambia reported they generally had difficulties in reading English; four reported no difficulty (two of whom scored the maximum of 30). When asked to read the English text, eight of the

Zambian low scorers could not read the English or Nyanja text, and were replaced. (Seven of the eight scored on the English test at or below the chance score of four; this melancholy figure at least serves to provide a degree of concurrent validation to the results.)

In Malawi, nine out of 12 high scorers reported that they generally found reading English difficult, and ten out of 12 low scorers. For both sets of testees, the reading investigation confirmed that most had some difficulty, and some severe difficulty, with low scorers unable to understand words that had been prejudged to be familiar, e.g. *sister, thirsty, everything, surprised.*

Implications for learning through the medium of English

The mean test score of approximately 12 out of 30 for both countries is not high, given that the test language was drawn from coursebooks at year 4 and below. It is difficult to see how the majority of these pupils could be learning through reading in English as prescribed in both countries from year 5 onwards. To extrapolate from these test scores to estimates of comprehension in content areas is problematic (c.f. Cummins and Swain 1986: 18). However, a reasonably generous view is that a score of 10 or less out of 30 is likely to be below the threshold: 56.4 per cent of Zambians were in this position, and 41.4 per cent of Malawians. Further, given that the test texts were taken from year 4 and below, then this conclusion certainly underestimates the percentage of year 5 pupils who cannot read adequately at their level.

A more accurate estimate is probably provided from similar cloze tests reported in Williams (1993), where subtests specifically targeted year 6 in 5 schools in each country. In Malawi the proportion of year 6 pupils not considered capable of reading adequately in English (a score of 7 or less on a 20 item subtest) was 78 per cent (N=158) and in Zambia 74 per cent (N=153). The latter proportion is remarkably close to the conclusion of the IIEP[10] (1996 Chapter 6: 15) that the percentage of year 6 Zambian pupils failing to reach 'the minimum level of mastery on the reading test' is about 74.2 per cent. These figures suggest that large numbers of pupils cannot adequately comprehend their English coursebooks, and almost certainly cannot understand their content subject coursebooks either (c.f. Chick 1992: 33 for South Africa).

In addition to the generally low levels of English reading, further analysis of the year 5 test scores also reveals the following differences between rural and urban children:

Table 20.4
English test means for Malawi and Zambia by location

	Malawi	N	Zambia	N
Rural	11.43	184	8.46	133
Urban	15.29	106	16.33	94

In Malawi and Zambia there are clear differences (over 3 and 7 points respectively) in favour of urban schools which just fail to achieve statistical significance ($p>0.05$).[11] However, when the data sets from the two countries are combined, the location effect is significant ($p < 0.02$). Furthermore, in Zambia the distribution of English test scores for all children displays a U-shape with low rural scores skewed towards the left, and high urban scores towards the right.

Findings for local languages

The test results on the local language modified cloze tests were:

Table 20.5
Results of local language reading tests for Malawi and Zambia

	N	Mean	SD	Max	Median	Min
Malawi	290	19.88	5.44	30	20.5	4
Zambia	227	4.4	3.70	22	3	0

The most striking feature is the superior performance of the Malawian children. In fact, the overall mean for Zambia is just above the chance level of 4. The results suggest that Malawian children read better in ChiChewa than Zambian children read in Nyanja. To obviate any suggestion that the Malawian version was easier, two Malawian schools also took the Zambian version of the test, achieving a mean of 18.66, very close to that which they achieved in the Malawian version.

Analysis of local language results by location reveals, for Malawi, an interesting contrast with English:

Table 20.6
Local language means for Malawi and Zambia by location

	Malawi	N	Zambia	N
Rural	19.43	184	3.68	133
Urban	20.65	106	5.41	94

The Malawi ChiChewa test results show much smaller differences with respect to location than do the English tests.[12] English seems to discriminate more against rural pupils than does ChiChewa, probably because both rural and urban children are exposed to ChiChewa in their social environments and so acquire it in roughly equal measure; English on the other hand is more available in urban environments. This issue does not arise for Zambia, for Nyanja means are again close to chance.

Local language reading investigation sessions

Of the 24 Malawian pupils selected, two chose to read the text silently, while the remainder read aloud. All these pupils read fluently with occasional deviances which were judged to be performance slips. Questions were handled with no difficulty; there was less hesitation, and almost every answer was acceptable. As a result, the researchers were confident that the text had been processed with understanding. In short, the individual sessions confirmed the test findings that most pupils (including those who were 'low-scoring' on the English test results) appeared to be competent readers of ChiChewa.

By contrast, the most striking feature of the Zambian pupils attempting the Nyanja passage was the very large proportion who said they were unable to read it, or who tried to read it and failed (on a text, furthermore, drawn from their own textbook). In the high-scoring group five out of 12 pupils either could not, or did not want to, read the Nyanja text aloud, while the same was true of all 12 low-scoring pupils. The general impression of the researchers concerning the seven pupils who managed to read the Nyanja text is that two had only a very general idea of what the text was about, while five appeared to have a reasonable comprehension, although they had difficulties with some individual words. Again the reading sessions confirm the test results of very low competence in reading Nyanja. Their poor overall performance in reading it is probably due the variety of Nyanja used in the text, and also lack of exposure to written Nyanja.

The variety of Nyanja in which Zambian children are competent is 'town Nyanja' (see Kashoki 1990: 137), a non-standard variety characterised by borrowings from English as well as other Zambian languages. The 'standard Nyanja' of the Zambian language coursebooks is a different variety, based on Malawian ChiChewa, which is generally regarded as a 'purer' form.[13] Zambian pupils are well aware of the differences between 'town Nyanja' and 'standard Nyanja', with one pupil commenting, '*When we are told to write, we are given different things, things that are spoken by other people, and not the Nyanja we speak.*' (Italics in transcriptions indicate translation from Nyanja.)

The probable reason for Malawian pupils' local language superiority is that ChiChewa is used as the language of instruction for the first four years. Malawian pupils are thus accustomed to seeing ChiChewa in written form. Zambian pupils on the other hand rarely see their local language in written form. Not only are Zambian languages not used as media of instruction, they are also neglected as subjects in primary school teaching, since they 'do not contribute in any way to the overall mark for secondary selection' (Ministry of Education 1992: 45). This neglect is also borne out by pupil comments such as: 'We sometimes do Nyanja, but it was a long time ago. We did it from time to time unless [sic] English, we learn English every day.'

Conclusion

The low levels of English reading proficiency revealed in this research suggest that the policy of using the language at primary level as a medium is highly questionable. However, people in both countries are enthusiastic about their politicians' prescriptions: although it may well be that they are victims of hegemony in their insistence on English, the question is 'what can we do about it?' (Davies 1996: 491). Families see primary school English as the first step towards the coveted white-collar job, which, although statistically unlikely, is a more realistic option than waiting on the demise of the global economic and intellectual empire of English-using institutions. However, one policy modification, especially for countries like Zambia, would be to reduce the role of English as a medium of instruction at primary level, in favour of the main local languages. (Recall that Malawian pupils' superiority in local language reading has not resulted in a lower performance in English; conversely, Zambia's focus on English to the virtual exclusion of the local languages has not paid off in terms of gains in English.) Political imperatives would still require English as a subject, but such a policy modification might be socially acceptable and educationally beneficial.

Family enthusiasm for English in the hope of enhancing children's individual mobility coincides with the politicians' choice of English to achieve unity and modernisation. Nevertheless, the dominance of English in schools has not been an unqualified success for these aims. As concerns unification, while English may have succeeded in preventing conflict between rival language groups, it has created division between those groups who have reasonable access to English, typically members of the relatively well-off urban classes, and those groups who do not, typically the members of poor rural classes. The test results for Zambia in particular, indicate national division, not unity. That the use of English, and not simply inequity in general education provision, is a factor is suggested by very large differences in Malawi for English scores, but very small differences for ChiChewa scores, between the rural and urban children.

As far as modernisation of the nation is concerned, one assumes this will be dependent upon a significant proportion of educated citizens. Here the use of English in primary schools is a double-edged sword: it is indeed educating a minority of individual pupils, but the majority who fail to acquire adequate competence continue their English-medium education in a miasma of incomprehension, and without comprehension there can be little development of academic skills. There is thus a danger that school is a stultifying, rather than an enlightening experience, exemplified by the eight Zambian pupils who could not read in any language. Again the Malawi results support the commonsense point that literacy in a known local language is relatively easier to achieve under the difficult circumstances currently prevailing. To the objection that there are few Nyanja books for Zambians to read and learn from, one can only respond that until more people become literate in it, this will continue to be the case, and also that these test results suggest there is little learning going on in English either. Further, if the concept of modernisation covers quality of life, then there is evidence that local language literacy yields benefits in health and fertility (Hobcraft 1993) and productivity (Moock and Addou 1994).

The situation concerning language in education in most sub-Saharan countries is complex. Solutions, because of social and economic tensions, are likely to be partial and slow, and it does not behove outsiders to be too glib in their views. However, if there is to be any progress towards the goal of education for all, then policy makers first need to acknowledge the testimony of their own children on the negative effects of current policies.

Notes

1 I am grateful to the UK Department of International Development for funding the research which this paper draws on. Invaluable help in collecting local language data came from: Hannock Mateche, Rosemary Mkumba, Benson Zigona (Malawi); Israel Chikalanga, Bridget Chipimo, Catherine Nakaanga, Martin Phiri (Zambia). My thanks to James Cooke for helpful comments on an early draft.

2 This paper follows Zambian English practice of omitting language prefixes (Chi-, Ici-, Si-, etc.) when discussing Zambia, and Malawian English practice of including them when discussing Malawi.

3 Until 1994 children paid school fees which never amounted to more than US$3 per year. From 1995 free primary education was instituted.

4 The time allocation for English at the time of this research was 5 x 30 minutes in years 1 and 2, rising to 7 x 30 minutes in years 3 and 4.

5 This format was selected from others after piloting, as by far the most pupil-friendly, and corresponding to exercises done in class. See Williams (1996) for further discussion.

6 It included five non-crucial lexical items judged to be difficult.

7 18% of the Malawian testees spoke a language other than ChiChewa at home, and 46% of the Zambians a language other than Nyanja. Test results showed a very small statistically non significant difference in favour of those who spoke the test language at home.

8 In order to help put pupils at their ease in the structured discussion and reading investigation sessions (held as a single session of 15 to 30 minutes), individuals chose two friends to accompany them and to join in the sessions.

9 Statistical analyses were performed by the Applied Statistics Department at Reading University, using the SAS package. Significance level is 0.05. The internal reliability of the tests (KR-21) varied from 0.75 to 0.95.

10 The International Institute for Educational Planning (IIEP) and the Zambian Ministry of Education conclusions result from a sample of 2,558 pupils in 157 schools nation-wide.

11 The statistician's written comment was 'It seems likely that a location effect is present in both countries, but that the small number of schools [in each country] prevents this being detected' (Department of Applied Statistics, Reading University, 1995).

12 In Malawi English also discriminates more than ChiChewa at the level of gender; boys outperform girls but the difference is less marked than the rural/urban differences.

13 Thus many Zambian children are more familiar with the 'town Nyanja' term mabrikisi (from the English 'bricks', but with Nyanja ma- as a plural marker, and Nyanja phonology) rather than the standard ncherwa.

References

Chick, J. K. 1992. English as a medium and as a subject in post-apartheid South Africa. *Southern African Journal of Applied Linguistics* 1 (1): 29–40.

Chikalanga, I. W. 1990. *Inferencing in the reading process.* Unpublished PhD Thesis, University of Reading.

Cummins, J. 1979. Cognitive/academic language proficiency, linguistic interdependence, the optimum age question and some other matters. *Working Papers on Bilingualism* 19: 197–205.

Cummins, J. and M. Swain. 1986. *Bilingualism in Education.* London: Longman.

Davies, A. 1996. Ironising the myth of linguicism. *Journal of Multilingual and Multicultural Development* 17 (2): 485–96.

Hobcraft, J. 1993. Women's education, child welfare and child survival: A review of the evidence. *Health Transition Review* 3 (2): 159–75.

IIEP, International Institute for Educational Planning, 1996. The Analysis of Education Research Data for Policy Development: the Zambian Case (mimeo report of the Southern African Consortium for Monitoring Educational Quality). Paris: UNESCO.

Kashoki, M. E. 1990. *The Factor of Language in Zambia.* Lusaka: Kenneth Kaunda Foundation.

Kishindo, P. J. 1990. An historical survey of spontaneous and planned development of Chichewa. In I. Fodor and C. Hagege (eds.) *Language Reform: History and Future*, Vol. V. pp. 59–82. Hamburg: Helmut Buske Verlag.

Ministry of Education [Zambia]. 1992. *Focus on Learning*. Lusaka: Ministry of Education.

Moock, P. R. and H. Addou. 1994. Agricultural productivity and education. In *The International Encyclopedia of Education*, Vol. I. Oxford: Pergamon Press.

Sharma, R. 1973. The Reading Skills of Grade 3 Children. *Psychological Service Report 2/1973.* Lusaka: Ministry of Education.

Sichinga, W. K. 1994. Language Statistics in Malawi. Unpublished mimeo. Zomba: Office of Statistics.

Skutnabb-Kangas, T. 1981. *Bilingualism or Not: The Education of Minorities.* Clevedon, Avon: Multingual Matters.

Wagner, D. A., J. E. Spratt and A. Ezzaki. 1989. Does learning to read in a second language always put the child at a disadvantage? Some counter-evidence from Morocco. *Applied Psycholinguistics* 10: 31–48.

Williams, E. 1993. First and second language reading proficiency of year 3, 4 and 6 children in Malawi and Zambia. *Reading in a Foreign Language* 10 (1): 915–29.

Williams, E. 1996. Reading in two languages at year five in African primary schools. *Applied Linguistics* 17 (2): 182–209.

Yahya-Othman, S. 1989. When international languages clash: The possible detrimental effects on development of the conflict between English and Kiswahili in Tanzania. In C. M. Rubagumya (ed.) *Language in Education in Africa,* pp. 42–53. Clevedon, Avon: Multilingual Matters.

Section Eight

The ethics of language testing

21 Cheating language tests can be dangerous

Bernard Spolsky
Bar-Ilan University, Israel

Recent newspaper accounts report the uncovering of a network that helped thousands of prospective American citizens cheat on a test conducted by a private agency for the Educational Testing Service. Part of the backwash from this event includes a congressional campaign to abolish the Immigration and Naturalization Service. While testing agencies have, in fact, spent huge sums of money to make it harder to cheat on high-stakes tests – the first product of the still promised millennial reform of TOEFL will be a more secure computerised version of the test – they have spent much less on making sure that tests do not cheat their takers or their users.

In this paper, I will celebrate Davies' concern for ethics in language testing by raising some questions about TOEFL, surely the best known, most widely used, and most profitable of all current language tests. Davies organised, at the 1996 AILA Congress in Jyväskylä, the first symposium devoted purely to the question of ethics in language testing. In doing this, he continued his long tradition of calling attention to major issues in the field. His 1968 collection of papers (Davies 1968), although not the proceedings of a meeting that its title suggests, helped to define the important directions of professional development for the field. The AILA colloquium, nearly three decades later (Davies 1997b), is another major step in professionalisation. It asks clearly, raising a question that had worried some of us for some time (Spolsky 1981, 1984), how to justify the use of instruments that we know to be imperfect.

It is important to be clear about that imperfection. At least since Professor Francis Ysidro Edgeworth discussed the statistics of examinations at meetings of the Royal Statistical Society over a century ago (Edgeworth 1888, 1890), we have known that examinations are, of necessity, flawed, their results blurred by the 'inevitable uncertainty' of measurement. There are all sorts of causes of measurement error, ranging from the necessary imperfection and heterogeneity of human judgement to the accidental lack of congruence between a test taker and his/her performance on any individual test. Edgeworth identified many of these causes and then calculated the probability of error in a number of contemporary examinations.

If uncertainty is certain in physical measurement, as Heisenberg established, how much more serious it must be in measurements of human qualities, where the very constructs remain issues of debate and controversy. At its best, the score on a test is no more than a chance approximation of the ability we hope to measure, and its use calls for the strictest ethical concern. A language tester, as a professional, must be guided by standards that make this clear. Neither Edgeworth a century ago nor Davies in his own considerations of this question more recently (Davies 1997a) would have us give up on the flawed instrument. Chancy as it may be, it is often all we have to avoid making decisions based on pure luck or prejudice. Both Edgeworth and Davies agree that examinations, imperfect as they are, are better than other methods of selection. They are lotteries biased in favour of the more talented. But they need to be used with care. The greater importance attached to the use, the greater care we are bound to take with the test score.

Faced by the challenge of Edgeworth, those who took his questions seriously devoted most of their energies to finding techniques for reducing the amount of error. Most of the work of the field of psychometrics has been driven by the privileged position given to reliability. Not everyone agreed. In spite of the fact that much of the earliest work in this area was done in England, and ignoring the pioneering objective testing of school subjects by Burt (1921) for the London County Council, English examiners have generally been fairly impervious to the call for objective tests. It was only as a result of a series of Carnegie-sponsored conferences (Monroe 1931, 1935, 1939) that Hartog (Hartog *et al.* 1941; Hartog and Rhodes 1935; Hartog and Rhodes 1936) was encouraged to carry out and publish research showing the lack of reliability in much English examining, but many examining boards continued in their lack of interest in these principles. In Scotland, reliability was taken more seriously, as witness Allen and Davies (1974).

In the US, on the other hand, the search for reliability and stability of scores soon became the main goal of the new psychometric profession. Encouraged, one suspects, by exaggerated accounts published by Yerkes (1921) of the usefulness of the mass intelligence testing he had sold to the US Army to separate out stupid recruits (Reed 1987), the objective testing movement flourished in the 1920s, and soon led to the growth of a major testing industry. The multiple-choice machine-scored test naturally appealed to this industrialised testing, and a secondary industry of psychometrists provided regular evidence of the psychometric purity of the results.

From our present perspective, I think their direction was wrong. Just as some of them misinterpreted the army testing to find support for racist immigration policies (Brigham 1923), so the deification of reliability and the subsequent glorification of objective testing has turned out to be a sterile path, distracting attention for too long a period from the more urgent task of learning how to use flawed instruments fairly. What happened to TOEFL is a good illustration (Spolsky 1995).

Looking back over 30 years later, it is understandable why TOEFL was an ideal candidate for industrialisation. Twice before, in the late 1920s and in the 1950s, the testing profession had responded to requests from the US Government for tests that would help block the loophole left in the Immigration Act by the provision of visas for students outside the quota. The test developed in 1929 (College Entrance Examination Board 1929) soon dropped into disuse, as few foreigners could afford to apply to US colleges, and government was not prepared to help. A similar fate met a post-war attempt to fill the gap (Saretsky 1984). But, by 1961, the stream of foreign students was starting to increase, and there was a growing demand for a new test that would measure the English proficiency of foreign students.

This time, however, the request for action was not addressed to the major establishment testing body (the College Entrance Examinations Board) or its growing offshoot (Educational Testing Service), or even to the active group of EFL testers at the University of Michigan, but to the newly founded Center of Applied Linguistics. There, Charles Ferguson, with the assistance of a small band of dedicated applied linguists and the active support of Melvin Fox at the Ford Foundation, was starting a number of initiatives whose products were to include not just TOEFL but also the TESOL organisation and many basic studies in language policy (Fox 1975; Fox and Harris 1964).

The task of organising a conference on English proficiency was given by Ferguson to Sirarpi Ohannessian, who invited key groups involved in foreign student affairs and in language testing to a meeting for '*the exchange of information on present testing needs and practices and the drafting of proposals for setting up appropriate machinery to prepare and administer annual English examinations which will set up standards of competency acceptable to universities and institutions in the United States*'. Ferguson opened the first morning session on 11 May 1961, after which John Carroll gave a keynote speech which is still required reading for language testers (Carroll 1961). Other background papers written for the conference were discussed the rest of the day. The second day dealt with criteria for test construction and the mechanics of test administration and implementation. A set of conference decisions was accepted and an interim committee was appointed to implement them.

Reading the full account of the conference, one realises both the strength of the institutional demand for action, and the extent to which it overlapped and built on existing testing programmes. In her report on the conference, the College Board representative, Katharine Salter, paid no attention to the more theoretical matters, but responded instead to what she considered its political action programme:

> *Contrary to our original view of the conference, which we gathered from bits of correspondence, it quickly became apparent that this group intended to put in motion all of the wheels necessary for the development of a new test of English language proficiency, including an aptitude test of language skills, under the joint sponsorship of groups represented at the meeting. There was no thought of adapting an existing test programme, or of asking an existing group, such as the College Board, to set up such a programme.* (Salter 1961)

All agreed that a new test was needed, and taking advantage of the state-of-the-art discussions of language testing, were generally agreed on the form of the test. The conference casts interesting light on the nature of applied linguistics and the implementation of its ideas. First, the whole exercise started not with a desire to apply some new notion in linguistic theory, but rather as what Henry Widdowson would call a principled effort to solve a language-related problem. As the papers make clear, and the statement of conference decisions reaffirms, the conference was called to find a practical solution to a socially relevant problem, the assessment of the English language proficiency of the increasing number of foreign students seeking to study in American universities.

The people called together to discuss this issue were American scholars and administrators with experience of language tests from two points of view: as test makers and as test users. A number of them had been trained as linguists, but the knowledge of linguistic theory was firmly counterbalanced by knowledge of psychometric theory, and both sets of theories were strongly constrained by practical experience and demands. This was not a meeting where a single linguistic theory would or could be proposed as the panacea for a problem. In this, the conference's work can be clearly distinguished from a number of less successful interventions by linguists who have proposed that some aspect of theory will form the basis for a new and successful method of teaching, for example, reading or foreign languages.

The conference was presented with a set of theoretical notions (mainly in Carroll's keynote paper, but also in other presentations and surely in the discussions), a number of possible models (especially the Michigan test directed by Robert Lado and the American University Language Center batteries), and a set of practical administrative and institutional constraints, among which funding was the most serious problem. Assuming a world without financial and practical limitations, the kind of battery that the language testers at the meeting would presumably have favoured would have consisted of a large objective section to test reading and grammar, improved (that is to say, more psychometrically reliable) versions of the speaking test used in the American University Language Center battery and of the composition writing test of the Michigan battery, and a language aptitude test that would help relate the synchronic measurement of the test to the diachronic prediction it was intended to make.

Such an ideal test, for which we are still waiting, would have doubtless been much more capable than the test battery that was actually developed of bridging the gap between traditional and modern tests, by combining the demands of psychometric reliability with those for naturalistic and integrative performance. In the circumstances, it seems probable that the greater intellectual value attached to objective testing principles, not unrelated to the then still fairly firm alliance between structural linguistic theory and behaviourist psychology in foreign language learning theory, meant that the conference opted for immediate use of the objective items, with the speaking test and the scored writing left for later development. Thus, Carroll's important call for integrative testing, with its relation to real-life situations, was not specifically echoed in the decisions, and was satisfied, in actual test development, by the use of mini-dialogues in the listening comprehension and of short connected passages in the reading comprehension. The absence of any spokesperson at the conference for the oral testing that, by 1961, was proceeding efficiently at the Foreign Service Institute (Wilds 1961), and the decreasing status of prognostic tests that had once held equal place with proficiency tests (Carroll 1960), made it easier for the practical arguments of a machine-scorable test to win out.

The conference thus recognised a tension, but was constrained to suggest a resolution of it that was heavily weighted towards the psychometric principles that drove the industrial practices at Educational Testing Service. Any doubts about the wisdom of omitting tests of speaking or writing were quickly pushed aside for 'later research', the common filing cabinet for any desirable but unfeasible academic idea. The conference came up with a very valuable set of prescriptions, that should have permitted designing the best possible testing programme, given the state of language testing knowledge and the general intellectual atmosphere of American language teaching theory and practice at the time. The research effort that was stressed in the decisions provided a way to deal with the areas where the participants wisely spotted weakness in that knowledge. As things turned out, the lack of resources and the institutional straitjacket that came with the financial bail-out meant that the research took much longer than the participants had anticipated, with the result that the test that was implemented was much narrower in its scope than might have been hoped.

The decision on specifications for the test was speedy and amicable, Katharine Salter (1961) reported to her colleagues at the College Board. The test, it was decided, should have two parts. The first should be an English proficiency test, 'an omnibus battery testing a wide range of proficiency and yielding meaningful (reliable) subscores in addition to total score'. It should take two and one-half hours and be aimed, at first, at the college level. The second part should be a language aptitude test, needed 'in view of the importance of predictions of subsequent English attainment ...'.

The idea of including an aptitude test is mentioned in the conference report in papers by Harris, Alatis and Marquardt (Center for Applied Linguistics 1961). Carroll's keynote paper referred to validating the proficiency test on the basis of its predictive power, just as one would validate an aptitude test, but he did not specifically propose including aptitude in the battery. However, he later recalled that though this was planned, it was never carried out; 'it seems that conferees hoped that I could work something out, but I never did, thinking the task too difficult or impractical, or not having the time' (Carroll 1989).

The next part of the story I will tell here very quickly; there are full details in Spolsky (1995). Test specifications were one thing, but getting an enterprise like this started turned out to be another. What followed was a tragedy or comedy in five acts. In the first, David Harris (working closely with Fred Godshalk at ETS) developed a plan, specifications and a budget for a new test, and, with Melvin Fox, set out in search of a financial backer. None of the government agencies who wanted the test were willing to pay, and no one but Ford would offer funding. In a side plot, some officers at College Board tried to shoot down the enterprise and seemed to have succeeded in making sure that Ford came up with only half the money needed. In the second act, the test was written, edited, printed and started. Its validity was shown by its correlations with existing tests. In the third act, the budget ran out, and no one would support independent continuation. In the fourth, two members of the executive committee (one from ETS and one from College Board) suggested handing it over to their institutions, and this was agreed to. Immediately, Ford found the rest of the money. In the fifth act, the test moved to Princeton as a joint College Board-ETS project, directed by a language tester for the first year. It continued in the red until, a short time later, College Board gave up its partnership, the language tester was replaced by an administrator, and TOEFL began its industrial career.

The language testers who were involved with TOEFL in its formative period – David Harris, Leslie Palmer and Fred Godshalk, in particular – had assumed that, once testing was in progress, they would be able to deal with a number of necessary but postponed issues, such as the aptitude tests (that Carroll knew about) and the direct testing of writing (that Godshalk was developing at ETS [Godshalk, Swineford and Coffman 1966]) and of speaking (well developed by then at the Foreign Service Institute). Had this been the case, TOEFL might well have broken out of the strict adherence to the principles of the psychometric-structuralist model of language testing, and taken advantage of the post-modern, communicative-integrative approaches that were already appreciated and being implemented in 1960.

For reasons that had nothing to do with the state of language testing theory, these hopes were to be disappointed or at least put into cold storage. Instead of carrying out the delayed research and incorporating the new ideas, the TOEFL programme, once it was swallowed by Educational Testing Service, developed an industrial infrastructure that was effective not just in making the test efficient and profitable, but also in resisting changes in it for as long as possible. There certainly was research, as time went on, but its directions were determined not by growth in understanding of language testing, but by a concern to defend the test against consumer complaints. TOEFL had become a product, like a car, and its proprietors were driven by considerations of marketing and profitability.

I have told this story as a background to asking some questions about ethics. I think it is clear that we are talking about a business enterprise, one that may well have started as a disinterested effort to provide public service, but has for a long time been a way of making money. Complex though its corporate structure may be – the Nader report on ETS (Nairn 1980) was frustrated by the cleverness of shifting responsibility for the tests to 'autonomous' boards that 'owned' tests and contracted with ETS for their production – and divided as the authority might be (it is nominally the TOEFL Board and not ETS that formally approves decisions like computerisation), the buck has to stop somewhere. But my concern in this paper is not with corporate responsibility, but with the extra-legal ethical responsibility of language testers for the results. True, we don't sit on the central decision-making bodies, but many of us work for ETS, and do its research, and sit on its committees. What then are our responsibilities?

I don't have a simple answer, and I suspect that it is a difficult one to formulate, as witness the time it has been taking the ILTA committee to come up with a code of practice for language testers. All of us have no difficulty with one point, that a professional language tester is responsible for developing the best test that resources permit. This is I think the core of the call by Alan Davies for professionalisation. Davies is more cautious than some of us, and will not go along with Hamp-Lyons who wants us to 'accept responsibility for all those consequences which we are aware of' (1997: 302).

TOEFL offers a case in which I suspect we have not been as outspoken as we might in pointing out the compromises in testing quality and shortcuts in guaranteeing full validation. As individuals, we have been feeble in our dealings with an industrial giant, giving the benefit of the doubt to the business argument not to tamper with a well-paying product in the face of our academic scepticism.

There have been many causes of this scepticism. The failure to insist on full validation, the lack of questioning of impact, the coyness in dealing with the long anchoring to the first sample population, the reluctance to deal with the dynamic nature of language proficiency, the slowness of modification, have all been decisions that suited the business needs of the test producer but failed to meet the needs of the users. A serious validation study remains a dim future prospect, millions of candidates later.

Our failure as a profession has been collective. Rather than trying to patch up tests to make them a little less uncertain, we should have started seriously a century ago to try to find ways of using inaccurate instruments as fairly as possible. This is what the new concern for test ethics is about, and we should be thankful to Alan Davies for his contribution to this as to so many other aspects of applied linguistics.

References

Allen, J. P. B. and A. Davies (eds.) 1974. *The Edinburgh Course in Applied Linguistics. Vol. 4.* London: Oxford University Press.

Brigham, C. C. 1923. *A Study of American Intelligence.* Princeton: Princeton University Press.

Burt, C. L. 1921. Mental and scholastic tests. Report by the Education Officer. London: London County Council.

Carroll, J. B. 1960. The prediction of success in intensive foreign language training (final revision). Laboratory for Research in Instruction, Graduate School of Education, Harvard University.

Carroll, J. B. 1961. Fundamental considerations in testing for English language proficiency of foreign students. In *Testing the English Proficiency of Foreign Students.* Washington, DC: Center for Applied Linguistics.

Carroll, J. B. 1989. Letter to B. Spolsky.

Center for Applied Linguistics. 1961. Testing the English proficiency of foreign students. Report of a conference sponsored by the Center for Applied Linguistics in cooperation with the Institute of International Education and the National Association of Foreign Student Advisers. Washington, DC: Center for Applied Linguistics.

College Entrance Examination Board. 1929. Twenty-ninth Annual Report of the Secretary. NY, College Entrance Examination Board.

Davies, A. (ed.) 1968. *Language Testing Symposium: A Psycholinguistic Perspective.* Oxford: Oxford University Press.

Davies, A. 1997a. Demands of being professional in language testing. *Language Testing* 14 (3): 328–39.

Davies, A. 1997b. Introduction: The limits of ethics in language testing. *Language Testing* 14 (3): 235–41.

Edgeworth, F. Y. 1888. The statistics of examinations. *Journal of the Royal Statistical Society* 51: 599–635.

Edgeworth, F. Y. 1890. The element of chance in competitive examinations. *Journal of the Royal Statistical Society* 53: 644–63.

Fox. M. J. (ed.) c.1975. *Language and Development: A Retrospective Survey of Ford Foundation Language Projects, 1952–1974.* NY: Ford Foundation.

Fox, M. J. and D. H. Harris. 1964. *English as a Second Language: Development and Testing.* NY: Ford Foundation.

Godshalk, F. I., F. Swineford and W. E. Coffman. 1966. The measurement of writing ability. Research Monograph Series. NY: College Entrance Examination Board.

Hamp-Lyons, L. 1997. Washback, impact and validity: Ethical concerns. *Language Testing* 14 (3): 295–303.

Hartog, P., P. B. Ballard, P. Gurrey, H. R. Hamley and C. Ebblewhite Smith. 1941. *The Marking of English Essays.* London: Macmillan and Company Ltd.

Hartog, P. and E. C. Rhodes. 1935. *An Examination of Examinations, Being a Summary of Investigations on Comparison of Marks Allotted to Examination Scripts by Independent Examiners and Boards of Examiners, Together with a Section on Viva Voce Examinations*. London: Macmillan and Company Ltd.

Hartog, P. and E. C. Rhodes. 1936. *The Marks of Examiners, Being a Comparison of Marks Allotted to Examination Scripts by Independent Examiners and Boards of Examiners, Together with a Section on Viva Voce Examinations.* London: Macmillan and Company Ltd.

Monroe, P. (ed.) 1931. Conference on examinations, Eastbourne, England, 1931. NY: Teachers College, Columbia University.

Monroe, P. (ed.) 1935. Conference on examinations, Folkestone, England, 1935. NY: Teachers College, Columbia University.

Monroe, P. (ed.) 1939. Conference on examinations, Dinard, France, 1938. NY: Teachers College, Columbia University.

Nairn, A. 1980. *The Reign of ETS: The Corporation that Makes up Minds.* Nader Foundation.

Reed, J. 1987. Robert M. Yerkes and the mental testing movement. In M. M. Sokal (ed.) *Psychological Testing and American Society 1890–1930.* New Brunswick: Rutgers University Press.

Salter, K. 1961. Memorandum to Mr Pearson: College Board Archives.

Saretsky, G. D. 1984. History of the EEFS. Unpublished manuscript, EEFS Papers, Educational Testing Service Archives.

Spolsky, B. 1981. Some ethical questions about language testing. In C. Klein-Braley and D. K. Stevenson (eds.) *Practice and Problems in Language Testing.* Frankfurt am Main: Verlag Peter D. Lang.

Spolsky, B. 1984. The uses of language tests: An ethical envoi. In C. Rivera (ed.) *Placement Procedures in Bilingual Education: Education and Policy Issues.* Clevedon, Avon: Multilingual Matters Ltd.

Spolsky, B. 1995. *Measured Words: The Development of Objective Language Testing.* Oxford: Oxford University Press.

Wilds, C. P. 1961. *Proficiency Ratings for Native Speakers.* Washington: Foreign Service Institute Archives.

Yerkes, R. M. (ed.) 1921. *Psychological Examining in the United States Army.* Washington DC: Government Printing Office.

22 Ethics, fairness(es), and developments in language testing

Liz Hamp-Lyons
Hong Kong Polytechnic University

I seem to have been struggling with questions to myself about the ethical aspects of language testing for a long time: in fact, this struggle goes back at least to 1985, as the following extract from a draft of a chapter of my dissertation shows:

> *Currently language testing seems to be moving to (what may be) ... referred to as an ethical phase. ... an ethical phase will not replace the previous phases (in LT) but in many contexts will exist alongside them. Also, a concern for ethicality is not a new development, for it has provided the underlying motivation for developments in language testing from the beginning. Rather, it may be a shift into another dimension or domain. Three features mark the current period as deserving the epithet 'ethical'. Firstly, an ethical imperative has meant that none of the groups concerned with language testing in earlier phases has been squeezed out: in fact, this shift has brought back classroom teachers in particular into this key area of their rightful concerns. Teachers' judgements and ratings are being accorded a place once again; teachers' responsibility for justifiable evaluations is being reasserted. In addition, testees themselves may be given a role, in self-evaluation, self-report, and peer evaluation. The scope may be widened still further, to include those concerned with the testee in language use, for instance, university supervisors, coursemates, flatmates, etc. The second feature is the increasing untenability of the position that ... the language tester is obliged to choose either reliability at the expense of (most kinds of) validity, or validity at the expense of reliability. Following from the period of initial enthusiasm for tests of communicative competence has come a concern to improve the reliability of these tests, while retaining the multidimensional validity that has been achieved. Closely allied to this is the third feature of the ethical phase, an increased attention to and sophistication in test validation activities.*

This draft continued by building up a rather gauche little diagram which purported to be a model of this 'ethical phase' in language testing. It resembled a house, of which the roof, the 'all-encompassing' structure, is ethicality.

Alan Davies' handwritten response to this draft, as my doctoral supervisor, says:

> *I'm still unhappy about the term Ethicality unless you stress the professional aspects and the humanistic orientation. I suppose we can distinguish Validity from its use (i.e. a test may be V. but you might not use it for E. reasons), but the E. is not, I suggest, then properly a quality of the test but a general attitude towards learners, learning, etc.*

I didn't at the time understand what Alan meant by 'professional aspects', but in recent papers he has given he has worked this through, and in his article in the 1997 *Language Testing* special issue (Davies 1997), he has brought together this thinking. Nor did I at the time understand why he referred to the 'humanistic orientation', since it seemed obvious to me that ethical concerns would be humanistic concerns as well as technical concerns. Only slowly over the years since then have I gradually understood that not everyone accepted these fundamental 'humanistic' underpinnings to work in language testing. Similarly, only slowly have I understood how complex these issues are, and that merely professing a humanistic or ethical concern does not make one's work ethical. As 'knowing' what is ethical has become more difficult in this age of cultural and moral relativism, ethics have become a more important issue in many fields. In the epistemological crisis engendered by postmodernism, it is much more difficult to assert that any decision – or measurement – is 'right' or 'true'. While this makes our lives as practising language testers more difficult, in many ways it also liberates us to think seriously about what would enable us to accept our own behaviours as contributing to the greater good of the greatest number of those whose lives we touch. In his comments on a paper of mine (Hamp-Lyons 1989) in his recent *Language Testing* paper, Alan Davies questions what he sees as my characterisation of ethics as 'made up of a combination of validity and backwash' and suggests that I may have been appealing to consequential validity. With hindsight, that is probably true; but the terminology of consequential validity was not in common use, nor was it clearly defined at that time (indeed, we might question how well it is defined even now!).

My 1985 draft turned out to be premature: once again with hindsight, the whole field of educational measurement was still rather naive in its views of the nature of ethical principles: it, and language testing within it, took too narrow a view of what the compass of our ethical responsibilities is. Few of us had thought about the meaning and responsibilities of ethics in sophisticated ways.

Only now is there any indication of a movement towards some agreement over professional ethics as related to social justice, and an understanding of how it is possible to hold a position such as that of philosopher Alasdair MacIntyre (1987), who sees ethics as as much about politics and economics as about right and wrong – what we might these days refer to as 'distributive justice'. But perhaps we all needed to pass through those naive early stages before we could learn to challenge our own thinking, our own expectations of ourselves, and set our sights higher, or in different directions. Certainly my own early exchange of views with Alan Davies, leaving me dissatisfied as it did, forced me to think harder about why I felt there were ethical issues that needed to be addressed in language testing, and that thinking was reflected in my 1989 paper, and in more recent work (Hamp-Lyons 1996, 1997).

In what follows[1] I explore some ideas generated by the recent considerable debate in educational measurement about 'fairness'. I take 'fairness' to be a member of a semantic set with 'morality' and 'ethics', and I ask: What is fairness? What makes a test fair? How do we know when a test is unfair? In keeping with the uncertainties of these relativist times, I find these questions increasingly difficult, and am increasingly unwilling to claim an ability to answer them. But I do feel that they all imply, and assume, some ideal model of 'fairness' that is somewhere 'out there', waiting for us, if we only knew where to look. The introduction to this chapter clearly suggests the unlikelihood of the existence of such a model or solution; therefore it will not surprise the reader that in this paper I do not propose to look for that ideal model; rather, I want to raise some of the complicating situations and questions that occurred to me while I was musing on the elusiveness of that ideal model. The questioning and reflective mode of this chapter, as well as its subject matter, is, I believe, appropriate as a contribution to this tribute to the work of Alan Davies over the years and his influence on the work of many other language testers, myself included.

1 If it is true that:
Language teaching as a field has not agreed what is the right way to teach or learn, and has not established a single dominant model for language teaching, it follows that students should be free to discover and then follow their own learning styles and learning strategies. Similarly, if it is true that:
Language testing has not discovered a single dominant model of how to test a student's learning, ability or performance, it follows that students should be free to consider their own learning history, their learning styles and strategies, and choose test and item types that best match their own learning profile. Tests, then, would need to exist in multiple forms so that each student could select a unique, appropriate pathway to demonstrating mastery, one which would be uniquely fair to her or him.

2 If it is true that:
Students' judgements of their own performances are heavily influenced by their teacher's degree of harshness or leniency towards error, and by the performance targets their teachers set for them and accept from them, it follows that teachers need to be benchmarked so that students will have better self-knowledge, so that they will not be misled by their teacher's encouragement to view themselves as more successful than they are, or by their teacher's criticisms to view themselves as less successful than they are. From this it follows that teachers would need to be tested to ensure that they comprehend and can consistently apply the appropriate criteria and standards to learners in their classes. Teachers entering new teaching situations – new school years, new kinds of learners, teaching new skills, would need to take a re-benchmarking course and would be required to pass the course before teaching this new kind of learner. This kind of fairness places the needs of the teacher below the needs of the learner, because it states that standards and criteria are not negotiable. It does not, however, contradict the previous kind of fairness, because standards and criteria are distinct from styles and strategies, which when the teacher is in turn a rater, she or he can still choose freely.

3 If it is true that:
Language testing has embraced post-modernism, and has accepted the fact that raters have personal philosophies and belief sets, and that it is a fiction to suppose that they can 'check these at the door', it follows that formal judgement systems should acknowledge this and figure out how to accommodate assessment systems to the rating styles and strategies of raters. Tests, then, would need to have multiple scoring alternatives so that each rater could select a unique, appropriate approach to scoring, one that would be uniquely fair to her or him.

4 If it is true that:
Teachers are educated and trained in many different ways, and that every teacher, through education, experience, personality, interests and skills is different, classes by different teachers will not be the same, even if the syllabus is. It follows that teachers should be free to teach according to their own personal 'style', and that they should be free to assess, and have their students assessed, by their personal style. When assessments match instruction, not only in content but in style, there will be least dissonance for the teacher, and therefore for the learners. Tests, then, would need to exist in multiple forms so that each teacher could select a unique, appropriate pathway for her or his students to demonstrate mastery, one which would allow students and teacher to be seen in their best light by assessing in areas and in ways where they have the most strength.

5 If it is true that:
Parents know their children best of all, have a set of social values, and have expectations of what their children should be able to do and how they should be doing it; if it is true that they also want to understand what happens in the classroom and the school much better than they do now, it follows that most kinds of tests will seem alienating for parents. Most tests are done in technical ways that exclude the parents, and they are reported in technical language, or simply with number scores which are not attached to actual examples of their child's performance. All this is clearly unfair to the parents. Tests would be fairer to parents if they were directly related to the content the children had been learning and that parents had been seeing in the homework assignments; they would be fairer to parents if they were scored in ways that parents could completely understand, and if parents were able to take part in the design of the test and its scoring method. Because parents understand their children's learning needs and problems so well, it would be fairer to parents if they could take part in test design and could be trained as raters of the tests. Tests will only be fair to parents if test results/reports make complete sense to them, either because the reports are transparently descriptive, or because parents have been trained in test report interpretation in their own children's context. There needs to be an appeal system that parents can use to challenge their child's test score or the way the child was tested.

Each of the fairnesses I have portrayed above focuses on being fair to one group of stakeholders: learners, raters, teachers, parents. It has not escaped me that there are some mutually contradictory strategies implied by these attempts to consider fairness from the viewpoint of different stakeholder groups. There are other stakeholder groups too: taxpayers, national and state Education Department officials, big business, political parties, and governments.

If some of the creations of views of students, parents, teachers, and test raters seem far-fetched, I only ask that you spend time just listening to these groups discussing how they learn, what they believe about good teaching, what they worry about in their child's education, etc. I will agree with you that some of the suggestions I have voiced seem outrageous to us, as language testers, but only if you will agree with me that such suggestions are real, that you too have heard these and comments like them discussed in student focus groups, parents' meetings, teachers' common rooms, among practising teachers taking Master's courses in Language Testing, or chatting over tea during a rating session. What is outrageous, if anything, is the difficulty of making our tests fit these fairnesses, not the views themselves. It seems to me that none of them should be taken too lightly. Once language testers accept that there is no single 'right answer' to issues in 'doing' language testing, we also have to listen seriously to all views.

My thinking has developed since that early exchange with Alan. I've learned that 'fairness' is such a difficult concept because there is no one standpoint from which a test can be viewed as 'fair' or 'not fair'. The language tester has no more inherent right to decide what is 'fair' for other people than anyone else does. But the language tester does have the responsibility to use all means to make any language test she or he is involved in as 'fair' as possible. As our technical skills expand, as our definition of 'a test' is refined, as our political consciousness of the power of tests is heightened, we raise our expectations of ourselves. Ethics is, as Alan pointed out then, a professional issue, because our conception of what our professional responsibilities are has expanded. 'Ethics', for the language tester, involves decisions about whose voices are to be heard, whose needs are to be met; about how a society determines what is best for the largest number when fairnesses are in conflict. Ethics is also more than a humanistic issue, as Alan also foresaw: language testing as a field is interestingly and challengingly about political and social needs and consequences, as much as it is about what is right and what is wrong. The time has arrived when we are obliged to critique everything that we do, and to take that critique onward and look at the impact we have on test takers, other stakeholder groups, and on society, and we must not flinch from accepting some responsibility for the uses made of the tests we have been involved in: the fascinating and important question is, where and when do we decide to let our responsibility drop?

Note

1 The rest of this paper is substantially based on a paper I prepared as a response to Henry Braun's plenary talk at the Language Testing Research Colloquium, 1998.

References

Davies, A. 1997. Demands of being professional in language testing. *Language Testing* 14 (3): 328–39.

Hamp-Lyons, L. 1989. Language testing and ethics. *Prospect* 5: 7–15.

Hamp-Lyons, L. 1996. Applying ethical standards to portfolio assessment of writing in English as a second language. In M. Milanovich and N. Saville (eds.) *Performance Testing, Cognition and Assessment: Selected Papers from the 15th Language Testing Research Colloquium*, pp. 151–64. Cambridge: Cambridge University Press.

Hamp-Lyons, L. 1997. Washback, impact and validity: Ethical concerns. *Language Testing* 14 (3): 295–303.

MacIntyre, A. 1987. *After Virtue*. Oxford: Oxford University Press.

23 The ethical potential of alternative language assessment[1]

Brian K. Lynch
University of Melbourne

Introduction

My paper will attempt to explore the ethical potential of alternative language assessment. Alternative, here, is defined as essentially different from traditional testing, the latter being well captured by the following quote from Foucault:

> *The examination as the fixing, at once ritual and 'scientific', of individual differences, as the pinning down of each individual in his own particularity, clearly indicates the appearance of a new modality of power in which each individual receives as his status his own individuality, and in which he is linked by his status to the features, the measurements, the gaps, the 'marks' that characterize him and make him a 'case'.* (Foucault 1975/1979: 192)

I will be investigating the way in which alternative assessment will need to be evaluated against criteria for validity which are different from those created for traditional testing. This will have implications for how ethical issues, especially those of fairness and power relations, are rendered in language assessment contexts.

Alternative assessment vs. traditional testing

Ultimately, the case for alternative assessment must be made on its own internal merits, as Worthen (1993) has argued. However, its very name invites a comparative investigation: 'alternative' to what? In general, the term contrasts with traditional testing, which is based on a 'testing culture' (Wolf *et al.* 1991). This culture emphasises the rank ordering of students, privileges quantifiable data for isolated, individual test performances, and in general promotes the idea of neutral, scientific measurement as the goal of educational evaluation. Underlying this culture is an 'epistemology of intelligence' which is '... tightly woven around the fundamental image of a unified scale of worth, ratified in biology, and verified in the search for enduring group differences' (p. 43) and assumes that intelligence is 'a unitary and immutable trait' (p. 36) that can be ranked, fixed and predictably located. Birenbaum (1996) further characterises the culture of testing as one in which teaching and testing are considered separate activities carried out by separate types of experts, the test development plan and criteria usually remain a mystery for the student (see also Peirce 1992), and the pencil-and-paper product becomes the sole focus of evaluation, usually reported in the form of a single score.

Alternative assessment, by contrast, is based on an 'assessment culture' (Wolf *et al.* 1991), characterised by an investigation of developmental sequences in student learning, a sampling of genuine performances that reveal the underlying thinking processes, and the provision of an opportunity for further learning. Underlying this culture is an 'epistemology of mind' that assumes 'the capacity of thoughtfulness is widespread, rather than the exclusive property of those who rank high, and our views of students' abilities are susceptible to change' and that '... learning at all levels involves sustained performances of thought and collaborative interactions of multiple minds and tools as much as the individual possession of information' (p. 48). Birenbaum (1996) points out that this model of assessment culture implies that teaching and assessment are integrated, the student is an active participant in the process of developing assessment criteria and standards, both the product and the process of assessment tasks are evaluated, and the evaluation is reported in the form of a profile that will usually be qualitative, at least in part, rather than a single score or other quantification.

Darling-Hammond (1994), drawing upon Glaser (1990), differentiates traditional testing from alternative assessment in terms of purpose and history. Testing is concerned with selection and placement, whereas assessment aims to measure achievement, to 'describe the nature of performance that results from learning' (Darling-Hammond 1994: 11). A distinction based on purpose, as with the distinction based on the notion of 'culture', is important, since assessment format or procedure alone will not always distinguish alternative from traditional. Take the example of portfolios, which are traditionally associated with alternative assessment. Depending on how the portfolio components are selected, assembled and evaluated, they may or may not be good exemplars of the characteristics of alternative assessment 'culture'. If the student does not actively participate in the selection of portfolio components, if those components are focused on entirely as 'products', if they are judged by external reviewers unfamiliar with the individual students and their learning context, and if the evaluation is reported only in the form of a single score, then this version of portfolio assessment begins to look more like traditional testing. If there is active student participation in the process of selecting the writing samples to be included, as well as in determining the criteria for evaluating the portfolio assemblage, and a reporting format that is, at least in part, a qualitative profile that examines the process of student writing as well as the end product, then this could be referred to as portfolio-based alternative assessment (Wolf *et al.* 1991: 57).

Ethics and validity

How, then, do we judge the ethical potential of alternative assessment? To examine ethical practice we need to focus on the rights of research participants to not be harmed (socially, psychologically, emotionally, physically) and to not be coerced or manipulated against their will. Following Hamp-Lyons (1989), I will propose to embed this discussion of ethics within the notion of validity; that is, within the framework that defines what the relationship between tester and testee should be; what the testee should be asked to do in order to demonstrate their ability; what the tester believes to be the nature of that ability; how the tester decides what counts as evidence. These validity issues colour the way the ethical questions are posed and answered. On one level, the basic ethical questions remain the same for both traditional testing and alternative assessment, as do the appropriate responses – no one believes that research participants should be harmed or coerced. However, depending on the way validity is conceptualised, the harm and coercion that the tester researcher is responsible for may be defined differently.

My other motivation for embedding the discussion of ethics within validity is that I believe it helps clarify the potential for ethicality that is particular to alternative assessment. The main reason for an 'alternative' assessment is, after all, a dissatisfaction with traditional testing. This dissatisfaction, especially within the context of its effects on instruction and educational reform, has been articulated in the general educational research literature. For example, Wolf *et al.* (1991: 31) assert that 'researchers and educators, families and students want assessment that offers rigorous and wise diagnostic information rather than the rankings of normal curves'. They go on to list the specific negative effects that traditional testing has had on education. Although admitting to its technical and psychometric merits, they claim '... if we scrutinize the practices and results of this technically elegant system, we find that it distorts instruction (Raizan *et al.* 1989; Romberg, Zarinnia and Williams 1989; Zessoules and Gardener, 1991), underscores inequities in access to education (Chachkin 1989; Hilliard 1990; O'Connor 1989), and forecloses debates over the standards that will be applied to their work' (Schwartz and Viator 1990) (p. 32).

Wiggins (1993) discusses these negative effects of traditional testing as resulting in curricula that do not prepare students for real world challenges.

Shepard (1993: 13) similarly warns that 'the evidence documenting the negative influence of traditional multiple-choice tests on what teachers teach and how they teach it is irrefutable' (ultimately citing, in particular, Darling-Hammond and Wise 1985; Shepard and Dougherty 1991; and Smith 1991). However, she goes on to caution against thinking that alternative assessment will necessarily have positive effects on instruction.

Similar dissatisfaction has been expressed in the applied linguistics and language testing research literature as well. Hamayan (1995) criticises the ability of standardised tests and 'other indirect approaches to assessment' to respond to the needs of educational reform and, in terms of English language learners from culturally and linguistically diverse backgrounds, to foster equity of educational opportunity and excellence. Shohamy (1996: 152–53) portrays dissatisfaction with traditional testing (which in the language testing literature can include performance tests, used in a somewhat different sense in the educational measurement literature) primarily as a failure to incorporate both 'achievement' and 'proficiency' components of language knowledge. Her use of the term 'alternative', however, is extended to mean 'complementary' methods (including traditional ones) of assessment (cf. Norris *et al.* 1998).

Analysing the ethical potential of alternative assessment: The framework

In addition to sharing the basic dissatisfaction with traditional testing that has been discussed, I also share the belief that the traditional testing validity framework is inappropriate for properly evaluating alternative assessment (cf. Moss 1994, 1996). Instead, I will focus my analysis on a framework developed by two researchers in programme evaluation, Guba and Lincoln (1989), who have developed validity criteria designed to be unique to alternative inquiry (in their case, 'constructivism'). They use 'authenticity' in place of 'validity' to further emphasise the alternative nature of their 'criteria' for judging research (in their case, programme evaluation) findings. These criteria are formulated to be uniquely relevant to the naturalistic, or constructivist, research paradigm (see Guba 1990) rather than being parallel to the traditional, or positivist validity typology (e.g. internal, statistical conclusion, external, and construct validity).

The authenticity criteria

Guba and Lincoln (1989) present the criterion of ontological authenticity as the degree to which the range of stakeholders and participants in a particular research setting are able to gain and use information as a result of the research process, so that they are able to improve 'their conscious experiencing of the world' (Guba and Lincoln 1989: 248). Educative authenticity is closely related to ontological authenticity, but adds the requirement that stakeholders and participants gain an understanding of the perspectives and meaning constructions of those outside their own group (e.g. teachers coming to understand the perspective of students). Catalytic authenticity refers to the degree to which something is actually done as a result of the research. Building upon this criterion, tactical authenticity refers to how well the stakeholders and participants are actually empowered to take the action that the research sets in motion. The evidence that is necessary for validity under these criteria comes from documenting discussions and testimony from the stakeholders and participants, conducting negotiation sessions concerning the developing interpretations and research findings, and systematic follow-up sessions as the research findings are translated into actions.

Fairness and power

The remaining criterion in Guba and Lincoln's framework, fairness, I will use as an interaction with issues of power. Fairness can be defined as treating all individuals equally and giving all individuals an equal opportunity to contribute to the research process or, in the case of assessment research, to demonstrate their ability. As suggested even in recent work on testing validity theory (e.g. Messick 1989, 1996), fairness will also need to address the consequences of assessment; that is, we need to examine the uses to which our assessment procedures are being put and the intended as well as unintended effects on the individuals being assessed. In the past, this may have been put aside as a concern for policy makers, not language testers. It is clear, however, that even traditional testing has evolved to the stage where the consequences of testing decisions cannot be separated from a determination of the validity and, therefore, the ethicality of the test (or, more properly, the inferences made from the test scores).

In examining fairness, there is an inevitable interaction with power. To a certain extent, the issues of ethics in research can be thought of as aspects or expressions of power and the potential for abusing that power (i.e. through deception, the violation of privacy, or taking action without consent). In relation to language assessment, power has been defined as 'who decides what will be done to whom' (Herron 1988). However, as Shohamy (1993) has done, power can also be defined in relation to the work of Foucault (1975/1979, 1976/1990, 1982). In particular, the notion of 'forms of power' versus 'relations of power' becomes important (Lynch and Jukuri 1998).

In Foucault's work on hospitals and prisons, there is an essentially negative and dark picture of power. In his book on the prison, *Discipline and Punish*, he depicts the examination, or traditional testing, as being 'at the centre of the procedures that constitute the individual as effect and object of power, as effect and object of knowledge' (1975/1979: 192). The basic forms of power are referred to by Foucault (1982) as domination, exploitation, and subjection. However, substituting an alternative assessment procedure, such as writing samples organised into a portfolio, will not necessarily change the power 'relations' within which these forms are realised (McNamara, personal communication). In his writing on the history of sexuality and subsequent essays (1976/1990, 1982), Foucault's concept of relations of power seems to allow for the possibility of power as something other than a negative social force – it allows for relations that resist the forms of power (Lynch and Jukuri 1998). This can be thought of, perhaps, as a potential for response to unethical assessment procedures which might be possible in alternative assessment procedures. At the very least, a consideration of power in the determination of ethicality in language assessment should uncover relationships that might remain implicit or hidden.

Applying the framework: Self-assessment

By way of example, I have selected self-assessment as a form of alternative assessment in order to apply the framework discussed above. As Herron (1988) has argued, the use of self-assessment techniques provides for an important change in the traditional distribution of power in educational decision making. In Foucault's terms, the traditional form of power, that of domination of student by teacher/assessor, is replaced, but replaced by what? If it is pure self-assessment, then the unilateral domination of student by teacher is replaced by an equally unilateral student to teacher domination, at least in the sense that the student controls the decision-making process and dictates to the teacher what the outcome of that process will be. Perhaps the form of power that is most active and relevant in both the traditional and the self-assessment process is 'subjection', or subjectification, rather than domination. Foucault (1982: 212) discusses subjection as both 'subject to someone else by control and dependence, and tied to his own identity by a conscience or self-knowledge'. With this analysis of the form of power inherent in assessment contexts, we see that replacing traditional teacher controlled assessment with self-assessment will not necessarily result in fairer, or more ethical practice. In part, this is perhaps a reason for the reluctance we often see in our students to engage in self-assessment – they know, or intuit, that the way in which they are tied to their own identity, the nature and limits of their self-knowledge, may in fact result in a form of subjection as equally unfair as one imposed by a teacher. It is a case of potentially being their own worst critic, their own worst enemy. Rather than being someone else's 'subject' in assessment or research, they become their own 'subject'.

Of course, this is why those who have studied and written about self-assessment have emphasised the need for training of teachers in the introduction of self-assessment (Cram 1995) and a recognition of the 'measure of affective and interpersonal competence' required on the part of students and teachers alike. If we examine more closely the proposals for using self-assessment, we see that most often it is proposed in conjunction with other strategies. For example, Herron (1988) argues against traditional assessment because it can be unreliable – different assessors can give widely different evaluations to the same work – and sees greater fairness resulting from including the student in the process.

> *The only way to avoid such injustice is to make the student party to the assessment procedure, and hence party to the general unreliability. I cannot cry injustice when I have been a free negotiating participant in the assessment of my work.* (Herron 1988: 60)

The student is included in the process through self-assessment and assessment by peers (see also Wilkes 1995). The inclusion of peer-assessment allows for the possibility of revising the self-assessment after feedback from peers. The teacher may also collaborate in this negotiation.

What results from this collaborative approach to assessment is the possibility of what Foucault (1982: 220) calls a 'relationship of power', which is defined as 'an action upon an action, on existing actions or on those which may arise in the present or the future' and in which ' "the other" (the one over whom power is exercised) is thoroughly recognized and maintained to the very end as a person who acts; and that, faced with a relationship of power, a whole field of responses, reactions, results, and possible inventions may open up'. Dennis Lynch and Stephen Jukuri (1998: 279) argue that implied in this definition is the requirement that relations of power be reciprocal and that the answer to the problem of power is not how to dissolve power relations but how to 'take advantage' of them, to attend to their potential for 'reversibility' (p. 282).

And it is in this potential that they see room for solutions to ethical problems, as they are being discussed here, in the composition classroom. In the language assessment context, the ethical problems posed by a subjection of the student by assessor can be responded to by the incorporation of a particular form of self-and-peer assessment into the teacher/assessor's procedures. This form needs to reflect Foucault's requirements for relations of power (and most importantly, Lynch and Jukuri's sense of reciprocality and reversibility) by the assessment process being multidirectional (self–peer; peer–self; student–teacher; teacher–student) with the possibility for constant and equal 'actions upon actions', or responses to the unfolding judgements of self, peer, and teacher. In this way, there is the potential for fair, non-harmful, and non-coercive assessment, dependent upon the ability to achieve true reciprocality (i.e. not having one individual or social role/identity become dominant).

This form of alternative assessment should meet the requirements of the authenticity criteria, as well. To achieve reciprocal relations of power, there needs to be an increase in one's understanding of one's own position as well as that of others (ontological and educative authenticity). And since these relations of power are actions (upon actions), and since in this form of assessment all participants are equally involved in generating and interpreting the assessment information, there is great potential for catalytic authenticity (an action taken on the basis of the assessment information) and tactical authenticity (student and teacher being prepared to move from their involvement in and close understanding of the assessment process to acting upon that information). Evidence for the use of self- and peer-assessment as resulting in validity has been summarised elsewhere (Cram 1995: 274–78), and can be seen to reflect the framework advocated here.

Conclusions

In examining the traditional testing approach to ethicality, we see a focus on creating fairness by controlling conditions and standardising procedures – everyone is treated the same, everyone is given an equal chance. The conditions that affect fairness are not explicitly rendered by traditional validity frameworks – they are kept in the background or removed from the testing context. Alternative assessment, on the other hand, explicitly builds a concern for ethicality into its evaluation of validity, as well as dealing with ethical issues such as fairness in a less controlling fashion than does traditional testing (i.e. through dialogue and negotiation). The conditions that affect ethicality and fairness are part of the data for evaluating validity; they are foregrounded in the discussion.

The issue of power is similarly handled in different ways by the two approaches, and this has implications for the ethical potential of each. Traditional testing addresses power by affirming the unidirectional relationship of domination or subjection between tester and testee; it defines roles of expertise that reaffirm this relationship and keep it implicit to the testing process. Alternative assessment can create the potential for resisting the forms of power characterised by domination and subjection, including that part of the assessment procedure where the results are interpreted. Certain forms of alternative assessment open the process up for the realisation of reciprocal relations of power, with the assessor, assessee and other stakeholders sharing responsibility for the process (see also Shohamy 1996).

In order for alternative assessment to receive a fair hearing from the language testing community and others interested in this approach, it needs to be evaluated with appropriate validity criteria, not those designed for traditional testing or parallel translations of those criteria. Although more work needs to be done in refining alternative validity criteria for use in language testing research, I have attempted to provide some preliminary ideas of what these might look like.

It is important to emphasise, however, that the use of alternative assessment formats will not automatically guarantee validity or ethicality. This has already been pointed out in the educational research literature by Darling-Hammond (original emphasis): '*changes in the forms of assessment are unlikely to enhance equity unless we change the ways in which assessments are used as well*: from sorting mechanisms to diagnostic supports; from external monitors of performance to locally generated tools for inquiring deeply into teaching and learning; and from purveyors of sanctions for those already underserved to levers for equalizing resources and enhancing learning opportunities' (Darling-Hammond 1994:7).

The approach to considering the ethical potential of alternative assessment that I have presented in this paper will hopefully help us to respond to the cautions that have been raised and to the calls for changes in the way assessments are used. The ethical potential for alternative assessment and, hence, for validity in assessment research and practice, is great. We need to continue the move beyond the image of the examination given in the initial quote from Foucault – we need to render assessment as an activity in which the individual is not 'pinned down' to a case-like identity determined by externally imposed 'measurements, gaps, and marks', but is allowed to take an active part in the process, even to resist or 'refuse what one is' by forming reciprocal and creative relations of power with assessment participants. This will require training in order for the negotiation among the stakeholders of the assessment context to avoid becoming an exercise in which strong personalities dominate and create a return to unilateral power relationships. The fact that it may be difficult, that it will require new forms of training and consciousness, as well as additional time and resources, is no reason to abandon the project.

Note

1 Revised version of a paper presented at the 31st Annual TESOL Convention; Orlando, Florida; 12 March 1997; Research Interest Section Academic Session: Research in Language Testing: Consequences and Ethical Issues

References

Birenbaum, M. 1996. Assessment 2000: Towards a pluralistic approach to assessment. In Birenbaum, M. and F. J. R. C. Dochy (eds.) *Alternatives in Assessment of Achievements, Learning Processes and Prior Knowledge*: 3–29. Dordrecht Netherlands: Kluwer Academic Publishers Group.

Chachkin, N. 1989. Testing in elementary and secondary schools: Can misuse be avoided? In B. Gilford (ed.), *Test Policy and the Politics of Opportunity Allocation: The workplace and the law*, pp. 163–87. Boston: Kluwer Academic Publishers.

Cram, B. 1995. Self-assessment: From theory to practice. Developing a workshop guide for teachers. In G. Brindley (ed.), *Language Assessment in Action, Research Series* 8, pp. 271–305. Sydney: National Centre for English Language Teaching and Research.

Darling-Hammond, L. 1994. Performance-based assessment and educational equity. *Harvard Educational Review* 64 (1): 5–30.

Darling-Hammond, L. and A. Wise. 1985. Beyond standardization: State standards and school improvement. *The Elementary School Journal* 85: 315–336.

Foucault, M. (1975) 1979. *Discipline and Punish: The Birth of the Prison* (tr. A. Sheridan). New York: Vintage Books/Random House, Inc.

Foucault, M. 1982. The subject and power. In H. L. Dreyfus and P. Rabinow (eds.), *Michel Foucault: Beyond Structuralism and Hermeneutics*, pp. 208–26. [pp. 208–16 written in English by Michel Foucault; pp. 216–26 translated from the French by Leslie Sawyer.] Brighton, UK: The Harvester Press.

Foucault, M. (1976) 1990. *The History of Sexuality: Volumes 1, 2, and 3* (tr. R. Hurley). New York: Vintage Books/Random House, Inc.

Glaser, R. 1990. *Testing and Assessment: O tempora! O mores!* Pittsburgh, PA: University of Pittsburgh, Learning Research and Development Center.

Guba, E. G. and Y. S. Lincoln. 1989. *Fourth Generation Evaluation*. Newbury Park, CA: Sage.

Guba, E. G. 1990. The alternative paradigm dialog. In E. G. Guba (ed.), *The Paradigm Dialog*, pp. 17–27. Newbury Park, CA: Sage.

Hamayan, E.V. 1995. Approaches to alternative assessment. *Annual Review of Applied Linguistics* 15: 212–226.

Hamp-Lyons, L. 1989. Language testing and ethics. *Prospect* 5 (1): 7–15.

Herron, J. 1988. Assessment revisited. In D. Boud (ed.), *Developing Student Autonomy in Learning*, pp. 55–68. London: Kogan Page.

Hilliard, A. G. 1990. Misunderstanding and testing intelligence. In J. Goodlad and P. Keating (eds.), *Access to Knowledge: An Agenda for our Nation's Schools*, pp. 145–57. New York: The College Entrance Examination Board.

Lynch, D. A. and S. D. Jukuri. 1998. Beyond Master and Slave: Reconciling Our Fears of Power in the Writing Classroom. *Rhetoric Review* 16 (2): 270–288.

Messick, S. 1996. Validity and washback in language testing. *Language Testing* 13: (3) 241–56.

Messick, S. 1989. Validity. In R. L. Linn (ed.), *Educational Measurement* (3rd ed.), pp. 13–103. Washington, DC: The American Council on Education and the National Council on Measurement in Education.

Moss, P. A. 1994. Can there be validity without reliability? *Educational Researcher* 23 (2): 5–12.

Moss, P. A. 1996. Enlarging the dialogue in educational measurement: voices from interpretive research traditions. *Educational Researcher* 25 (1): 20–28.

Norris, J. M., J. D. Brown, T. Hudson, and J. Yoshioka. 1998. *Designing Second Language Performance Assessments*. Honolulu, HI: Second Language Teaching and Curriculum Center, University of Hawaii.

O'Connor, M. C. 1989. Aspects of differential performance by minorities on standardized tests: Linguistic and socio-cultural factors. In B. Gilford (ed.), *Test Policy and the Politics of Opportunity Allocation: The Workplace and the Law*, pp. 129–81. Boston: Kluwer Academic Publishers.

Peirce, B. N. 1992. Demystifying the TOEFL reading test. *TESOL Quarterly* 26 (4): 665–89.

Raizan, S. *et al.* 1989. *Assessment in Elementary School Science: Publication no. 303*. Andover, MA: National Center for Improving Science Instruction.

Romberg, T. A., E. A. Zarinnia and S. R. Williams. 1989. *The Influence of Mandated Testing in Mathematics Instruction: Grade 8 Teacher Perceptions.* Madison: National Center for Research in Mathematical Science Education.

Schwartz, J. and K. Viator (eds.) 1990. *The Prices of Secrecy: The Social, Intellectual, and Psychological Costs of Current Assessment Practices.* Cambridge, MA: Educational Technology Center.

Shepard, L. A. 1993. The place of testing reform in educational reform: A reply to Cizek. *Educational Researcher* 22 (4): 10–13.

Shepard, L. A. and K. C. Dougherty. 1991. Effects of high-stakes testing on instruction. Paper presented at the American Educational Research Association, Chicago.

Shohamy, E. 1993. The power of tests: the impact of language tests on teaching and learning. *NFLC Occasional Papers* June: 1–19.

Shohamy, E. 1996. Language testing: Matching assessment procedures with language knowledge. In M. Birenbaum and F. J. R. C. Dochy (eds.), *Alternatives in Assessment of Achievements, Learning Processes, and Prior Knowledge*, pp. 143–60. Dodrecht, Netherlands: Kluwer Academic Publishers Group.

Smith, M. L. 1991. Put to the test: The effect of external testing on teachers. *Educational Researcher* 25: 307–33.

Wiggins, G. 1993. Assessment: Authenticity, context, and validity. *Phi Delta Kappa* 75 (3): 200–14.

Wilkes, M. 1995. Learning pathways and the assessment process: A replication of a study on self- and peer-assessment in the ESL classroom. In G. Brindley (ed.), *Language Assessment in Action,* Research Series 8, pp. 307–21. Sydney: National Centre for English Language Teaching and Research.

Wolf, D., J. Bixby, J. III, and H. Gardener. 1991. To use their minds well: Investigating new forms of student assessment. *Review of Research in Education* 17: 31–74.

Worthen, B. R. 1993. Critical issues that will determine the future of alternative assessment. *Phi Delta Kappa* 74 (6): 444–54.

Zessoules, R. and H. Gardener. 1991. Authentic assessment: Beyond the buzzword and into the classroom. In V. Perrone (ed.), *Assessment in Schools: Issues and Possibilities.* Washington, DC: The Association for Supervision and Curriculum Development.

Section Nine

Language testing and SLA

24 Quantitative evaluation of vocabulary: How it can be done and what it is good for

Batia Laufer
University of Haifa

Vocabulary proficiency testing: The need for change

'Lexical knowledge' is defined differently by different people. Naive native speakers would probably classify a word as either 'known' or 'unknown', depending on whether they are able to link its form to a particular meaning. Most researchers, however, agree that lexical knowledge is not an all-or-nothing phenomenon, but involves degrees of knowledge. Some suggest it should be construed as a continuum, or continua, consisting of several levels and dimensions of knowledge (Faerch, Haastrup and Phillipson 1984; Palmberg 1987; Henriksen 1996). At one end of the continuum there might be 'potential vocabulary' (easily recognisable cognates in a learner's L1, Palmberg 1987), or a vague familiarity with the word's meaning (Faerch *et al.* 1984). The other end of the continuum would be the ability to use the word correctly.

The continua approach (Henriksen 1996) consists of a partial-precise comprehension continuum, a depth of knowledge continuum and a receptive-productive continuum. Others describe lexical knowledge as a taxonomy of components (e.g. form, grammatical pattern, meaning, function, relation with other words) each of which can be associated with word comprehension, or word use (Laufer 1990; Nation 1990).

The multifaceted nature of word knowledge means that deepening the knowledge of individual words can be viewed as one aspect of progress in vocabulary learning in general, and in second language learning in particular. Yet progress in L2 vocabulary learning is mostly described in terms of a gradual increase in the learner's vocabulary size, since the most striking difference between foreign learners and native speakers is in the quantity of the words that each group possesses.[1]

An ideal test of a learner's total vocabulary, therefore, would need to measure the breadth of knowledge, i.e. how many words s/he knows and also the depth of knowledge, and how well each word is known. However, the vocabulary sample for such a test would not only have to be large enough to represent the testee's total vocabulary, but would also need to allow for each word to be tested on all aspects of knowledge. While vocabulary depth tests (which try to test as many aspects of word knowledge as possible) are available, the sample of items is not representative (Wesche and Paribakht 1996; Schmitt 1996). Quantitative tests, on the other hand, tend to measure only a single aspect of vocabulary knowledge such as comprehension (Nation 1983), the lexical quality of writing (Arnaud 1992) or the lexical richness of writing (Laufer and Nation 1995).

It is, therefore, not possible to assess general lexical proficiency using an existing test. Yet such an assessment would be invaluable for the purposes of student placement or admission into an educational institution, since lexical knowledge is related to reading, writing, and general language proficiency, as well as academic achievement. Measuring lexical proficiency is also important for research into vocabulary acquisition, as progress in vocabulary involves a gradual increase in the learner's vocabulary size and depth.

Measuring global vocabulary knowledge: The multiple tests approach

Since assessing lexical proficiency is important for both education and research and since no single test of vocabulary size and depth is available, a 'multiple test' approach, using a battery of quantitative tests, each measuring a different aspect of vocabulary knowledge, is suggested. These tests are: the Vocabulary Levels Test (Nation 1983, 1990), which measures passive vocabulary size, a test of controlled productive ability (Laufer and Nation 1999), which measures elicited active vocabulary size, and the Lexical Frequency Profile (Laufer and Nation 1995), which measures lexical richness in composition.

Whilst the importance of aspects of knowledge not included in the above tests, such as understanding peripheral meanings, or awareness of a word's paradigmatic and syntagmatic relations, should not be underestimated, it is argued that the types of vocabulary knowledge tested by these three tests are the most basic in L2 learning.

The advantages of the multiple tests approach for vocabulary measurement are twofold. Firstly, the combined results can provide a comprehensive picture of learners' vocabulary at different stages of language learning. Secondly, by comparing test results for each individual, we can investigate the relationship between different aspects of lexical knowledge in the same learners and the changes that may occur in these relationships as learning progresses. These findings are likely to be useful for learner evaluation and placement purposes, for teaching and research.

Testing passive vocabulary size

The 'Vocabulary Levels Test' tests the understanding of the most basic and frequent meanings of the target words. The target test items are samples from five levels of word frequency: the 2000 most frequent words, the third thousand most frequent words, the fifth thousand, the University World List (Xue and Nation 1984)[2] and the tenth thousand most frequent words. Learners are required to match groups of three words out of six with their paraphrases as in

For example:

1.	original		
2.	private	complete	(key: 6)
3.	royal		
4.	slow	first	(key: 1)
5.	sorry		
6.	total	not public	(key: 2)

The target words are tested in isolation because we are only interested in the students' sight vocabulary, that is, the number of words they can understand without any contextual clues. The answers are dichotomously scored as correct (1 point) or incorrect/blank (0 points). There are five sections in the tests corresponding to each of the five frequency levels. Each section consists of 18 items to give a maximum score of 90.

Testing elicited productive vocabulary size

The 'Test of Controlled Productive Ability' (Laufer and Nation 1999) is modelled on the passive levels test and uses the same vocabulary frequency bands and items. In this test, however, the items are not provided but elicited in short sentences. In order to avoid elicitation of non-target words which may fit the sentence context, the first letters of the target words are provided.

For example:

They will restore the house to its orig__________ state.

This test elicits a cued recall of words and it resembles real life situations where, for example, a speaker tries to access the word which best fits a context that has been specified by an interlocutor.

The items are dichotomously scored as correct or incorrect/blank. An item is considered correct when it is semantically correct, i.e. the appropriate word is used to express the intended meaning. An item is still marked as correct, if it uses the wrong grammatical form (e.g. stem instead of past tense) or contains an unobtrusive spelling error (e.g. * *recieve* instead of *receive*). Items marked incorrect include non-words, like *origan*, or existing words which are incorrect in the context, like *origami* in the example above. As in the test of passive vocabulary size, there are five frequency levels, each comprising 18 items, with a maximum score of 90. In both tests the raw score can be converted into an approximate number of word families the learner knows.

These two tests are available in four parallel versions so that when subjects are tested on both the passive and active tests, or on one of them twice (e.g. in pre- and post-testing) the same items do not reappear.

Testing lexical richness

In contrast to elicited productive knowledge, free productive knowledge has to do with the use of words without any specific prompts as is the case in free composition. The distinction between controlled and free productive vocabulary is necessary, as learners who use infrequent vocabulary when prompted will not necessarily choose to use it in other situations, e.g. when writing letters, reports, compositions, or giving oral presentations.

Free productive vocabulary can be tested by having learners write a composition which is analysed in terms of the proportion of frequent and non-frequent vocabulary. The analysis is performed by the Lexical Frequency Profile (LFP) measure, which shows the percentage of words used from different vocabulary frequency levels in a piece of writing. Consider, for example, a composition which consists of 200 word families. Of these, 150 belong to the first 1,000 most frequent words, 20 to the second, 20 to the University Word List and 10 are not in any list. If we convert these numbers into percentages out of the total of 200 word families, the LFP of the composition is 75%–10%–10%–5%. The entire calculation is done by a computer program which matches vocabulary frequency lists with the learners' compositions after they have been typed into the computer. The profile is calculated for tokens, i.e. all words in the composition, for types, i.e. different words in the composition, and for word families, i.e. groups of base words and their common derivatives.

For the LFP analysis to be performed, the compositions are typed into the computer. During this process, spelling errors that do not distort the word are corrected whilst proper nouns (which are not considered as belonging to the lexis of a given language) and words that are semantically incorrect (e.g. wrong meaning or wrong collocation) are omitted as well since they cannot be regarded as known by the learners.

The LFP can be converted into a condensed profile consisting of the percentage of basic 2,000 words (i.e. the sum of scores on the first two lists) and the percentage of the beyond-2,000 words (i.e. the sum of scores on the University Word List and 'not on the lists').[3] In the above example, the 'beyond 2,000' score is 15% (10+5).

The LFP is topic independent, that is, it is stable for compositions on different topics written by the same students, as long as these are of a general nature and do not involve infrequently used jargon words. (For a detailed discussion of the LFP, see Laufer and Nation 1995.)

Examples of quantitative studies of L2 vocabulary learning

In this section, three studies which were carried out using a combination of vocabulary measures will be discussed.

Vocabulary growth over one year of study

In this study, the three measures of vocabulary were used to investigate both the development of passive, controlled productive and free productive vocabulary knowledge over a one-year period and the changing relationships amongst these three types of knowledge (Laufer 1998). This was done by comparing EFL learners in grades 11 and 12 respectively. As the groups were similar on all variables (i.e. syllabus, teachers, materials, socio-economic status) except years of instruction, any difference between the groups may reasonably be attributed to the difference in years of instruction – six and seven years respectively. In addition to this cross-sectional comparison, a within-subject comparison was carried out investigating relationships among the three areas of vocabulary knowledge.

Table 24.1 presents the results of the three tests. Each score represents a group mean score. The (P) passive and (CA) controlled active results are presented in word families after converting the raw scores on the respective Levels tests. The CA/P ratio is the proportion of CA words out of the P words and was calculated as follows: CA vocabulary divided by P vocabulary x 100%. (FA) free active vocabulary is expressed as a percentage of non-frequent words, i.e. words that are not in the 2,000 most frequent words in the language.

Table 24.1
The effect of one year of study on vocabulary knowledge

	Passive (in word families)	C A	CA/P ratio	Free active (% beyond 2,000)	
10th graders	1,900	1,700	89%	7.1%	(n=26)
11th graders	3,500	2,550	73%	6.7%	(n=22)

These results show that, as might be expected, passive vocabulary has increased the most, followed by controlled active vocabulary, with free active vocabulary developing least over the one-year period.[4]

Passive–active vocabulary relationships and the context of learning

The second study looked at the effect of language learning context (EFL or ESL) on the relationship between passive and active vocabulary. The two learning contexts are distinguished by the amount of input, opportunities for communicative output and requirements for memorisation and controlled use of vocabulary (teacher-designed tasks).

For the study, EFL learners in Israel and ESL learners in Canada were divided into 'intermediate' and 'advanced' groups on the basis of their passive (P) vocabulary scores. In this way matched EFL and ESL groups were established. The pair of groups labelled 'intermediate' scored between 37 and 62 (out of 90) on the passive vocabulary size test, while the 'advanced' groups scored between 63 and 86.

Table 24.2 presents the mean scores of the three types of vocabulary knowledge by learner's P vocabulary level. P and CA results are given in raw scores. The table also shows the differences between ESL and EFL learners on each of the three scores by means of a t-test.

Table 24.2
Comparison of vocabulary test scores of EFL and ESL learners at the intermediate and advanced levels of passive vocabulary knowledge

Vocabulary scores	Intermediate P			Advanced P		
	EFL (n=30)	ESL (n=29)	Diff.	EFL (n=30)	ESL (n=74)	Diff.
P	50	52.7	n.s.	72.2	72.1	n.s.
CA	37	30.3	p<.005	51.6	45.9	p<.05
Ratio	74%	57.5%	p<.0005	71.4%	63.2%	p<.005
FA	10%	9.8%	n.s.	15.8%	12.3%	p<.005

Both groups of EFL learners had greater controlled active vocabulary than their ESL counterparts, and the more advanced EFL learners also had higher free active vocabulary. These results may at first look surprising, as they suggest that the EFL context, which is disadvantaged in terms of language input and opportunities for practice, is nevertheless more conducive to the activation of passive vocabulary. The results make good sense, however, if one accepts that language learning is conditional upon mental effort and enforced output (Swain 1995). These are characteristic of the conscious learning and formal instruction characteristic of EFL contexts.

The larger P–CA gap and lower FA vocabulary of the ESL learners mean, mathematically, that if we compare EFL and ESL learners with similar CA or FA, the ESL learners will have a larger passive vocabulary than the EFL learners. This may be the result of exposure to a large number of lexical items in the ESL learners' environment. Thus, an ESL context may facilitate the rapid growth of passive vocabulary even though their activation may lag behind that of EFL learners. The EFL context, on the other hand, appears to be more conducive to activation of the vocabulary that is being learnt.[5]

Activating passive vocabulary: 'traditional' versus communicative language teaching

The third study looks at the effect of teaching methodology on vocabulary learning. Educationists believe that using vocabulary in communicative tasks is more beneficial to developing active vocabulary than requiring learners to memorise isolated words, or leaving them to their own devices. Language teachers in Israel have been using the communicative teaching method for years. In the People's Republic of China, on the other hand, communicative language teaching has only recently been introduced and is still not followed wholeheartedly.

In order to investigate the effect that different teaching methods might have on active vocabulary, groups of EFL adolescent and adult learners in Israel (end of high school and university learners) and China (university learners) were compared on passive and controlled active vocabulary size. Two groups of similar passive vocabulary size were identified and compared on their controlled active vocabulary. In addition, the compositions of second year English department students in Israel and China respectively were analysed for lexical richness. The topic of the compositions was the same in both contexts: arguments for and/or against China's 'one child' policy.

Table 24.3 presents the means for passive vocabulary scores, controlled active vocabulary and the CA/P ratio. Table 24.4 shows the lexical profiles of the compositions. Chinese and Israeli learners were compared by t-tests on each vocabulary test and the CA/P ratio. None of the differences was significant.

Table 24.3
Teaching method and controlled active vocabulary

	Passive	Controlled active (out of 90)	CA/P ratio
Method 1 (Israel, n=46)	58	41.4	72.5%
Method 2 (Chinese, n=31)	56.6	38.9	69.2%
difference	not sign.	not sign.	not significant

Table 24.4
Teaching method and free active vocabulary

	Free active (% of beyond 2,000 words)
Method 1 (Israel, n=46)	11.6%
Method 2 (Chinese, n=43)	13 %
difference	not significant

Tables 24.3 and 24.4 show that learners with similar passive vocabularies in the two teaching methods also have similar active vocabularies. These results may look surprising at first, as it is generally believed that Communicative Language Learning is more beneficial for language performance than non-communicative approaches. However, one explanation may be that learning style is more important to the outcome than teaching style. Interviews with learners, teachers and British Council English Language Officers in China revealed that motivated Chinese learners rehearse the new vocabulary in isolation and memorise chunks of language from texts. They also practise new words in a self-generated context silently or in conversations with peers. Apparently, this method is just as effective as using words in the communicative tasks designed by the Israeli teachers. The 'Chinese method' has provided the learners with 'virtual input' (Sharwood-Smith 1998) and resulted in pushed output (Swain 1995), both of which are associated with learning.

Summary and conclusion

The three studies illustrated how quantitative measures of vocabulary can help researchers to investigate a number of vocabulary learning issues: the development of different aspects of lexical knowledge, changes in the passive–active vocabulary relationship over time and the changes it undergoes as lexical knowledge grows, and the effect of language learning context and teaching methodology on the activation of passive vocabulary.

As for the development of lexical knowledge, the first study suggests that the three dimensions of lexical knowledge develop at different rates as learners proceed in their L2 learning, with active vocabulary developing more slowly than passive vocabulary. With regard to the passive-controlled active vocabulary ratio, Studies One and Two show that it is not stable, but seems to decrease with increase in passive vocabulary (Study One), or to stabilise. (In Study Two, there were no significant differences in the CA/P ratios between intermediate and advanced learners, both in EFL and ESL contexts.) As for the effect of the traditional and communicative teaching methods on the activation of passive vocabulary, Study Three suggests that the type of teaching method may be less important than is generally believed. Learners may compensate for the shortcomings of non-communicative teaching by developing effective vocabulary learning strategies.

Further applications of a combination of quantitative vocabulary measures could include investigation of lexical attrition, the relationship between lexical knowledge and language proficiency in general, and of ultimate attainment of L2 knowledge. Whilst there may well be alternative methods for measuring vocabulary, it is nevertheless important for quantitative vocabulary knowledge to be measured and investigated, since the quantity of learners' vocabulary is indicative of the quality of their language.

Notes

1 For example, graduates of Israeli high schools are expected to have learnt about 3500–4000 word families in English as a foreign language while 18-year-old native speakers of English are reported, according to modest estimates, to have mastered 18,000–20,000 word families at the end of high school (Nation 1990).
2 Comprising 836 words.
3 For advantages of the beyond 2,000 measure, see Laufer 1995.
4 For a detailed description and discussion of the study, see Laufer 1998.
5 For a detailed description and discussion of the study, see Laufer and Paribakht 1998.

References

Arnaud, P. 1992. Objective lexical and grammatical characteristics of L2 written compositions and the validity of separate component tests. In P. Arnaud and H. Bejoint Eds., *Vocabulary and Applied Linguistics,* 133–145. London: Macmillan.

Faerch, C., K. Haastrup and R. Phillipson. 1984. Learner Language and Language Learning. Clevedon, Avon: Multilingual Matters.

Henriksen, B. 1996. *Semantisation – a key process for vocabulary learning and use*. Paper presented at 11th AILA Conference, Jyväskylä, Finland.

Laufer, B. 1990. Ease and difficulty in vocabulary learning: Some teaching implications. *Foreign Language Annals* 23: 147–56.

Laufer, B. 1995. Beyond 2000: A measure of productive lexicon in a second language. In L. Eubank, L. Selinker and M. Sharwood-Smith Eds., *The Current State of Interlanguage,* 265–72. Philadelphia PA: John Benjamins.

Laufer, B. 1998. The development of passive and active vocabulary in a second language: same or different? *Applied Linguistics* 19: 255–71.

Laufer, B. and P. Nation. 1995. Vocabulary size and use: Lexical richness in L2 written production. *Applied Linguistics* 16: 307–22.

Laufer, B. and P. Nation. 1999. A vocabulary size test of controlled productive ability. *Language Testing* 16: 36–51.

Laufer, B. and T. S. Paribakht. 1998. Relationship between passive and active vocabularies: Effects of language learning context. *Language Learning* 50: 365 – 91.

Nation, I. S. P. 1983. Testing and teaching vocabulary. *Guidelines* 5: 12–25.

Nation, I. S. P. 1990. *Teaching and Learning Vocabulary.* New York, NY: Heinle and Heinle.

Palmberg, R. 1987. Patterns of vocabulary development in foreign-language learners. *Studies in Second Language Acquisition* 9: 201–20.

Schmitt, N. 1996. *How much depth is there in vocabulary size tests?* Paper presented at the 11th AILA World Congress, Jyväskylä, Finland.

Sharwood-Smith, M. 1998. Cognitive processes in second language development, input enhancement and the role of consciousness. http://www. let.uu.nl/MYOZK.htm#englishplace

Swain, M. 1995. Three functions of output in second language learning. In G. Cook and B. Seidelhoffer Eds., *Principles and Practice in Applied Linguistics: Studies in Honour of H. G. Widdowson,* 125–44. Oxford: Oxford University Press.

Wesche, M. and T. S. Paribakht. 1996. Assessing second language vocabulary knowledge: Depth versus breadth. *The Canadian Modern Language Review* 53 (1): 13–40.

Xue Guoyi and I. S. P. Nation. 1984. A University Word List. *Language Learning and Communication* 3: 215–29.

25 Some thoughts on testing grammar: An SLA perspective

Rod Ellis
Auckland University

Introduction

Traditionally, the testing of grammar has involved indirect system-referenced tests (Robinson and Ross 1996).[1] Such tests are supported by the belief that grammar is central to learning a language and by the availability of psychometric techniques for developing reliable tests. However, the testing of grammar is also an important part of many tests based on models of communicative language proficiency. Modular models of communicative competence such as those proposed by Canale and Swain (1980) and Bachman (1990) include 'grammatical competence' – the knowledge required to understand and produce grammatical sentences in a language. Such models suggest that communicative language proficiency can be measured by obtaining separate measures of the components that comprise it. Thus, they provide a theoretical basis for system-referenced testing in general and for testing one component of proficiency (such as grammar) in isolation from other components (e.g. sociolinguistic or discourse competence).[2] Furthermore, system-referenced tests of grammar based on such models continue to be of the indirect rather than the direct kind, doubtless because these are much easier to administer and to score. For example, the Test of English as a Foreign Language (TOEFL), perhaps the best known and most widely used test of language proficiency, tests a well-established set of grammatical items by means of unspeeded multiple choice selections and grammaticality judgements, methods that Lado (1961) would recognise as familiar.

The question that arises, however, is 'how valid is such a system-referenced approach to grammar testing?' This chapter seeks to address this question by drawing on SLA research, in particular, that research that has investigated variability in learner-language. The aim is to put forward a number of 'provisional specifications', which language testers might like to consider.

The nature of L2 grammatical knowledge

A general distinction is made in cognitive psychology and in SLA between **implicit** and **explicit** linguistic knowledge (see N. Ellis 1994). Implicit knowledge is the knowledge of a language that is typically manifest in some form of naturally occurring language behaviour, such as conversation. It has two major characteristics: it is intuitive and it can be rapidly processed. Explicit knowledge is knowledge about a language. Two types of explicit knowledge can be distinguished. Explicit knowledge in the form of **metalanguage** consists of knowledge of the technical and semi-technical terms for describing a language. Explicit knowledge in the form of **analysed** knowledge involves an awareness of linguistic form and of form-function mappings which can exist independently of whether learners possess the metalanguage needed to verbalise their knowledge. Explicit knowledge, in contrast to implicit knowledge, is accessed only slowly. Even fully automatised explicit knowledge cannot be accessed as rapidly as implicit knowledge.

This psycholinguistic modelling of the L2 learners' knowledge raises important questions for language testing. What kind of knowledge do testers want to test? How can they test it? Traditional grammar tests – and we have already noted that some contemporary tests have continued in the same mode – have largely ignored these questions, assuming that 'knowledge of grammar' is undifferentiated in nature such that a pencil-and-paper test, like the TOEFL, can provide an adequate measure of what a learner knows. In contrast, SLA researchers have long recognised the heterogeneous nature of learners' grammatical knowledge and the need, therefore, to obtain varied samples using different kinds of tests in order to establish what a learner knows (see, for example, VanPatten and Sanz 1995).

Testers can choose to measure (1) implicit knowledge, (2) explicit knowledge as metalanguage, (3) analysed explicit knowledge, or, of course, any combination of these. In part, their decisions will need to reflect the kind of grammatical proficiency deemed relevant to the particular population of subjects being tested. For example, if the population consists of learners planning to enrol in an academic programme, then, arguably, the test would need to measure both implicit knowledge and analysed explicit knowledge but probably not metalanguage.[3] A case for testing metalanguage could be made, however, if it can be shown that this contributes to learners' overall L2 proficiency. However, recent studies by Alderson, Clapham and Steel (1997) and Han and Ellis (1998) suggest that this is not the case. In other populations (e.g. a group of L2 learners planning to study linguistics), a test of metalanguage might be deemed relevant. In part, though, the decision about what kind of knowledge to test will be theoretically rather than practically motivated. If, as the psycholinguistic model outlined above suggests, it is implicit knowledge that is primary in the sense that this is the kind of knowledge that language users rely on most to generate output, particularly in unplanned discourse, then testers will need to find ways of testing what grammar learners know implicitly.

This constitutes a considerable challenge. Most grammar tests probably do not provide reliable measures of learners' implicit knowledge. Consider again the TOEFL. The TOEFL Test and Score Manual (1997) explicitly informs us that the language tested is 'formal' rather than 'conversational' (p. 12), presumably because of the wish to exclude the grammar of colloquial spoken English. More importantly, the manual also informs us that 94% of examinees are able to complete all the questions in the grammar section, thus indicating that 'speed is not an important factor' (p. 29). Clearly, the designers of the TOEFL consider this a desirable characteristic of the test. However, because learners are under no time pressure, they will be able to access their explicit knowledge in answering the questions. In fact, there is no way of knowing what kind of grammatical knowledge the test measures, as the design of the test makes it possible for learners to achieve correct answers using either their implicit knowledge or their analysed explicit knowledge. It is perhaps not surprising that many learners attempt to prepare for the TOEFL by learning explicit rules of grammar.

How, then, can implicit knowledge of grammar be measured? This is a question of considerable importance to SLA researchers, for it is implicit rather than explicit knowledge that is deemed indicative of whether acquisition has taken place. The solution usually adopted is to devise a task that calls for the unmonitored use of the target feature in unplanned discourse. Typically, this requires performance-referenced testing by means of a communication task. The problem with such a solution, however, is that it is extremely difficult to devise tasks that make the use of specific grammatical features essential (see Loschky and Bley-Vroman 1990). From the language tester's point of view, this makes such a solution unworkable for, as Davies (1990) has pointed out, 'test measurement is also a practical matter' (p. 6). Whereas the failure of a task to elicit the use of a specific grammatical structure may not totally negate the value of a teaching task, it constitutes an obvious failure in the case of a testing task. However, the very nature of implicit knowledge suggests another solution. As we noted above, implicit knowledge is easily accessed because it is represented in a form that makes for automatic use. It is possible, therefore, that pressurising learners to perform a discrete-item grammar test under a time constraint will oblige them to draw on their implicit knowledge. In other words, far from it being desirable to eliminate speed as a factor, as assumed by the designers of TOEFL, it is possible that a speeded test may actually be necessary to ensure that implicit, as opposed to explicit knowledge, is tested.

There is some evidence to support such a conclusion. Han and Ellis (1998) found that scores on a timed grammaticality judgement test (their intermediate-level subjects were given 3.5 seconds to judge each sentence) loaded on a different factor from scores on an untimed version of the same test. The timed test factored together with an oral production test while the untimed test factored with a measure of metalingual knowledge. Han and Ellis argue that the two factors might be appropriately labelled 'implicit' and 'explicit knowledge'. Furthermore, they found that whereas the untimed test produced significant correlations with the learners' TOEFL scores, the timed test did not. This study suggests that there may be a significant difference in the kind of grammatical knowledge a test measures, depending on whether the test is performed under time pressure. It also suggests that timed discrete-item tests may be an effective way of measuring implicit knowledge.

Another solution to the problem of testing implicit knowledge might be to design **interpretation tests** (i.e. tests that require learners to process a grammatical structure in the input by reading or listening and then to demonstrate that they have comprehended it). Such tests have been developed for researching the comparative effects of input processing instruction and production practice (e.g. VanPatten and Cadierno 1993; VanPatten and Oikkenon 1996). In one version of such tests, learners listen to (or read) a sentence and then select the picture that matches its meaning. VanPatten has argued that interpretation tests tap more directly into learners' implicit knowledge. Such a claim, of course, remains speculative. However, timed interpretation tests seem especially likely to prevent learners from accessing their explicit knowledge. Also, there is really no sound theoretical reason why grammar should be tested solely through production. Davies (1990) notes that, for practical reasons, tests are typically receptive rather than productive, so it is surprising that grammar tests have traditionally tested only production.

The order and sequence of acquisition

One of the principal findings of SLA research is that learners progress through an **order** of acquisition (see R. Ellis 1994, Chapter 3). That is to say, they acquire some grammatical structures before others. For example, where English is concerned, 'verb+*ing*' is acquired early whereas '3rd person-*s*' is acquired much later and subject relative pronouns are acquired before object relative pronouns. Furthermore, there is convincing evidence that the order of acquisition is largely universal. Various explanations for the existence of such an order have been proposed but these need not concern us here. The important point from the tester's point of view is that grammatical structures are not equivalent in difficulty, if difficulty is equated with the order in which the structures are acquired.

Not only do learners acquire different grammatical structures in a definite order, they also pass through stages in the acquisition of any particular grammatical feature. That is, they manifest **sequences** of acquisition. For example, in acquiring English negatives learners begin with anaphoric '*no*', progress to external negation (e.g. 'No Mary live here'), then to internal preverbal negation using '*no/don't*' + verb (e.g. 'Mary no live here'), and finally, to internal post-verbal negation incorporating auxiliary verbs (e.g. 'Mary doesn't live here'). Again, such sequences, while influenced in minor ways by the learner's L1, have been shown to be robust and universal.

It follows, therefore, that learners can manifest development even without acquiring the target form. This is because some interlanguage forms are more 'advanced' than others. For example, a learner who overgeneralises the use of the irregular past tense form to produce errors such as '*goed*' can be considered more advanced than a learner who uses the simple form of the verb ('*go*') in contexts requiring the past tense. As Corder (1967) long ago pointed out, errors provide evidence of learning.

These well-attested facts of L2 acquisition pose a number of problems to language testers concerning both the choice of content of a grammar test and the method of testing. Testers have long recognised the importance of ensuring that the items they test are at an appropriate level of difficulty for the learners taking the test. For example, Bachman (1990) comments that 'the precision of test scores will be lessened to the extent that the test includes tasks at levels of difficulty that are inappropriate for the ability level of the group being tested' (p. 36). There are two steps involved in the selection of items: first, the tester makes an initial selection based on some set of theoretical principles for determining the level of difficulty of individual grammatical features (and, more likely than not, the tester's own experience of teaching and testing) and second, the tester then trials the chosen items on a sample drawn from the population the test is intended for and analyses the results using, for example, item response theory to maximise the fit between the items and the learners. Information about the order of acquisition is of obvious relevance to the initial choice of grammatical items. To date, however, the initial choice has been guided by the same general and vague notions of difficulty that inform the design of structural syllabuses (see Krahnke 1987). These are self-evidently unsatisfactory. For example, a feature like 3rd person-*s* is generally perceived of as 'simple', yet it is late-acquired. From an acquisitional perspective, therefore, this feature would be considered 'difficult'.

This conflict between traditional criteria and the findings of SLA reflects the distinction between explicit and implicit knowledge discussed above. The traditional criteria relate to explicit knowledge; 3rd person-*s* is a relatively easy grammatical feature to understand (see Krashen 1982). In contrast, the SLA findings speak to implicit knowledge; 3rd person-*s* is a relatively difficult grammatical feature to acquire. Again, then, we see the necessity of testers determining what kind of grammatical knowledge they wish to test, as different principles will be required to guide the selection of grammatical content for a test of implicit and explicit knowledge. To date, testers have paid little attention to the order in which learners acquire different grammatical features. This may reflect the fact that the tests they have constructed permit learners to use their explicit knowledge.

The findings relating to sequence of acquisition are even more troubling to testers. Measures of grammatical knowledge are invariably based on target-language norms. That is, a testing item is scored according to whether learners display a knowledge of the correct target-language form. Thus, in a multiple choice item such as the one below, choice C would be considered correct and the other choices incorrect.

Mary _______ a salad for lunch yesterday.
A. eat
B. eated
C. ate
D. eating

An acquisitional perspective, however, suggests the need to take account of interlanguage norms as well as target-norms. Thus, B might be considered a more advanced interlanguage norm than A or D on the grounds that it is acquired later. One way of acknowledging this might be to devise a scalar scoring system (i.e. award 2 marks for C, 1 mark for B and 0 marks for A and D) instead of the dichotomous system usually applied to such testing items. An acquisition perspective might also be applied to grammaticality-judgement items. For example, learners are likely to find the sentence:

Mary eat a salad for lunch yesterday.

easier to judge as ungrammatical, particularly in a timed test, than the sentence:

Mary eated a salad for lunch yesterday.

even though both are ungrammatical when judged against target language norms. Again, the ability to judge such sentences correctly might be differentially rewarded, depending on the level of difficulty they pose the learner. To some extent, then, testers may be able to overcome the problem of basing measures of grammatical knowledge entirely on target language norms.

Variable L2 performance

SLA research has provided convincing evidence that learner-language, like native-speaker language use, is inherently variable (see Tarone 1988 for a review of the relevant research). The extent to which this variability is solely a performance phenomenon, as claimed by Gregg (1990), or is indicative of a heterogeneous competence, as argued by Tarone (1990) and Ellis (1990), remains controversial. This issue is also of importance to the language tester for, as Bachman (1990) points out, there is a need to decide what kinds of performance are most relevant and representative of the targeted abilities. Clearly, then, the language tester can benefit from an understanding of the sources of variability in learner-language.

There is widespread recognition that the **linguistic context** affects language learners' use of grammatical structures. That is, learners supply one variant of the structure in one context and another variant in a different context. Consider this example:

* Maria lives in New Jersey but she work in Manhattan.

In the main clause, the verb is correctly marked for 3rd person-*s* ('lives') but in the subordinate clause, the simple form of the verb ('work') is erroneously used. Linguistic contexts can be weighted according to whether they favour the use of the target form (or, perhaps, a more advanced interlanguage form). Thus, learners are more likely to supply a form such as 3rd person-*s* in a 'heavy' context, such as main clauses, than in a 'light' context, such as subordinate clauses. The language tester, then, needs to give careful thought to the linguistic contexts in which specific grammatical features are tested. Testing features in 'heavy' contexts may provide an over-estimation of what learners actually can do (and, arguably, of what they actually know). Conversely, testing features in 'light' contexts may lead to an under-estimation. One possibility might be to test items such as 3rd person-*s* twice, once in a heavy context and once in a light context. Alternatively, the choice of context might be made with reference to the learner's overall 'level of proficiency', a test for beginners focusing primarily on heavy contexts and a test for more advanced learners including light contexts. Whatever, the effects of linguistic context cannot be ignored in the design of a grammar test.

The **sociolinguistic context** is the second source of systematic variability. Again, there is plenty of evidence to show that situational factors such as the addressee influence L2 performance (and, in the opinion of some, interlanguage development). Tarone and Liu (1995), for example, show that a Chinese boy's use of English varies according to whether he is speaking to his teacher, other students or a familiar adult (the researcher). Tarone and Liu found that new grammatical structures were most likely to appear first in conversation with the familiar adult and least likely with the teacher. Such a finding is of obvious importance for the administration of tests such as the

ACTFL, where test takers are required to interact with an unfamiliar adult (comparable in status to the teacher in Tarone and Liu's study). Such tests may lead to a serious under-estimation of the learners' grammatical proficiency.

Contextual factors, such as the addressee, induce **style shifting** (Tarone 1983). In Labovian terms, this means that learners vary according to whether they manifest a careful or vernacular style or some style in between. The choice of linguistic forms varies according to the style the learner selects. Stylistic variation is a complex phenomenon. Whereas early research indicated that target language variants (or more advanced interlanguage variants) occurred more frequently in the learner's careful style and (less advanced) interlanguage variants in the vernacular style, subsequent research (e.g. Tarone 1985) has shown that vernacular language use can be more target-like. A grammar test, whether of the pencil-and-paper kind (where the addressee is some distant examiner) or of the interview kind, is likely to tap the learner's careful style. As such, it can provide only a partial and incomplete measurement of grammatical proficiency. Again, it is not clear how this problem can be addressed as there are obvious problems in creating situations that tap into the learner's vernacular style. It may be that all that the tester can do is acknowledge the difficulty of measuring anything other than careful language use.[4]

It is much easier for the language tester to take the third source of systematic variability – **psycholinguistic context** – into consideration. This refers to the conditions of language comprehension and production that influence learners' choice of linguistic forms. The condition that has attracted the most attention is planning time. A spate of recent studies (e.g. Foster and Skehan 1996; Mehnert 1998) have shown that giving learners the opportunity to plan prior to production leads to both greater grammatical accuracy and complexity when performing communicative tasks. Wigglesworth (1997) reports the results of a study designed to investigate the effects of giving low and high proficiency learners one minute to plan prior to performing different testing tasks. She tentatively concludes that the planning time assisted the high proficiency learners with regard to both grammatical accuracy and complexity but not the low proficiency learners.[5]

The question facing testers, then, is whether to incorporate planning time into grammar tests, whether of the contextualised kind involving communicative tasks, as in Wigglesworth's study, or the discrete-point kind, as in the TOEFL. One line of argument is that tests should 'bias for the best' (Swain 1984), which would favour the allocation of planning time. A more convincing argument, however, is that it will depend on what kind of knowledge the tester wishes to test (see earlier discussion). Giving learners planning time may enable them to make fuller use of their existing knowledge; no planning time may force them to rely more on those knowledge forms that have been deeply learned and are readily accessible. In part, it will depend on what type of language use (planned or unplanned) is relevant to particular test takers. In many cases, test designers might want to sample learners' performance with and without planning. An encouraging finding of both Mehnert's and Wigglesworth's studies for the design of tests is that even one minute of planning time can have a marked effect on grammatical accuracy. This makes the provision of planning time in a test practical.

It should be noted that planning time and time pressure constitute separate factors in the design of a test. Planning time concerns whether learners have the chance to prepare *before* they perform, which may assist the selection of the learners' more advanced interlanguage forms; time pressure concerns whether they have the chance to deliberate *while* performing, which may be conducive to monitoring. Thus, we can envisage four different kinds of tests:

1 planning/untimed;
2 planning/timed;
3 no planning/untimed; and
4 no planning/timed.

However, to date, no study has investigated the differential effects of permuting these two variables in this way on learners' use of grammatical forms.

Summary and conclusion

The purpose of this chapter has been to examine grammar testing from the perspective of SLA research with a view to developing a number of 'provisional specifications' that language testers might like to consider. These specifications will be summarised with reference to the three steps that Bachman (1990) suggests are involved in test measurement.

Defining constructs theoretically:

Language testers need to:

1 distinguish implicit and explicit knowledge;
2 reconsider the notion of 'task difficulty' by taking into account the 'order' of acquisition;
3 reconsider the use of target language norms as the sole criteria of what learners know;
4 consider sources of variability in determining which kind of performance they wish to measure.

Defining constructs operationally:
Language testers should consider:

1 using indirect system-referenced tests that incorporate a time pressure factor as a practical way of measuring implicit knowledge;
2 testing implicit grammatical knowledge by means of interpretation tests as well as production tests;
3 designing testing tasks (e.g. multiple choice) so as to give credit to learners who demonstrate a knowledge of advanced interlanguage forms;
4 determining task difficulty with reference to factors that induce variability (e.g. the social status of the addressee, linguistic context and the opportunity to plan).

Quantifying observations:

Direct system-referenced tests quantify observations in terms of the number of items deemed 'correct', with the scores generally treated as comprising an interval scale. However,

1 Learners' grammatical knowledge might be more usefully characterised in scalar rather than dichotomous terms, with points awarded for the display of advanced interlanguage forms as well as target language forms.
2 Scores may need to be weighted to reflect the level of difficulty of a given grammatical structure.

Davies (1990) points out that 'the fundamental argument/debate in language testing over the last 25 years has been basically about the meaning/realization of language behaviour' (p. 137). Similarly in SLA there has been debate over how to obtain valid and reliable measures of what L2 learners know. The debate arises because there is no direct measure of competence; what learners 'know' can only be deduced from what they 'do'. In a sense, then, all testing is 'performance testing'. The task facing the researcher/tester is to decide what kind of performance to test. The problem, as Clark (1972) recognised long ago, is that 'there will always be the possibility of a discrepancy between student performance on a test and his performance in the real-life situations which the test is intended to represent' (p. 125). Overcoming this problem (or, perhaps, minimising it, as it is uncertain whether ultimately it can ever be overcome), arguably requires the expertise of both SLA researchers and language testers.

Notes

1 Robinson and Ross (1996) distinguish system-referenced and performance-referenced tests, both of which can be direct or indirect. Grammar tests are almost invariably of the system-referenced kind and usually direct.

2 In contrast, performance-referenced tests have not been used to test grammar. Such tests are directed at identifying a set of 'work plans' (Clark 1972) that can be tested. Interestingly, however, measures of grammar derived from the performance of such tasks have been found to correlate significantly with overall performance scores (e.g. McNamara 1996).

3 Since the advent of structuralist and behaviourist approaches to teaching grammar, there has been a widespread rejection of testing metalanguage, or even of including metalingual terms in testing rubrics. This rejection has been theoretically driven. The recent research provides an empirical basis for avoiding metalanguage in proficiency testing.

4 It would be wrong to equate careful language use (a sociolinguistic construct) with the use of explicit knowledge (a psycholinguistic construct). In fact, careful language use, like vernacular language use, may draw on both implicit and explicit knowledge. However, as careful language use involves some degree of conscious attention to the choice of linguistic forms, it may favour the use of explicit knowledge.

5 Whereas the research conclusively shows that planning time assists complexity, rather more mixed results have been obtained for its effects on accuracy, with some studies showing a quite clear effect (e.g. Foster and Skehan 1996 and Mehnert 1998) and others no effect.

References

Alderson, C., C. Clapham and D. Steel. 1997. Metalinguistic knowledge, language aptitude and language proficiency. *Language Teaching Research* 2: 93–121.

Bachman, L. 1990. *Fundamental Considerations in Language Testing*. Oxford: Oxford University Press.

Canale, M. and M. Swain. 1980. Theoretical bases of communicative approaches to second language teaching and testing. *Applied Linguistics* 1: 1–47.

Clark, J. 1972. *Foreign Language Testing: Theory and Practice*. Philadelphia, PA: Center for Curriculum Development.

Corder, S. P. 1967. The significance of learners' errors. *International Review of Applied Linguistics* 5: 161–9.

Crookes, G. 1989. Planning and interlanguage variation. *Studies in Second Language Acquisition.* 11: 183–99.

Davies, A. 1990. *Principles of Language Testing*. Oxford: Basil Blackwell.

Ellis, N. (ed.) 1994. *Implicit and Explicit Learning of Languages.* London: Academic Press.

Ellis, R. 1990. A response to Gregg. *Applied Linguistics* 11: 384–91.

Ellis, R. 1994. *The Study of Second Language Acquisition.* Oxford: Oxford University Press.

Foster, P. and P. Skehan. 1996. The influence of planning and task type on second language performance. *Studies in Second Language Acquisition* 18: 299–323.

Gregg, K. 1990. The variable competence model of second language acquisition and why it isn't. *Applied Linguistics* 11: 364–83.

Han, Y. and R. Ellis. 1998. Implicit knowledge, explicit knowledge and general language proficiency. *Language Teaching Research* 2: 1–23.

Krahnke, K. 1987. *Approaches to Syllabus Design for Foreign Language Teaching.* Englewood Cliffs, NJ: Prentice Hall.

Krashen, S. 1982. *Principles and Practice in Second Language Acquisition.* Oxford: Pergamon Press.

Lado, R. 1961. *Language Testing: The Construction and Use of Foreign Language Tests.* London: Longman and Green.

Loschky, L. and R. Bley-Vroman. 1990. Creating structure-based communication tasks for second language development. *University of Hawaii Working Papers in ESL* 9: 161–209.

McNamara, T. 1996. *Measuring Second Language Performance*. London: Longman.

Mehnert, H. 1998. The effects of different lengths of time for planning on second language performance. *Studies in Second Language Acquisition* 20: 52–83.

Robinson, P. and S. Ross. 1996. The development of task-based assessments in English for academic purposes programs. *Applied Linguistics* 17: 455–476.

Swain, M. 1984. Large-scale communicative testing: A case study. In S. Savignon and M. Berns Eds., *Initiatives in Communicative Language Teaching.* Reading, MA: Addison-Wesley.

Tarone, E. 1983. On the variability of interlanguage systems. *Applied Linguistics* 4: 143–63.

Tarone, E. 1985. Variability in interlanguage use: A study of style-shifting in morphology and syntax. *Language Learning* 35: 373–403.

Tarone, E. 1988. *Variation in Interlanguage*. London: Edward Arnold.

Tarone, E. 1990. On variation in interlanguage: A response to Gregg. *Applied Linguistics* 11: 392–400.

Tarone, E. and G. Liu. 1995. Situational context, variation, and second language acquisition theory. In G. Cook and B. Seidlhofer (eds.), *Principle and Practice in Applied Linguistics: Studies in Honour of H. G. Widdowson*. Oxford: Oxford University Press.

TOEFL Test and Score Manual. 1997. Princeton, NJ: Educational Testing Service.

VanPatten, B. and T. Cadierno. 1993. Explicit instruction and input processing. *Studies in Second Language Acquisition* 15: 225–41.

VanPatten, B. and C. Sanz. 1995. From input to output: Processing instruction and communicative tasks. In F. Eckman *et al.* Eds., *Second Language Acquisitions Theory and Pedagogy*. Mahwah, NJ: Lawrence Erlbaum Associates, Publishers.

VanPatten, B. and S. Oikennon. 1996. Explanation versus structured input in processing instruction. *Studies in Second Language Acquisition* 18: 495–510.

Wigglesworth, G. 1997. An investigation of planning time and proficiency level in oral test discourse. *Language Testing* 14: 85–106.

26 Measuring development and ultimate attainment in non-native grammars

Antonella Sorace
University of Edinburgh
Daniel Robertson
University of Leicester

Background

It is generally recognised that the original 'Interlanguage Hypothesis' developed by Corder (1967, 1981) set out the framework and the central questions for much research on adult second language acquisition (SLA) in the last two decades. One of the issues addressed by Corder was that of the nature of the 'interlanguage continuum', and particularly the definition of the learner's 'starting point'; this was essentially the question of the extent of L1 influence on the learner's initial hypotheses about the target language. Corder suggested that interlanguage knowledge progresses along a 'developmental continuum', which starts not from the L1 but from a 'basic universal grammar', corresponding to the 'core' of all natural languages; in some cases, however, interlanguage grammars follow a 'restructuring continuum', starting with the L1, which the learner progressively reanalyses in the direction of the L2 grammar. Equally important in the early debate was the question of the 'final point' of the interlanguage continuum, and the recognition that native-like competence is an ideal target that most learners approximate to but never attain because they 'fossilise' at an earlier stage. The basic intuition underlying these ideas is that interlanguage grammars are natural languages in their own right, that is, they are subject to the same kind of constraints, and should be analysed with the same tools, as fully developed languages.

While Corder's theories clearly were on the right track, they had a speculative flavour that, with hindsight, is easy to ascribe to a lack of conceptual and methodological tools for analysis; like other early second language theorists (e.g. Krashen 1981), he was in a sense 'ahead of his time', which meant that many of the innovative concepts he proposed could not receive either a full theoretical interpretation, or an empirical validation, until much later.

It is thus not surprising that current theoretical second language acquisition research engages in the same debate that Corder's pioneer research opened up thirty years ago, but from the vantage point of modern linguistic theory, psycholinguistics and experimental psychology. As in early interlanguage theory, the principal objects of enquiry are, on the one hand, the identification of Universal Grammar (UG) constraints on the learner's initial state and, on the other hand, the characteristics of the final state(s) that can be attained. A definition of the initial state has to do, as Corder suggested, with the question of whether and to what extent L1 knowledge informs the learner's hypotheses. A definition of 'attainable' final state is necessary in second language acquisition because, unlike L1 acquisition, the final state is not uniformly and deterministically attained; rather, final states often diverge both from the target and from each other. At the same time, the developmental question, namely the nature of intermediate interlanguage grammars, is of special importance in SLA precisely because the final state is not known in advance (see Zobl 1995 for similar arguments).

Theories of the initial state differ, sometimes considerably (see Schwartz and Eubank 1996), but they all assume (a) some degree of L1 transfer, and (b) the existence of UG constraints at all stages of the acquisition process. Simplifying somewhat, three positions can be identified according to the extent to which the L1 is hypothesised to shape the initial state. The 'Minimal Trees' hypothesis (Vainikka and Young-Scholten 1994, 1996) assumes that lexical projections ('content' categories such as Noun, Verb, Adjective and Preposition) and their associated linear order transfer from the L1, but functional categories (i.e. abstract categories such as Tense and Agreement) do not; instead these are added progressively by lexical learning, in an order determined by their hierarchical position. This position, like Corder's 'developmental continuum', predicts that, all other things being equal, learners follow the same route, regardless of their L1. In contrast, the 'Full Transfer/Full Access' position (Schwartz and Sprouse 1994, 1996) argues that the L1 grammar *in toto* constitutes the L2 initial state; learners' progress consists of a gradual restructuring of their grammars which is failure-driven, that is, led by exposure to input that cannot be accommodated in terms of the current grammar. Like Corder's idea of a restructuring continuum, this position predicts that learners will follow different (L1-dependent) routes among the ones permitted by UG, and may end up with representations that are divergent from the target, but still 'possible' in terms of UG. An intermediate position is the 'Weak Transfer' or 'Valueless Features' hypothesis (Eubank 1994, 1996), according to which both lexical and functional projections from the L1 transfer, but the 'strength' of the features of functional heads – the engine of movement in current generative linguistic theory – does not. Learners acquire feature values on the basis of exposure to the morphology of the L2. The prediction of this theory is that until the feature values have been acquired, early interlanguage grammars present unconstrained variation.

Regardless of the form attributed to the initial state, the consensus emerging from this research is that non-native grammars may be non-convergent with respect to the target but nevertheless are UG-constrained. This generalisation implies the abandonment of the 'identity assumption' (Sorace 1996b), according to which the only evidence for UG constraints on the acquisition of a second language (L2A) is the correspondence between learner and native grammars, or the similarity in the sequences of stages followed by child and adult acquirers. The focus of most recent research is no longer invariance, but rather limits on variance. This new perspective allows for the possibility that non-native grammars may exhibit certain subtle features that distinguish them from native grammars. It has been shown, for example, that non-native grammars may take paths that are divergent from the target, and yet display features that are found in other natural languages (see White 1996 for a review).

Furthermore, even learners who are capable of native-like performance often have knowledge representations that differ systematically from those of native speakers (Sorace 1993); final states can therefore be not only indeterminate, or incomplete (as assumed by the early concept of 'fossilisation') but also divergent. Indeed, divergence in ultimate attainment is to be expected precisely because the adult learner's initial state is different from the child's. However, divergence is a very elusive feature to investigate, since it may not be manifested in the learner's production.

Another particularly elusive feature that typically characterises interlanguage grammars, and makes them divergent from the target, is optionality. The term refers to the availability of two alternative realisations of the same syntactic construction, which typically are not in random distribution; rather, learners' patterns of preferences for one variant over the other change systematically in the course of development (Sorace 1996b, in press; Sorace *et al.* 1999). Optionality is common in L1 acquisition, and is frequently ascribed to the underspecification of functional categories, which is in turn due to the child's following a maturational schedule. However, L1 optionality is a transient phenomenon, whereas it can be protracted and even permanent in L2 grammars. For example, Robertson and Sorace (1999) show that the grammar of very advanced German learners of English still exhibits the V2 constraint (see Section 2 for more details), while White (1990/1991) and Eubank (1994), among others, attempt an explanation of the long-lived optionality of adverb placement in French learners of English. The pervasiveness of optionality in L2A may be due to the fact that L2 learners often do not receive sufficiently robust evidence to be able to expunge non-target optional variants, regardless of whether these are derived from the L1 or not. Optionality, however, is not necessarily the hallmark of a 'rogue' grammar (contrary to what is suggested in e.g. Towell and Hawkins 1994):

since it is a property of natural language grammars, it can be accounted for on the basis of the same mechanisms.

Given the multiplicity of non-overt paths and patterns of attainment that characterise L2 acquisition, the empirical investigation of non-native grammars requires sophisticated techniques that are sensitive enough to capture non-overt states of indeterminacy, divergence, or optionality. Magnitude estimation is one of these techniques.

An illustrative example: Losing the V2 constraint

To illustrate the use of magnitude estimation in the investigation of interlanguage development, we consider now some results from a study which makes crucial use of the technique (Robertson and Sorace 1999). The study was prompted by evidence from a corpus of essays written by German first-year undergraduate students of English that the interlanguage (IL) grammar at this stage has traces of the 'verb-second (V2) constraint' of the L1 (German) grammar. Examples such as the following will be familiar to those who teach English to German learners:

1 First of all one has to realise that in the past new developments always affected society. Whether it was the radio or the car it doesn't make any difference. **Always have been conservative warnings** that the harms would outweigh the positive consequences. But nevertheless these warnings couldn't stop the development.
2 Although in a highly developed country, like Germany, the majority of the people are well off, **for many kids is living with their parents** a nightmare.
3 I like to watch people thoroughly. In streets and in trains, in station halls and in narrow elevators, **everywhere do human beings perform plays**: short plays, dramas and comedy.

What these examples (the relevant parts are printed in bold) have in common is the fact that the first clausal-constituent is not the subject of the clause. In such circumstances the grammar of German requires that the finite verb should occupy the second position; the subject (if there is one) is displaced to third position, giving rise to so-called 'subject-verb inversion'. The V2 constraint is the requirement that the finite verb in German main declarative clauses must occupy the second position in the sentence.

The evidence of subject-verb inversion in the written IL of these learners suggests that the IL grammar is characterised by a 'residual' V2 constraint. However, it is clearly not the case that the V2 constraint is categorical in its application, since not all learners at this level make this kind of mistake, and even those who do use the form do not use it consistently (see Robertson and

Sorace, in press, for details). These considerations give rise to a number of empirical questions. First, if there is evidence of the sporadic application of a V2 constraint at advanced levels, do learners at lower levels apply the constraint more frequently? Secondly, do the IL grammars of even the most advanced German learners of English retain traces of the constraint? Thirdly, if the constraint is ultimately eliminated from the grammar, does this process occur gradually, or 'catastrophically' as a result of a radical restructuring of the grammar?

In order to answer these questions it is necessary to devise some means of measuring the strength of the V2 constraint in the IL grammar. There are two kinds of evidence which are potentially relevant to hypotheses about interlanguage development: language production (written or spoken) or language intuitions (usually in the form of judgements of acceptability). Production data have two disadvantages for an investigation of this type: subject-verb inversion is infrequent, so a large corpus would be necessary before reliable frequency counts could be obtained, and production data do not provide evidence as to the status of constructions which are unacceptable (i.e. incompatible with the IL grammar). In contrast, acceptability judgements enable one to focus with some precision on constructions which are of interest, and they also make it possible to measure the extent to which sentences are unacceptable.

For these reasons, the study required a methodology which measures the strength of preference for the verb-second construction at different points on the developmental continuum. In order to do this, acceptability judgement tests using magnitude estimation with native speakers of German were carried out at five levels: Grade 8 (G08: average age 14, n = 64), Grade 10 (G10: average age 16, n = 70), Grade 12 (G12: average age 18, n = 71), first-year university (UN1: average age 20, n = 21), and fourth-year university (UN4: average age 24+, n = 24). The tests were also administered to two groups of native speakers of English: fifth-formers at a Scottish secondary school (NS1: average age 16+, n = 15) and first-year undergraduates (NS2: average age 18+, n = 24).

For materials, pairs of sentences with non-subject sentence-initial constituents were constructed, where one sentence of the pair made use of subject-verb inversion and the other did not. Each experimental sentence was preceded by a sentence which provided a context for the felicitous application of the V2 constraint. The examples below are representative:

4 Context: I hate the smell of cigarettes.
a. Because of this I have always refused to allow smoking in my house.
b. *Because of this have I always refused to allow smoking in my house.

Both of these test sentences begin with a discourse adverbial ('Because of this'), and, as we have indicated, in such circumstances the finite verb must appear in the second position in German, giving rise to subject-verb inversion. Thus, the German equivalent of (4a) would be ungrammatical, while the German equivalent of (4b) would be grammatical (except for the fact that the non-finite verb would be clause-final in German). The judgements are of course reversed in English.

In a typical experiment using magnitude estimation to quantify judgements of linguistic acceptability, the procedure is as follows. A range of different sentence types and distractors is used and the sentences are presented to the subject in random order. The subject is instructed to assign any number that seems appropriate to the first sentence to indicate its acceptability, and to assign numbers to subsequent sentences to indicate their acceptability in proportion to the acceptability of the first sentence. Thus, if the first sentence is given the number 4, and the next sentence is judged to be twice as acceptable as the first, the subject will give the second sentence the number 8. The subjects are told that there are no upper or lower limits to the numbers that they can use, so long as the numbers are greater than zero. In particular, they are told that they can use numbers less than 1. (For more details of the procedure, see Bard, Robertson and Sorace 1996.)

For the analysis, the raw responses are transformed into logs, and the strength of preference for each sentence-pair is calculated as the difference between the logs for each sentence. To give an example, suppose the subject assigns the number 10 to sentence (4a) and the number 2 to sentence (4b). The difference between the logs of these two numbers is 2.3026 -0.6931 = 1.6095. When exponentiated, this difference represents a ratio: $e^{1.6095} = 5.00$, which is of course the ratio of 10 / 2 = 5. These differences can be treated as the dependent variable in the experimental design, and the results can be reported in terms of this 'strength of preference' score. For the experiment being reported here, one-way ANOVAs were conducted, with strength of preference as the dependent variable and level of development (as determined by group membership) as the independent variable. The source of significant effects was identified by means of Tukey's test for the posthoc comparison of means.

As we have indicated, the strength of preference for V3 over *V2 was tested by means of several similar constructions which shared the feature that *V2 is grammatical in German but ungrammatical in English. The dependent variable in this analysis is the mean of the strength of preference scores for ten different V3/*V2 constructions. Figure 26.1 shows the mean strength of preference for V3 over *V2 by all groups in all V3/*V2 constructions[1]:

The effect of level is significant ($F[6,282] = 2.62$, $p = 0.0174$).

A Tukey test shows that this effect is due to significant differences between the mean strength of preference of the first-year university group UN1 and the three lower-level non-native speaker groups G08, G10 and G12. No other comparisons are significant.

Figure 26.1
Overall mean performance for V3 over *V2

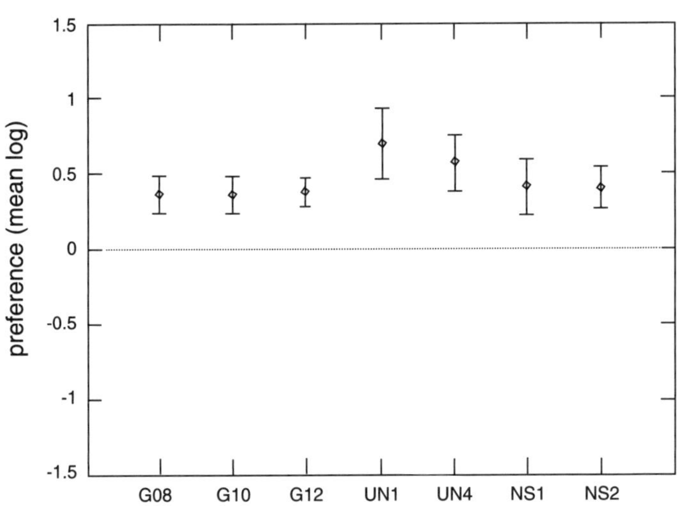

The main generalisation which emerges from these results is that all groups (including the lowest-level non-native speaker group G08) show a determinate preference for the grammatical V3 structures over the ungrammatical *V2 structures. There is some evidence of development, in the significant differences between the first-year university group and the three lower-level non-native speaker groups, but this is not compelling, especially as there are no significant differences between the most advanced non-native speaker group and the three lower-level groups.

Discussion and conclusion

Recall that the study was designed to find evidence for the existence of a residual V2 constraint in the IL grammar of German learners of English. It is clear that there is no evidence for such a constraint in the grammar of these learners considered as a group, even at the lowest level. It is difficult to reconcile this conclusion with the evidence from our corpus of undergraduate essays that there is a residual V2 constraint in the IL grammars of advanced learners.

The explanation which we propose for this apparent conflict between the corpus evidence and the experimental evidence is that the V2 constraint is an **optional feature** of the IL grammar across the whole range of the developmental continuum. Closer examination of the corpus shows that only a minority of the writers (at a level equivalent to the UN1 group in the experimental study) make use of the V2 construction, and those who do use it use it only occasionally. There is therefore variation in the group and in the individual in the application of the V2 constraint. The experimental evidence points to a similar conclusion: at each level, a minority of subjects shows an overall preference for the ungrammatical *V2 sentences over the grammatical V3 sentences, but none of these subjects is completely consistent in their preferences. The proportion of subjects at each level who show an overall preference for *V2 over V3 decreases gradually from a high point of 18 per cent in the lowest-level group (G08) to a low of 4.5 per cent in the UN4 group. The evidence of the corpus and the experimental study taken together suggests strongly that the V2 constraint is an optional feature of the IL grammar, even at the most advanced levels.

Aside from its theoretical interest, this conclusion is of interest for methodological reasons. The method of choice for most SLA researchers who wish to quantify judgements of acceptability has usually been a dichotomous scale ('Correct' or 'Incorrect') or some variant of a Likert-type scale (e.g. Five points on a scale between 5 = 'Correct' to 1 = 'Incorrect'). As Sorace (1996a) has pointed out, such scales have severe limitations: in particular, they do not allow for the application of parametric statistics in the analysis. The advantage of magnitude estimation in this respect is that magnitude estimates provide measurement on at least an interval scale, making it possible to make use of the full range of parametric statistical techniques. These techniques include, crucially in the present context, the use of ANOVA with complex experimental designs, including repeated measures designs (Winer 1971; Girden 1992) and multiple comparison tests, both planned and unplanned (Maxwell 1980; Keselman 1982; Klockars and Sax 1986; Toothaker 1993). Such tests provide powerful and well-recognised procedures for estimating the statistical significance of differences between means; in particular, they make it possible to detect changes in the acceptability of particular sentence types from one stage of IL development to the next.

In sum, magnitude estimation of linguistic acceptability provides a sensitive and reliable technique for the measurement of change (between groups) and difference (between sentence types) in interlanguage grammars. This is well demonstrated in a number of studies conducted at the University of Edinburgh in recent years, including those of Yuan 1993, Ratwatte 1994, and Dube 1998. It is not too fanciful to suggest that this, and related, work at

Edinburgh represents the fruit of a marriage between the speculative tradition in interlanguage studies initiated by Pit Corder and a rigorous approach to measurement in applied linguistics as insisted upon by Alan Davies (Allen and Davies 1977, Davies 1990).

Note

1 The error bars show the 95 per cent confidence limits for estimation of the population means. The confidence limits provide a useful 'eyeball' test for statistically significant differences among the means: where the confidence limits for two means do not overlap, the difference between the means is statistically significant.

References

Allen, J. P. B. and A. Davies. 1977. *The Edinburgh Course in Applied Linguistics, Volume 4: Testing and Experimental Methods.* London: Oxford University Press.

Bard, E. G., D. Robertson and A. Sorace. 1996. Magnitude estimation of linguistic acceptability. *Language* 72: 32–68.

Bhatia, T. and W. Ritchie (eds.) 1996. *Handbook of Second Language Acquisition.* New York, NY: Academic Press.

Corder, S. P. 1967. The significance of learners' errors. *International Review of Applied Linguistics* 5: 161–70.

Corder, S. P. 1981. *Error Analysis and Interlanguage.* Oxford: Oxford University Press.

Davies, A. 1990. *Principles of Language Testing.* Oxford: Blackwell.

Dube, S. 1998. The initial hypothesis of Zulu L2 syntax. Unpublished PhD dissertation, University of Edinburgh.

Eubank, L. 1994. Optionality and the initial state in L2 development. In Hoekstra and Schwartz: 369–88.

Eubank, L. 1996. Negation in early German–English interlanguage: More valueless features in the L2 initial state. *Second Language Research* 12: 73–106.

Girden, E. R. 1992. *Anova Repeated Measures.* Newbury Park, CA: Sage Publications.

Hoekstra, T. and B. D. Schwartz Eds. 1994. *Language Acquisition Studies in Generative Grammar.* Amsterdam: John Benjamins.

Keselman, H. J. 1982. Multiple comparisons for repeated measures means. *Multivariate Behavioral Research* 17: 87–92.

Klockars, A. J. and G. Sax. 1986. *Multiple Comparisons.* Newbury Park, CA: Sage Publications.

Krashen, S. D. 1981. *Second Language Acquisition and Second Language Learning*. Oxford: Pergamon Press.

Maxwell, S. E. 1980. Pairwise multiple comparisons in repeated measures designs. *Journal of Educational Statistics* 5 (3): 269–87.

Ratwatte, H. 1994. Activating vs resetting functional categories in SLA: The acquisition of AGR and TNS in English by Sinhalese first language speakers. Unpublished PhD dissertation, University of Edinburgh.

Robertson, D. and A. Sorace. 1999. Losing the V2 constraint. In E. Klein and G. Martohardjono (eds.), *The Development of Second Language Grammars: A Generative Approach*, pp. 317–61. Amsterdam: John Benjamins.

Schwartz, B. and L. Eubank. 1996. What is the 'L2 initial state'? *Second Language Research* 12: 1–6.

Schwartz, B. and R. Sprouse. 1994. Word order and nominative case in non-native language acquisition: A longitudinal study of (L1) Turkish interlanguage. In Hoekstra and Schwartz, pp. 317–68.

Schwartz, B. and R. Sprouse. 1996. L2 cognitive states and the 'Full Transfer/Full Access' model. *Second Language Research* 12: 40–72.

Sorace, A. 1993. Divergent vs incomplete representations of unaccusativity in non-native grammars of Italian. *Second Language Research* 9: 22–47.

Sorace, A. 1996a. The use of acceptability judgements in second language acquisition research. In Bhatia and Ritchie, pp. 375–409.

Sorace, A. 1996b. Permanent optionality as divergence in non-native grammars. Paper presented at the 6th Meeting of the European Second Language Association (EUROSLA), Nijmegen, Holland.

Sorace, A. In press. Near-nativeness, optionality and L1 attrition in Proceedings of the 12th International Symposium of Theoretical and Applied Linguistics. Thessaloniki: Aristotle University of Thessaloniki.

Sorace, A., C. Heycock and R. Shillcock (eds.). 1999. *Language Acquisition: Knowledge Representation and Processing*. Amsterdam: Elsevier.

Toothaker, L. E. 1993. *Multiple Comparison Procedures*. Newbury Park, CA: Sage Publications.

Towell, R. and R. Hawkins. 1994. *Approaches to Second Language Acquisition*. Clevedon, Avon: Multilingual Matters.

Vainikka, A. and M. Young-Scholten. 1994. Direct access to X'-Theory: Evidence from Korean and Turkish adults learning German. In Hoekstra and Schwartz, pp. 265–316.

Vainikka, A. and M. Young-Scholten. 1996. Gradual development of L2 phrase structure. *Second Language Research* 12: 7–39.

White, L. 1990/1991. The verb-movement parameter in second language acquisition. *Language Acquisition* 1: 337–70.

White, L. 1996. Universal grammar and second language acquisition: Current trends and new directions. In Bhatia and Ritchie, pp. 85–120.

Winer, B. J. 1971. *Statistical Principles in Experimental Design.* New York, NY: McGraw-Hill.

Yuan, B. 1993. Directionality of difficulty in second language acquisition of Chinese and English. Unpublished PhD dissertation, University of Edinburgh.

Zobl, H. 1995. Converging evidence for the acquisition-learning distinction. *Applied Linguistics* 16: 35–56.

Section Ten

Beyond language testing

27 Fossilisation: Moving the concept into empirical longitudinal study

Larry Selinker, University of London
ZhaoHong Han, Columbia University

Introduction

Fossilisation, since its reality was suggested – for better or worse – in Selinker (1972), has been a widely recognised and significant feature of what we think we know about second language acquisition. This has been true not only for research discussions but, more importantly, for many teachers as they try to solve the difficult daily problems of second language pedagogy. Teachers often are deeply interested in and have strong opinions about this phenomenon, looking to second language acquisition for clarification and advice. Additionally, fossilisation has appeared to take on popular tones, even appearing in some current dictionaries. It may be that the concept of fossilisation is the only second language acquisition concept that is discussed in broader intellectual circles. It is important, therefore, for us to take stock of the status of this central concept[1] while subjecting it to further scrutiny in an empirical longitudinal sense.

A review of the literature reveals that there has been little advance on what Hyltenstam captured in 1988. Fossilisation remains a phenomenon noted, much puzzled over, little understood, but most importantly, described poorly and certainly not in the necessary longitudinal sense. It seems that a curious intellectual flip-flop has occurred; put in Chomskian (1965) terms, what we have here is not the logically prior description before explanation, but worse: explanation without description. Why have we not moved beyond the situation described by Hyltenstam? One reason, as just hinted, is that there are limited longitudinal fossilisation data accessible for perusal by researchers, and no agreed means of measuring lack of change in language development over time. This situation, as we suggest in our conclusion to this paper, presents a challenge for language testers.

Our goal in this brief paper is to provide some useful guidelines for colleagues needing to interpret the literature on fossilisation and to conduct the longitudinal studies which we feel are necessary to produce convincing empirical evidence of the phenomenon.

Exploring the theory of refossilisation

It is our conclusion – after much discussion with colleagues[2] and much soul searching – that the concept of fossilisation remains elusive for two reasons: first, because of the uncertain theoretical status of the concept, and second, due to the empirical problem of deciding which interlanguage data count as 'fossilised' and which do not. Although these two difficulties have often been conflated, we believe they should be treated as separate issues. In terms of theory, we have not gone beyond what was discussed in Selinker and Lakshmanan (1992) and in Flynn and O'Neil (1988), who state that from the point of view of both linguistic theory and second language acquisition theory: 'we are yet unable to explain the nature of plateaus in learning with adult learners often reported in the literature' (p. 18). Flynn and O'Neil's basic list of research questions still remains a priority, namely:

– *Why do some adults, beyond simply phonological problems, seem never to fully master the L2?*

– *Can these plateaus be explained in terms of a lack of exposure to the essential data base?*

– *Does this suggest an interaction with other domains of cognition (and) something quite deep about the nature of UG?* (Flynn and O'Neil 1988: 18–19).

Finally, they raise a question that places fossilisation concerns squarely within the realms of human cognition:

– *Is it possible to argue that there is an independent domain-specific faculty for language while at the same time maintaining that it is so inextricably tied to other aspects of cognition that it is difficult to affect one area without affecting many others?* (Flynn and O'Neil 1988: 19).

To these, Selinker and Lakshmanan add:

– *Can we produce in principle a list of 'fossilizable structures' that can be theoretically predicted?* (Selinker and Lakshmanan 1992: 212).

The complex question of which interlanguage structures are to be counted as 'fossilised' and which not remains a tough one and will be raised later in the context of our discussion of other kindred concepts such as stabilisation and backsliding.

The fossilisation literature

One complication is that over the past decades, fossilisation has been discussed within two distinct traditions: developmental and ultimate attainment (cf. Rutherford, 1984). The former tradition encompasses a wide range of perspectives, but often emphasises the sociolinguistic (Preston 1989; Tarone, 1994); the latter, interestingly, analyses the problem almost exclusively in terms of one or another form of universal grammar. In the developmental tradition, we find the nub of the fossilisation question to be:

– *How do we as observers know that interlanguage development has ceased?*

In the ultimate attainment tradition, the question is put slightly differently:

– *How do we as observers know that the attainment to date is in fact ultimate and that final steady state grammar, if such a thing exists, has been reached?*

When the focus is on putative 'near-natives'[3] (Coppieters 1987; Birdsong 1992; Sorace 1993; White and Genesee 1996), as is apparently more and more the case, answering this latter question is particularly crucial.

Furthermore, in searching through the vast SLA literature since the early 1970s, it becomes apparent that indirect inquiries into fossilisation appear to be proliferating, whereas direct inquiries remain sparse. Among the few papers dealing directly with the issue of fossilisation are: Vigil and Oller (1976); Schumann (1978); Selinker and Lamendella (1978, 1979); Stauble (1978); Lowther (1983); Tollefson and Firn (1983); Mukattash (1986); Kellerman (1989); Hyltenstam (1988); sections of Preston (1989); Thep-Ackrapong (1991); Washburn (1992);Selinker and Lakshmanan (1992). Most of these provide some theoretical, but disconnected, arguments and some new empirical data. It is beyond the scope of this paper to review this literature comprehensively; we will simply point the reader to Selinker and Lamendella (1978) which deals in detail with the Vigil and Oller study, and to the useful though limited literature reviews in Washburn (1992), Selinker and Lakshmanan (1992). Problematic features of these studies (such as varying and imprecise definitions of fossilisation; assumed rather than demonstrated fossilisation; using data from one point in time; using corrective feedback as metric; and conflating stabilization with fossilisation) have been extracted and will be discussed passim throughout this paper.

Attempts at definitions and theoretical interpretations

Evolving definitions

'Fossilisation' was initially defined thus:

> *...fossilisable linguistic phenomena are linguistic items, rules, and subsystems which speakers of a particular NL native language tend to keep in their IL interlanguage relative to a particular TL target language, no matter what the age of the learner or amount of explanation and instruction he receives in the TL. Fossilisable structures tend to remain as potential performance, reemerging in the productive performance of an IL even when seemingly eradicated.*
>
> (Selinker 1972: 215)

In retrospect, it is clear that this earliest definition of fossilisation delineates six basic properties: first, fossilisation is equivalent to cessation of development; second, fossilisable features pertain to each and every aspect of interlanguage, including phonetic, phonological, morphological, syntactic, semantic, lexical, discoursal and pragmatic features; third, fossilisable features are persistent and resistant; fourth, fossilisation hits both adult L2 learners and child L2 learners; fifth, fossilisable features usually manifest themselves as backslidings in performance, with reemergence of forms being a key indicative marker; finally, note that in this definition fossilisation concerns specific persistent interlanguage features that are to be discovered empirically.

As might be expected, these early definitions have developed over time and this is detailed in Selinker (1992). In 1979, Selinker and Lamendella defined the phenomenon of fossilisation as a 'permanent cessation of IL learning before ... all levels of linguistic structure' of the target language (TL) have been mastered, doubting if such mastery is possible (p. 373). Here Selinker and Lamendella make a strong statement about the permanent nature of fossilisation. In retrospect, one can read into their discussion a tendency to associate fossilisation with both traditions, developmental and ultimate attainment. There is however one important development here: fossilisation is no longer viewed as confined to cessation of development of subsystems but also as pertaining to overall systems, culminating in fossilised competence. Moreover, comparing this definition with the earlier definition, there is here an emphasis on cessation of learning as a cognitive process over the persistent appearance of interlanguage forms.

In Selinker (1992), fossilisation is defined as 'a cessation of IL learning, often far from TL norms' (p. 243). The issue here may boil down to the argument that, as long as learners do not get expected target language norms in all discourse domains controlled by the learner, there is a failure to reach a competence comparable to that of a native speaker and thus fossilisation has occurred. An additional development appears in Selinker (1996), where there is an attempt to come to grips with both L2 competence and L2 performance in one conceptual framework where the concept of fossilisation is related to variation which at times is target-like and at other times non-target-like. That is, the fossilisation can itself be seen in the variation percentages.

Thus, the failure of 'native-speakerhood', even if defined in the literature in different ways, has consistently been predicated on a preprogrammed cognitive condition that fossilisation will occur 'no matter what the learner does' (see all Selinker references). This failure has led to the study of where the learner ends up, which has been called 'ultimate attainment' and to this we now turn.

Concern with ultimate attainment and 'the logical problem' of second language acquisition

The association of fossilisation with L2 learner ultimate attainment has led to queries from a number of quarters into such central issues as the nature of interlanguage, interlanguage competence, and interlanguage processing mechanisms, as well as to a new understanding of the relationship of SLA to UG and L1 acquisition. A key question which has definitional consequences for fossilisation is: how one can explain the so-called 'logical problem of second language acquisition', namely that:

> *few adults are completely successful; many fail miserably, and many achieve very high levels of proficiency, given enough time, input, effort and given the right attitude, motivation and learning environment.*
> (Bley-Vroman 1989: 49)

Bley-Vroman leads from this concern to his 'fundamental difference hypothesis' where what is accessible from universal grammar must be instantiated in the native language. This widely-debated hypothesis can be reframed, in terms of fossilisation, as follows:

– What is fossilisable relates intimately to what is accessible through universal grammar and that, in turn, relates solely to what has been instantiated in the native language.

In this view, which we subscribe to (cf. Selinker and Lakshmanan 1992), language transfer as a causal variable in the formation of interlanguages is a privileged factor.

In contrast, we find that, in one UG version, the ultimate attainment question is phrased as:

> *...why some learners 'fossilize' with divergent ILGs interlanguage grammars whereas others successfully attain a native-like grammar, why some parameters are successfully reset whereas others are not, why positive L2 input is only sometimes successful as a trigger for grammar change?* (White 1996: 115)

What is common to both of the above positions is what we might call a cross-learner perspective. But this is not the only way one can frame ultimate attainment and the logical problem of second language acquisition. We think there is an additional useful way to conceptualise this problem, viz. a within-learner perspective, where there may very well be fossilisation in one discourse domain and not another, and in one subsystem and not another. This latter approach, we feel, is the only one open to longitudinal study of fossilisation and will reveal a number of interesting paradoxes, most often in the same learner's interlanguage, paradoxes such as:

– systematicity AND variability in the same learner's interlanguage
– permeability AND impermeability in the same learner's interlanguage
– stability AND instability in the same learner's interlanguage
– transition AND non-transition in the same learner's interlanguage.

We believe that future studies will reveal strong evidence for the coexistence of these contrasting phenomena. If we are right, an either/or (UG or not) perspective is uncalled for[4] and we need rather to pinpoint the complex dual- (and even multiple-) contextual nature of the subject matter. Primarily we hypothesise in terms of overlapping discourse domains, which might explain why we are likely to find instances of both acquisition *and* fossilisation within a single learner's interlanguage production.

Before we leave definitions of fossilisation, we should note that Nunes (1996), among others, sees it as one of the extreme challenges for SLA theory to explain, not just success with L2 but also failure, and failure is what most dictionary definitions of fossilisation focus on.

Distinguishing various types of stabilisation

In terms of building up a prolegomenon towards understanding (permanent) fossilisation, including identifying instances of fossilisation, it seems essential to examine the nature of stabilisation since this has been a central feature of fossilisation brought out in most definitions. Stabilisation can be defined as the persistence of an interlanguage form over time.[5] Some researchers have interpreted stabilisation as the harbinger of fossilisation (e.g. Schumann 1978; Stauble 1978; Perdue 1993). Interestingly, others have distinguished the two in that stabilisation is correctable and fossilisation is not (cf., e.g. Lin and Hedgcock 1996) – a notion which clearly has important pedagogical implications. Since stabilisation itself can apparently be both short-term and long-term, we have to ask both what 'stabilisation' is and whether it is always a prelude to fossilisation.

As we read the literature, we gather hints on three, not necessarily mutually exclusive, major possibilities that are attachable to the phenomenon of stabilisation of interlanguage form:

1 First, stabilisation could be a temporary stage of 'getting stuck', a natural stage in all learning, though it might have peculiar second language acquisition attributes (Selinker and Lamendella, 1978; Selinker 1992). One place to look for such evidence in the literature would be the theoretical (and Dulay and Burt 1974; Pienemann 1989). Another potential source of evidence would be empirical studies demonstrating 'non-equipotentiality', a feature Schachter (1996) identifies as central to adult L2 acquisition.[6]

2 A second possibility attachable to the phenomenon of stabilisation is that stabilisation itself could involve a permanent cessation of interlanguage development/learning (Selinker 1992; Selinker and Lamendella 1978; Selinker and Lakshmanan 1992). Only in such a case does the issue of fossilisation indistinguishable from stabilisation arise. To equate the two would, however, be problematic given the evidence suggesting that stabilisation can be both short-term and long-term, itself an indication that, as noted by Long (1993), there are different processes involved. While primarily addressing the theme of age-related effects on SLA, Long sees an important difference between short-term and long-term studies in that the former, in his view, speak only to rate of acquisition but not to absolute abilities. Would there be a parallel in the case of stabilisation? In other words, could it be the case as well that short-term stabilisation is a natural product of learning, whereas long-term stabilisation fossilises? If this were true, then only longitudinal evidence would be relevant to fossilisation claims.

3 The third possibility is that stabilisation could be interlanguage restructuring or reanalysis in terms of progressing towards a target language norm, whatever the surface form might look like (Selinker and Lamendella 1978; Selinker 1992). Huebner (1983) noted that at some points the change across time is linear, and that at others there are marked discontinuities. In our view, it is possible that the 'discontinuities' in development appear as 'stabilised' forms which mask the restructuring that is taking place. Another possible case of 'masked change' could be seen in what Kellerman (1983) characterises as 'U-shaped' behaviour. Here, we speculate that the dip in the 'U' may appear persistent or suspended, and the learner's performance at this stage would therefore probably be considered as 'fossilised' by those who view continued non-target-like behaviour as evidence of fossilisation. But in actuality, restructuring is taking place leading to the later observed upsurge in interlanguage development. The question remains: how do we uncover this change when the change may itself be masked? This is another example of our needing to study what is not there, itself a major problem for us (cf. Kaplan and Selinker 1997). Evidence of this third type of stabilisation, i.e. what might be termed superficial stabilisation, may however be available in Klein (1993). Focusing on the acquisition of temporality, Klein suggests that such stabilisation is particularly prevalent in interlanguage development beyond what he terms 'the basic variety'[7]:

> *Further development is slow, gradual and continuous ... For a long time, we observe a coexistence of correct and incorrect usages from the point of view of the TL, and learning is a slow shift from the former to the latter, rather than the product of a sudden insight.*
>
> (Klein 1993: 108–9)

This 'slow, gradual and continuous' development is only discernible through longitudinal study as reflected in Klein (1993).

A further difficulty in distinguishing different types of stabilisation is noted by Huebner (1983), who points out that the dynamics of acquisition can sometimes be blurred by the instrumental measures used in researching interlanguage systems with masked change.[8] A case in point is Schumann's fossilisation data of Alberto, an adult native speaker of Spanish who was seen during the 10-month observation to have 'evidenced very little linguistic development' (Schumann 1978: vii) in the acquisition of English negation. In Schumann's quantitative analysis of the data, frequencies and percentages are both counted on as important indicative variables. Recently, Berdan (1996) has reanalysed the corpus by means of a generalised model of logistic regression, incorporating short-term time as a continuous variable. In contrast to previous findings, this analysis reveals 'slow but steady change on the part of Alberto' (PC), justifying the author's conclusion that 'Alberto was in the process of acquiring negation' (Schumann 1978: 206).

Surface manifestations of stabilisation leading to potential fossilisation

Now if, as many believe, stabilisation is a necessary prelude to fossilisation, then, might stabilisation/fossilisation form a progressive continuum or cline progression (Selinker and Lamendella 1978)? Whichever is the case, we must ask: How do we operationalise stabilisation when it is a prelude to fossilisation? To tackle this question, we refer here to four possible manifestations of stabilisation at an interlanguage performance level that may potentially lead to fossilisation: non-variant appearance, backsliding, stabilised inter-contextual variation, and stabilised intra-contextual variation.

Non-variant appearance

When stabilisation forms a potential continuum with fossilisation, it can manifest itself non-variantly despite continuous exposure to natural as well as pedagogical L2 data – a mark of both persistence and resistance on the part of the subject. This appears to be the case in a longitudinal study of the late Prime Minister Rabin's news interlanguage-English (for further details see Selinker and Douglas in preparation) and in another longitudinal study of

Thai-Norwegian interlanguage (Han and Selinker in press). In this latter study, we have located a non-variant interlanguage structure (null subject – i.e. what is *not* there) in the context of adverb fronting. This phenomenon persists despite positive and explicit negative evidence of full subject in the input.

Backsliding

Getting back to the spirit of the original 1972 definition of fossilisation, we feel we have to tie our conception of fossilisation in some clear way to backsliding (Schachter 1988), which would be manifested in the variational reappearance over time of interlanguage structures that appear to have been eradicated. We know of no studies here, so a hypothetical, but plausible, experiential example will have to suffice. Suppose a Turkish-speaking learner of English produced a sentence like 'I listened a concert yesterday' and then ceased producing this form for some time. Then, he is heard to say 'I listened to a concert yesterday' in a number of different contexts, until one day he reverts to 'I listened a concert yesterday' in similar contexts. If one could find attested examples such as these, it would seem to us that learning and fossilisation can be disentangled because learning has clearly not stopped, with the stabilised form returning only occasionally under some conditions.

Teasing apart backsliding from natural variability (cf. discussion in Gass and Selinker 1994: 180) is however tricky. Brown (1996) reminds us that:

> *...if we acknowledge that in all learning, in first or second language learners, progress is not achieved in a series of discrete stages but rather in bursts and backdrifts and overlapping usages, the question of how such a volatile system of knowledge might be represented in the mind is indeed a live one.* (Brown 1996: 4)

Again we are tempted to think that only longitudinal studies with distributed databases can seriously illuminate the nature of the backsliding phenomenon.

Stabilised inter-contextual variation

By stabilised inter-contextual variation, we refer to a situation in which target-like and non-target-like forms alternate contextually. It may be that this type of variation is amenable to learner control. Here, in contexts which require more monitoring, target-like forms are used, whereas in contexts requiring less monitoring, non-target-like forms are used. To help visualise the scenario, we may cite a few sentences from the database of an on-going longitudinal case study of a Chinese-speaking informant using English as L2, which one of the authors is currently engaged in (Han 1998). In writing to his colleague on email, the informant writes:

(1) The long paper is still here, have not finished yet, especially waiting for your version.

Whereas, to his boss on email, he writes:

(2) Most of the contents in the paper can still be used. The referee is probably correct, but examples of publishing details and more cases after a short paper are seen everywhere.

Sentence (1) contains what is usually called a pseudo-passive (with null subject), a common Chinese-English sentence (Schachter and Rutherford 1979; Rutherford 1983; Yip 1995; Yip and Matthews 1995). If one were to look at data from this informal domain alone, one might conclude that the subject did not know the passive. However, in sentence (2), he produces what looks like an English passive, showing that he has the structure and some degree of control over its use (cf. Han 1998 for further details). While it is not the concern of the present paper to pinpoint the underlying structural connections between (1) and (2), for our purpose here, it is important to highlight the fact that (1) and (2), as well as other structures similar to (1) and (2), have been seen used consistently in different contexts. Another possibility to be explored is that fossilisation may be contextually governed, occurring in one context, whereas control and learning may be possible in another (cf. Selinker and Douglas 1985 for theoretical discussion of this possibility and 1987 for suggestive evidence).

Stabilised intra-contextual variation

A fourth possible surface manifestation of stabilisation leading to potential fossilisation is what we call stabilised intra-contextual variation. Unlike stabilised inter-contextual variation, here variation occurs within the same context on a random basis. At the level of interlanguage production, these interlanguage forms could appear as what Schachter (1996) sees as 'fossilized variation', i.e. random error variation, for which she offers us the following picture:

> *A perfectly fluent adult nonnative speaker (NNS) of English will produce 'I see him yesterday' and shortly thereafter produce 'I saw him yesterday' apparently on a random basis.*
>
> (Schachter 1996: 160)

Whereas inter-contextual variation seems to us subject to learner control, intra-contextual variation may be beyond learner control, thus presenting a most potent form of potential fossilisation. Note that these various surface manifestations may be the key to why there are very different approaches to studying fossilisation, with each focusing on a slightly different phenomenon.

Conclusion

We have attempted to characterise in this paper the complex nature of the concepts of stabilisation/fossilisation and to identify some of the many questions which still remain to be addressed. The current lack of clarity in the field of SLA about these concepts should be worrying both for ourselves and for those outside our discipline who depend on us for understanding of this basic cognitive phenomenon. To make headway in this area, we need, as researchers, to pay close attention to the often untidy and theoretically recalcitrant phenomena which we encounter in our struggle to understand from the outside observer perspective those learner-internal processes which lead to short- or long-term cessation of interlanguage development.

We have made a case for longitudinal studies of stabilisation/fossilisation, despite the inevitable difficulties in setting them up and maintaining them, because without such studies, there is no way we can be sure that *no* change has occurred in an interlanguage form over time. We have also tried to argue here that, as we contemplate how we can establish the pre-requisites to organising such studies, there are certain issues we can no longer avoid. Thus, before we can approach such central cognitive issues as: Does fossilisation exist only in second language acquisition or can one find this in other human mental modules? we need to produce at the very least either a theoretically driven or an empirically discovered list of fossilisable structures. We must also arrive at unambiguous definitions of theoretical terms; clear connections between related theoretical terms; and clear criteria as to what we consider to be reasonable degrees of proof. We need this also to see whether our cognitive view of fossilisation as primarily a mental process belonging to an individual mind makes empirical sense.

We can now ask: What role for the language tester? We wish to state that not only can language testers provide much help in this research but that the benefit can be mutual. Testers can devise long-term pre- and post-testing procedures which are sensitive not only to language development but also to any lack of development which may be attributed to fossilisation. Fossilisation researchers need to employ some form of elicitation device, 'language test' in the broadest terms, to collect the longitudinal data we have called for. Language testers have a lot to offer fossilisation research, provided that, as advocated by Bachman and Palmer (1996) and Douglas (2000), they take greater account of context in their test design. By paying serious attention to contextual features (what Bachman and Palmer call 'task characteristics') testers can help account for the kind of variation in fossilisation performance referred to above.

Context-sensitive elicitation procedures, designed by language testers in collaboration with SLA researchers and administered at different stages in the learner's development, can help elucidate the complex nature of fossilisation phenomena – permeability, systematicity, stability, transition – alluded to above. Such co-operation between SLA researchers and language testers can be mutually beneficial, with the 'tests' themselves becoming more valuable in principle by providing more useful information about learner systems in general.

Notes

1 As far as we can tell, the last state-of-the-art discussion of this concept was in Selinker and Lamendella (1981), where the phenomenon was described from a neurolinguistic perspective which is clearly out of date.
2 Here Alan Davies has particularly helped us over the years to bridge the conceptual gap between interlanguage thought and language testing (see e.g. the introduction to the important volume Davies 1984). For this chapter, we have had important discussions about fossilisation and language testing with Dan Douglas and Lyle Bachman.
3 One thing we are sure about: language tests as a measure of near-nativeness are highly suspect, but that is the subject of another paper.
4 Cf. E. Klein (1993: 237) who comes to the same conclusion.
5 We are constantly being asked how much time is enough to decide whether a form has fossilised or not and there seems to be no precise answer, either theoretically motivated or empirically determined. Moving the discussion to stabilisation does not change this difficult issue. Our contention is that the time needed to discern stabilisation may depend on individual variables, but is surely subject to such factors as the subjects' learning conditions, personal learning history and knowledge of the target language. This has methodological implications in that it may be the case that studying fossilisation in beginners would need longer observation of stabilised interlanguage forms than studying advanced subjects who have learnt an L2 for, say, ten years.
6 Schachter (1996) notes the importance of the fact that L2 learners typically find some languages more difficult than others, integrating this with psychotypology notions.
7 W. Klein (1993) divides the entire acquisitional processes into three major steps: pre-basic varieties; basic varieties and further development. He claims that fossilisation is most likely to hit learners in the stage of basic variety because of satisfaction of communicative needs and lack of compelling factors to motivate further development.
8 This relates to our previous question of the difficulty of studying what is not there.

References

Bachman, L. F. 1989. Language testing-SLA research interfaces. *Annual Review of Applied Linguistics* 9: 193–209.

Bachman, L. F. and A. S. Palmer, 1996. *Language testing in Practice*. Oxford: Oxford University Press.

Berdan, R. 1996. Disentangling language acquisition from language variation. In R. Bryley and D. Preston (eds.), *Second Language Acquisition and Linguistic Variation.* Amsterdam: Benjamins.

Birdsong, D. 1992. Ultimate attainment in second language acquisition. *Language* 68: 706–55.

Bley-Vroman, R. 1989. What is the logical problem of foreign language learning? In S. Gass and J. Schachter (eds.), *Linguistic Perspectives on Second Language Acquisition.* Cambridge: Cambridge University Press.

Brown, G. (ed.) 1996. *Performance and Competence in SLA*. Cambridge: Cambridge University Press.

Chomsky, N. 1965. *Aspects of the Theory of Syntax.* Cambridge, MA: MIT Press.

Coppieters, R. 1987. Competence differences between native and near-native speakers. *Language* 63 (3): 544–73.

Davies, A. 1984. Introduction to Interlanguage. In A. Davies, T. Howatt and C. Criper (eds.), *Interlanguage*. Edinburgh: Edinburgh University Press.

Douglas, D. 2000. *Assessing Language for Specific Purposes: Theory and Practice*. Cambridge: Cambridge University Press.

Douglas, D. and L. Selinker. 1985. Principles for language tests within the 'discourse domains' theory of interlanguage: Research, test construction and interpretation. *Language Testing* 2: 205–26.

Dulay, H. and M. Burt. 1974. Natural sequences in child second language acquisition. *Language Learning* 24: 37–53.

Flynn, S. and W. O'Neil. 1988. *Linguistic Theory in Second Language Acquisition*. Dordrecht: Kluwer Academic Publishers.

Gass, S. and Selinker, L. 1993 (eds.) *Language Transfer in Language Learning*. Rowley, MA: Newbury House.

Gass, S. and L. Selinker. 1994. *Second Language Acquisition: An Introductory Course*. Hillsdale, NJ: Lawrence Erlbaum Associates Publishers.

Han, Z.H. 1998. Fossilization: An investigation into L2 learning of a typologically distant language. Unpublished PhD dissertation. University of London.

Han, Z.H. and L. Selinker (in press). Error resistance: Towards an empirical pedagogy. *Language Teaching Research* 3(3): 248–75.

Huebner, T. 1983. *A Longitudinal Analysis of the Acquisition of English.* Ann Arbor, MI: Karoma.

Hyltenstam, K. 1988. Lexical characteristics of near-native second language learners of Swedish. *Journal of Multilingual and Multicultural Development* 9: 67–84.

Kaplan, T. and L. Selinker. 1997. Empty, null, deleted, missing, omitted, absent ... items in interlanguage. Review article of E Klein 1993. *Second Language Research* 13 (2): 170–86.

Kasper, G. 1997. Can pragmatic competence be taught? Plenary presented at 1997 TESOL Annual Convention, Orlando.

Kasper, G. 1996. The development of pragmatic competence. In E. Kellerman, B. Weltens, T. Bongaerts (eds.), *EuroSLA* 6: *A selection of papers* (= *Toegepaste Taalwetenschap in Artikelen* 55), 103–20.

Kellerman, E. 1983. 'Now you see it, now you don't'. In Gass and Selinker 1993.

Kellerman, E. 1989. The imperfect conditional: Fossilization, cross-linguistic influence and natural tendencies in a foreign language setting. In K. Hyltenstam and L. Obler (eds.), *Bilingualism across the Life Span.* Cambridge: Cambridge University Press.

Klein, W. 1993. *Toward Second Language Acquisition: A Study of Null-Prep.* Dordrecht: Kluwer Academic Publishers.

Lin, Y.-H. and J. Hedgcock, 1996. Negative feedback incorporation among high-proficiency and low-proficiency Chinese-speaking learners of Spanish. *Language Learning* 46(4): 567–611.

Long, M. H. 1993. Maturational constraints on language development. *Studies in Second Language Acquisition* 12: 251–85.

Lowther, M. 1983. Fossilization, pidginization and the monitor. In L. Mac-Mathuna and D. Singleton (eds.), *Language Across Cultures.* Dublin: Association for Applied Linguistics.

Mukattash, L. 1986. Persistence of fossilization. In Nehls-Dietrich (ed.), *Interlanguage Studies*, pp. 59–75. Heidelberg: J. Groos.

Nunes, D. 1996. Issues in second language acquisition research: Examining substance and procedure. In Ritchie and Bhatia, pp. 349–72.

Perdue, C. 1993. *Adult Language acquisition: Cross-linguistic Perspectives. Volume I: Field Methods*. Cambridge: Cambridge University Press.

Pienemann, M. 1989. Is language teachable? *Applied Linguistics* 10: 52–79.

Preston, D. 1989. *Sociolinguistics and Second Language Acquisition.* Oxford: Basil Blackwell.

Ritchie, W. C. and T. K. Bhatia. (eds.) 1996. *Handbook of second language acquisition.* San Diego, CA: Academic Press.

Rutherford, W. 1983. Language typology and language transfer. In Gass and Selinker (eds.) 1993.

Rutherford, W. 1984. Description and explanation in interlanguage syntax: State of the art. *Language Learning* 34: 127–155.

Schachter, J. 1996. Maturation and the issue of Universal Grammar in second language acquisition. In Ritchie and Bhatia (eds.).

Schachter, J. 1988. Second language acquisition and universal grammar. *Applied Linguistics* 9(3): 219–35.

Schachter, J. and W. Rutherford. 1979. Discourse function and language transfer. *Working Papers in Bilingualism* 19: 1–12.

Schumann, J. 1978. *The Pidginization Process: A Model for Second Language Acquisition.* Rowley, MA: Newbury House.

Selinker, L. 1972. Interlanguage. *International Review of Applied Linguistics* 10 (2): 209–31.

Selinker, L. 1992. *Rediscovering Interlanguage.* Longman

Selinker, L. 1996. On the notion of interlanguage competence in early SLA research: An aid to understanding some baffling current issues. In G. Brown, K. Malmkjaer and J. Williams (eds.) *Performance and competence in second language acquisition.* Cambridge: Cambridge University Press.

Selinker, L. and D. Douglas. 1985. Wrestling with 'context' in interlanguage theory. *Applied Linguistics* 6: 190–204.

Selinker, L. and D. Douglas. 1987. The problem of comparing 'episodes' in discourse domains in interlanguage studies. *ESCOL' 86: Proceedings of the Eastern States Conference on Linguistics.*

Selinker, L. and J. Lamendella. 1992. Transfer and fossilisation: the multiple effect principle. In S. Gass and L. Selinker (eds.) *Language Transfer in Language Learning*, pp. 197–216. Amsterdam: John Benjamins.

Selinker, L. and J. Lamendella. 1978. Two perspectives on fossilisation in interlanguage learning. *Interlanguage Studies Bulletin,* 3: 143–91.

Selinker, L. and J. Lamendella. 1979. The role of extrinsic feedback in interlanguage fossilisation: A discussion on 'rule fossilisation: A tentative model'. *Language Learning,* 29: 363–75.

Selinker, L. and J. Lamendella. 1981. Updating the interlanguage hypothesis: A neurofunctional perspective. *Studies in Second Language Acquisition,* 3.2: 201–20.

Sorace, A. 1993. Incomplete vs. divergent representations of unaccusativity in non-native grammars of Italian. *Second Language Research* 9 (1): 22–47.

Stauble, A. 1978. The process of decreolization: a model for second language development. *Language Learning* 28: 29–54.

Tarone, E. 1994. 'Interlanguage'. In R. E. Asher (ed.) *The Encyclopedia of Language and Linguistics,* pp. 4: 1715–1719.

Thep-Ackrapong, T. 1991. Fossilization: A Case Study of Practical and Theoretical Parameters. Unpublished PhD dissertation. Illinois State University.

Tollefson, J. and J. Firn. 1983. Fossilization in second language acquisition: an inter model view. *RELC Journal* 14 (2). 19–34.

Vigil, N. A. and J. W. Oller. 1976. Rule fossilization: A tentative model. *Language Learning* 26 (2): 281–295.

Washburn, G. 1992. Fossilization in second language acquisition: A Vygotskian perspective. Unpublished PhD dissertation. University of Pennsylvania.

White, L. 1996. Issues of maturation and modularity in second language acquisition. In Ritchie and Bhatia (eds.).

White, L. and F. Genesee. 1996. How native is near-native? The issue of ultimate attainment in adult second language acquisition. *Second Language Research* 12: 233–65.

Yip, V. 1995. *Interlanguage and Learnability: From Chinese to English.* Amsterdam: John Benjamins.

Yip, V. and S. Matthews. 1995. I-interlanguage and typology: The case of topic-prominence. In L. Eubank, L. Selinker, and M. Sharwood-Smith (eds.), *The Current State of Interlanguage*, pp. 17–30. Amsterdam: John Benjamins.

28 The unbearable lightness of being a native speaker

John C. Maher
International Christian University, Tokyo

Language testing firmly tackles such concepts as 'native speaker' ... and 'language' and gives them definition and operational effect.
Alan Davies, *Language Testing and Evaluation* (1992: 138)

Linguist: Now, does your language have minimal pairs?
Native-Speaker Informant (Kiowa Indian): No, but we do have small apples.
Eugene Nida, *Informants or Colleagues* (1981: 169)

... an air of paradox.
Noam Chomsky, *Aspects of the Theory of Syntax* (1965: 21)

Definition and operational effect

The airy form of the Native Speaker steps light-of-foot through the house of language, past the halls of linguistic philosophy, theoretical linguistics and bilingualism, along to phonetics and language teaching. It visits them all. Its presence is elemental and inspiring and to some observers unbearable. It is a necessary though somehow nameless being.

Writing in *Aspects of the Theory of Syntax* (1965: 21), Chomsky ruminates on the fact that the notion of native speaker is cloaked in 'an air of paradox'. Without doubt, the theory of the autonomy of the native speaker, as it stands, yields paradoxical results. Its weight shifts lightly from one foot to another as it casts off one definition and then assumes another. There is an unbearable lightness in the indeterminate but somehow compelling figure of the native speaker. To continue to survive, the native speaker has long assumed different, disputed identities by shifting guise among a range of properties. Easy come, easy go. Thus, the native speaker: spontaneously uses language for communication, acquires the first language in childhood, knows the rules governing the native language, i.e. has intuitions about the language beyond knowledge of his/her own idiolectal grammar, can joke effectively, has the unique capacity to interpret and translate into the L1, detects lexical, semantic, syntactical absurdity, senses ambiguity, has an intuitive understanding of the social functions of language in use, has the unique capacity to write creatively, e.g. poetry, has a massive memory stock of lexical items.

Now this, now that. Amidst all these guises the ambiguous native speaker is a figure of magic realism. This oxymoron encapsulates Chomsky's description of the 'air of paradox' contained within the native speaker – a being of flesh and blood but also denizen of the territory of the Ideal. The native speaker is capable of calling forth to interrupt the plane of the real world the fantasy and myth that sustains the imagination. It is a multiple reality which depicts both concretely and imaginatively, an alternate to (his) story. It involves the presentation of the highest level of abstraction as, simultaneously, ordinary reality.

Paradoxical results threaten the validity of these definitions and the paradoxes are strange and interesting as Davies has brilliantly shown (Davies 1991: 146–52). The problems have been deemed sufficiently damaging by many observers of the native speaker to prompt calls for the tumbril, the guillotine, for an end to the entire native speaker story. *A Festschrift for the Native Speaker* has been compiled (Coulmas 1981). Other voices are raised:

> *The whole mystique of the native speaker ... should preferably be quietly dropped from the linguist's set of professional myths about language.*
>
> (Ferguson 1983: viii)

> *Native Speaker is ... a sad and sorry figure: royalty without a realm, a relative ruler without roots in reality. We may even say that Native Speaker looks a distant relative of that other famous linguistic refugee: Chomsky's Ideal-Speaker/Hearer*
>
> (Mey 1981: 72)

Along with its alleged pretensions to kingship, the native speaker was employed in language studies for ceremonial effect. In the 1960s, the native speaker became linked inexorably with the paraphernalia of being an expert-informant. In this work, the linguist thus donned the cloak of the magic haymaker separating the wheat from the chaff: finding instances that are ungrammatical and tossing them out.

> *You are a native speaker of English; in ten minutes you can produce more illustrations on any point in English grammar than you will find in many millions of words of random text.*
>
> (Francis 1979: 110)

Thus, the native speaker became a ceremonial totem in the business of gathering and talking about data. Sometimes the native speaker-linguist became more valuable than other kinds of language data available. There is surely more to the native speaker than this.

The fact is, however, that language teachers, learners and educators continue to make use of the notion native speaker. This apparently ambiguous being is evidently doing something right, or being in the right place at the right time. The concept has what Davies has termed 'operational effect'. What is the reason for the longevity of the concept?

Values and necessities

> *The native speaker, [is] a product of the debate over idealism in philosophy.* (Davies 1994: 2719)

Although the lineage of the concept native speaker can be traced back to the Idealist vs Nominalist speculations in medieval philosophy, only in recent times has the concept presented itself both as a potentially (1) valuable construct and (2) necessary construct. Firstly, the native speaker has value because it suggests a way of treating language problems. Linguistics is the thoughtful study of language and the subject matter of language is infinite. This crucial fact imposes upon those who do linguistics the necessity of choosing selective points of view in order to organise the facts of language. One such point of view is the locus of the Native Speaker. It is a polyvalent concept. It comes into being in response to the demands of linguistic theory.

Linguistics constantly strives to address the questions that language poses by making theories of language. Theories and the metaphors of theory unravel and change over time: now *Stammbaumtheorie,* now typological universals. It is *de rigueur* to expect from linguistics explanations of language and to expect also that explanations must involve a theory of language. However, to assume that a theory of language expresses the essence or true nature of language is to appeal to the so-called scientificness of linguistics and to do so is to go down a difficult path. A theory is not a picture and describes nothing. A theory is the finger pointing, not the moon itself, and the native speaker is more likely to be the moon-viewer than the lunar object itself. A theory is a rule-book of symbols that directs how to do the work to be done. For example, the star forms of Indo-European languages are a phonetic algorithm of similarities between the vocabularies of the languages in the phylum. They are a guide for making certain analyses of the structure of vocabulary items and are not themselves a 'picture of the history' of the Indo-European languages. The relevant question is, therefore, not how a theory like 'native speakerness' approximates to a template of reality but, as de Saussure emphasised, the value of a theory [only] lies in providing persuasive explanations of more or less '*principes constants*':

> *Il est vrai que les valeurs dépendent aussi et surtout d'une convention immuable, la règle du jeu, qui existe aussi en matière de langue; ce sont les principes constants de la sémiologie.*
>
> (de Saussure 1980: 126)

Likewise, matters of judgement of a concept *qua* concept (e.g. the hypothesis of the Native Speaker) are typically preceded by questions and puzzles rather than a set of answers, as Frege pointed out: 'We grasp the content of a truth before we recognize it as true' (Frege 1969: 7–8). The existence of the Native Speaker is subject to the constraining influences of need. When the need for Native Speaker theory declines, the theory will move on elsewhere. It remains only a real presence *sub specie functionalitatis*. In this sense, its existence is temporary, both real and fantastical.

Second, the Native Speaker is fundamental to proper explanation. It is part of the operation of **ideal-type** theory of the sort employed by Weber and Marx. Thus, for the sake of theoretical explanation we do two things: first, devise the notion of the ideal speaker–hearer; second, leave out – for the sake of theory – extraneous factors in language acquisition such as time. The latter step is consistent with the notion of Universal Grammar which constructs an instantaneous 'grammar' or 'theory' of what language looks like. Thus, nothing in the actual progress of language acquisition will affect the unfolding of this theory. Ideal-type theory (Max Weber's term) is typical of social science methodology which starts from the imperative that not all judgements should be of empirical fact. Thus, justification for the careful separation of grammatical from agrammatical utterances was methodologically-driven and concerned the proper requirements necessary for the work of idealisation and abstraction which in turn are needed to formulate theory. That this is indeed legitimate work is well elaborated by Chomsky (see Maher and Groves 1997: 7–20).

Traditionally, the grammarian travels down the road with the blinds down, working on a more or less uniform set of phenomena representing language, bracketing variability as non-essential to the task in hand. The grammarian thus imposes standardisation and, in addition, decontextualises it. The sociolinguist, Hymes' 'person in the social world', proceeds with the windows open, observing and making sense of the way in which language is affected by the changing scenery – the various contexts of its use. The limitations of this useful but limited dichotomy can be illustrated by imagining all of language as a dynamic moving object forever captured in a meteor shower of social relations. Language moves forward or back, this way and that only by consideration of the alternatives in meaning that are available to the speaker – hearer. The Hallidayan conception of language as a social semiotic is relevant here as that view considers the contextual features which impinge on the choices of the speaker. The Native Speaker stands at the centre of a hypothesis about language's meaning.

The lightness of the native speaker consists in its habitation in an ideal world. The difficulty initially expressed by sociolinguistically-minded linguists towards the habitus of a native speaker sitting in a homogeneous speech community was their conflation of the notion of **ideal-type** with **pure-type**. Thus, we are liable to confuse ideal-type, a necessary theoretical construct to elaborate other parts of a formulation, with **pure type** – an empirically describable entity – you, me as wholly capable native speakers. However, this misconstruing had desirable consequences because from this emerged the notion 'communicative competence'.

The age of the competence

> *The position taken up by communicative competence is that knowing what to say is never enough; it is also necessary to know how to say it.*
>
> (Davies 1994: 2723)

The native speaker and freedom

Seven centuries of native speakership have elapsed. In the mid-20th century, the field of sociolinguistics regrouped around the same issues of language, state and the individual addressed by Renaissance linguists Pietro Bembo, Poggio Bracciolini, Biondo di Forli and others. Sociolinguistics found new impetus by rebounding off Chomsky's biologic – psycholinguistic formulation of the ideal native speaker. 'The monolithic idealized notion of linguistic competence was ... inadequate' (Verhoeven 1997: 390). A linguistic 'competence' which was not social and which left out situation, purpose, domain and variety was deemed insufficient by a new wave of anthropologically-minded linguists.

In the 1960s–1970s, there emerged also an attractive and timely resource. The charismatic new field of ethnomethodology, now tilting at mainstream sociology, was concerned with the theory of how a speaker constructs and orders speech. It was, in fact, a theory of (native) speaker competence.

'Competence' embodied the *Zeitgeist* of the age, analogue of the universalist ideologies of the 1960s. In the formulation of the period, competence is an inher-ent inher-itance. It is the essential fact of being human. It expresses a universal democracy. Let us describe this further.

Competence is beyond the reach of power relations. It is deep within the individual (viz. Maher and Groves 1997). The 'social logic' of the concept competence conformed to the essential thrust of Chomsky's anarchist philosophy. Our genetic inheritance reinforces language to make it free-standing, non-plastic, able to withstand the powerful pressures of environment. Language is remarkably constant. Just as this unique linguistic endowment keeps language from becoming the bending branch ever at the mercy of the forces of the social wind so also human nature, at its deepest level, is impervious to the blows of outside forces. Oppressive political systems can never ultimately control our minds. We are free men and women. As Chomsky writes in *For Reasons of State*:

> *Language, in its essential properties and the manner of its use, provides the basic criterion for determining that another organism is a being with a human mind and the human capacity for free thought and self-expression, and with the essential human need for freedom from the external constraints of repressive authority.*
>
> (Chomsky 1973: 394)

In this conception, the language of the native speaker is a shared property. There is unity in diversity. We need to obtain a kind of psychic distance from language and see the common characteristics for what they really are rather than being bewitched by the diversity of Babel. The native speaker embodies the universalism of the *Übermensch*, autonomous and rooted in the essentially libertarian structures of the mind. Chomsky, again reflecting on language and freedom:

> *... it is reasonable to suppose that just as intrinsic structures of mind underlie the development of cognitive structures, so a 'species character' provides the framework for the growth of moral consciousness, cultural achievement and even participation in a free and just community. It is, to be sure, a great intellectual leap from observation on the basis for cognitive development to particular conclusions on the laws of our nature ... to the conclusion that human needs and capacities will find their fullest expression in a society of free and creative producers, working in a system of free association in which 'social bonds' will replace 'all fetters in human society'.*
>
> (Chomsky 1973: 133–34)

Rewriting Babel

The connection between a philosophy of language and a philosophy of anarchism glimmers constantly on the horizon of Chomsky's work but, being not understood fully, paradoxically played no part in the revolutionary deliberations of the 1960s. In other ways, however, the exaltation of competence, as a focal point of a *fin de siècle*, necessitated a re-ordering of the other more familiar metaphors.

The Native Speaker proposed by Chomsky was rigorously Platonic and biblical. The native speaker embodied a necessarily pure and Ideal Form to which the commonality of humankind approximated. The Native Speaker was also Man before the Fall unconstrained by the prison house of the social world. In this respect, for the successful birth of late-20th century multiculturalism/multilingualism there was need to reverse two fundamental orders of metaphor: the religious and the psychological. This was accomplished notably by a radical assault on 'Babel' (George Steiner, Einar Haugen, Roland Barthes) and a redefinition of personal psychology (Jung), the latter rejecting the mechanistic topology of the mind proposed by Freud. The rewriting of Babel was undertaken by Einar Haugen after the model of the 'happy bilingual' (not 'the sad bilingual' in the confused prison of many sounding tongues). Now the speaker–hearer takes pleasure, not punishment, in Babel. No longer a confusion, the mix of languages that we experience in our multicultural *vie ordinaire* is an invitation to delight in the spiral Tower of Languages. For Roland Barthes, the text provided by social life now invites 'cohabitation', an irrepressible androgyny of opportunity, a cipher of sexual pleasure – '*jouissance*' : 'the subject accedes to *jouissance* by the cohabitation of languages, which work side by side; the text of pleasure, it is a happy Babel' (Barthes 1972: 10).

This led Barthes to propose the written text itself as the site where active, creative processing is carried out by the reader (an echo of Chomsky's emphasis upon the creative abilities of the speaker). Thus, readers possess literary competence, that is, the capability to handle literary language by constructing the meanings of the text, reading in meanings which are not apparently in the text.

The impact of Jung on the 1960s cannot be underestimated. Jung's formulation of psychological competence complemented the biological theory of Chomsky. I have suggested, elsewhere, that Jungian theory resonates with the notion of universal grammar:

> *The human psyche is composed of innate forms always potentially present, giving direction and form to their actualization in images and action. The collective unconscious is universal; it is shared by everyone ...*
>
> (Jung 1928: 157)

Sociolinguists, in one introductory textbook after another, hastened to demolish Chomsky's asocial definition of competence. They were only to take it back privately to the potter's wheel to refashion it according to the new urgencies of the age. Competence was the prophetic fulfilment of 20th century post-positivist philosophy: Ryle, G. E. Moore, Wittgenstein. It was a celebration of J. L. Austin's 'the plain man' or the 'Logic' of the 'Non-Standard' English [sc. Culture]. The players in the theatre of competence can be classified thus:

1 Common-sense competence (G. E. Moore),
2 Ordinary language competence (Wittgenstein),
3 Speech-act competence (J. L. Austin and J. Searle),
4 [Cultural competence] (Levi-Strauss),
5 [Communicative competence] (Jurgen Habermas),
6 [Sociolinguistic competence] (Dell Hymes),
7 [Cognitive-developmental competence] (Jean Piaget),
8 [Competence of conversational accomplishment] (Schlegoff).

The theme competence has been played throughout linguistic history in various versions. The dichotomy between 'competence' and 'performance', '*langue*' and '*parole*' (de Saussure) was prefigured in the *opera* of the Roman grammarians, notably Varro whose search for paradigmatic regularity led him to postulate the influential concept *analogia* ('proportion') which is the interface between language and the speaker–hearer vs. 'customary usage' of what we now call sociolinguistic reality. A thousand years later, Canale and Swain (1980) outlined the *novo ordo rerum* by noting that any updated definition of the native speaker competence would have to include at least four aspects: grammatical competence (mastery of phonological rules, sentence formation, morphosyntactic rules, etc.); discourse competence (knowledge of rules concerning the cohesion and coherence of various types of discourse); strategic competence (mastery of verbal and non-verbal strategies to compensate for breakdowns and to enhance the effectiveness of communication); sociolinguistic competences (the mastery of sociocultural conventions within varying social contexts). The explosion of the idea of competence and the Native Speaker's move to centre stage was the work of magic reality in which linguistics performed its proper function as the work of replenishment. Through the re-invention of competence by means of the Native Speaker – 'The Competent One' – the old reality of the well-known, traditional and exhausted was turned into something inventive and ambiguous: a magic and ever-so-light reality.

An ending but not a conclusion

> *The native speaker, like Lewis Carroll's snark, is a useful and enduring linguistic myth ... like the snark ...*
>
> (Davies 1994: 2719)

In a story which is both realistic and magic the Native Speaker *knows*. The Native Speaker is haloed by an important trait: 'insight', or intuition. They are related terms. I suggest that this insight is one type of imaginative understanding and it is for this reason that it is, as Chomsky noted, unstable, i.e. we do not always have smooth access to it. Insight is the window by which we interpret other people's behaviour. It is not the possession of an abstruse technique. An important aspect of insight is the ability to recognise resemblances between apparently different experiences of language and its world of lects. We arrive at insight about language because meaning is defined, as Saussure saw, by a web of oppositions and contrasts, that is, 'by everything that exists outside of it' (de Saussure 1959: 115). The Native Speaker is able to deal with oppositions and contrasts because the speaker's identity itself is comprised of such lectal oppositions. In an echo of Saussure, Wittgenstein invoked resemblance-theory as a means of explaining how we make sense of the complicated network of similarities, overlapping and criss-crossing which sometimes have overarching similarities and sometimes similarities of smaller detail: *'ein kompliziertes Netz von Ahnlichkeiten, die einander ubergreifen und kreuzen. Ahnlichkeiten im Grossen und Kleinen'* (Wittgenstein 1960 quoted in Slobin 1979: 152, 195).

The expression 'native speaker' does not point to an orderly fact but it is a simple and creative symbolisation of how we come to 'know' language. It is because this knowing is not at all straightforward that we encounter trouble with our Native Speaker. The Native Speaker *knows* but the knowing is more than having knowledge of language. The Native Speaker HAS knowledge of language, but there is more to having than possession. Here one is inclined to conclude that terminology, like the specialised expression 'The Native Speaker' (article included), is equally the result of the human tendency to mythmake as it is to rationalise and the native speaker might just serve the metafunction of mythic symbol, i.e. an explanatory emblem (ritual, icon, etc.). Returning to the main question, what is the relation, as Davies stresses, between the knowledge held by the living and breathing native speaker and the idealised knowledge possessed by the 'native speaker' when placed in inverted commas? This reels in a question that keeps circling, 'what is basic to knowledge?'

Perhaps we might answer the question by starting to destabilise the notion of possession, i.e. the sense in which a person is said to possess knowledge of language. There are alternatives even to this model. We could say, for instance, that the native speaker 'appropriates' language. Whereas the Native Speaker can be said to possess steady state biological competence of language, a combined competence which takes in also the world of social relations seems to invoke the need for a formulation different from (mere) possession. Rather, language is 'appropriated' (*Aneignung,* the making of a thing one's own) a term borrowed from Marx which emphasizes the human development aspect of knowing language including the operational meanings in language that we receive through experience with expert persons in the surrounding environment (for reference see Leont'ev 1965 and Ishiguro

1996). The interpretations that can be placed upon the Native Speaker as Knower are endless.

I suggest that both symbolisation and rationalisation are necessary to the formulation of the concept 'native speaker'. To know language seems both, on the one hand, to reproduce the nature of language somehow 'as it is', (essentially), but at the same time to frame language in concepts and concept-clusters which are themselves a creation of thought. The Kantian solution to this traditional philosophical dilemma, what he called his 'Copernican revolution', was to take intellectual knowing as a copy of something else but to find in the forms of knowing themselves a measure of meaning. Thus, a native speaker knows and this knowing is more than a perfect record of the thing called language. The concept 'native speaker' is thus an intellectual form or what Chomsky would want to call an 'organ' of knowing. In this sense, it constitutes a symbolic form in much the same way that art and science and language itself are symbolic forms. From one symbolic plane emerged another pivotal notion, 'competence'.

Native speakers constantly move along the periphery of an autonomous community of knowledge. This is an epistemology of language on a large, group scale. More or less, in continuous contact with the group language grammar, native speakers (more or less) 'reach the same conclusion' 'have similar thoughts'. The feeling of rightness prevails. The knowledge brought by the Native Speaker is a moment of invention, the instantiation of an imaginary realm within the real.

The paradox is not that an 'idealised, monolithic' Ideal Native Speaker must somehow exist beside the flesh and blood of the Social Native Speaker but rather that the very notion of 'speech community' and 'state' as the real-world *habitus* of its Native Speaker counterpart is equally a magic–realist conception. The notions 'state' and 'community' are, even at best, dubious realities of daily life. They are also subject to mythmaking and ambiguity. This path leads us back to the anarcho-philosophical observation point of Chomsky and to another discussion. For the moment, let us say that the Native Speaker inhabits an airy terrain of the imagination and speculation continually 'divesting' itself of the clothing of close definition. It possesses an unbearable lightness of being. And this must be so.

The last word remains with Davies upon whose speculations about the Native Speaker this paper can be viewed as an exegesis. For Davies, it is the Medieval philosophical path, the *via negativa*, wherein lies firm ground:

> *Even if I cannot define a native speaker I can define a non-native speaker negatively as someone who is not regarded by him/herself or by native speakers as a native speaker. No smoke and mirrors this; rather, it is in this 'sense' only that the native speaker is not a myth, the sense that gives reality to feelings of confidence and identity. They are real enough even if on analysis the native speaker is seen to be an emperor without clothes.*
>
> (Davies 1991: 167)

Davies is surely right to pivot the Native Speaker on the delicate axis of myth and reality and it is because of this ambiguity that the being of the Native Speaker will no doubt continue, lightly and exquisitely, to survive.

References

Barthes, R. 1972. *Le Plaisir du Texte*. Paris: Editions du Seuil.

Canale, M. and Swain, M. 1980. Theoretical bases of communicative approaches to second language testing and teaching. *Applied Linguistics* 1: 11–47.

Chomsky, N. 1965. *Aspects of the Theory of Syntax*. Cambridge, MA: The MIT Press.

Chomsky, N. 1973. *For Reasons of State*. London: Fontana.

Coulmas, F. (ed.) 1981. *A Festschrift for the Native Speaker.* Berlin: Mouton.

Davies, A. 1978. Language Testing 1. Survey. *Cambridge Language Teaching Surveys*: 145–59.

Davies, A. 1992. Language Testing and Evaluation. In W. Grabe and R. Kaplan (eds.), *Introduction to Applied Linguistics*: 125–139. Reading, MA: Addison-Wesley.

Davies, A. 1990. *The Principles of Language Testing*. Oxford: Blackwell.

Davies, A. 1991. *The Native Speaker in Applied Linguistics.* Edinburgh: Edinburgh University Press.

Davies, A. 1994. Native Speaker. In E. Asher (ed.), *The International Encyclopedia of Language and Linguistics*: pp. 2719–25. Oxford: Elesevier Sueime Ltd.

Frege, G. 1969. *Posthumous Writings.* English Edition, Oxford: Blackwell.

Francis, W. N. 1979. Problems of assembling and computerizing large corpora. In H. Bergenholtz and B. Schaeder (eds.), *Empirische Textwissenschaft*, pp. 110–23. Königstein/Ts.: Scriptor Verlag.

Ferguson, C. 1983. Language Planning and language change. In J. Cobarrubias and J. Fishman (eds.), *Progress in Language Planning*. Berlin: Mouton.

Ishiguro, H. 1996. *On the relation between new voices and old voices: What does a newcomer appropriate?* Paper presented at the 2nd Conference for Sociocultural Research, Geneva.
Jung, C. G. 1928. *Contributions to Analytical Psychology.* London: Kegan Paul, Trench, Trubner and Co.
Leont'ev, A. N. 1965. *The Mental Development of the Child.* Vachnik: Moscow.
Maher, J. and J. Groves. 1997. *Introducing Chomsky.* Cambridge: Icon.
Mey, J. 1981. Right or wrong, my Native Speaker: Estant les régestes du nobel souverain de l'Empire linguistique avec un renvoi au mesme Roy. In Coulmas, pp. 69–84. The Hague: Mouton.
Nida, E. 1981. Informants or Colleagues. In Coulmas (ed.). *A Festschrift for the Native Speaker*, pp.169–74. Berlin: Moulton.
de Saussure, F. 1959. *Course in General Linguistics*. Trans. Wade Baskin. London: Collins/Fontana.
de Saussure, F. 1980. *Cours de Linguistique Générale.* Ed. T. de Mauro Payot.
Slobin, D. J. 1979. *Psycholinguistics.* Glenview, IL: Scott, Foresman.
Verhoeven, L. 1997. Sociolinguistics and Education. In Coulmas (ed.), *The Handbook of Sociolinguistics*, pp. 389–404. Oxford: Blackwell.
Wittgenstein, L. 1960. *The Blue and Brown Books.* Oxford: Blackwell.

Section Eleven
The publications of Alan Davies

The publications of Alan Davies

Books published

1999. *Introduction to Applied Linguistics: From Practice to Theory.* Edinburgh: Edinburgh University Press.
1999. *Language Testing Dictionary* (first author with A. Brown, C. Elder, K. Hill, T. Lumley and T. McNamara). UCLES/Cambridge: Cambridge University Press.
1997. *The Bilingual Interface Project.* Canberra: Department of Employment, Education Training and Youth Affairs (with P. McKay, B. Devlin, J. Clayton, R. Oliver and S. Zammitt).
1991. *The Native Speaker in Applied Linguistics.* Edinburgh: Edinburgh University Press.
1990. *Principles of Language Testing.* Oxford: Basil Blackwell.

Books edited

1986. *Language in Education in Africa.* Edinburgh: Centre for African Studies, University of Edinburgh.
1984. *Interlanguage.* Edinburgh: Edinburgh University Press (first editor with A. Howatt and C. Criper).
1982. *Language and Learning in Home and School.* London: Heinemann.
1982. *Language and Ethnicity.* Special issue (Vol 3/3) of *Journal of Multilingual and Multicultural Development.*
1978. *The Teaching of Comprehension.* ETIC Occasional Paper. British Council.
1977. *Testing and Experimental Methods.* Volume 4 in *Edinburgh Course in Applied Linguistics.* Oxford: Oxford University Press.
1977. *Language and Learning in Early Childhood.* London: Heinemann.
1975. *Problems of Language and Learning.* London: Heinemann.
1968. *Language Testing Symposium.* Oxford: Oxford University Press.

Articles published as sole author

1999. Ethics in educational linguistics. In Bernard Spolsky (ed.), *Concise Encyclopedia of Educational Linguistics,* pp. 21–25. Amsterdam: Elsevier.

1999. Native Speaker. In Bernard Spolsky (ed.), *Concise Encyclopedia of Educational Linguistics,* pp. 532–39. Amsterdam: Elsevier.

1999. Standard English: Discordant voices. *World Englishes* 18 (2): 171–86.

1997. Real language norms. VIEWS, *Working Papers of Institüt für Anglistik und Amerikanistik,* University of Vienna 6(2): 4–18.

1997. What second language learners can tell us about the native speaker: Identifying and describing exceptions. *Melbourne Papers in Language Testing* 5 (2): 1–27.

1997. Response to a reply. *Journal of Multilingual and Multicultural Development* 18 (3): 248.

1997. Introduction: The limits of ethics in language testing. *Language Testing* [special issue] 14 (3): 235–41.

1997. Demands of being professional in language testing. *Language Testing* 14 (3): 329–39.

1997. Australian immigrant gatekeeping through English language tests: How important is proficiency? In V. Kohonen, A. Huhta, L. Kurki-Suonio and S. Luoma (eds.), *Current Developments and Alternatives in Language Assessment:* Proceedings of LTRC '96, pp. 71–84. Jyväskylä: University of Jyväskylä and University of Tampere.

1996. Ironising the myth of linguicism. *Journal of Multilingual and Multicultural Development* 17 (6): 485–96.

1996. Outing the tester: Theoretical models and practical endeavours in language testing. In G. M. Blue and R. Mitchell (eds.), *Language and Education*, pp. 60–69. Clevedon, Avon: British Association for Applied Linguistics in association with Multilingual Matters Ltd.

1995. Introduction: Measures and reports. *Melbourne Papers in Language Testing* 4 (2): 1–11.

1995. Testing communicative language or testing language communicatively: what? how? *Melbourne Papers in Language Testing* 4 (1): 1–20.

1995. The role of the segmental dictionary in professional validation: Constructing a dictionary of language testing. In A. Cumming and R. Berwick (eds.), *Validation in Language Testing*, pp. 222–35. Clevedon, Avon: Multilingual Matters.

1995. Proficiency or the native speaker: What are we trying to achieve in ELT? In G. Cook and B. Seidlhofer (eds.), *Principles and Practice in Applied Linguistics: Studies in Honour of H. G. Widdowson*, pp. 145–57. Oxford: Oxford University Press.

1994. The observer's paradox. In *Encyclopedia of Language and Linguistics,* pp. 2863–2864. Oxford: Elsevier Science Ltd.

1994. Politicized language. In *Encyclopedia of Language and Linguistics,* pp. 3211–3214. Oxford: Elsevier Science Ltd.

1994. Native Speaker. In *Encyclopedia of Language and Linguistics,* pp. 2719–2725. Oxford: Elsevier Science Ltd.

1994. Pedagogy by glossary: Defining the limits of an LSP by writing a dictionary. In R. Khoo (ed.), *LSP—Problems and Prospects. Anthology Series* 33, pp. 80–96. Singapore: SEAMEO Regional Language Centre.

1993. Is proficiency always achievement? *Journal of English and Foreign Languages* [special issue] CIEFL, Hyderabad (10 and 11): 79–89.

1993. Simply defining: Constructing a dictionary of language testing. In M. L. Tickoo (ed.), *Simplification: Theory and Application. Anthology Series* 31, pp. 101–13. Singapore: SEAMEO Regional Language Centre.

1992. The notion of the native speaker. *Focus on English* 7 (2 and 3): 3–15.

1992. Speculation and empiricism in applied linguistics. *Melbourne Papers in Language Testing* 1(2): 1–18.

1991. The notion of the native speaker. *Journal of Intercultural Studies* 12 (2): 35–45.

1991. The Language Testing Centre, Melbourne: Projects and purposes. *NLLIA Occasional Paper No 4.* Melbourne: National Languages Institute of Australia.

1991. Performance of children from non-English speaking background on the New South Wales Basic Skills Tests of Numeracy. *Language, Culture and Curriculum* 4 (2): 149–61.

1991. An evaluation model for English language teaching projects in South India: The policy of change. *Australian Review of Applied Linguistics* 14 (2): 73–86.

1991. Language testing in the 1990s. In J. C. Alderson and B. North (eds.), *Language Testing in the 1990s: The Communicative Legacy*, pp. 136–49. London: Modern English Publications, Macmillan.

1991. Language testing and evaluation. In W. Grabe and R. Kaplan (eds.), *Introduction to Applied Linguistics*, pp. 125–39. Reading, MA: Addison-Wesley.

1991. Correctness in English. In M. L. Tickoo (ed.), *Languages and Standards: Issues, Attitudes, Case Studies. Anthology Series 26:* 51–67. Singapore: SEAMEO Regional Language Centre.

1991. British applied linguistics: The contribution of S. Pit Corder. In R. Phillipson, E. Kellerman, L. Selinker, M. Sharwood-Smith and M. Swain (eds.), *Foreign/Second Language Pedagogy Research*, pp. 52–60. Clevedon, Avon: Multilingual Matters Ltd.

1990. The study of language. In A. Wilkinson, A. Davies and D. Berrill (eds.), *Spoken English Illuminated*, pp. 91–100. Milton Keynes, UK: Open University Press.

1990. The spoken language. In A. Wilkinson, A. Davies and D. Berrill (eds.), *Spoken English Illuminated*, pp. 101–11. Milton Keynes, UK: Open University Press.

1990. Operationalising uncertainty in language testing. In J. de Jong and D. Stevenson (eds.), *Individualizing the Assessment of Language Abilities*, pp. 179–195. Clevedon, Avon: Multilingual Matters Ltd.

1989. Is international English an interlanguage? *TESOL Quarterly* 23 (3): 447–67.

1989. Communicative competence as language use. *Applied Linguistics* 10 (2): 157–70.

1989. Testing reading speed through text retrieval. In C. N. Candlin and T. F. McNamara (eds.), *Language, Learning and Community*, pp. 115–124. Sydney: National Centre for English Language Teaching and Research.

1989. From Knox to Fox. *InterArts*, Edinburgh (9): 15–17.

1988. Thirty years of applied linguistics. *Edinburgh University Bulletin.*

1988. Operationalising uncertainty in language testing: An argument in favour of content validity. *Language Testing* 5 (1): 32–48.

1988. Talking in silence: Ministry in Quaker meetings. In N. Coupland (ed.), *Styles of Discourse*, pp. 105–137. London: Croom Helm.

1988. Communicative language testing. In A. Hughes (ed.), *Testing English for University Study.* ELT Documents No. 127. London: Modern English Publications and British Council.

1987. Certificate of Proficiency in English. In J. C. Alderson, K. Krahnke and C. W. Stansfield (eds.), *Reviews of English Language Proficiency Tests.* Washington, DC: TESOL Publications.

1987. How language planning theory can assist first language teaching. In R. Shuy and O. Tomic (eds.), *The Relationship of Theoretical and Applied Linguistics*, pp. 157–75. Plenum Press.

1986. Language loss and symbolic gain: The meaning of institutional maintenance. In T. Van Els *et al.* (eds.), *Language Attrition in Progress*, pp. 117–27. Dordrecht: Foris.

1986. Indirect ESP testing: Old innovations. In M. Portal (ed.), *Language Testing*, pp. 55–67. NFER/Nelson.

1985. Words or discourse: What should reading tests measure? *Regional Institute of English Journal.* Bangalore, 2(1): 1–25.

1985. Standard and dialect English: The unacknowledged idealisation of sociolinguistics. *Journal of Multilingual and Multicultural Development* 6 (2): 183–92.

1985. John Oller and the restoration of the test. *System* 13 (2): 99–104.
1985. Doing reading: Questions for the foreign language reader. *Teaching English:* 18 (3) 23–8. Centre for Information on the Teaching of English, Edinburgh.
1985. Follow my leader: Is that what language tests do? In Y. P. Lee, C. Y. Y. Fok, R. Lord and G. Low (eds.), *New Directions in Language Testing*, pp. 3–13. Oxford: Pergamon.
1985. Commentator 1 on E. Thumboo, English literature in a global context. In R. Quirk and H. G. Widdowson (eds.). *English in the World*, pp. 61–3. Cambridge: Cambridge University Press.
1984. Validating three tests of English language proficiency. *Language Testing* 1 (1): 50–69.
1984. ESL expectations in examining: The problem of English as a foreign language and English as a mother tongue. *Language Testing* 1 (1): 82–96.
1984. The interaction of language and culture. In T. Corner (ed.), *Education in Multicultural Societies*, pp. 60–7. New York: St Martins Press.
1984. Simple, simplified and simplification: What is authentic? In J. C. Alderson and A. H. Urquhart (eds.) *Reading in a Foreign Language*, pp. 181–98. London: Longman.
1984. Idealisation in sociolinguistics: The choice of the standard dialect. In D. Schiffrin (ed.), *GURT 84: Meaning, Form and Use in Context. Linguistic Applications*, pp. 229–39. Washington, DC: Georgetown University Press.
1984. Computer-assisted language testing. *CALICO Journal* 1 (5): 41–42, 48.
1984. Procedures in language test validation. In A. Hughes (ed.), *Proceedings of the Seminar: Testing English beyond the High School: 9–11 May 1984,* pp. 83–91. Istanbul: Bogazici University.
1988. Procedures in language test validation. In A. Hughes (ed.), *Testing English for University Study.* ELT Documents No. 127. London: Modern English Publications and British Council.
1983. The validity of concurrent validation. In A. Hughes and D. Porter (eds.), *Current Developments in Language Testing*, pp. 141–46. London: Academic Press.
1982. Spaces between silences: Verbal interaction in Quaker meetings. *Nottingham Linguistic Circular* 11 (1): 44–63.
1982. Introduction in A. Davies (ed.), *Language and Ethnicity. Journal of Multilingual and Multicultural Development* [Special Issue] 3 (3): 153–61.
1982. Introduction. In A. Davies (ed.), *Language and Learning in Home and School*, pp. vi–xi. London: Heinemann.
1982. Criteria for evaluation of tests of English as a foreign language. In J. B. Heaton (ed.), *Language Testing,* pp. 11–16. London: Modern English Publications.

1981. Reaction to the Palmer and Bachman and to the Vollmer papers. In J. C. Alderson and A. Hughes (eds.), *Issues in Language Testing*, pp. 182–186. London: British Council.
1979. Second language lessons for the teaching of reading. In A. Cashden (ed.), *Language, Reading and Learning*, pp. 120–136. Oxford: Blackwell.
1978. Language testing: Part two. Survey article. *Teaching and Linguistics Abstracts* 11 (4): 215–31.
1978. Language testing: Part one. Survey article. *Language Teaching and Linguistics Abstracts* 11 (3): 145–59.
1978. Textbook situations and idealised language. *Work in Progress* No. 11: 120–33. Department of Linguistics, University of Edinburgh.
1977. The construction of language tests. In J. P. B. Allen and A. Davies (eds.), *Testing and Experimental Methods, Vol. 4* in *Edinburgh Course in Applied Linguistics*, pp. 38–104. Oxford: Oxford University Press.
1977. Introduction. In J. P. B. Allen and A. Davies (eds.) *Testing and Experimental Methods, Vol. 4* in *Edinburgh Course in Applied Linguistics*, pp. 1–10. Oxford: Oxford University Press.
1977. Introduction. In A. Davies (ed.), *Language and Learning in Early Childhood*, pp. 1–14. London: Heinemann.
1976. Registers in English Teaching. In C. S. Butler and R. R. K. Hartmann (eds.), *A Reader on Language Varieties*, pp. 95–104. Exeter Linguistics Studies No.1, University of Exeter.
1976. Do foreign students have problems? In *ELT Documents* 75/3. London: British Council. Also in A. P. Cowie and J. B. Heaton (eds.), *English for Academic Purposes,* pp. 34–36. Reading: BAAL 1977.
1975. Two tests of speeded reading. In R. Jones and B. Spolsky (eds.), *Testing Language Proficiency*, pp. 119–27. Washington, DC: Center for Applied Linguistics.
1975. Introduction. In A. Davies (ed.), *Problems of Language and Learning*, pp. 1–7. London: Heinemann.
1973. Literature for children (Unit 2). In *Reading Development* (PE261), *A Post Experience Course*, pp. 1–49. Milton Keynes: The Open University.
1973. Tests für den fremdsprachlichen Unterricht. In *Testen bearbeitet von Heinrich Schrand Cornelsen*, pp. 23–24. Berlin: Velhagaen und Glasing.
1973. Printed media and the reader (Units 8 and 9). In *Reading Development* (PE261), *A Post Experience Course,* pp. 1–85. Milton Keynes: The Open University.
1971. Language aptitude in the first year of the UK secondary school. *Regional English Language Centre Journal* 2 (1): 4–19.
1971. Aptitude for and proficiency in French in the first year of the UK secondary school. In G. Perren and J. Trim (eds.), *Applications of Linguistics*, pp. 177–81. Cambridge: Cambridge University Press.
1970. *The Pedigree of Nations.* Ramjham, Kathmandu, Nepal. 6 (3): 26–33.

1969. Language testing. In *Leistungsmessung in Sprachunterricht,* pp. 27–51. Marburg: Informationszentrum für Fremdsprachenforschung.
1969. The notion of register. *Educational Review* 64–77.
1969. Improving writing. *English in Education* 3 (3): 64–77.
1969. Error analysis. In *Leistungsmessung in Sprachunterricht*, pp. 109–123. Marburg: Informationszentrum für Fremdsprachenforschung.
1968. Some problems in the use of language varieties in teaching. *Educational Review* 20 (2): 107–22.
1968. Oral English testing in West Africa. In A. Davies (ed.), *Language Testing Symposium,* pp. 151–179. Oxford: Oxford University Press.
1968. Introduction. In A. Davies (ed.), *Language Testing Symposium*, pp. 1–10. Oxford: Oxford University Press.
1967. The English proficiency of overseas students. *British Journal of Educational Psychology* 37 (2): 165–174.
1965. Linguistics and the teaching of spoken English. In A. Wilkinson (ed.), *Spoken English.* University of Birmingham Educational Review Occasional Publications, No. 2: 17–39.

Joint articles

1998. Performance on ESL examinations: Is there a language distance effect? *Language and Education* 12: 1–17. [with C. Elder]
1997. Review of literature on acquiring literacy in a second language. In P. McKay, A. Davies, B. Devlin, J. Clayton, R. Oliver and S. Zammitt (eds.), *The Bilingual Interface Project*, pp. 17–74. Canberra: DEETYA. [first author with E. Grove and M. Wilkes]
1997. Language distance as a factor in the acquisition of literacy in English as a Second Language. In P. McKay, A. Davies, B. Devlin, J. Clayton, R. Oliver and S. Zammitt (eds.), *The Bilingual Interface Project*, pp. 91–107. Canberra: DEETYA. [with C. Elder]
1996. Is grammar good for you? The relationship between metalinguistic knowledge and success in studying a language at university. *Melbourne Papers in Language Testing* 5 (1): 35–55. [with C. Elder, J. Hajek, D. Manwaring and J. Warren]
1996. Comparing test difficulty and text readability in the evaluation of an extensive reading programme. In M. Milanovic and N. Saville (eds.), *Performance Testing, Cognition and Assessment*, pp. 165–183. Cambridge: Cambridge University Press. [first author with A. Irvine]
1990. Designing instruments to measure language proficiency. In E. Wylie (ed.), *Assessment of Proficiency in Japanese as a Foreign Language,* pp. 94–103. Canberra: Asian Studies Council. [first author with A. Brown]
1988. English Language Testing Service Research Report 1 (1). *ELTS Validation Project Report*, British Council/UCLES. [with C. Criper]

1986. Evaluation of the Bangalore Project. *Journal of English Language Teaching (India)* 21 (4). [with A. Beretta]

1986. English proficiency in the Kathmandu Valley Colleges: A preliminary investigation. *Indian Journal of Applied Linguistics* 12 (1–2): 127–136. [first author with T. Kansakar]

1985. Evaluation of the Bangalore Project. *English Language Teaching Journal* 39 (2): 121–7. [with A. Beretta]

1977. Research on spoken language in the primary school. In A. Davies (ed.), *Language and Learning in Early Education*, pp. 143–86. London: Heinemann. [with C. Criper]

1974. Reading and writing. In S. P. Corder and J. P. B. Allen (eds.), *Edinburgh Course in Applied Linguistics* Volume 3, pp. 155–201. Oxford: Oxford University Press. [first author with H. G. Widdowson]

1971. English Proficiency in the Valley Colleges: A preliminary investigation. *Journal of Tribhuvan University* 6 (1). [first author with T. Kansakar]

Important notes, reviews and review articles

1997. Obituary of Stephen Pit Corder. *BAAL Newsletter* 57: 23–5.

1997. Response to the letter from Michael Stubbs. *BAAL Newsletter* 56: 26–7.

1997. Review of M. Clyne *et al.* 1986. *An Early Start: Second Language at Primary School,* Melbourne: River Seine Publishers and M. Clyne *et al.* 1995. *Developing Second Language from Primary School: Models and Outcomes,* Deakin: NLLIA. *Australian Language Matters* 5 (1).

1997. Review of F. Genesee and J. A. Upshur. 1996. *Classroom-Based Evaluation in Second Language Education.* Cambridge: Cambridge University Press. *Studies in Second Language Acquisition.*

1996. Review of T. Crooks and G. Crewes (eds.), 1995. *Language and Language Development.* Denpasar. Bali. *Australian Language Matters* 4 (3).

1996. What do they know? Language awareness amongst tertiary students of LOTE. *Australian Language Matters* 4 (4). [with C. Elder, J. Hajek, D. Manwaring and J. Warren]

1996. Academic performance and level of English proficiency. *Development Update.* British Council, Manchester.

1995. Charles Carpenter Fries and Structure of English. *BAAL Newsletter* 49: 22–4.

1995. Review of G. Brindley (ed.), *Language Assessment in Action. Research Series 8.* Sydney, Australia: NCELTR, Macquarie University. *TESOL Journal* 5 (1): 44–5.

1992. Review of J. C. Alderson and A. Beretta (eds.), 1992. *Evaluating Second Language Education.* Cambridge: Cambridge University Press. *Language Testing* 9 (2): 207–9.

1991. Review of R. Fasold. 1990. *The Sociolinguistics of Language.* Blackwell. *Journal of Language and Social Psychology* 10 (4): 292–5.

1991. Review Article: Change of state? A comparison of two volumes L. Michaels and C. Ricks (eds.), *The State of the Language, 1980* and *1990. Language and Education* 5 (4): 287–94.

1991. Review of B. Spolsky. 1990. *Conditions for Second Language Learning.* Oxford: Oxford University Press. *Language Culture and Curriculum* 4 (2): 168–72.

1990. Review of M. J. Ball (ed.), 1988. *The Use of Welsh.* Clevedon, Avon: Multilingual Matters. *The Modern Language Journal* 74 (2): 269–70.

1990. Review of B. Corcoran and E. Evans (eds.), 1987. *Readers, Texts, Teachers,* Open University Press: Milton Keynes. *Language and Education* 4 (1): 77–9.

1989. Review of R. Fasold. 1985. *The Sociolinguistics of Society,* London: Blackwell. *Journal of Language and Social Psychology* 8 (2): 86–9.

1988. 30 years of Applied Linguistics at Edinburgh. *Edinburgh University Bulletin* p.10.

1985. Review of D. Sutcliffe 1982. *British Black English.* Oxford: Blackwell. *Applied Linguistics* 6 (1): 93–9.

1984. Review of J. W. Oller (ed.), 1983. *Issues in Language Testing Research.* Rowley, MA: Newbury House. *Language Testing* 1 (1): 11–115. 1982. Review of A. Wilkinson *et al.* 1980. *Assessing Language Development.* Oxford: Oxford University Press. *Journal of Curriculum Studies,* pp. 208–10.

1981. Review of M. Jones and A. R. Thomas (eds.), 1977. *The Welsh Language.* University of Wales Press (for Schools Council). *Modern Language Journal,* pp. 122–23.

1981. Review of J. Munby. 1978. *Communicative Syllabus Design.* Cambridge: Cambridge University Press. TESOL *Quarterly,* pp. 332–36.

1981. Review of C. Harrison. 1980. *Readability in the Classroom.* Cambridge: Cambridge University Press. *Journal of Research in Reading* 4 (2).

1980. Review of T. Aitken and T. McArthur (eds.), 1979. *Languages of Scotland.* Edinburgh: W and R Chambers. *Modern Language Journal,* pp. 239–40.

1978. Review of E. J. Gibson and H. Levin (eds.), 1975. *The Psychology of Reading.* Cambridge, MA: MIT Press. *Journal of Research in Reading* 1 (2): 145–49.

Audio/video recordings

1996. *Mark My Words: Assessing second and foreign language skills.* [with A. Brown, C. Elder, R. Evans, E. Grove, K. Hill, N. Iwashita, T. Lumley and C. O'Shannessy.] Multimedia Education Unit, University of Melbourne.

Editorship

Co-editor of *Language Testing* 1992–1996.
Co-editor of *Applied Linguistics* 1985–1989.

Notes on the contributors

J. CHARLES ALDERSON

J. Charles Alderson is Professor of Linguistics and English Language Education at Lancaster University. He holds an MA in German and French from Oxford University and a PhD in Applied Linguistics from Edinburgh University. He is the author of numerous articles and books on language testing, reading in a foreign language and language education. He is series co-editor with Lyle Bachman of the CUP series *Cambridge Language Assessment Series* and he is co-editor with Lyle Bachman of the journal *Language Testing*.

JOAN AUCHTER

Joan Auchter is the Executive Director of the General Educational Development Testing Service (GEDTS) of the American Council on Education (ACE). In addition to authoring numerous publications and articles, she is a frequent speaker at national and state conferences, speaking on topics that range from the programmatic (such as the future of GED) to policy (such as accreditation requirements for adults) to technical (such as test translation and adaptation methodology).

LYLE F. BACHMAN

Lyle F. Bachman is Professor of Applied Linguistics and TESL at the University of California, Los Angeles. His current professional interests include the development and validation of tests of language ability, the technology of test design and development, and the interfaces between language testing and other areas of applied linguistics research. His publications include *Fundamental Considerations in Language Testing, Language Testing in Practice* (with Adrian S. Palmer), and *Interfaces between Second Language Acquisition and Language Testing Research* (co-edited with Andrew D. Cohen). He has also published numerous articles in the area of language testing and evaluation. He is currently editor of the journal *Language Testing*, and co-editor of the *Cambridge Language Assessment Series*.

ROSEMARY BAKER

Rosemary Baker has worked on the development of language proficiency tests, and has taught in the areas of language teaching, language testing and research methods in applied linguistics. Her major research interests are the assessment of language impairment resulting from stroke and Alzheimer's dementia in bilinguals and speakers of English as a second language, and communication abilities in ageing in these populations.

JAYANTI BANERJEE

Jayanti Banerjee is a PhD student in the Department of Linguistics and Modern English Language at Lancaster University, UK. Her current research interests are in the development and validation of questionnaires and interview schedules and qualitative research methods.

GEOFF BRINDLEY

Geoff Brindley is Senior Lecturer in the Department of Linguistics and Research Co-ordinator in the National Centre for English Language Teaching and Research (NCELTR) at Macquarie University, Sydney, Australia. He has worked as an EFL and ESL teacher, teacher educator, researcher and evaluator in Australia, Asia, Europe and North America. He is the author and editor of a wide range of books and articles on TESOL curriculum design, second language acquisition and language proficiency assessment.

ANNIE BROWN

Annie Brown has been a Research Fellow in the Language Testing Research Centre since its inception in 1990. She has been involved in numerous test development and research projects, and her main interests are the assessment of oral proficiency, and rater and interviewer behaviour. Annie is particularly interested in the use of discourse analysis and verbal protocols in the examination of test processes, and is currently completing a PhD investigating the discourse of oral proficiency interviews.

CHRISTOPHER BRUMFIT

Christopher Brumfit is Professor of Education with reference to Language and Linguistics, and Director of the Centre for Language in Education, at the University of Southampton, UK. He has been Head of the Research and Graduate School of Education and Dean of the Faculty of Educational Studies for much of the past 15 years. Before that he taught in primary and secondary schools in Britain and Africa, in a teacher training College in Birmingham, and in the universities of Dar-es-Salaam and London. He has published over 30 books and many papers on language teaching, literature teaching, and language in education. In recent years he has concentrated on work on the role of explicit knowledge in language teaching, on language policy, and on literature in education.

CAROLINE CLAPHAM

Caroline Clapham lectures in the Department of Linguistics at Lancaster University, UK. One of her most recent publishing activities was to be editor of *Language Testing and Assessment*, Volume 7 of Kluwer Academic's *Encyclopedia of Language and Education* (1997). She is also co-editor of *Language Testing Update.*

ANDREW D. COHEN

Andrew D. Cohen, Department of English as a Second Language and Graduate Faculty in Linguistics, is Director of the National Language Resource Centre at the Centre for Advanced Research on Language Acquisition (CARLA), University of Minnesota. He is also Secretary General of the International Association of Applied Linguistics (AILA). Along with numerous articles on language teaching, learning, testing, and research methods, his recent books include *Assessing Language Ability in the Classroom* (Heinle and Heinle 1994), *Strategies in Learning and Using a Second Language* (Longman 1998), and a volume co-edited with Lyle Bachman, *Interfaces Between Second Language Acquisition and Language Testing Research* (Cambridge University Press 1998).

DAN DOUGLAS

Dan Douglas is Professor in the TESL/Applied Linguistics Program, English Department, Iowa State University. His major research interests include language testing, language for specific purposes, and second language acquisition. He has taught and conducted research in Botswana, Hawaii, Scotland, England, Sudan, and Japan.

CATHERINE ELDER

Cathie Elder is Associate Professor in the Institute of Language Teaching and Learning at the University of Auckland and a former Director of the Language Testing Research Centre at the University of Melbourne. Her major research interests are in the area of language testing and language programme evaluation and she is co-author of the *Dictionary of Language Testing* (Cambridge University Press). She has a particular interest in policies and practices relating to the teaching and assessment of foreign and immigrant languages.

ROD ELLIS

Rod Ellis is currently Professor and Director of the Institute of Language Teaching and Learning at the University of Auckland. Previously he has worked in teacher education in Zambia, the United Kingdom, Japan and the USA. His publications include *Understanding Second Language Acquisition, Instructed Second Language Acquisition, The Study of Second Language Acquisition* and *SLA Research and Language Teaching.* He will shortly publish *Learning a Second Language Through Interaction* (John Benjamins). In addition, he has written a number of English language textbooks.

PATRICK GRIFFIN

Patrick Griffin (BA MEd PhD FACE) is Professor of Educational Assessment, Director of the Collaborative Centre for Assessment Research in the Faculty of Education at the University of Melbourne. He is the author of 12 books in the area of assessment, evaluation, monitoring and reporting. He has led many research and development projects of national and international significance which, together with his publications, have had major impact in several nations on four continents. Patrick was an Australian member of the IELTS revision team in 1997/98. During that project, he provided psychometric input to the project and was based for a time at the University of Lancaster.

ELISABETH GROVE

Lis Grove is a Research Fellow in the Language Testing Research Centre at the University of Melbourne, where she also teaches in the Centre for Communication Skills and ESL. Since joining the LTRC in 1993, she has been involved in a number of research and test development projects, and her main interests are specific-purpose testing in health care and medical education. She is also interested in second language pedagogy and curriculum development, particularly in the area of English for Academic Purposes.

LIZ HAMP-LYONS

Liz Hamp-Lyons is Chair Professor in English and Head of the Department of English at the Hong Kong Polytechnic University. She has published extensively in the fields of second language writing and in language testing; her most recent book is *Assessing College Writing Portfolios: Principles for Practice, Theory, Research,* Cresskill, NJ: Hampton Press, 1999 (with Bill Condon). Her current research interests are in writing assessment, language testing ethics and paradigms, and in language teacher education.

ZHAOHONG HAN

ZhaoHong Han is Assistant Professor of Languages and Education at Teachers College, Columbia University, USA. Her recent research efforts include trying to understand fossilisation in the presence of a typologically-distant L1.

KATHRYN HILL

Kathryn Hill is a Research Fellow at the University of Melbourne Language Testing Research Centre and at the Australian Council for Educational Research. Her research interests include the use of feedback in test development, rater characteristics, and issues regarding the teaching and learning of languages other than English in schools.

NORIKO IWASHITA

Noriko Iwashita is a Research Fellow at the Language Testing Research Centre in the Department of Linguistics and Applied Linguistics at the University of Melbourne and a former lecturer in Japanese as a foreign language. She has recently completed her PhD thesis on the role of conversation in the acquisition of Japanese as a second language and has conducted a number of major research projects at the interface between language testing and second language acquisition.

BATIA LAUFER

Batia Laufer is Associate Professor in the Department of English Language and Literature at the University of Haifa where she teaches courses in English as a foreign language as well as on a range of topics in linguistics and applied linguistics, including vocabulary acquisition, the structure of English, issues in second language research and language assessment. She has published widely and has presented papers at numerous scholarly conferences. Her publications include D. D. Sim and B. Laufer-Dvorkin *Reading Comprehension Course – Selected Strategies* (Collins 1982), B. B. Sim and B. Laufer-Dvorkin *Vocabulary Development* (Collins 1984) and B. Laufer-Dvorkin (ed.) *Similar Lexical Forms in Interlanguage* (Gunter Narr 1991).

TOM LUMLEY

Tom Lumley is Assistant Professor in the Department of English, The Hong Kong Polytechnic University, where he is also an Associate of the Asian Centre for Language Assessment Research (ACLAR). Before coming to Hong Kong, he worked for seven years at the Language Testing Research Centre at the University of Melbourne. His major area of research interest is language assessment, particularly performance assessment, including applications of Rasch measurement.

BRIAN LYNCH

Brian Lynch is Senior Lecturer in Applied Linguistics at the University of Melbourne. He has worked on English language programmes in Australia, China, Mexico, and the United States, and has published in the areas of programme evaluation and language testing.

JOHN MAHER

John Maher is Professor of Linguistics in the Department of Communication and Linguistics, International Christian University, Tokyo. Of British and Irish nationality, he was educated at the universities of London, Michigan and Edinburgh. He was interpreter for the Ainu Association delegation to the United Nations in Geneva and has featured in language-related discussions on the BBC, ABC, NHK and FM Japan. His publications include *English as an International Language of Medicine* (University of Michigan Press 1992), *Bilingualism in Japan* [In Japanese] (Kenkyusha 1991), *Linguistic Theory in Language Teaching* (Bonjinsha 1993), *Towards a New Order* [In Japanese] (Kokusai Shoin 1993), *Diversity in Japanese Culture and Language* (Kegan Paul 1994), *Multilingual Japan* (Multilingual Matters 1995) and *Introducing Chomsky* (Icon 1997).

ROSAMOND MITCHELL

Rosamond Mitchell is Reader in Education at the University of Southampton, England, where she directs an MA programme in applied linguistics. She formerly studied and worked in the Department of Applied Linguistics at the University of Edinburgh, and at the University of Stirling. She is an ex-editor of *Applied Linguistics*, and a past Chair of the British Association for Applied Linguistics. Her research interests have to do with classroom foreign language learning, grammar pedagogy and language in education policy.

HELEN MOORE

Helen Moore is currently writing her PhD dissertation at the Ontario Institute for Studies in Education at the University of Toronto, Canada. Prior to that she was a Senior Lecturer in the Graduate School of Education, La Trobe University, Melbourne, Australia, with responsibility for TESOL education programmes. Her dissertation is concerned with how educational and bureaucratic agendas concerning ESL curriculum and assessment came into conjunction in Australia from 1991 to 1996.

TIM MCNAMARA

Tim McNamara is Associate Professor in Applied Linguistics and Director of the Language Testing Research Centre at the University of Melbourne. His research interests include performance assessment in second languages, particularly in occupational and academic contexts; the applications of Rasch measurement in language testing; and theories of performance in second language performance assessment. Among his publications are *Measuring Second Language Performance* (Addison-Wesley Longman 1996) and *Language Testing* (OUP 2000).

KIERAN O'LOUGHLIN

Kieran O'Loughlin is Lecturer in TESOL in the Department of Language, Literacy and Arts Education at the University of Melbourne. He is also an Associate of the Language Testing Research Centre at the same university. His research interests include language assessment and social identity in language learning and teaching. He has published articles in *Language Testing, Prospect, Australian Review of Applied Linguistics, On-CALL* and *TESOL in Context.*

PAULINE REA-DICKINS

Pauline Rea-Dickins has recently moved to the Graduate School of Education, University of Bristol. She teaches, researches and publishes in areas of language programme evaluation, testing and school-based assessment. Her current funded research project is concerned with the assessment of learners for whom English is an additional language in Key Stage 1 of the National Curriculum in England and Wales.

JOHN READ

John Read is Senior Lecturer in Applied Linguistics at Victoria University of Wellington, New Zealand, where he teaches courses in language testing, research methodology and academic writing. His primary research interests are in second language vocabulary assessment and the testing of English for academic and occupational purposes. He is the author of *Assessing Vocabulary* (Cambridge University Press 2000).

DANIEL J. REED

Daniel Reed is Director of Assessment at the Centre for Advanced Research on Language Acquisition (CARLA), the University of Minnesota. He has been working with the Assessment Team there to develop a four-skill test battery, the Minnesota Language Proficiency Assessments (MLPA). He has also given presentations at international conferences on topics related to proficiency-oriented assessment and has published articles based on his research in these areas. Prior to joining CARLA, he was an assistant professor and research associate in the Program in TESOL and Applied Linguistics at Indiana University, Bloomington, Indiana.

DANIEL ROBERTSON

Daniel Robertson has taught EFL in Italy, Scotland and Germany. He completed a PhD in Applied Linguistics at the University of Edinburgh under the supervision of Alan Davies and Antonella Sorace. Since completing his PhD in 1991 he has worked as a full-time researcher on two projects at the University of Edinburgh. In 1997 he took up a post as Lecturer in Education at the University of Leicester, where he teaches on the MA in TESOL and the EdD (Doctorate in Education) programmes. He is currently conducting research into the acquisition of English by L1 Chinese speakers and the discourse of language learning tasks.

LARRY SELINKER

Larry Selinker is Professor of Applied Linguistics and Director, Centre for Interlanguage Studies at Birkbeck College, University of London. He is currently interested in pushing the frontiers of the intersection of 'Interlanguage and Virtual Life', and is primarily engaged in two sorts of interrelated online activities: distance interlanguage analysis, especially with several universities in Spain, and a new part-distant, part-virtual PhD progamme in applied linguistics.

ANTONELLA SORACE

Antonella Sorace holds degrees from the University of Rome and the University of Southern California, and a PhD in Linguistics from the University of Edinburgh, where she currently is a Reader. Her research interests are second language acquisition theory, the syntax-semantics interface, Romance linguistics, and psycholinguistics.

BERNARD SPOLSKY

Bernard Spolsky, Professor of English at Bar-Ilan University since 1980 and about to retire, is the author of *Measured Words: The Development of Objective Language Tests* (Oxford 1995). His most recent books, all published in 1999, are *Sociolinguistics* (Oxford), *The Languages of Israel* (Multilingual Matters) and *Concise Encylopaedia of Educational Linguistics* (Elsevier). He is currently working on a book on urban sociolinguistics and two projects on immigrant language learning.

CHARLES W. STANSFIELD

Charles W. Stansfield (PhD, Florida State University, 1973) is President of Second Language Testing, Inc. He has served as a professor of Spanish at the University of Colorado, director of Peace Corps training in Nicaragua, director of various language testing programmes at Educational Testing Service, and director of the ERIC Clearinghouse for Languages and Linguistics.

ELAINE TARONE

Elaine Tarone serves on the faculty of the MA Program in English as a Second Language at the University of Minnesota as a Professor, and directs the Centre for Advanced Research on Language Acquisition at the same university. She has written about second language acquisition since 1972.

CAROLYN E. TURNER

Carolyn E. Turner is Associate Professor and Director of Graduate Programs in the Department of Second Language Education at McGill University in Montréal, Québec, Canada. Her main focus/commitment is language testing and evaluation within educational settings. She carries this out through her teaching, research, service to the community, and publications. In addition, she works with outside organisations on testing matters (e.g. Ministry of Education in Québec, Educational Testing Service concerning the TOEFL family of tests). Recently she has devoted much time to large-scale educational projects involving empirically derived rating scales and the impact of their use.

CYRIL WEIR

Cyril Weir is the Director of the Centre for Research in Testing, Evaluation and Curriculum at the University of Surrey, Roehampton. His primary research interests are testing EAP proficiency and the methodology of language programme and project evaluation. His published work includes *Communicative Language Testing* (Prentice Hall 1990), *Understanding and Developing Language Tests* (Prentice Hall 1993), Weir and Roberts, *Evaluation in ELT* (Blackwell 1994), Urquhart and Weir, *Reading in a Second Language* (Longman 1998).

HENRY WIDDOWSON

Henry Widdowson is currently Professor of English at the University of Vienna and was formerly Professor of Applied Linguistics at the University of Essex and Professor of TESOL at the University of London. He was a founding editor of the journal *Applied Linguistics* and has written extensively on discourse analysis, stylistics, and language education. Among his publications are *Teaching Language as Communication* (1978), *Learning Purpose and Language Use* (1983), two volumes of *Explorations in Applied Linguistics* (1979, 1984), *Aspects of Language Teaching* (1990), *Practical Stylistics* (1992), *Linguistics* (1996), all published by Oxford University Press. The last is a title in the series *Oxford Introductions to Language Study*, of which he is the editor.

EDDIE WILLIAMS

Eddie Williams works at the University of Reading's Centre for Applied Language Studies where he is Director of the Literacy in Learning Unit. His principal interests are in the areas of reading, language education policies and evaluation. He has carried out a number of projects for the British Council, the Council of Europe and UNESCO in many parts of the world. Recently he has been carrying out research for the DFID in Sub-Saharan African countries, including Malawi, Rwanda, South Africa and also Zambia, where his research on reading has helped to shape Ministry of Education policy. He has published widely on the theory and practice of reading in a second language.

Author Index

A

Adams, R. 103, 107
Addou, H. 208, 210
Airasian, P. W. 140, 148
Alderson, J. C. 23, 31–38, 42, 43, 47, 48, 51, 107, 130, 134, 135, 138, 139, 141, 142, 147, 149–161, 260, 307–310, 313, 315
Allen, J. P. B. 213, 219, 272, 310, 312
Allwright, D. 152, 160
American Educational Research Association 116, 238
American Federation of Teachers 128, 134
American Psychological Association 116
American Speech-Language-Hearing Association 61, 71
Angelis, P. 24, 31
Angoff, W. H. 97–99, 104, 106
Anivan, S. 95
Arnaud, P. 242, 249
Australian Association of Speech and Hearing 61, 71
Australian Bureau of Statistics 61, 71

B

Bachman, L. F. 16, 17, 20, 23, 31, 46, 47, 49–51, 93, 109–116, 129, 134, 140, 147, 194, 198, 251, 255, 257, 259, 261, 286–288, 310, 315, 317
Baglioni, A. J. 72
Baker, R. 61–71, 316
Banerjee, J. 138, 142, 147, 150–160, 316
Bard, E. G. 269, 272
Barnwell, D. 84, 87, 93
Barratt-Pugh, B. 134
Barrs, M. 132, 134
Barthes, R. 298, 302
Bates, E. 62, 63, 72
Bayles, K. A. 67, 72
Becher, T. 178, 189
Bejoint, H. 249

Berdan, R. 283, 288
Beretta, A. 312, 313
Bernard, H. R. 76, 79
Berrill, P. 308
Berry, J. W. 79, 85
Berry, V. 93
Berwick, R. 31, 85, 86, 149, 306
Bhatia, V. 53–55, 59, 272–274, 289, 290, 291
Birdsong, D. 278, 288
Birenbaum, M. 229, 237, 239
Bixby, J. 239
Black, H. 132, 134
Bley-Vroman, R. 288
Bloor, T. 34, 37, 43
Blue, C. M. 306
Bottomley, Y. 178, 185, 189
Bouffler, V. 134
Boyd, S. 195, 198
Breen, M. 127, 133, 134
Bremer, K. C. 165, 175
Breslow, M. J. 80
Brigham, C. C. 213, 219
Brindley, G. 8, 10, 94, 122, 123, 125–127, 134–136, 178, 189, 191, 198, 199, 237, 239, 312, 316
Brislin, R. W. 76, 79
Broeder, M. 175
Broadfoot, P. 132, 134, 177, 189
Brookhart, S. 126, 135
Brown, A. 7, 9, 10, 84–86, 93, 305, 311, 316
Brown, G. 95, 184, 288, 290
Brown, J. D. 94, 130, 135, 238
Brown, M. 135
Brumfit, C. J. 2, 4, 18, 20, 152, 160, 317
Burchell, G. 190
Burns, A. 178, 189
Burt, C. L. 213, 219
Burt, M. 281, 288
Butcher, L. S. 62, 72
Butler, C. S. 310
Byrnes, H. 95

C

Cadierno, T. 254, 263
Cashden, A. 310
Candlin, C. 308
Campbell, D. T. 75, 80
Canale, M. 14, 15, 20, 23, 31, 129, 135, 251, 261, 299, 302
Carroll, J. B. 22, 29, 31, 112, 116, 131, 135, 214–217, 219
Carter, R. 43
Centre for Applied Linguistics 190
Chachkin, N. 230, 237
Chalhoub-Deville, M. 84, 93
Chapelle, C. 31, 52, 93
Chaudron, C. 152, 160
Cheng, L. 139, 141, 147
Chick, J. K. 204, 209
Chikalanga, I. W. 201, 208, 209
Chitty, C. 163, 175
Chomsky, N. 13, 90, 292, 293, 295–298, 300–303, 320
Christian, D. 74, 80
Cizek, G. S. 126, 127, 135, 138
Clapham, C. 33–43, 47, 50, 52, 107, 134, 252, 261, 317
Clark, J. L. 175, 261
Clayton, J. 305, 311
Clyne, M. 61, 72, 312
Coffman, W. E. 217, 220
Cohen, A. D. 82–96, 315, 317
Cohen, R. N. 80
Colberg, M. 74, 79
College Entrance Examinations Board 214
Collins, A. 140, 147, 320
Colman, J. 189
Conklin, N. 127, 136
Cook, G. 60, 250, 263, 306
Coppieters, R. 278, 288
Corbel, C. 178, 185, 189
Corder, S. P. 261, 272
Corson, D. 149
Coulmas, F. 293, 302, 303
Cram, B. 234, 235, 237
Criper, C. 97, 107, 201, 288, 305, 311, 312
Crookes, G. 112, 116, 261
Coupland, N. 308

Cumming, A. 135, 198
Cummins, J. 210
Cushing Weigle, S. 23, 31

D
Dalton, J. 178, 185, 189
Darling-Hammond, L. 229, 231, 236, 237
Daugherty, R. 163, 175
Davies, A. 4, 10, 31, 32, 52, 59, 93, 147, 210, 219, 227, 262, 272, 288, 302
de Jong, J. 24, 32, 199, 308
Department for Education 175
Department of Education and Science 175
Department of Immigration and Multicultural Affairs (DIMA) 188, 195
Derewianka, B. 134
Detmer, E. 84, 94
Devlin, B. 305, 311
Dickerson, L. 53, 59
Dickson, P. 165, 175, 176
Donitsa-Schmidt, S. 148
Dougherty, K. C. 231, 238
Douglas, D. 31, 45–52, 54, 60, 84, 93, 283–288, 290, 317
Dube, S. 271, 272
Duff, P. 112, 116
Dwyer, S. 60

E
Edgeworth, F. Y. 212, 213, 220
Educational Testing Service 31, 32, 80, 93, 212, 214, 216, 218, 220, 263, 323, 324
Elder, C. 7, 8, 10, 33, 43, 85, 93, 143, 147–149, 305, 311, 312, 314, 318
Ellis, R. 53, 59, 166, 175, 251–263, 318
Employment and Skills Formation Council 178, 181, 190
Eubank, L. 250, 272, 291
Evans, R. 7, 10, 313, 314
Ezzaki, A. 210

F

Faerch, C. 241, 250
Falodun, J. 112, 116
Faltis, C. J. 95
Ferguson, C. 214, 293, 302
Ferman, I. 248
Figueroa, E. 74, 80
Firn, J. 278, 290
Fitzgerald, S. 135
Fitz-Gibbon, C. T. 154, 160
Flynn, S. 277, 288
Foddy, W. 151, 157, 160
Fodor, I. 210
Fok, C. Y. Y. 135, 136, 309
Foster, P. 258, 261, 262
Foucault, M. 179, 180, 187, 190, 228, 232–237
Fox, M. J. 214, 217, 220
Francis, W. N. 293, 302
Frederiksen, J. R. 140, 147
Frederiksen, N. 148
Frege, G. 295, 302

G

Gabbard, S. H. 80
Gane, M. 190
Gardener, H. 239
Garrett, P. 33, 43
Gass, S. 112, 116, 284, 288, 289
GED Testing Service 73, 77, 79, 80
Genesee, F. 278, 291, 312
Gillette, S. 60
Gillis, S. 106, 107
Girden, E. R. 271, 272
Glaser, R. 229, 237
Glenn, J. III. 239
Godshalk, F. I. 217, 220
Goh, K. M. 197, 198
Goodlad, J. 237
Gordon, C. 190
Grabe, W. 135, 136, 302, 307
Greenbaum, S. 43

Gregg, K. 257, 262
Griffin, P. 97 107, 318
Gross, M. 98, 107
Grove, E. 7, 10, 311, 318
Groves, J. 295, 296, 303
Guba, E. G. 231, 232, 237
Guilford, J. P. 97, 98, 107

H

Haas, N. S. 148
Haastrup, K. 241, 250
Hagan, P. 177, 178, 190
Hagege, C. 210
Hagiwara, M. P. 84, 93
Hajek, J. 43, 311, 312
Haladyna, T. H. 140, 148
Haladyna, T. M. 74, 80
Halstead, M. 178, 190
Halleck, G. B. 86, 87, 94, 95
Halliday, M. A. K. 18–20, 189, 190
Hamayan, E. V. 231, 237
Hambleton, R. 76, 79, 80
Hamp-Lyons, L. 96, 138–141, 143, 147, 148, 218, 220, 230, 237, 319
Han, Y. 252, 254, 262
Han, ZH. 276–292, 319
Handscombe, J. 175
Harris, D. P. 22, 32, 214, 217, 220
Hartmann, R. R. K. 310
Hartog, P. 213, 220
Hasselgren, A. 83, 94
Hatch, E. 152, 161
Hawkins, E. 167, 175, 176
Hawkins, R. 266, 274
Hawthorne, L. 191, 195, 198, 199
Heaton, J. B. 309, 310
Hedgcock, J. 289
Henriksen, B. 241, 250
Herrington, R. 151, 161
Herron, J. 232, 233, 234, 237
Heycock, C. 273
Hickson, L. M. H. 72

Hill, K. 7, 10, 32, 85, 94, 314, 319
Hilliard, A. G. 230, 237
Hobcraft, J. 208, 210
Hoekstra, T. 272–274
Hoinville, G. 152, 161
Hood, S. 178, 189, 190
Hooper, J. 166, 176
Horak, T. 151, 161
House, H. 134
Howatt, A. 288, 305
Hudson, C. 134
Hudson, T. 89, 94, 238
Huebner, T. 282, 283, 288
Hughes, J. A. 152, 161, 308–310
Huhta, A. 93–95, 306
Hunter, I. 177, 180, 190
Hyltenstam, K. 176, 178, 289
Hymes, D. 13–15, 17–21, 295, 299

I

International Instutite for Educational Planning (IIEP) 209, 210
Icke, V. 60
IELTS 23, 24, 31, 86, 93, 97, 106, 107, 147, 151, 153, 154, 156–159, 161, 192–199, 318
Ingram, D. 181, 190
Ingram, E. 6, 22, 32
Ishiguro, H. 301, 302
Iwashita, N. 7, 10, 314, 319

J

Jackson, E. 190
Jacobson, W. 58, 59
James, C. 33, 43, 126, 208
James, M. 135
Johns, A. 53, 59
Johnson, D. 54, 59
Johnson, K. 18, 20
Johnson, T. 190
Jones, M. 190, 313
Jones, R. 310
Jowell, R. 161

Joyce, H. 190
Jukuri, S. D. 232 234, 238
Jung, C. G. 298, 303

K
Kane, M. 97, 107
Kanagy, R. 116
Kansakar, T. 312
Kaplan, T. 282, 289, 302, 307
Kashoki, M. E. 201, 206, 210
Kasper, G. 289
Keating, P. 237
Kellaghan, T. 140, 148
Kellerman, E. 278, 282, 289, 307
Kelly, A. V. 163, 175
Kenyon, D. 87, 94
Kertesz, A. 64, 72
Keselman, H. J. 271, 272
Khoo, S. T. 103, 107, 307
Kishindo, P. J. 202, 210
Klein, E. 273, 282, 283, 287, 289
Klein, W. 287, 289
Klein-Braley, C. 220
Klockars, A. J. 271, 272
Kogan, M. 178, 190, 237
Kohonen, V. 93–95, 306
Krahnke, K. 255, 262, 308
Krashen, S. 33, 43, 255, 262, 264, 273
Kuehn, K. 57, 59
Kurki-Suonio, L. 93–95, 306

L
Lado, R. 9, 22, 32, 215, 251, 262
Lakshmanan, U. 277, 278, 280, 282, 290
Lamendella, J. 278, 279, 281–283, 287, 290
Larsen-Freeman, D. 166
Laufer, B. 241–250, 320
Lawton, D. 163, 175
Lawton, T. A. 148
Lazaraton, A. 84, 86, 94, 152, 161
Lee, Y. P. 135, 136, 309

Leech, G. 43
Leont'ev, A.V. 301, 303
Levine, L. 55, 56, 59
Lin, Y. 281, 289
Linacre, J. M. 82, 94
Lincoln, Y. S. 231, 232, 237
Lingard, B. 177, 190
Linn, R. L. 116, 148, 238
Litwin, M. S. 154 – 156, 158, 161
Liu, G. 53, 60, 257, 258, 263
Loner, W. J. 79
Long, M. 166, 282, 289
Lord, R. 135, 136, 309
Loschky, L. 253, 262
Low, G. D. 135, 136, 152, 161, 309
Lowe, Jr. P. 83, 94
Lowther, M. 278, 289
Lumley, T. 7, 10, 85, 94, 134, 305, 314, 320
Lunz, M. E. 82, 96
Luoma, S. 93 – 95, 306
Lynch, B. 23, 31, 86, 94, 228 – 239, 320
Lynch, D. A. 238
Lyster, R. 173, 176

M

MacIntyre, A. 224, 227
Mac-Mathuna, L. 289
Macpherson, R. J. S. 177, 178, 190
Madaus, G. F. 140, 148
Maguire, H. H. 55, 59, 60
Maher, J. 292–303, 320
Malmkjer, K. 95
Manidis, M. 190
Manwaring, D. 43, 311, 312
Martin, C. 175, 176, 208
Masters, G. 103, 107
Matthews, S. 285, 291
Mavrommatis, Y. 127, 135
Maxwell, S. E. 271, 273
McDowell, C. 191, 199
McGroarty, M. E. 95

McIntyre, P. 83, 94
McKay, R. B. 76, 80, 305, 311
McNamara, T. 5–10, 46, 47, 52, 82, 86, 87, 94, 130, 131, 136, 142, 148, 191, 199, 233, 261, 262, 305, 308, 321
Meara, P. 43
Mehnert, H. 258, 255, 261, 262
Meiron, B. 92, 95
Meldman, M. A. 85, 95
Mendelsohn, D. 136
Messick, S. 112, 116, 140, 148, 232, 238
Mey, J. 293, 303
Milanovic, M. 142, 148, 311
Miller, P. 190
Minister of Immigration 192–199
Ministry of Education (Zambia) 194, 201, 207, 209, 324, 325
Mitchell, R. 152, 160, 163–176, 306, 321
Monroe, P. 213, 220
Moock, P. R. 208, 210
Mori, M. 55, 56, 59
Morris, L. L. 154, 160
Moss, P. A. 231, 238
Mukattash, L. 279, 289
Myles, F. 266, 276

N

Nairn, A. 218, 220
Nakamoto, J. M. 80
Nash, R. 152, 161
Nation, I. S. P. 241–243, 245, 249
National Council on Measurement in Education 116, 128, 238
New Zealand Immigration Service 191, 192, 195, 199
New Zealand Official Yearbook 196, 199
Nida, E. 292, 303
Nilipour, R. 63, 72
Nolen, S. B. 140, 148
Norris, J. M. 231, 238
North, B. 32, 83, 92, 95, 134, 135, 307, 316
Northern Examinations Board (NEAB) 31, 32
Nunan, D. 55, 59
Nunes, D. 281, 289

O

O'Connor, M. C. 230, 238
Oikennon, S. 263
Oliver, R. 305, 311
Oller, J. W. 20, 93, 278, 291, 309, 313
O'Neil, W. 277, 288
Oppenheim, A. N. 152, 161
Orem, R. 175
O'Shannessy, C. 10, 314

P

Page, B. 167, 176
Palmberg, R. 241, 250
Palmer, A. S. 16, 20, 40, 49–51, 109–112, 114, 116, 129, 134, 286, 310, 315
Palmer, L. 22, 32, 217
Paradis, M. 62–66, 70, 72
Paribakht, T. S. 242, 249, 250
Paris, S. G. 141, 148, 210, 302
Parks, S. 55, 59, 60
Pavlou, P. 83, 95
Peirce, B. N. 228, 238
Perdue, C. 281, 289
Perren, G. 310
Perrone, V. 239
Phillips, J. A. N. 167, 176
Phillips, M. 176
Phillipson, R. 241, 250, 307
Pica, T. R. 112, 116
Pienemann, M. 281, 289
Pike, L. 23, 32
Pollitt, A. 95
Portal, M. 308
Porter, D. 85, 95, 125
Preston, D. 277, 278, 288, 289
Pusey, M. 177, 190

Q

Quirk, R. 37, 43, 309

R

Rachor, R. 135
Raizan, S. 230, 238
Ranney, S. 55, 56, 60
Ranta, E. 173, 176
Rasch, G. 86, 87, 92, 94, 96, 98, 100, 103, 104, 106, 107, 320, 321
Ratwatte, H. 271, 273
Read, J. 191, 194, 199, 322
Rea-Dickins, P. 22, 28, 32, 322
Reed, D. J. 82, 86, 95, 322
Reed, J. 213, 220
Reynolds, R. W. 80
Rhodes, E. C. 213, 220
Richards, J. C. 93
Richmond, J. 33, 43
Riggenbach, H. 84, 94
Rimarcik, J. L. 57, 58, 60
Ritchie, W. C. 272–274, 289–291
Roberts, C. 175
Roberts, J. 117, 125
Robertson, D. 264, 266, 267, 269, 272, 273, 322
Robinson, P. 251, 261, 262
Rohl, M. 134
Romberg, T. A. 230, 238
Ross, S. 86, 95, 251, 261, 262
Roth, J. L. 148
Rubagumya, C. M. 210
Rutherford, W. 277, 285, 289, 290

S

Sajavaara, K. 47, 48, 52
Salter, K. 214–216, 220
Sangster, R. L. 80
Sanz, C. 252, 263
Saretsky, G. D. 214, 220
Saville, N. 142, 148, 227, 311
Sax, G. 271, 272
Schachter, J. 281, 284, 285, 287, 288, 290
Schiffrin, D. 309
Schmitt, N. 242, 250
Schneider, G. 92, 95
School Curriculum and Assessment Authority 176

Schumann, J. 278, 281, 283, 290
Schwartz, B. 230, 238, 265, 272, 273, 274
Scott, D. 190, 303
Seidlhofer, B. 60, 263, 306
Selinker, L. 46, 48, 50, 52, 54, 55, 60, 84, 93, 250, 276–290, 307, 323
Sharwood-Smith, M. 248, 250, 291, 307
Shillcock, R. 273
Shohamy, E. 52, 83, 92, 93, 95, 139, 140, 147, 148, 231, 232, 235, 238, 239
Shuy, R. 308
Sichinga, W. K. 202, 210
Simon, B. 163, 175
Singleton, P. 289
Sireci, S. G. 74, 80
Skehan, P. 15, 16, 21, 33, 43, 47–49, 52, 258, 261, 262
Skutnabb-Kangas, T. 200, 210
Slobin, D. J. 300, 310
Smith, D. 179, 190, 231, 239
Smith, M. L. 141, 148
Sokal, M. M. 220
Sorace, A. 34, 43, 264, 266–278, 290, 322, 323
Spolsky, B. 49, 52, 90, 95, 129, 139, 212–214, 216, 217, 219–221, 306, 310, 313, 323
Spratt, J. E. 200, 210
Sprouse, R. 265, 273
Stahl, J. A. 82, 96
Stansfield, C. 24, 31, 32, 73, 74, 80, 83, 87, 94, 308, 323
Stauble, A. 278, 281, 290
Steel, D. 33, 35–38, 42, 43, 252, 261
Stevenson, D. 127, 130, 136, 220, 308
Stiggins, R. 127, 136
Stubbs, M. 166, 176, 312
Sturgess, A. 181, 188, 190
Sunderland, J. 85, 96
Swartvik, J. 43
Swain, M. 14, 20, 23, 31, 129, 135, 194, 200, 204, 210, 247, 248, 250, 251, 258, 261, 262, 299, 302, 307
Swain, P. 194, 199
Swales, J. 53, 55, 60

T

Tarnai, I. 80
Tarone, E. 53, 54, 56, 58, 60, 257, 258, 262, 263, 277, 290, 323
Taylor, B. 71
Taylor, O. L. 175
Teschner, R. V. 93
Thep-Ackrapong, T. 278, 290
Thorndike, R. L. 107
Tickoo, M. L. 307
TOEFL (Test and Score Material) 8, 22–24, 31, 32, 93, 118, 141, 147, 158, 212, 214, 217, 218, 238, 251–254, 258, 263, 324
Tollefson, J. 278, 290
Tomic, O. 308
Tomoeda, C. K. 67, 72
Toothaker, L. E. 271, 274
Torrance, H. 135, 136
Towell, R. 266, 274
Trim, J. 310
Trimble, L. 53, 60
Trites, J. 58, 60
Turner, C. E. 84, 96, 138–146, 148, 324

U

University of Cambridge Local Examinations Syndicate (UCLES) 10, 26, 31, 32, 107, 142, 147, 148, 150, 151, 160, 161, 199, 305, 311
Upshur, J. A. 84, 96, 139, 143, 144, 145, 148, 149, 312
Urquhart, A. H. 47, 51, 309, 324
Utley, D. 167, 176

V

Vainikka, A. 265, 274
Van Els, T. 308
Van Maele, J. 85, 92, 96
VanPatten, B. 252, 254, 263
Vasseur, M.-T. 175
Vaughan, C. 83, 96
Verhoeven, L. 24, 32, 296, 303
Viator, K. 230, 238
Vigil, N. A. 278, 291
Vonk, W. 273

W

Wagner, D. A. 200, 210
Warner, O. 76, 80
Wall, D. 134, 138, 140, 141, 147, 149
Walton, A. R. 52
Warren, J. 43, 311, 312
Washburn, G. 278, 291
Watanabe, Y. 238, 241, 249
Watson-Gegeo, K. A. 138, 149
Weir, C. J. 24, 27, 32, 117–125, 324
Werner, O. 80
Wesche, M. 242, 250
White, L. 266, 274, 278, 280, 291
Widdowson, H. G. 12 – 21, 45, 47, 52, 60, 215, 250, 263, 306, 309, 312, 324
Wiggins, G. 230, 239
Wigglesworth, G. 7, 8, 10, 87, 96, 147, 148, 149, 191, 198, 258, 259, 263
Wilds, C. P. 216, 221
Wilkes, M. 234, 239, 311
Wilkinson, A. 308, 311, 313
Willett, J. 166, 176
Williams, E. 125, 200 – 210, 325
Williams, J. 195, 290
Williams, S. R. 230, 238
Winer, B. 271, 274
Winetroube, S. 151, 161
Wolf, D. 228, 229, 230, 239
Wolfram, W. 74, 80
Worrall, L. E. 72
Worthen, B. R. 228, 239
Wright, B. D. 98, 103, 107
Wulfeck, B. 62, 63, 72
Wylie, E. 181, 190, 311

X

Xue Guoyi 250

Y
Yahya-Othman, S. 201, 210
Yerkes, R. M. 213, 220, 221
Yip, V. 285, 291
Yoshioka, J. 238
Young, A. 197, 199
Young, R. 53, 60, 83, 96
Young-Scholten, M. 265, 274
Yuan, B. 271, 274

Z
Zammitt, S. 305, 311
Zarinnia, E. A. 238
Zessoules, R. 230, 239
Zobl, H. 265, 275